The Science-Backed
Perimenopause Weight Loss
Plan to Reclaim Your Energy,
Balance Your Hormones,
and Feel Confident After 40

EMPOWERED
WEIGHT LOSS

**Sarah Gibson, MPAS, PAC, HWC
and Abbey Walsh, MS, CNS, LDN**

Empowered Weight Loss

Medical Disclaimer
This book is intended for educational and informational purposes only and is not a substitute for professional medical advice, diagnosis, or treatment. The authors and publisher are not providing medical care or establishing a provider–patient relationship. Always consult a qualified healthcare professional before making changes to your diet, supplements, exercise routine, medications, or treatment plan.

Paperback ISBN: 978-1-963732-31-3
Hardcover ISBN: 978-1-963732-32-0

Published by

The Publishing Pad
www.thepublishingpad.com

Table of Contents

Introduction

If you're reading this, you may have noticed changes in your body that no one prepared you for. Energy feels harder to come by. Sleep isn't as restorative as it used to be. Weight shifts despite doing "all the right things." And sometimes—maybe more often than you'd like to admit—you just don't feel like yourself anymore. That feeling scares you because deep down, you're wondering if the woman you used to be is gone for good, and no matter what you try, you can't figure out how to get her back.

You're not imagining it. You're not broken. And you're definitely not alone.

This book was written for you—and for every woman who's been told her labs are "normal" while feeling anything but.

We are Sarah Gibson and Abbey Walsh, two women with different backgrounds, different areas of expertise, and remarkably similar breaking points.

We came to this work not just as professionals, but as women who lived the frustration, the shame, and the exhaustion of doing everything "right" and still feeling dismissed and stuck. Each of us reached a rock-bottom moment where the answers we desperately needed weren't found in conventional medical advice—and our bodies began asking questions we couldn't ignore any longer.

What follows begins with our personal stories. Not because this book is about us, but because these experiences shaped the questions we asked, the research we pursued, and the comprehensive system we ultimately built together—a system that has now helped over 1,800 women reclaim their health, their bodies, and their lives.

These aren't just stories. They're proof that what you're experiencing is real, fixable, and worth fighting for.

You're Not Broken—Your Body Is Just Speaking a Different Language.

Sarah's Story

I was standing in my bathroom at two a.m., the cold tile floor beneath my bare feet, staring at a number that refused to change. The scale mocked me with its indifference. Eight months. Eight brutal months of punishing myself in every way imaginable, and I'd lost two pounds.

Two. Pounds.

I'd done a medically supervised seventeen-day water fast—seventeen days of nothing but water and electrolyte salts, dizziness, headaches, and clinging to the edge of my sanity. I'd trained for and completed a full marathon. Twenty-six point two miles. My joints screamed with every step, but I kept running because I thought suffering was the answer. I tried strict keto until I dreamed about bread. I tried intermittent fasting, white-knuckling every minute until I could finally eat something. I counted every calorie, weighed every morsel, eliminated every "bad" food.

Nothing. Worked.

I'm a board certified, master's degree physician associate and had practiced medicine for over twenty years. I worked in trauma and emergency medicine, making split-second life-or-death decisions. I'd delivered countless diagnoses, prescribed thousands of treatments, helped save lives.

But I couldn't save myself. And that truth was suffocating.

This wasn't supposed to happen to me. I was the high-performer. The one who controlled everything through sheer willpower and discipline. In my twenties, if I needed to lose five pounds, I'd simply cut carbs for a week and move more. Problem solved. My body followed orders.

But now, in my thirties, after having four children back to back, my body had become a stranger. Nothing I threw at it made any difference. I was sixty pounds heavier than I'd ever been, and every strategy that used to work was now completely, utterly useless.

The weight wasn't even the hardest part. It was hating my own body. It was the soul-crushing reality that my efforts didn't match my results—that I could do everything "right" and still fail.

It was opening my closet every morning and feeling a wave of depression wash over me. Nothing fit. Nothing looked right. I was avoiding running into anyone who "knew me skinnier" because I couldn't bear the look in their eyes—or worse, the carefully neutral expression that pretended not to notice.

I was showing up as an exhausted mom for my kids and a barely surviving partner for my husband. This wasn't the woman I wanted to be. This wasn't the life I'd worked so hard to build.

So I did what any medical professional would tell their patient to do. I went to my doctor.

"Your labs are fine," he said, his eyes fixed on the computer screen instead of me. "It's just part of getting older. You need to eat less and exercise more."

I sat there, stunned into silence.

I wanted to scream. I wanted to shake him. I wanted to make him understand that I WAS eating less—less than I'd ever eaten in my life. I WAS exercising more—I'd just run twenty-six miles, for God's sake. But the words caught in my throat because somewhere deep down, I was starting to believe maybe he was right. Maybe this was just aging. Maybe I was the problem.

"But I—" I started.

He was already standing up, already moving toward the door. Already done with me.

I walked out of that office feeling smaller than I'd ever felt. Not because of my weight but because of the shame. The crushing, suffocating shame that followed me everywhere.

The shame of hiding in photos at family gatherings. The shame of wearing black every single day to try to disappear. The shame of avoiding social situations because I didn't want people to see what I'd become. The shame of looking in the mirror and not recognizing the exhausted, defeated woman staring back.

But worst of all was the professional shame. The voice in my head that whispered constantly, *If you can't even manage your own weight, how can you tell patients to do better? You're a fraud. A failure. You're supposed to know how bodies work, and yours is broken beyond repair.*

I felt trapped in a nightmare where I was doing everything right and getting punished anyway.

There was no way to eat less than a seventeen-day fast. There was no way to exercise more than marathon training. I'd reached the absolute limits of human willpower—and my body still refused to budge.

Late one night, unable to sleep again, I found myself back in medical journals. Not the ones I'd studied in school but deeper research about women's hormones, about perimenopause, about metabolic changes. I was determined not to let this be the rest of my life. I refused to give up—I was going to find answers.

That's when everything changed.

What I discovered wasn't in any of my conventional medical training. The medical establishment wasn't talking about the profound hormonal shifts that make midlife weight loss nearly impossible. They weren't addressing the five specific hormone imbalances that stack up like dominoes during perimenopause, each one triggering the next, creating a perfect metabolic storm that no amount of calorie restriction or exercise can overcome.

This wasn't about willpower. It wasn't about trying harder. It wasn't about my moral failure or lack of discipline.

It was about science. The real reason women struggle with weight loss— and how these five hormone imbalances sabotage everything. When I tested myself, I had every single one.

For the first time in years, my body made sense. My weight wasn't a character flaw; it was biology. My fatigue wasn't laziness; it was my body's desperate attempt to survive under impossible conditions. My body wasn't broken; it was responding exactly as designed to the perfect storm of insulin resistance, thyroid dysfunction, vitamin D deficiency, cortisol dysregulation, and sex hormone chaos.

I wasn't failing. My body was protecting me the only way it knew how.

Once I identified my imbalances and started treating them comprehensively, everything changed. I focused on healing my body instead of punishing it—listening to the signals, monitoring how my body responded, using food as medicine, adjusting movement to support rather than deplete me. I rebuilt my relationship with food through simple, sustainable strategies and lifestyle changes that actually worked with my biology.

The weight that had clung to me for years finally started to release. My confidence began returning. The depression lifted. I wasn't white-knuckling my way through each day anymore.

I started to feel like myself again. Not the broken version I'd become but the woman I'd been before all of this started.

The traditional medical model had failed me. It took six years of suffering to figure out what was actually wrong. But once I did, everything transformed. I healed my body and lost sixty pounds in eight months—eating more, exercising less, listening to my body, and healing what was actually broken.

My prediabetes reversed. I got off blood pressure medication. The anxiety and depression that had shadowed me for years finally lifted.

And then I did what I do best: I became determined to create a system so that no woman would have to suffer like I did. I built the medical practice I wished had existed for me, one that actually understands women's bodies, tests comprehensively, treats root causes, and doesn't dismiss our symptoms as "just aging."

Abbey's Story

I'd struggled with my weight and body image since high school. I was a late bloomer to begin with, and then birth control pills were handed out like candy for my period cramps. Before my body even found its own natural rhythm, I was manipulating it with synthetic hormones.

The obsession with calories began shortly after. I'd skip lunch at school. Wake up at dawn to hit the gym with my dad. Try every diet under the sun—South Beach, Atkins, obsessive calorie counting. By my senior year, I was eating little more than a can of green beans for every meal. If I could write a letter to my younger self now, I would tell her how short this phase of life would be and how desperately her body needed nourishment, not deprivation.

I opened my first boutique gym in 2012. Falling in love with fitness combined with the metabolism of my twenties helped me break the chains of calorie counting. I was strong, lean, and free.

But even though I was finally feeling good, I noticed something troubling: My most dedicated members—wonderful women in their forties and fifties who showed up religiously, sometimes staying for two classes a night—weren't getting results.

They were working out HARD. They were eating clean. They were doing everything "right." But they weren't losing weight.

I knew it wasn't for a lack of effort. These women were warriors. So what was going on?

I had a master's degree in nutrition and dozens of fitness certifications. I knew what should work. What was the difference between what was working for me in my twenties and what wasn't working for them in their forties?

I made it my mission to find out.

But then, in my thirties, I found myself living the exact struggle I'd been studying.

I experienced secondary infertility after the birth of my first child. Nearly seven years passed before I was able to conceive a pregnancy that carried to term. Seven years of trying for another baby. Seven years of seeing two pink lines and feeling hope surge through me, only to have that hope ripped away weeks later. Again. And again. And again.

Every miscarriage felt like my body was betraying me. Every negative pregnancy test felt like failure. Every well-meaning comment about "at least you have one" felt like a knife twisting deeper.

During those years, my body felt like it didn't belong to me anymore. For so many years teaching fitness classes and working as a nutritionist, I'd been able to keep my weight under control. But now I had so many symptoms, and my clothes didn't fit anymore.

I would stand in my closet and cry. The version of myself I'd worked so hard to build—strong, confident, in control—had disappeared. I made excuses to avoid social events because I couldn't bear for people to see what I'd become. I was back to extreme restricting, the same disordered patterns I thought I'd left behind forever in high school.

If I couldn't control whether I could have another child, at least I could control how I looked. At least I could control my weight. At least I could have my confidence back.

Except I couldn't.

No matter what I did, nothing worked. The symptoms kept getting worse—fatigue so crushing I could barely get through teaching my classes, aching joints that made even simple movements feel like wading through cement, freezing all the time and layering on sweaters in summer while everyone else was comfortable.

My periods had become a nightmare. Heavy, painful, unpredictable. I'd find myself terrified of bleeding through in public, having to plan my entire life around my cycle. I canceled my commitments. I'd wake up drenched in sweat, sheets soaked through from night sweats, and then lie there for hours watching the minutes crawl by on the clock—3:17... 3:42... 4:03...

And then there was the anxiety.

I'd never been an anxious person before. But now it felt like someone was choking me. My chest would tighten out of nowhere. My heart would race.

When you don't sleep, you become miserable fast. The fatigue pushed me to lean harder into caffeine, which only amped up the anxiety and cortisol dysregulation. I was trapped in a vicious cycle I couldn't break.

My relationship with my husband suffered under the weight of it all. The grief from losing pregnancy after pregnancy. The complete absence of my libido. The version of me he'd fallen in love with—energetic, confident, vibrant—had disappeared, replaced by someone exhausted and defeated and barely holding it together.

Meanwhile, the scale kept climbing to numbers I'd only seen during pregnancy—except I wasn't pregnant. I kept losing pregnancies instead.

I'll never forget sitting on my kitchen floor at nine p.m., surrounded by portioned containers, food scales, and my carb counting app open on my phone, sobbing so hard I could barely breathe.

"I don't even know what I can cook for dinner," I choked out to my husband. "I don't have enough macros left for the day."

I was eating barely any carbs, loading up on fat and moderate protein—meticulously tracking every gram. I was doing everything my education told me should work. Everything I'd successfully taught hundreds of clients.

And yet I was failing myself spectacularly.

I'd later discover through food freedom work and DNA testing that this approach was the worst thing I could do for my hormone health and weight loss goals given my unique biology. But in that moment, on that kitchen floor, all I knew was that nothing made sense anymore.

I went to doctor after doctor, desperate for answers. I was dismissed by all my providers, told it was unfortunate but there was no rhyme or reason for my recurrent miscarriages.

"Your labs are in normal range," they'd say, barely looking up from their computers.

"But something is clearly wrong," I'd insist. "I'm exhausted. I can't sleep. My periods are out of control. I keep losing pregnancies."

"These things just happen sometimes," they'd respond with practiced sympathy.

I'd walk out of those appointments feeling smaller each time. Dismissed. Unheard. Like my suffering didn't matter because the numbers on paper said I was "fine."

But I wasn't fine. I was drowning.

The professional shame was almost worse than the physical symptoms. Who was I to have a master's degree in nutrition and own a gym where I helped others lose weight and reclaim their health—but the moment *my* health got complicated, I couldn't figure out how to fix myself?

My initial struggles growing up with body image issues had led me to the wellness field in the first place. My gym members' struggles pushed me to dig deeper into midlife hormonal shifts and why what worked for women in their twenties didn't work the same for women in their forties and beyond. But my personal hormone struggles made me become a pioneer and advocate for women to get the care they deserve.

I did all the testing on myself. I discovered what imbalances were holding me back. I implemented every natural intervention I used with my clients—

optimizing my nutrition, taking targeted supplements, adjusting my fitness routine, prioritizing sleep and stress management.

I was able to support my thyroid hormone conversion and lower my TSH. I took herbs to lower inflammation. I ate nutrient-dense whole foods to support hormone production.

But deep down, I knew it wasn't enough.

My thyroid still wasn't optimized. My progesterone was still too low. I was doing everything within my scope as a nutritionist, and I was still suffering.

That realization was both devastating and clarifying.

I needed prescription support. I needed thyroid medication for an underactive thyroid that wasn't "out of range enough" for conventional doctors to care about. I needed progesterone replacement, not just herbs and supplements trying to coax my body into making more.

I needed help beyond what I could provide myself—and that was the hardest pill to swallow.

For some women, all the natural interventions are enough. Nutrition, supplements, lifestyle changes—they can work beautifully. I'd seen it happen hundreds of times with my clients.

But for some of us—for women with more complex hormone imbalances, for women whose bodies need more comprehensive support—natural isn't enough. We need both. We need the functional approach *and* the medical intervention. We need someone who understands the whole picture and isn't afraid to use every tool available.

Once I finally got the prescription support I needed—once my thyroid was properly optimized and my progesterone was replaced—everything changed. My sleep improved. The anxiety lifted. My periods normalized. The weight that had clung to me despite all my efforts finally started to release. My energy returned. My libido came back. I felt like myself again.

And I got pregnant. After seven years of loss and grief and feeling like my body would never cooperate, I carried a healthy pregnancy to term and welcomed my second child.

My body wasn't broken. It just needed the right support—support that combined my expertise in nutrition and lifestyle with proper medical intervention.

When Two Experts Become Unstoppable

By the time we met, we were both already getting results with women. Sarah had built a thriving medical weight loss practice, leveraging her expertise in diagnostics, lab interpretation, and prescriptive interventions. Abbey had transformed countless lives through her mastery of advanced nutrition strategies, fitness personalization, and targeted supplement protocols.

We were each successful in our own right. We knew enough about each other's domains to make recommendations that worked. But we also recognized our limitations—and more importantly, we saw the extraordinary potential in what we could create together.

Combining Sarah's medical precision with Abbey's nutritional and fitness expertise birthed something remarkable. Results didn't just double—they increased by a factor of ten.

Women who had plateaued were breaking through. Women with complex medical histories were finally getting comprehensive care. Women who'd been told their cases were "too complicated" were thriving.

Traditional medical providers were referring patients to us consistently. We were asked to speak on stages, appear in media outlets, and were referenced as experts in perimenopausal weight loss.

That's when we knew we had something bigger than two separate practices. We had a system.

Together, we created **The Matrix Method**—a comprehensive, replicable framework that works for every single woman, every single time, regardless of medical history, physical limitations, nutritional needs, or fitness level.

This wasn't a theoretical framework built on research and ideas. This was a battle-tested system forged from treating thousands of real women with real struggles—women just like us, women just like you.

Two experts. One mission. A method that actually works.

But here's what really matters: We didn't just create a theoretical framework based on research and ideas. We created a system that gets women results. Every. Single. Time.

In the past few years, we've helped over 1,800 women lose weight, balance their hormones, and reclaim themselves. Not women who read a book and maybe implemented some ideas. Women who went through our comprehensive program and transformed their lives.

Women like Jennifer, a lifelong athlete who hit the gym daily but gained twenty pounds during perimenopause—until we discovered her insulin resistance and thyroid dysfunction and helped her lose the weight within three months.

Women like Lisa, who was told she'd never get off her diabetes medication—until we addressed her five hormone imbalances and she not only lost thirty-five pounds but also reversed damage and no longer needed medication.

Women like Julie, whose oncologist said weight loss was "medically impossible" given her cancer treatment history—until she lost forty-seven pounds and her oncologist asked for our protocols to share with other patients.

Throughout this book, you'll meet many of these women. Their stories are woven into every chapter because they illustrate something crucial: This isn't theory. This is what happens in real life when you finally address what's actually broken.

Here's what sets us apart: We do this work. Every single day. All day, every day.

We review labs. We adjust protocols. We collaborate with oncologists about cancer survivors. We work with endocrinologists about complex thyroid cases. We problem-solve when the first approach doesn't work and figure out what will.

We've seen every pattern, every combination of hormone imbalances, every complicating factor. No amount of education can replace that kind of real-world, in-the-trenches experience. You can read every research paper ever published on insulin resistance, but until you've worked with hundreds of women who have it—seeing how it presents differently in someone with

PCOS versus someone in menopause versus someone with a cancer history—you don't truly understand it.

We have that insight. We've built that expertise. And we're giving it to you in this book.

Why We Wrote This Book

Because we were you.

Sarah stood in that bathroom at two a.m., a medical professional who couldn't fix her own body. Abbey suffered through multiple miscarriages while doctors dismissed her symptoms as normal.

We know what it's like to feel broken. To be told you're fine when you know you're not. To try everything and get nowhere. To wonder if this is just your life now.

And we're here to tell you: Nothing is wrong with you.

Your body isn't broken. It's not lazy. It's not sabotaging you. Your body is speaking a very specific language, the language of hormone imbalances, and until now, nobody has given you the translation guide.

This book is that guide. It's everything we wish someone had told us when we were in our own breaking point moments. It's the roadmap we followed to heal ourselves. It's the system we've used to help 1,800 women transform their lives. It's the knowledge we've gained from being in the trenches, solving the puzzle of complex hormone imbalances in real women with real lives.

And it's the key to your empowered weight loss.

Not weight loss through deprivation, punishment, or willpower. Not weight loss that disappears the moment you stop restricting. Empowered weight loss—the kind that comes from understanding your body, addressing root causes, and giving your metabolism what it actually needs to function properly.

The kind that's sustainable because you're not fighting your biology; you're supporting it. The kind that comes with energy returning, brain fog lifting, sleep improving, and feeling like yourself again. The kind that changes everything.

Who This Book Is For

This book is for the woman who's in perimenopause, menopause, or post-menopause and struggling with weight that won't budge no matter what you try.

You've been told "it's just aging" or "eat less, move more" by doctors who dismiss your symptoms. You've tried every diet and exercise program under the sun with minimal or temporary results. You know something is genuinely wrong, but you can't get anyone to take you seriously or run comprehensive testing.

You feel exhausted, foggy, achy, anxious, and unable to sleep. You don't feel like yourself anymore. You may have complex medical conditions that make standard weight loss programs or hormone replacement therapy unsuitable.

You're ready to understand what's actually happening in your body so you can make informed decisions about your health. You want science-based, medically sound information without being talked down to or oversimplified.

If you're nodding your head right now, this book is for you.

What Makes This Book Different

Most weight loss programs focus on the symptom—excess weight—without addressing why your body is storing fat in the first place. We dig deeper to identify the specific hormone imbalances driving your weight gain and treat those root causes comprehensively.

But here's what really sets this book apart: It's not written by researchers theorizing about hormone balance. It's written by practitioners who do this work every single day.

Every protocol in this book has been tested on hundreds of women. Every recommendation has been refined through real-world application. When we tell you to request specific lab tests, it's because we've seen how those tests reveal patterns that standard testing misses—in patient after patient. When we give you optimal lab ranges to aim for, it's because we've tracked those markers in hundreds of women and seen exactly where they need to be for symptoms to resolve and weight to move.

This isn't pseudoscience or wellness trends. Every recommendation is backed by peer-reviewed research, clinical experience , and proven medical protocols. We cite our sources, explain the mechanisms, and give you real science in accessible language.

We respect your intelligence. You don't need to be scolded or shamed. You need information, understanding, and effective tools. We don't stop at "eat better and exercise more"; we give you specific lab tests to request, optimal ranges to aim for, supplement protocols, prescription options, lifestyle modifications, and advanced strategies. We cover every tool in the toolbox because different women need different solutions.

Throughout this book, you'll meet real women who have walked this journey. You'll hear how Maria finally understood why her HIIT classes weren't moving the scale. You'll discover how Karen went from planning a hysterectomy to managing her symptoms naturally. You'll learn how women with cancer histories, autoimmune diseases, and complex medical conditions achieved results they were told were impossible.

Their stories will help you see yourself, understand you're not alone, and believe that change is possible. But more than that, these stories will show you what's possible for you and how to achieve your desired result.

How to Use This Book

This book is organized into three parts, each building on the previous one to give you complete understanding and practical tools. You can choose to read this cover to cover, get a deep understanding of what is happening in your body, and start healing right away, or you can skip to the protocols if you already have a diagnosis and are looking for treatment. Either way, the answers are here.

Part I: Understanding Why You're Struggling with the Scale explains exactly what's happening in your body during perimenopause and beyond. You'll learn about the five hormone imbalances that stack up to create the perfect storm for weight gain and metabolic dysfunction. Each chapter covers one hormone imbalance in depth—what the hormone does, how the imbalance develops, what it feels like in daily life, how to test for it, and real patient stories from our practice. Don't skip Part I. Understanding the "why" is crucial for making informed decisions and advocating for yourself with healthcare providers.

Part II: Nutrition, Foundations & Lifestyle covers the essential strategies that must be in place before any supplement or medication can work effectively. We'll teach you the "Home Base" habits—adequate protein, vegetables, hydration, and sleep—that form the foundation everything else builds upon. You'll learn why gut health matters for hormone metabolism and how to optimize your nutrition for hormone balance. These aren't optional extras; they're the foundation that makes everything else possible.

Part III: The Comprehensive Approach brings everything together. You'll learn how The Matrix Method works and why personalized medicine matters. We provide detailed treatment protocols for each of the five hormone imbalances, including optimal lab ranges to aim for, prescription medication options, evidence-based supplement protocols, and lifestyle integration strategies. You'll see how these treatments work synergistically because treating one imbalance while ignoring the others rarely produces lasting results.

The book culminates with Julie's complete transformation story—a woman whose doctors said weight loss was medically impossible, who went from planning to end her life to planning a baby shower and excited to meet her first grandchild. Her journey demonstrates what becomes possible when you address all five hormone imbalances comprehensively, even with the most complex medical history imaginable.

Setting Realistic Expectations

Before you continue, we need to be honest with you about what this journey actually looks like.

This is not a quick fix. Real, lasting transformation takes three to six months minimum, often longer. This is not easy—it requires commitment, consistency, and often some uncomfortable conversations with healthcare providers who might not understand what you're asking for. We'll give you the tools to advocate for yourself, but you'll need to use them.

This is not just about weight loss. Yes, the scale matters. But this is fundamentally about optimizing your health, reducing disease risk, and feeling like yourself again. Weight loss is a side effect of fixing what's broken, not the primary goal.

Individual results vary. Your journey might look different from the women you'll read about in this book. You might lose more or less. You might improve dramatically in energy and symptoms while the scale moves slowly. Every body is different, and we respect that.

For some women, lifestyle changes alone aren't enough, and that's not failure—that's biology. After working with 1,800 women, we know exactly when supplements will be sufficient and when you need prescription support. We'll help you understand the difference.

This book is educational, not medical advice. You need proper medical supervision for testing, diagnosis, and treatment. Never stop or start medications without professional guidance.

But here's what we can promise you: If you follow the roadmap in this book, if you get comprehensive testing, if you address all five hormone imbalances rather than just one or two, if you build the foundation before expecting medications to work miracles, you will see results.

Maybe that means finally sleeping through the night or having energy to play with your grandchildren. Maybe it means the scale moving steadily downward over months. Success looks different for every woman. But it's real, it's achievable, and it's waiting for you.

A Note About Safety

Please read this carefully: This book provides information about hormone health, metabolic optimization, and weight management.

It is NOT a substitute for medical advice, diagnosis, or treatment.

Always consult qualified healthcare providers before starting any new supplement regimen, changing your diet significantly, beginning a new exercise program, or stopping or starting any medications. Some supplements and medications interact with each other or with pre-existing conditions. What's safe for one woman may not be safe for another.

This book is a tool to help you understand your body and advocate for yourself. Use it wisely and in partnership with qualified medical professionals.

Your Journey Starts Now

We've walked the path you're on. We've felt the frustration, the shame, the exhaustion, the bewilderment of trying everything and getting nowhere. We've faced the medical gaslighting that told us we were fine when we knew we weren't.

We've stood where you're standing right now. And we found the way through.

Not through willpower. Not through working harder. Not through trying yet another diet. But through understanding the language your body is speaking and giving it what it actually needs.

The five hormone imbalances you'll learn about in Part I are identifiable, testable, and treatable. The symptoms that feel like your new normal can improve dramatically. The weight that feels permanently stuck can move. The energy that disappeared can return.

We know this because we've seen it happen—1,800 times and counting.

You're not broken. You're not weak. You're not lazy. You're a woman navigating one of the most profound physiological transitions of your life with almost no support, outdated information, and doctors who dismiss your symptoms as "just aging."

That ends now.

You deserve to understand your own body. You deserve comprehensive care. You deserve to feel like yourself again. You deserve empowered weight loss—the kind that comes from knowledge, understanding, and treating root causes rather than just symptoms.

Welcome to the journey. We're honored to guide you.

Turn the page. Become Empowered.

Sarah Gibson, MPAS, HWC, PAC and
Abbey Walsh, MS, CNS

Understanding Why You Are Struggling With The Scale

What the Heck Is Happening in My Body?

If you're reading this book, chances are you've noticed changes in your body. Perhaps dramatically, perhaps gradually, but undeniably—your body is not responding the way it used to.

You might be in your late thirties, noticing the first subtle shifts. Or you're in your mid-forties, bewildered by symptoms that appear out of nowhere. Maybe you're in your early fifties, dealing with changes that have been building for years, wondering if you'll ever feel like yourself again.

Regardless of where you are in this journey, one thing is certain: You deserve to understand what's actually happening in your body. Not vague platitudes about "getting older" or dismissive comments about "just part of being a woman" but real, science-based explanations for the profound physiological changes you're experiencing.

Let's start with the basics—the terminology that will help you understand and advocate for yourself throughout this transition.

Defining the Stages: It's Not Just "Menopause"

Most people use the term "menopause" to describe this entire phase of life, but that's imprecise and contributes to the confusion surrounding women's health during these years. There are actually four distinct reproductive stages, and understanding them is crucial.

Premenopause: Starting at Puberty

Premenopause encompasses the reproductive lifespan from your first menstrual period (menarche, typically occurring between ages 10-15) until the onset of perimenopause. During these years, often spanning three decades or more, your ovaries function optimally, producing relatively consistent levels of estrogen and progesterone in predictable monthly cycles.

Here's what most women don't understand: Premenopause isn't a static, unchanging phase. Your hormones don't maintain the exact same levels from age twenty to age forty. Instead, this phase has its own subtle evolution. Women in their early twenties typically experience peak fertility and the most robust hormonal production. By the early to mid-thirties, subtle shifts begin. Fertility starts declining, menstrual cycles may shorten slightly (often from 28-30 days to 26-27 days), and estrogen levels can begin their gradual descent, though still within normal ranges.

These changes are so subtle that most women don't notice them, and they don't typically cause symptoms. Your body is still operating within its designed parameters—ovulation occurring regularly, hormone levels remaining sufficient to support metabolic function, bone density, cardiovascular health, brain function, and all the other systems that depend on adequate estrogen and progesterone.

What makes the distinction between late premenopause and early perimenopause challenging is that there's no definitive blood test or clear biological marker that says "perimenopause starts today." Rather, it's a gradual transition marked by emerging symptoms—changes in cycle regularity, new or worsening PMS symptoms, subtle shifts in body composition, sleep disruption, or metabolic changes that signal that your ovaries are beginning to struggle with consistent hormone production.

This is why understanding your baseline—how your body functions during your premenopausal years—is so valuable. The women who navigate perimenopause most successfully are often those who understand what "normal" looked like for them before the transition began.

Perimenopause: The Transition (Age 35-55, typically 10-15 years)

Perimenopause—literally "around menopause"—is the transitional period leading up to menopause itself. This is when hormones start to shift, symptoms start to emerge, and most women start to struggle more with the scale.

Starting as early as age thirty-five (though more commonly in the early to mid-forties), your body starts producing less estrogen and progesterone. This isn't a smooth, gradual decline but rather an erratic, unpredictable fluctuation that can last 10-15 years. Some months your hormones might be relatively normal; other months they plummet. Some menstrual cycles might be heavy and prolonged; others might be light or skipped entirely. This inconsistent fluctuation in hormone levels is responsible for vague symptoms and impacts other parts of the body. The variability is maddening, but it reflects the complex interplay of multiple hormonal systems attempting to recalibrate as your reproductive function winds down.

Menopause: One Day in Time

Here's something most women don't realize: Menopause is technically just one single day. It's defined as the point at which you've gone twelve consecutive months without a menstrual period. That's it. One day, twelve months after your final period, you've officially reached menopause. If you have gone eleven consecutive months and then get a menstrual period, the clock starts again. The average age of menopause in the United States is fifty-one, but the normal range extends from the mid-forties to the mid-fifties.

Post-Menopause: The Rest of Your Life

Post-menopause encompasses everything after that single day of menopause—essentially, the rest of your life. During this phase, your ovaries produce minimal estrogen and progesterone, and your adrenal glands and adipose tissue take on increased responsibility for producing what sex hormones your body still makes.

Many women assume symptoms will end once they reach menopause, but this isn't necessarily true. While some symptoms (particularly those related to fluctuating hormones, like irregular periods and some mood volatility) do resolve, others (like hot flashes, sleep disruption, vaginal dryness, and metabolic changes) can persist for years or even decades without appropriate intervention.

The post-menopausal years also bring increased health risks—accelerated bone loss, cardiovascular changes, cognitive shifts—that make this time crucial for proactive health management. How you navigate perimenopause and early post-menopause significantly impacts your health trajectory for decades to come.

Why Does This Transition Take So Long?

One of the most frustrating aspects of perimenopause is its extended timeline. Ten to fifteen years of symptoms? Why can't the body just make this transition quickly and be done with it?

The answer lies in the profound recalibration your endocrine system must undergo. For three to four decades, your ovaries have been the primary producers of estrogen and progesterone with production carefully orchestrated by a complex feedback loop involving your hypothalamus, pituitary gland, and ovaries—the hypothalamic-pituitary-ovarian (HPO) axis.

As your ovarian reserve depletes (you're born with all the eggs you'll ever have, and they've been steadily diminishing over the years), your ovaries become less responsive to the pituitary's signals. Your brain, sensing lower hormone levels, then increases production of follicle-stimulating hormone (FSH) and luteinizing hormone (LH), essentially shouting louder at your ovaries to produce more hormones.

Sometimes this works, creating temporary hormone surges that can actually produce higher-than-normal estrogen levels. Other times your ovaries simply can't respond adequately, resulting in significant hormone deficiencies.

Meanwhile, your body is attempting to shift sex hormone production to secondary sites—primarily your adrenal glands and, to a lesser extent, your fat tissue. But this transition doesn't happen overnight. Your adrenal glands must upregulate enzyme systems, increase production capacity, and essentially learn to take over a function they previously only supplemented.

Dr. Mary Claire Haver, in her groundbreaking book *The New Menopause*, emphasizes that this transition period is not a disease state but rather a natural physiological process that has been profoundly understudied and under-supported by the medical establishment. She notes that while every woman goes through this transition, the severity and nature of symptoms vary dramatically based on factors including:

- **Genetic predisposition**: Your mother's and grandmother's experiences with menopause provide clues about your likely trajectory
- **Baseline health status**: Women entering perimenopause with existing metabolic dysfunction, insulin resistance, thyroid issues, or chronic inflammation typically experience more severe symptoms
- **Stress levels**: Both acute and chronic stress significantly amplify perimenopausal symptoms
- **Body composition**: Lean muscle mass and body fat percentage influence hormone production and metabolism
- **Lifestyle factors**: Nutrition, exercise patterns, sleep quality, and toxin exposure all impact how you experience this transition
- **Medical history**: Previous pregnancies, use of hormonal birth control, gynecological surgeries, and other health events shape your hormonal landscape

This explains why some women breeze through perimenopause with minimal symptoms while others are absolutely debilitated. It's not about pain tolerance or attitude—it's about the complex interplay of genetics, life circumstances, and accumulated health factors.

The Weight Gain Mystery: Why Women and Men Are Different

Now let's address one of the most frustrating aspects of perimenopause: the seemingly inexplicable weight gain, particularly around the midsection.

First, we need to establish a fundamental biological truth that the fitness and diet industries often ignore: **Women are not just smaller versions of men**. Our bodies are designed differently, function differently, and respond to

dietary and exercise interventions differently. Understanding this difference
is crucial to understanding your weight struggles.

The Biological Imperative

Women grow the population. Not metaphorically, not aspirationally—literally. Women are the sex responsible for conception, gestation, birth, and
lactation. This represents an extraordinary metabolic demand. Pregnancy
alone requires approximately 80,000 additional calories over nine months.
Breastfeeding can require an additional five hundred calories daily for
months or years.

Research on famine and pregnancy outcomes reveals a sobering reality:
Women who are malnourished or starving face significantly elevated risks
of maternal and fetal mortality during pregnancy. The metabolic demands
of creating and sustaining new life are simply too great for a body that lacks
adequate energy reserves.

Men who are starving, by contrast, can still successfully father children. Their biological role in reproduction—a single act requiring minimal
metabolic investment—doesn't require the substantial energy reserves that
women need.

This difference in reproductive biology has shaped our physiology at the
most fundamental level. Compared to men, women:

- **Lose weight more slowly**: Our bodies resist fat loss more stubbornly because, from an evolutionary perspective, maintaining energy
  reserves protects reproductive capacity.
- **Gain weight more easily**: We store fat more efficiently because,
  historically, having adequate fat stores meant surviving pregnancy
  and lactation.
- **Experience more intense hunger cues**: Our appetites are more
  sensitive and harder to ignore because our bodies are wired to prioritize energy acquisition.
- **Have a higher percentage of body fat at equivalent fitness levels**:
  Even very fit women typically have 6-10 percent more body fat than
  men of comparable athletic ability.

Beyond sex-based differences, everyone, male and female, experiences age-related muscle loss called sarcopenia. But here again, women get the short end of the biological stick.

Men experience sarcopenia at a rate of approximately 1.5 percent per decade after age thirty. Women lose muscle mass at a rate of 3.5 percent per decade—more than twice as fast.

We'll go over this phenomenon in further detail in Part 2, but just keep it in mind because it is a key factor in how many calories your body burns as you get older.

None of this is due to moral failing or lack of discipline. It's biology. Your body is doing exactly what it was designed to do to ensure survival and reproductive success. The problem is that these evolutionary adaptations, while protective in environments of scarcity, work against us in our current environment of abundance, and they become even more problematic during perimenopause when hormonal shifts amplify these tendencies.

The Five Hormone Imbalances: A Comprehensive Framework

When most people, including most healthcare providers, discuss perimenopause or menopause, they focus almost exclusively on sex hormones: estrogen, progesterone, and sometimes testosterone. This makes sense; these are the hormones most directly involved in reproductive function, and their decline defines the menopausal transition.

But focusing solely on sex hormones misses critical pieces of the metabolic puzzle, particularly when it comes to weight management.

After analyzing thousands of lab panels, we've identified five specific hormone imbalances that directly impact a woman's ability to lose weight during perimenopause and menopause. We call these the **Five Metabolizer Types:**

1. **The Locked Metabolizer (Insulin Resistance):** Impaired glucose metabolism and insulin signaling

2. **The Burnout Metabolizer (Cortisol Dysregulation):** Disrupted stress hormone patterns
3. **The Slow Burner Metabolizer (Thyroid Dysfunction):** Suboptimal thyroid hormone production or conversion
4. **The Hormonally Hijacked Metabolizer (Sex Hormone Imbalance):** Declining or imbalanced estrogen, progesterone, and testosterone
5. **The Shadow Metabolizer (Vitamin D Deficiency):** Inadequate levels of this crucial hormone (yes, it's actually a hormone, not a vitamin)

Each of these imbalances independently impacts metabolism, fat storage, energy production, and appetite regulation. When multiple imbalances coexist—which is common during perimenopause—they create synergistic effects that make weight loss feel virtually impossible through diet and exercise alone.

Understanding Your Metabolizer Pattern

Here's what we've learned: **Every woman has a primary metabolizer type**—the main hormone imbalance that's driving most of her symptoms and weight struggles. But most women also have two, three, or even four additional metabolizer subtypes contributing to the overall picture.

For example, you might be primarily a **Locked Metabolizer** (insulin resistance is your biggest issue), but you also have characteristics of cortisol dysregulation and vitamin D deficiency. Or you might be primarily **Hormonally Hijacked** (sex hormone imbalance is dominant), but you're also showing signs of having thyroid dysfunction.

This is why the symptom quizzes at the end of each chapter are so valuable. They help you identify:

- **Your primary metabolizer type:** The imbalance causing the most severe symptoms and likely driving your weight gain
- **Your subtypes:** The additional imbalances compounding the problem and making everything harder to fix

You might score high on one quiz and moderate on three others. That tells you something important: You have one dominant imbalance and three contributing factors. All of them need to be addressed for complete healing, but your primary type might need the most aggressive intervention.

Why Understanding All Five Matters

Understanding all five metabolizer types is crucial for several reasons:

- **Complete Assessment:** Not all women have all five imbalances, but all five need to be evaluated to create a comprehensive treatment plan. You can't know what you don't test. The symptom quizzes give you clues about which types you might be, but only lab testing provides definitive answers.

- **Alternative Pathways:** For women who cannot or choose not to use hormone replacement therapy (HRT), whether due to medical contraindications, personal preference, or fear, addressing the other four imbalances can still produce significant results. You're not limited to only one intervention.

- **Synergistic Effects:** Treating multiple imbalances simultaneously produces dramatically better results than addressing just one. For example, optimizing insulin sensitivity while also supporting thyroid function and managing cortisol creates metabolic improvements that exceed what any single intervention could achieve.

- **Personalization:** Every woman's hormonal picture is unique. Some women are primarily Locked Metabolizers with minimal thyroid issues. Others are primarily Burnout Metabolizers with relatively intact insulin sensitivity. Understanding your specific pattern—your primary type and your subtypes—allows for targeted, personalized treatment rather than one-size-fits-all approaches.

- **The Cascade Effect:** These five hormone systems don't operate independently. They influence each other in complex ways. Often, your primary metabolizer type triggers or worsens your subtypes. For instance, being a Burnout Metabolizer (high cortisol from chronic stress) can create or worsen insulin resistance, making you also a

Locked Metabolizer. Being Hormonally Hijacked (low estrogen) can slow your thyroid conversion, making you also a Slow Burner. The Shadow Metabolizer (vitamin D deficiency) amplifies every other imbalance, making all of them harder to fix.

A Critical Note About Self-Assessment

The symptom quizzes in each chapter are powerful tools for identifying likely patterns, but they are not diagnostic tests.
They help you understand which metabolizer types you might be so you can:

- Have informed conversations with healthcare providers
- Request appropriate lab testing
- Understand why you might be struggling

But **symptoms overlap significantly** between different hormone imbalances. Fatigue could be from cortisol dysregulation, thyroid dysfunction, insulin resistance, sex hormone imbalance, or vitamin D deficiency—or all five. Weight gain around the middle could be due to insulin resistance, cortisol issues, or sex hormone imbalance. Brain fog appears in nearly every pattern.

This is why **we strongly recommend comprehensive lab testing** rather than treating based on symptoms alone. The only way to know definitively which metabolizer types you are—and which is your primary driver—is through appropriate blood work that assesses all five systems simultaneously.

In the upcoming chapters, we'll explore each of these five metabolizer types in detail—what they are, how they affect your body, what symptoms indicate their presence, and which lab tests reveal their status. You'll complete symptom quizzes for each type to help identify which ones are most problematic for you and which might be your primary metabolizer type versus subtypes.

Weight Gain as Symptom, Not Problem

One final crucial concept before we dive into the individual hormone chapters: weight gain is not the problem. It's a symptom of the problem.

This might seem like semantic hair-splitting, but understanding this distinction is fundamental to achieving lasting results.

Symptoms are your body's way of communicating that something is out of balance. They're signals, not the underlying issue itself. When you only treat symptoms without addressing their root cause, you get temporary relief at best and often create additional problems.

Consider a fever. If you take acetaminophen (Tylenol), your fever will decrease, the thermometer reading will go down. But if you don't identify and treat the infection causing the fever, you haven't actually solved anything. You've masked the symptom while the underlying problem continues—potentially worsening because you're not addressing it.

The same is true for perimenopausal weight gain.

You can force the scale down through severe caloric restriction. You can exercise compulsively to burn more calories. You can use appetite suppressants or stimulants. These interventions might temporarily move the number on the scale, but if you haven't addressed the underlying hormonal imbalances—if you haven't identified whether you're a Locked Metabolizer, a Burnout Metabolizer, a Slow Burner, Hormonally Hijacked, or operating as a Shadow Metabolizer—you haven't actually fixed anything.

The moment you stop the extreme restriction or excessive exercise—which you eventually must, because these approaches are unsustainable—the weight returns. Often with interest, because the metabolic stress of extreme interventions can worsen the underlying hormonal imbalances.

For women going through perimenopause who are already doing the "right things"—eating well, exercising consistently, managing stress as best they can—yet still experiencing weight gain, the root cause is hormonal dysregulation. You have one or more metabolizer types that are sabotaging your efforts.

Additional Clarification

Let's be clear about who we're talking to. If you've drastically changed your eating habits—going from balanced nutrition to daily consumption of fast food, processed snacks, and excessive alcohol—and you've gained weight, the root cause is obvious. If you've gone from regular exercise to a completely sedentary lifestyle and you've gained weight, again, the cause is clear.

In those scenarios, the solution is also clear: Address the behavior changes. Return to nutritious eating. Resume regular physical activity.

This book is specifically for women who haven't changed anything—or who have actually increased their efforts—yet can't control the number on the scale. Women who are eating well and exercising consistently but are still experiencing weight gain. Women whose efforts don't match their results.

That's hormonal weight gain. That's what happens when you're operating as one or more of these metabolizer types, where underlying imbalances disrupt your metabolism regardless of your diet and activity level. And that's what requires the comprehensive approach we'll explore in this book.

What to Expect in the Coming Chapters

Over the next five chapters, you'll gain deep understanding of each metabolizer type that commonly affects women during perimenopause and menopause:

Chapter 1: The Locked Metabolizer (Insulin Resistance) explores the metabolic dysfunction that makes your body store fat instead of burning it, creates intense cravings, and produces frustrating weight loss resistance even with perfect diet compliance.

Chapter 2: The Burnout Metabolizer (Cortisol Dysregulation) examines what happens when chronic stress overwhelms your adrenal glands, disrupting your sleep, tanking your energy, and stealing the raw materials needed to make sex hormones.

Chapter 3: The Slow Burner Metabolizer (Thyroid Dysfunction) investigates how this master metabolic regulator can be suboptimal even when your labs are "normal," slowing your metabolism and creating that maddeningly sluggish feeling.

Chapter 4: The Hormonally Hijacked Metabolizer (Sex Hormone Imbalances) covers not just estrogen and progesterone deficiency but also the complex patterns of estrogen dominance, progesterone deficiency, and testosterone decline that create distinct symptom patterns.

Chapter 5: The Shadow Metabolizer (Vitamin D Deficiency) reveals why vitamin D—actually a hormone, not a vitamin—is crucial for hormone production, insulin sensitivity, inflammation control, and maintaining healthy weight, and why "normal" levels are nowhere near optimal.

Each chapter follows the same structure:

1. **Biological mechanisms:** What this hormone does and why it matters
2. **Research foundation:** The science demonstrating this hormone's role in weight and metabolic health
3. **Symptom patterns:** How imbalance manifests in your daily experience
4. **Lab testing:** Which tests reveal this imbalance
5. **Symptom quiz:** A self-assessment tool to help identify whether this metabolizer type is affecting you and whether it might be your primary type or a subtype

As you read through these chapters, we recommend:

Take the symptom quizzes seriously: Be honest about what you're experiencing. These aren't pass/fail tests; they're tools to help you identify which metabolizer types you are—your primary type and your subtypes. If you score high on one quiz and moderate on two or three others, that tells you something important about your hormonal pattern.

Take notes: Keep track of which symptoms resonate most strongly, which metabolizer types seem most relevant to your situation (both primary and subtypes), and questions you want to ask healthcare providers.

Don't diagnose yourself: These quizzes and symptom lists help identify likely imbalances, but they're not substitutes for proper testing. Symptoms can overlap between different conditions, and the only way to know definitively which metabolizer types you are—and which is primary—is through appropriate lab work.

Prepare to advocate: Use the information you learn to have informed conversations with healthcare providers. If your doctor dismisses your concerns, you'll have specific questions to ask and specific tests to request.

Understand the interconnections: As you read, notice how these five hormone systems influence each other. These systems don't operate in isolation, which is why comprehensive assessment and treatment is so important. Your primary metabolizer type often triggers or worsens your subtypes.

At the end of Part I, after you've completed all five hormone chapters and taken all five symptom quizzes, we'll provide resources for getting the comprehensive lab testing you need. We'll give you a PDF you can print and take to your healthcare provider, requesting specific tests that will reveal your hormonal status and confirm which metabolizer types you are. If your provider won't order these tests, we'll provide information about ordering them independently through our practice.

The goal of this part is not to overwhelm you with information but to empower you with understanding. You deserve to know what's happening in your body. You deserve to have language for your experience, to know your metabolism type and the contributing subtypes. And you deserve to have a roadmap for what to test and why.

Only then can you develop a truly personalized treatment plan that addresses your specific hormonal pattern—your primary metabolizer type and all your subtypes—rather than applying generic approaches that may or may not be relevant to your situation.

Remember: these are easy things to test. They're available through traditional medicine (though not always interpreted through the functional medicine lens you need). If you're ready, let's begin with The Locked Metabolizer—the hidden metabolic saboteur that affects the majority of women during perimenopause and makes weight loss feel impossible despite perfect diet compliance.

Insulin Resistance—
The Locked Metabolizer

You're eating less than you ever have. You're at the gym five or even six days a week. And still the scale climbs. And even if the number on the scale stays the same, your body composition is changing. Weight starts being stored around your middle, creating a thick spare tire that makes every pair of pants feel too tight. An hour after lunch, you crash so hard you can barely keep your eyes open. The cravings are relentless—urgent, demanding, impossible to ignore. You're starving an hour after eating a full meal.

You go to your doctor desperate for answers. "Your labs are fine," he says. "Just eat less and exercise more." But you're already doing that. You're doing everything, and it's getting worse. What they didn't tell you is that your cells are locked. Glucose can't get in to be burned for energy. It's trapped in your bloodstream, getting converted to fat and stored around your organs. Every meal—even healthy ones—gets stored instead of burned. Your metabolism isn't just slow. It's *locked*.

This is why we call this pattern "The Locked Metabolizer." When you have insulin resistance, your metabolism literally becomes locked in storage mode. The key that should open your cells to let energy in—insulin—no longer works properly. The lock is jammed. And no matter how little you eat or how much you exercise, your body can't access the fuel it needs to perform optimally because everything is stored as fat instead of being burned for energy. You're metabolically locked.

Insulin resistance is a top metabolic dysfunction commonly seen during perimenopause and menopause, yet it remains one of the most underdiagnosed and undertreated conditions in women's health.

Left unaddressed, insulin resistance progresses into prediabetes and eventually type 2 diabetes, setting the stage for cardiovascular disease, kidney failure, vision loss, and numerous other serious complications. But here's the empowering truth: If caught early and addressed appropriately, insulin resistance is reversible. Understanding insulin resistance is crucial not just for weight management but for your long-term health.

So let's explore what insulin resistance actually is, why it develops during perimenopause, how it manifests in your daily life, and—most important-ly—how to identify whether it's affecting you.

What Is Insulin and Why Does It Matter?

To understand insulin resistance, we first need to understand metabolism at its most fundamental level.

Metabolism is simply the process of converting what you eat—whether protein, fat, carbohydrates, or sugar—along with stored energy from your liver (as glycogen) or from body fat into usable fuel. Regardless of the source, all of these must ultimately be converted into one thing: glucose.

Glucose is your body's universal energy currency. It's carried throughout your bloodstream, attached to red blood cells, circulating constantly, ready to be delivered wherever it's needed.

Here's how the system works when everything is functioning properly:

When a cell anywhere in your body needs energy—maybe a muscle cell during exercise, a brain cell during concentration, a heart cell pumping blood, that cell essentially raises its hand, signaling that it needs fuel.

This signal triggers your pancreas to release insulin into your bloodstream. That insulin then travels to the cell that needs the energy and binds to specific insulin receptors on the cell's surface—think of this as inserting a key into a lock. When insulin binds correctly, it triggers a cascade of intra-cellular signals that allow glucose transporters to move to the cell surface, creating channels through which glucose can enter the cell where it can be burned for energy.

The cell gets the fuel it needs. Your blood sugar remains stable. Your energy stays consistent. The system maintains balance. This is where the "calories in, calories out" principle works as expected—you consume energy, your body uses that energy efficiently, and weight remains stable.

Everyone's happy.

When the System Breaks: Understanding Insulin Resistance

Now let's explore what happens when this elegant system malfunctions.

Insulin resistance is a condition in which cells throughout the body—particularly in muscle, liver, and fat tissue—become less responsive to insulin's signals. With insulin resistance, the initial steps occur normally. You eat food. It's converted to glucose. Glucose circulates in your bloodstream. A cell signals that it needs energy. Your pancreas dutifully releases insulin.

But here's where things go wrong: When insulin arrives at the cell and attempts to bind to the receptor—when the "key" enters the "lock"—the lock doesn't work properly. This could happen for several reasons: The insulin signal is blunted; glucose transporters can't efficiently move to the cell surface; glucose cannot enter the cell adequately.

That cell, which calmly signaled that it needed energy, cannot access the abundant fuel just outside its membrane. From the cell's perspective, despite adequate (or even excess) glucose in the bloodstream, it's experiencing an energy shortage.

Your body responds to this cellular energy deficit with a cascade of metabolic adaptations:

- **Metabolism slows:** Your body attempts to conserve energy by reducing its metabolic rate. This is an adaptive response to perceived energy scarcity at the cellular level. Your body wants to burn the least amount of fuel possible to conserve your energy, and by doing this... This is why women with insulin resistance often say they

Part I: Understanding Why You Are Struggling With The Scale

"barely eat anything" yet still gain weight—their metabolic rate has downshifted significantly.

- **Energy levels plummet:** If cells cannot efficiently utilize glucose for energy production (Adenosine Triphosphate or ATP), you experience profound fatigue. Think about it: When you have more energy, you are more productive in your day. But if your body perceives a lack of fuel, it reduces energy output to conserve resources it perceives as scarce. This manifests as persistent fatigue, difficulty getting through the day, and that characteristic "sluggish" feeling.

- **Glucose gets stored as fat:** Unable to deliver glucose into cells for energy, your body must do something with the excess circulating glucose. It converts it to triglycerides through a process called de novo lipogenesis, primarily in the liver, and stores it as fat—particularly around your midsection. This abdominal (visceral) fat deposition isn't random; it's metabolically active tissue that, unfortunately, further worsens insulin resistance by releasing inflammatory cytokines and free fatty acids that interfere with insulin signaling.

- **The pancreas releases more insulin:** Sensing that glucose isn't getting into cells adequately (detected as elevated blood glucose), your pancreas produces increasing amounts of insulin, trying to overcome the resistance and force the system to work. This creates hyperinsulinemia—chronically elevated insulin levels. While this compensation may maintain relatively normal blood glucose for years, the high insulin levels themselves contribute to further metabolic dysfunction, increased fat storage, and progression of insulin resistance.

- **The vicious cycle perpetuates:** Insulin resistance leads to higher insulin levels (hyperinsulinemia), which in turn leads to more fat storage (particularly visceral fat), worsening insulin resistance through inflammatory mechanisms that require even more insulin. This positive feedback loop progressively worsens metabolic health, slowing metabolism, depleting energy, and promoting weight gain despite dietary efforts.

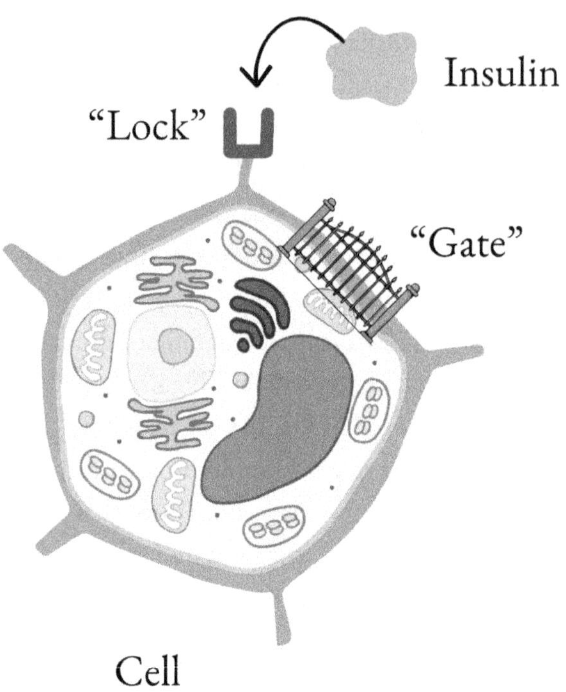

The Estrogen Connection: Why This Happens During Perimenopause

If insulin resistance can affect anyone at any age, why does it become so prevalent during perimenopause and menopause, striking even women who never had blood sugar issues earlier in life?

The answer is simple: **ESTROGEN**.

Estrogen is not merely a reproductive hormone—it's a master metabolic regulator that affects the whole body. The decline in estrogen during the menopausal transition has been identified as an independent risk factor for developing insulin resistance, separate from the effects of aging alone.

Among its many metabolic roles, estrogen:

1. **Enhances insulin sensitivity:** Estrogen, particularly 17β-estradiol, improves insulin signaling at the cellular level through multiple mechanisms. It enhances insulin receptor expression, improves insulin receptor substrate (IRS) signaling, and facilitates glucose

transporter function. When estrogen declines during perimenopause, tissues—particularly skeletal muscle and the liver—become less responsive to insulin's signals. Research has demonstrated that postmenopausal women have significantly reduced insulin sensitivity compared to premenopausal women of similar age and body composition.

2. **Regulates hepatic glucose production:** Estrogen helps suppress gluconeogenesis (glucose production) in the liver. Estrogen signaling through hepatic estrogen receptors modulates the expression of genes involved in glucose production. When estrogen levels drop, hepatic glucose output increases, flooding the bloodstream with glucose even when dietary intake is appropriate and blood glucose is already elevated. This excess endogenous glucose production, combined with reduced peripheral glucose uptake due to insulin resistance, creates a perfect storm for hyperglycemia and metabolic dysfunction.

3. **Influences fat distribution and adipocyte function:** Premenopausal women, under estrogen's influence, tend to store fat subcutaneously in the hips and thighs—a "gynoid" pattern. This subcutaneous fat is relatively metabolically inert. As estrogen declines during menopause, fat distribution shifts dramatically toward an "android" pattern with increased visceral (abdominal) fat accumulation. This shift has profound metabolic consequences. Visceral adipose tissue is metabolically active, releasing free fatty acids directly into portal circulation, producing inflammatory adipokines (including TNF-α, IL-6, and resistin), and secreting less of the insulin-sensitizing hormone adiponectin. These factors directly interfere with insulin signaling in liver and muscle tissue, creating and perpetuating systemic insulin resistance.

4. **Modulates inflammatory pathways:** Estrogen possesses anti-inflammatory properties, partly through its effects on immune cell function and cytokine production. Its decline during perimenopause allows a pro-inflammatory state to emerge. Chronic low-grade inflammation is now recognized as a key driver of insulin resistance,

Chapter 1: Insulin Resistance—The Locked Metabolizer

with inflammatory cytokines directly interfering with insulin signaling pathways at the molecular level.

5. **Affects mitochondrial function:** Emerging research suggests estrogen plays important roles in mitochondrial function and biogenesis. Mitochondria are the cellular powerhouses that produce ATP from glucose. Estrogen deficiency may impair mitochondrial efficiency, further compromising cellular energy metabolism.

A comprehensive review published in *The American Journal of Pathology* by De Paoli, Zakharia, and Werstuck (2021) thoroughly examines the role of estrogen in insulin resistance, concluding that "the hormonal shifts during menopause, specifically the decline in estrogen, are a potential risk factor for insulin resistance independent of age." The authors detail multiple mechanisms through which estrogen loss promotes insulin resistance and emphasize that postmenopausal women are significantly more susceptible to developing insulin resistance, impaired glucose tolerance, and metabolic weight gain compared to premenopausal women.

Additional research has shown that:

- Women who undergo surgical menopause (removal of ovaries) experience more rapid development of insulin resistance compared to those going through natural menopause.
- Hormone replacement therapy (HRT) with estrogen has been shown to improve insulin sensitivity in postmenopausal women.
- The timing and severity of insulin resistance development correlates with the rate and magnitude of estrogen decline.

The decline in estrogen doesn't just correlate with insulin resistance: It directly causes it through multiple, well-characterized biological mechanisms. This is why a woman who had perfectly normal blood sugar metabolism throughout her twenties and thirties can suddenly develop significant insulin resistance in her mid-forties despite making no changes to her diet, exercise, or lifestyle.

It's not your fault. It's biology. It's the predictable metabolic consequence of hormonal changes that every woman experiences during the menopausal transition.

The Dangers Beyond Weight Gain

While insulin resistance profoundly impacts weight management, its health implications extend far beyond the number on the scale. Understanding these risks underscores why early detection and reversal is so critical.

Insulin resistance and the resulting chronic hyperglycemia (elevated blood glucose) and hyperinsulinemia (elevated insulin) create widespread tissue damage through several mechanisms:

Advanced Glycation End Products (AGEs)

When glucose is chronically elevated, it can spontaneously react with proteins, lipids, and nucleic acids in a process called glycation. These reactions produce advanced glycation end products (AGEs), which accumulate in tissues and alter their structure and function. AGEs contribute to vascular stiffness, oxidative stress, and inflammation—all key factors in diabetic complications.

One particularly important glycation reaction occurs with hemoglobin, the oxygen-carrying protein in red blood cells. When hemoglobin is glycated, it becomes hemoglobin A1c (HbA1c). Since red blood cells live approximately 120 days (about 3-4 months), measuring the percentage of hemoglobin that's glycated gives us a three-month average of blood glucose control.

Microvascular Complications

Chronic hyperglycemia and insulin resistance cause particular damage to small blood vessels (microvasculature) throughout the body. The mechanisms include endothelial dysfunction, increased oxidative stress, inflammation, and accumulation of AGEs in vessel walls. The areas most vulnerable to microvascular damage include:

The eyes: The tiny vessels in the retina (retinal capillaries) are exquisitely sensitive to glucose-induced damage. Diabetic retinopathy—characterized by vessel leakage, hemorrhage, and eventually new abnormal vessel growth—is a leading cause of blindness in adults. Early detection and glucose control can prevent or slow this progression.

The kidneys: The glomeruli—microscopic filtering units in the kidneys—contain delicate capillary networks. Chronic hyperglycemia damages these structures, leading to diabetic nephropathy. Early signs include microalbuminuria (small amounts of protein in urine), which can progress to overt kidney disease and eventual kidney failure requiring dialysis or transplantation. Diabetes is the leading cause of end-stage renal disease in developed countries.

The nervous system: Peripheral nerves and their tiny nutrient blood vessels are vulnerable to glucose-induced damage, resulting in diabetic neuropathy. This manifests as pain, tingling, numbness, or loss of sensation—particularly in the feet and hands in a "stocking-glove" distribution. Loss of protective sensation in the feet contributes to unnoticed injuries, which, combined with impaired wound healing (another complication of diabetes), can lead to serious infections and ulcerations.

Macrovascular Complications

Insulin resistance and diabetes dramatically accelerate atherosclerosis (hardening and narrowing of larger arteries), increasing risk for:

Cardiovascular disease: Insulin resistance is a major component of metabolic syndrome and is strongly associated with coronary artery disease, heart attack, heart failure, and cardiovascular death. In fact, cardiovascular disease is the leading cause of death in people with diabetes.

Cerebrovascular disease: Stroke risk is significantly elevated in people with insulin resistance and diabetes, due to both large vessel atherosclerosis and small vessel disease.

Peripheral vascular disease: Reduced blood flow to the extremities, particularly the legs and feet, combined with neuropathy and impaired wound healing, creates the "diabetic foot"—a serious complication that can lead to non-healing ulcers, infections, gangrene, and amputation.

The Progression from Insulin Resistance to Diabetes

Insulin resistance typically exists for years before frank diabetes develops. During this time, your pancreas compensates by producing more and more insulin to maintain normal blood glucose levels. Eventually, pancreatic beta cells become exhausted or damaged from this chronic overwork, and insulin production declines. At this point, blood glucose rises above the diabetic threshold, and the diagnosis of type 2 diabetes is made.

This progression is not inevitable. If caught during the insulin resistance phase—before beta cell exhaustion—the condition is largely reversible through appropriate interventions. This is the critical window of opportunity that perimenopause presents.

In traditional medicine, we often cannot intervene until you've progressed to prediabetes or frank diabetes—at which point years of metabolic dysfunction have occurred and complications may already be developing. We're trained to treat disease states, not optimize metabolic health or prevent disease progression.

But catching insulin resistance early—identifying it through sensitive markers like fasting insulin, HgbA1c, and HOMA-IR, reversing it through comprehensive interventions, and healing the underlying metabolic dysfunction? That's true prevention. That's taking control of your health trajectory before irreversible damage occurs.

This is precisely why addressing insulin resistance during perimenopause is so crucial. You have a window of opportunity to reverse this condition, restore metabolic health, and prevent progression to diabetes and its devastating complications.

What Insulin Resistance Feels Like: Recognizing the Symptoms

Insulin resistance doesn't announce itself with a single dramatic symptom. Instead, it manifests as a constellation of experiences that, taken together, create a picture of metabolic dysfunction.

The Energy Roller Coaster

Perhaps the most common complaint is about energy—or the lack thereof. Women with insulin resistance describe feeling perpetually sluggish, like they're moving through molasses. But it's not just constant low energy; it's a specific pattern:

You might wake up feeling somewhat okay, push through the morning on willpower and caffeine. Then, about one to two hours after eating—particularly after a carbohydrate-containing meal—you crash hard. That post-meal fatigue isn't just normal afternoon tiredness—it's reactive hypoglycemia and cellular energy deficit.

Here's what happens: You eat a meal containing carbohydrates. Your blood glucose rises. Your pancreas, dealing with insulin resistance, releases excessive insulin to manage the glucose load. This large insulin surge can actually overshoot, driving blood glucose down too rapidly (reactive hypoglycemia). You experience profound fatigue, difficulty concentrating, shakiness, and intense hunger despite having just eaten.

This pattern often repeats throughout the day. You eat, hoping for energy, and instead experience a crash. You feel foggy, have difficulty concentrating on simple tasks, and find yourself reaching for sugar or caffeine just to function—which perpetuates the cycle.

The Cravings That Won't Quit

Insulin resistance creates intense, almost overwhelming cravings—particularly for carbohydrates and sugar. These aren't normal "I'd enjoy a cookie" cravings. They're urgent, demanding, difficult-to-ignore signals that feel almost desperate.

The mechanism is partly biological: High insulin levels drive blood glucose down, triggering hunger signals. But there's also a cellular component: Because glucose isn't efficiently entering cells, your body perceives energy scarcity and generates powerful hunger signals trying to solve what it interprets as starvation, even though blood glucose may be elevated.

The cravings intensify if you go extended periods without eating—anything over 12-14 hours, such as overnight fasting or skipping meals. Your body, sensing that cells aren't getting adequate fuel despite available glucose, sends increasingly urgent hunger signals.

Many women describe feeling like they're fighting their own bodies, white-knuckling through cravings while simultaneously knowing that giving in leads to more weight gain and perpetuates the cycle. It's exhausting and demoralizing.

The Inexplicable Weight Gain

Despite eating carefully—perhaps even eating less than you used to—weight accumulates. Not randomly distributed but specifically around your midsection. Your pants get tighter around the waist even if your legs stay the same. Your waistline expands. You develop the characteristic "apple shape" or "spare tire" around the middle.

This visceral fat accumulation is characteristic of insulin resistance and metabolic syndrome. It's not about eating too much. It's about your body's inability to efficiently burn what you're eating for fuel, defaulting instead to storage mode. High insulin levels signal fat storage, particularly in visceral adipose tissue. Every meal, even healthy ones, contributes to fat accumulation because the metabolic machinery isn't working properly.

Additional Warning Signs

As insulin resistance progresses, additional symptoms may emerge:

Increased thirst and urination: When blood glucose exceeds the kidney's reabsorption threshold (typically around 180 mg/dL), glucose spills into the urine, pulling water with it through osmotic diuresis. This leads to frequent urination (polyuria) and compensatory increased thirst (polydipsia).

Skin changes:

- **Acanthosis nigricans:** Dark, velvety patches of skin appear in body folds—neck, armpits, groin, under breasts. This hyperpigmentation is directly related to insulin resistance; high insulin levels stimulate skin cell growth in these areas.

- **Skin tags:** Small, benign growths often appear on the neck, armpits, or other areas. Their presence is associated with insulin resistance and metabolic syndrome.

Blurred vision: Fluctuating blood glucose levels cause fluid shifts in the lens of the eye, temporarily affecting its shape and focusing ability. This can cause vision to blur and fluctuate, particularly after meals when glucose peaks.

Frequent infections: Particularly yeast infections (candidiasis) and urinary tract infections. Elevated glucose creates an environment where bacteria and yeast thrive. Additionally, insulin resistance impairs immune function, making infections more frequent and harder to clear.

Slow wound healing: High glucose and insulin resistance impair multiple aspects of wound healing: reduced neutrophil function, impaired fibroblast activity, decreased collagen production, and compromised blood flow. Cuts, scrapes, and surgical incisions take notably longer to heal.

Fatty liver: Excess glucose is converted to triglycerides in the liver through de novo lipogenesis. When this exceeds the liver's ability to export triglycerides, fat accumulates in hepatocytes, creating non-alcoholic fatty liver disease (NAFLD). This is detectable on imaging (ultrasound, CT, MRI) and can progress to inflammation (NASH), fibrosis, and eventually cirrhosis.

The Frustration Factor: Why Nothing Works

Here's what makes insulin resistance so maddening for women trying to lose weight: Traditional weight loss advice doesn't just fail—it can make things worse.

"Eat less and exercise more" is the standard recommendation. But when insulin resistance is present, this approach is physiologically inadequate. Here's why:

The Biology Prevents Weight Loss

If glucose literally cannot enter cells efficiently due to impaired insulin signaling, no amount of caloric restriction will fix that fundamental biological problem. You can restrict calories—eating 1200, 1000, or even fewer calories daily and still gain weight because:

- Your metabolism slows in response to caloric restriction AND due to insulin resistance.
- High insulin levels (hyperinsulinemia) signal fat storage regardless of caloric intake.
- Whatever you eat is preferentially stored as fat rather than efficiently burned for energy.
- Your body cannot access stored fat for fuel when insulin is chronically elevated.

Exercise Alone Is Insufficient

You can exercise intensely—hours at the gym, long runs, high-intensity boot camps—and see minimal results. In fact, excessive exercise without adequate fueling and recovery can worsen the situation by:

- Elevating cortisol (which we'll discuss in the next chapter), which worsens insulin resistance
- Creating an even larger perceived energy deficit, which slows metabolism further

- Breaking down muscle tissue (which worsens metabolic rate) without adequate recovery nutrition
- Increasing inflammation, which impairs insulin signaling

This is the experience we hear repeatedly: "I'm eating less than I ever have. I'm working out more than I ever have. And I'm still gaining weight. What is wrong with me?"

You have a metabolic condition that requires appropriate diagnosis and treatment, not just more willpower or restriction.

Women with undiagnosed insulin resistance spend years—sometimes decades—spinning their wheels. Trying diet after diet: keto, paleo, low-fat, intermittent fasting, calorie restriction, meal replacements. Trying exercise program after exercise program: CrossFit, running programs, boot camps, personal training. Growing increasingly frustrated and hopeless as nothing produces lasting results.

They visit doctors who run basic labs, find fasting glucose at 95 mg/dL (just barely within the "normal" range of <100), and declare everything fine. Maybe they check HbA1c and find it at 5.4%—well below the traditional prediabetic threshold of 5.8%—and again reassure the patient that everything is normal.

But it's not fine. You feel terrible. You're exhausted constantly. You're gaining weight despite enormous effort and discipline. And you're being told it's just part of getting older, or you're not trying hard enough, or you should eat even less and exercise even more.

The problem isn't effort. The problem is that the underlying insulin resistance hasn't been identified and addressed. And without correcting the metabolic dysfunction, no amount of dietary restriction or exercise intensity will produce sustainable weight loss.

Part I: Understanding Why You Are Struggling With The Scale

Testing for Insulin Resistance: Getting the Right Labs

Standard annual physical labs typically include only fasting glucose. While this can identify advanced prediabetes or diabetes, it's a relatively insensitive marker for earlier insulin resistance. By the time fasting glucose is significantly elevated, you've likely had insulin resistance for years, and pancreatic compensation is beginning to fail.

This is why testing for insulin resistance specifically—not just fasting glucose but the more sensitive markers—is so important. You cannot treat what you don't know exists. And without proper diagnosis and targeted treatment, no amount of willpower, restriction, or exercise will overcome the underlying metabolic dysfunction.

For the right labs, we use more sensitive, earlier markers that reveal insulin resistance long before glucose becomes abnormal:

Hemoglobin A1c (HbA1c)

This test measures the percentage of hemoglobin (the oxygen-carrying protein in red blood cells) that has been glycated—bonded with glucose. Because red blood cells live approximately 120 days (3-4 months), HbA1c provides a long-term picture of average glucose levels rather than a single point-in-time measurement.

This test is particularly valuable because it's not affected by what you ate the night before your blood draw, whether you fasted properly, or stress-induced glucose fluctuations. It reflects your glucose control over months, providing a more stable and reliable assessment than fasting glucose alone.

Importantly, HbA1c can reveal glucose dysregulation even when fasting glucose appears normal. Some women have normal fasting glucose (under tight pancreatic control) but experience significant post-meal glucose spikes that aren't captured by fasting measurements. HbA1c reflects the cumulative glycemic exposure and can identify this pattern.

Fasting Insulin

While fasting glucose measures the sugar in your blood, fasting insulin measures how much insulin your pancreas is producing to manage that glucose. This is crucial because elevated fasting insulin is often the earliest detectable sign of insulin resistance, appearing years before glucose becomes abnormal.

Here's what's happening: Your cells are becoming resistant to insulin. Your pancreas compensates by producing more insulin to overcome that resistance. Glucose remains normal (or even low-normal) because the extra insulin is successfully managing it, but this compensation comes at a cost. The high insulin levels themselves promote fat storage, worsen insulin resistance over time, and eventually exhaust the pancreas.

Elevated fasting insulin indicates that your body is working harder, producing excess insulin just to maintain even normal glucose levels. The system is already dysfunctional; it's just still compensating. This is your window for intervention before compensation fails and glucose rises into the diabetic range.

HOMA-IR (Homeostatic Model Assessment of Insulin Resistance)

If you only have fasting glucose and fasting insulin levels, you can still screen for insulin resistance with the HOMA-IR (Homeostasis Model Assessment of Insulin Resistance).

HOMA-IR is a calculated index that combines fasting glucose and fasting insulin to provide a single number representing insulin resistance severity:

HOMA-IR = (Fasting Glucose [mmol/L] × Fasting Insulin [μIU/mL]) / 22.5

Or if glucose is measured in mg/dL (common in the US):

HOMA-IR = (Fasting Glucose [mg/dL] × Fasting Insulin [μIU/mL]) / 405

This calculation assesses the relationship between glucose and insulin, providing insight into how well your body is managing glucose metabolism.

A higher HOMA-IR score indicates greater insulin resistance—meaning more insulin is required to maintain a given glucose level.

Because it's based on fasting labs, HOMA-IR is a single time-point estimate (and fasting insulin can vary), whereas HbA1c reflects average glycemia over roughly 2–3 months. Clinically, HOMA-IR can be helpful when fasting glucose appears "normal" because insulin may rise earlier in the progression toward dysglycemia—so the combination can reveal metabolic strain that might be missed by glucose alone.

Our Preferred Approach

We typically recommend checking both HbA1c (for the three-month trend in glucose control) and fasting insulin (for current pancreatic compensation and early insulin resistance detection). This combination provides both historical perspective and current assessment, giving the most complete picture of metabolic status.

For women with significant symptoms or risk factors, we may also calculate HOMA-IR or order additional tests such as:

- Fasting lipid panel (triglycerides, HDL cholesterol—components of metabolic syndrome)
- Liver enzymes (to assess for fatty liver)
- Inflammatory markers (high-sensitivity CRP)

These tests are readily available through standard laboratories, covered by most insurance plans when appropriately ordered, and provide crucial information that standard glucose testing alone misses.

When you meet with your healthcare provider, specifically request these tests if they're not already ordered. If your provider is reluctant, explain that you're experiencing symptoms consistent with insulin resistance and want to catch any metabolic dysfunction early before it progresses to diabetes.

Note: Optimal ranges and detailed interpretation will be covered in Part III, along with comprehensive treatment protocols for reversing insulin resistance.

Insulin Resistance Symptom Quiz

Insulin resistance doesn't always announce itself clearly. For many women, it shows up as subtle, everyday symptoms that are easy to dismiss or normalize, especially during perimenopause. Use the checklist below to identify which symptoms apply to you.

Medical History & Risk Factors:

- ☐ Personal history of diabetes
- ☐ Family history of diabetes (parent, sibling)
- ☐ Personal history of gestational diabetes
- ☐ Family history of gestational diabetes
- ☐ Personal history of PCOS (polycystic ovary syndrome)
- ☐ Personal or family history of heart disease or stroke
- ☐ Elevated cholesterol or triglycerides
- ☐ High blood pressure (hypertension)
- ☐ Diagnosis of prediabetes or elevated blood sugar in the past
- ☐ Thyroid disorder
- ☐ Low physical activity level (sedentary lifestyle)
- ☐ History of smoking (current or past)
- ☐ History of taking certain medications (corticosteroids, antipsychotics, some blood pressure medications)

Current Symptoms & Experiences:

- ☐ Chronic fatigue and low energy levels throughout the day
- ☐ Energy crash or extreme tiredness 1-2 hours after eating (especially after carbohydrate-containing meals)
- ☐ Feeling persistently sluggish or foggy, difficulty thinking clearly
- ☐ Difficulty concentrating on simple tasks or remembering things
- ☐ Slow metabolism (feeling like you "can't lose weight no matter what")
- ☐ Weight gain, particularly around the midsection/abdomen
- ☐ Difficulty losing weight despite appropriate diet and exercise

☐ Intense cravings for salt or sugar, particularly in afternoon/evening
☐ Frequent hunger, even shortly after eating a meal
☐ Increased thirst (drinking more fluids than usual)
☐ Frequent urination (waking at night to urinate, needing bathroom frequently during day)
☐ Skin tags (small, soft skin growths on neck, armpits, or other areas)
☐ Darkening of skin in body folds (neck, armpits, groin, under breasts)
☐ Blurred vision or vision changes
☐ Frequent yeast infections (vaginal, oral, or skin)
☐ Recurrent urinary tract infections
☐ Slow healing of cuts, scrapes, or wounds
☐ Diagnosis of fatty liver on imaging studies

Scoring: Count your total checked items: ____________

Interpreting Your Results:

0-3 symptoms: Low likelihood of significant insulin resistance, though testing can still be valuable as some women with insulin resistance have minimal symptoms, particularly in early stages

4-7 symptoms: Moderate likelihood of insulin resistance; testing is recommended to assess metabolic status

8-12 symptoms: High likelihood of insulin resistance; testing is strongly recommended, and addressing this should be a priority

13+ symptoms: Very high likelihood of significant insulin resistance with possible progression toward prediabetes; comprehensive testing and metabolic evaluation is critical

Important Reminders:

- This quiz is a screening tool to help identify likely insulin resistance, not a diagnostic test.
- Insulin resistance can be present even with few symptoms, particularly in early stages.

- The only way to definitively diagnose insulin resistance is through appropriate laboratory testing.
- Regardless of your score, if you're experiencing unexplained weight gain, persistent fatigue, or metabolic symptoms during perimenopause, testing for insulin resistance is warranted.
- Symptoms can vary widely between individuals in both presentation and severity.
- Bring this completed quiz to your healthcare provider to facilitate discussion about appropriate testing.

Chapter Summary

If there's one thing to understand about insulin resistance—about being a Locked Metabolizer—it's this: The decline in estrogen during perimenopause leads to insulin resistance in the majority of women and can cause weight gain, metabolic dysfunction, and profound fatigue, even if you're eating well and exercising consistently. This is not your fault. This is biology.

Your metabolism has become locked in storage mode. The key—insulin—no longer opens your cells to let energy in. Everything gets stored as fat instead of being burned for fuel. This is why eating less and exercising more doesn't work when you're a Locked Metabolizer. You're not battling a lack of willpower. You're battling a fundamental biological dysfunction where your cells literally cannot access the fuel they need.

This is why focusing solely on sex hormone replacement therapy, while important, misses a crucial piece of the metabolic puzzle. If we don't address insulin resistance—if we only replace estrogen and progesterone without correcting the insulin signaling dysfunction and cellular metabolic impairment—we leave women struggling with weight management, at risk for diabetes, and vulnerable to all the serious health complications that follow.

The empowering truth: insulin resistance is reversible. With proper diagnosis through appropriate laboratory testing and comprehensive treatment (which we'll detail in Part III), you can:

- Restore insulin sensitivity and normal glucose metabolism
- Heal and optimize your metabolic function
- Lose weight sustainably without extreme restriction
- Regain consistent energy throughout the day
- Quiet intense cravings and normalize hunger signals
- Dramatically reduce your risk of progressing to prediabetes, diabetes, and all their associated complications
- Improve your long-term health trajectory and reduce cardiovascular disease risk

But first, you need to know it's there. You need to request the right tests—specifically HbA1c and fasting insulin, not just fasting glucose. And you need to stop blaming yourself for a biological, metabolic condition that requires medical intervention and comprehensive treatment—not just more willpower, restriction, or exercise intensity.

Insulin resistance is common during perimenopause. It's not a personal failure. It's a predictable consequence of hormonal shifts that can and should be addressed as part of comprehensive perimenopausal care.

Looking Ahead

In the next chapter, we'll explore the second major hormone imbalance affecting weight and well-being during perimenopause: cortisol dysregulation and adrenal dysfunction. You'll discover why stress isn't just mental or emotional but has profound physical and metabolic consequences—including its direct impact on insulin sensitivity, weight gain, and your ability to produce adequate sex hormones. You'll learn why managing cortisol is essential not just for feeling better emotionally but for metabolic health, sustainable weight loss, and successful aging.

Cortisol Dysregulation and Adrenal Fatigue—The Burnout Metabolizer

You wake up exhausted despite sleeping seven hours. You drag yourself through the morning fueled by coffee and willpower. By mid-afternoon, you hit a wall—your energy crashes completely. You push through somehow, making it to evening, when you finally have time to rest. But when you lie down to sleep, your mind starts racing. Or you fall asleep easily, only to wake at two or three a.m. with your brain spinning, unable to fall back asleep for hours.

Meanwhile, your waistline is expanding despite your best efforts. You snap at your family over minor inconveniences. You feel simultaneously exhausted and wired, depleted yet anxious, burned out but unable to truly rest.

If this describes your experience, you're likely dealing with cortisol dysregulation and adrenal fatigue, the second major hormone imbalance that affects weight and well-being during perimenopause. You're what we call a Burnout Metabolizer.

The term "Burnout Metabolizer" captures exactly what's happening in your body. You're not just emotionally burned out, though you may feel that way. Your metabolism itself is experiencing burnout. Your adrenal glands are depleted from years of chronic stress, unable to produce hormones efficiently. Your body is stuck in survival mode, breaking down your own muscle tissue for energy while simultaneously storing fat around your middle. You're running on empty, yet your system won't shut down to truly rest and recover. Your metabolism has burned out, and it's taking everything else down with it.

Part I: Understanding Why You Are Struggling With The Scale

Understanding cortisol and its far-reaching effects throughout your body is crucial not just for weight management but for your overall health, energy, mental well-being, and quality of life. When cortisol patterns are disrupted, virtually every system in your body suffers. But here's the empowering message: High-performing women can't necessarily escape their demanding lives, but they CAN change how stress impacts their bodies. Once you understand the mechanisms and implement targeted interventions, damage can be reversed, symptoms can disappear, and your adrenal glands can resume producing the hormones—including sex hormones—they were meant to make.

What Is Cortisol and Why Does It Matter?

Cortisol is often called the "stress hormone" and for good reason: It's the primary hormone your body releases in response to any perceived threat or stressor. Cortisol is produced by your adrenal glands, two small glands that sit atop your kidneys.

The stress response that cortisol mediates was designed to be short-term and temporary—a quick, adaptive reaction to immediate danger. Think of the classic "running from a tiger" scenario. In that moment, cortisol and related stress hormones create rapid physiological changes that enhance your chances of survival.

The Acute Stress Response: How It's Supposed to Work

Here's what happens during a healthy short-term stress response:

1. **You experience a trigger:** Something threatening occurs: a predator, an accident, a sudden danger.
2. **Stress hormones flood your system:** Your hypothalamus signals your pituitary gland, which signals your adrenal glands to release

cortisol, adrenaline, and noradrenaline. This is the hypothalam-ic-pituitary-adrenal (HPA) axis in action.

3. **Your body is flooded with glucose:** Cortisol triggers the liver to release stored glucose into the bloodstream, providing immediate energy for your muscles and brain to respond to the threat.

4. **Your cardiovascular system ramps up:** Blood vessels constrict (increasing blood pressure), and your heart rate increases. This delivers more oxygen-rich blood throughout your body, particularly to large muscle groups that need to run or fight.

5. **Non-essential functions are suppressed:** Your body conserves energy by temporarily shutting down systems that aren't immediately necessary for survival. Digestion slows or stops. Reproductive function is suppressed. Immune responses are dampened. Growth and tissue repair pause. The logic is simple: If you're running from a tiger, your body doesn't need to digest lunch, ovulate, fight off a cold, or build new tissue. It needs every bit of energy focused on immediate survival.

6. **The threat is neutralized:** You escape the tiger. You survive the crisis. The immediate danger passes.

7. **Hormone levels return to normal:** Cortisol drops back to baseline. Your body resumes normal function. Digestion restarts. Immune function recovers. You can rest, repair, and recover.

This system is brilliant, adaptive, and life-saving when stress is acute and temporary. The problem? Modern life has created a situation where stress is chronic, unrelenting, and never-ending—and our bodies are paying a devastating price.

The Problem: When Stress Never Ends

The stress response was never designed to be constantly activated. When stress becomes chronic—when the "tiger" never goes away, or when you face multiple "tigers" simultaneously and continuously—your body remains in a perpetual state of emergency response.

Consider the reality of most women's lives. Demanding careers with constant deadlines and pressure. Financial worries—mortgages, college tuition, retirement savings. Raising children while managing their schedules, emotional needs, and development. Running a household with endless tasks, decisions, and responsibilities. Caring for aging parents who need increasing support. Relationship challenges. Health concerns. The pressure of societal expectations. And the invisible mental load of coordinating everyone's schedules and anticipating everyone's needs. For most women, stress isn't occasional; it's constant, layered, and unrelenting.

When stress is chronic and cortisol remains elevated for extended periods, all those temporary adaptive changes become ongoing problems. That temporarily elevated blood sugar? It becomes chronically high, creating insulin resistance and setting the stage for prediabetes and type 2 diabetes. The cardiovascular strain that was helpful for a quick sprint away from danger? It becomes chronic hypertension that damages blood vessels and strains your heart, dramatically increasing your risk for heart disease and stroke.

And those systems that were temporarily suppressed? When they remain suppressed long-term, serious dysfunction develops. The body was never meant to sustain this emergency state indefinitely. Doing so creates widespread dysfunction and puts you at significant risk for type 2 diabetes, cardiovascular disease and hypertension, chronic fatigue and burnout, increased abdominal fat and metabolic syndrome, digestive disorders, fertility problems, weakened immune function and frequent infections, sleep disorders and insomnia, cognitive impairment and memory problems, thyroid dysfunction, anxiety and depression, and accelerated aging. This isn't hyperbole or exaggeration; these are well-documented consequences of chronic stress and sustained cortisol elevation, backed by decades of research across multiple medical specialties.

Chapter 2: Cortisol Dysregulation and Adrenal Fatigue—The Burnout Metabolizer

Why Perimenopause Creates the Perfect Storm

If chronic stress is harmful for everyone, why does it become particularly problematic for women during perimenopause? The answer lies in the convergence of multiple stressors and hormonal shifts happening simultaneously during this life stage.

By the time women reach perimenopause—typically mid-forties to early fifties—they've often been managing high-stress lives for decades. Building careers, raising children, maintaining relationships, managing households, meeting endless demands and expectations. But perimenopause brings additional unique stressors that create what can only be described as a perfect storm.

Many women find themselves in what's called the "sandwich generation"—simultaneously caring for growing children that are getting ready to leave the "nest" while also supporting aging parents who need increasing help. The demands from both directions are relentless and emotionally draining. At the same time, career pressures often peak during these years. Women in their forties and fifties may be in senior positions with maximum responsibility, or they're fighting to maintain relevance in youth-oriented industries, or they're trying to re-enter the workforce after years focused on family. The professional stress is intense.

But perhaps most challenging is that the physical symptoms of perimenopause themselves create additional stress. Disrupted sleep from night sweats and insomnia. Unpredictable periods that can be embarrassingly heavy or painfully cramping. Hot flashes that strike at the worst moments. Brain fog that makes you feel like you're losing your edge. Mood changes that make you feel unlike yourself. Weight gain despite eating the same way you always have. Declining energy that makes everything feel harder. Every symptom adds to your overall stress burden, and stress worsens every symptom. The cycle feeds itself.

There's also a physiological component that makes things worse. Declining estrogen during perimenopause allows inflammatory processes to increase throughout the body. Chronic inflammation drives cortisol production, trying to dampen that inflammation. But elevated cortisol paradoxically worsens inflammation over time. It's another vicious cycle that's difficult to break without intervention.

Sleep becomes increasingly disrupted—not just from night sweats but from cortisol pattern changes we'll discuss shortly. And sleep deprivation is itself a profound stressor that elevates cortisol, which further disrupts sleep. The sleep-cortisol cycle becomes self-perpetuating.

Then there's the psychological stress of not recognizing your own body. The weight gain, the changing shape, the declining strength, the joint aches and pains—the physical changes of perimenopause can feel like a betrayal. Many women describe feeling like strangers in their own bodies. Not recognizing yourself creates significant psychological stress that manifests physically through elevated cortisol.

The cumulative effect is this: By perimenopause, most women have been functioning in a state of chronic stress for years or decades. Their stress management reserves are depleted. And then the additional stressors of this life stage—the sandwich generation squeeze, the physical symptoms, the sleep disruption, the body changes—push many women past their breaking point into complete burnout.

The Adrenal Gland's Impossible Job

Here's where the hormonal component becomes crucial, and it's something most doctors never discuss with their patients. As we established in the Introduction, when your ovaries begin producing less estrogen and progesterone during perimenopause, your adrenal glands are supposed to partially compensate by increasing sex hormone production. This is how the female body is designed to transition through menopause—ovarian production decreases, adrenal production increases, and the transition happens more smoothly.

But here's the problem: Your adrenal glands are already overtaxed from years of chronic stress. They're already working at capacity, possibly beyond capacity. And now they're being asked to also ramp up production of sex hormones to compensate for declining ovarian function.

They simply can't do both adequately. Something has to give. And what gives is sex hormone production because your body always prioritizes survival over reproduction.

This is where understanding the "pregnenolone steal" becomes important.

The Pregnenolone Steal: Why Stress Steals Your Hormones

All steroid hormones in your body—cortisol, progesterone, estrogen, testosterone, and DHEA—are made from the same starting material: cholesterol. Yes, the same cholesterol you've been told to watch in your diet is actually the foundation of your entire hormone system.

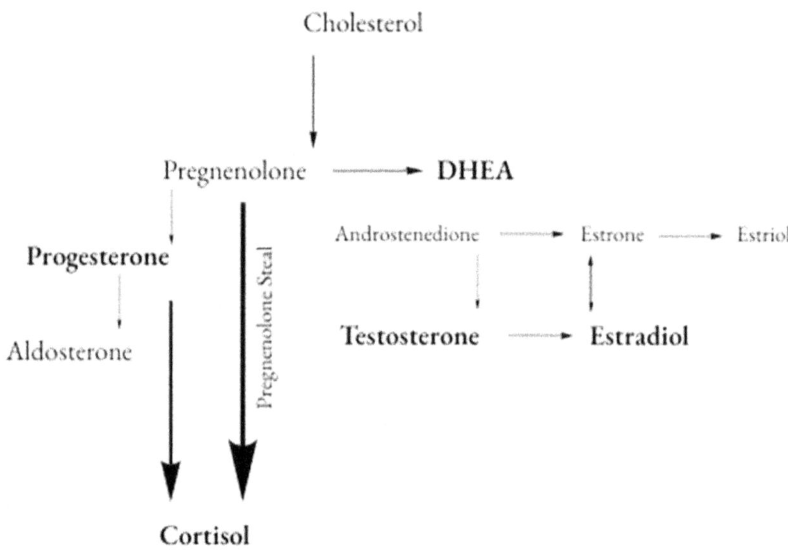

The Hormone Production Pathway:

Cholesterol → Pregnenolone → Either:
- Stress hormone pathway → Cortisol

- Sex hormone pathway → DHEA → Progesterone, Estrogen, Testosterone

Pregnenolone is sometimes called the "mother hormone" because it's the precursor to all other steroid hormones. But here's the critical point: Your body has a limited supply of pregnenolone at any given time, and when you're under chronic stress, your body must decide how to allocate that limited resource.

From an evolutionary perspective, the decision is clear. If you're under threat—if you're being chased by a predator, if food is scarce, if you're in constant danger—reproduction is not a priority. Immediate survival is. So when your adrenal glands receive constant signals that you're under threat through chronically elevated demand for cortisol, they prioritize survival over reproduction. They preferentially shunt pregnenolone toward cortisol production rather than toward sex hormone production.

This is what functional medicine practitioners call the "pregnenolone steal" or "cortisol steal." Cortisol production literally steals the raw materials that should be going toward making progesterone, estrogen, and testosterone.

The result:
- High cortisol (or erratic patterns)
- Low sex hormones, particularly progesterone and DHEA
- Worsening of all perimenopausal symptoms

Now layer perimenopause on top of this. During perimenopause, your ovarian production of sex hormones is already declining significantly. Your body is supposed to shift sex hormone production to the adrenal glands to partially compensate and smooth the transition. But if your adrenal glands are already depleted from years of chronic stress and are prioritizing cortisol production just to keep you functioning, they cannot adequately take over sex hormone production.

This creates a devastating combination:
- Ovaries are producing less estrogen and progesterone
- Adrenal glands should compensate but can't because they're overwhelmed making cortisol

Chapter 2: Cortisol Dysregulation and Adrenal Fatigue—The Burnout Metabolizer

- Result: Severe sex hormone deficiency combined with cortisol dysregulation
- All perimenopausal symptoms worsen dramatically

This is why addressing stress and cortisol during perimenopause isn't optional or just about "self-care" or "managing stress better" in some vague wellness sense. It's physiologically essential. If you don't manage cortisol and support adrenal function, you cannot optimize sex hormone production, and you'll continue to suffer despite other interventions, including hormone replacement therapy.

When Stress Rewires Your Brain and Body

Cortisol doesn't just affect your adrenal glands and sex hormones. Because cortisol receptors exist throughout virtually every tissue in your body, chronic elevation creates widespread dysfunction across multiple systems. Let's walk through the major effects, understanding that these aren't separate issues—they're all connected through the common thread of chronic cortisol elevation.

Feeling "On Edge"—Hypervigilance and Irritability

Chronic stress keeps your sympathetic nervous system—your fight-or-flight response—activated constantly. This creates a state of persistent hyperarousal where you're constantly feeling on alert, unable to relax even in safe situations. You find yourself hypervigilant, unconsciously scanning your environment for potential threats. You startle easily at sudden noises or movements. You're irritable and quick to anger, with what people describe as a "short fuse." You're ready to snap at people over minor inconveniences that wouldn't normally bother you. You feel anxious and keyed up, like you can never fully calm down. And you're emotionally reactive, overreacting to situations in ways that don't feel like your normal self.

The neurobiological basis is fascinating and disturbing. Chronic cortisol exposure literally alters your brain structure and function. Your amygdala—

your brain's threat detection and emotional response center—becomes enlarged and hyperactive. It's constantly searching for danger, interpreting neutral situations as threatening. Meanwhile, your hippocampus—involved in memory and contextual understanding—actually shrinks, reducing your ability to distinguish real threats from perceived ones. And your prefrontal cortex, responsible for executive function and emotional regulation, shows reduced activity.

The result is a brain that's primed for threat detection and reaction with dramatically reduced capacity for rational thinking and emotional regulation. You're physiologically stuck in a defensive, reactive state.

Women describe this experience in remarkably consistent ways:

- "I feel like I'm always waiting for the other shoe to drop."
- "I can't turn my brain off."
- "Everything feels overwhelming."
- "I have no patience anymore."
- "I fly off the handle at the smallest things."
- "I'm exhausted but wired at the same time."

Weight Gain and Difficulty Losing Weight

This is perhaps the most frustrating effect for women trying to manage their weight during perimenopause. Chronic cortisol elevation directly promotes weight gain and prevents weight loss through multiple mechanisms.

First, fat located around your organs—called visceral fat—has significantly more cortisol receptors than fat located elsewhere on your body. This means that when cortisol is elevated, it signals fat to be stored on those visceral adipose receptors, increasing that characteristic belly fat or "muffin top" that seems impossible to lose.

Second, cortisol causes you to crave foods that are high-calorie, high-fat, high-sugar "comfort" foods. Because with elevations in cortisol, your body is craving relief or reward, and those foods are the ones that give you a quick boost of "feel-good" hormones. This is also what is referred to as "emotional eating" because your body is craving that reward.

Chapter 2: Cortisol Dysregulation and Adrenal Fatigue—The Burnout Metabolizer

Third, as we discussed in Chapter 1, elevated cortisol actually makes insulin resistance worse. High insulin plus high cortisol equals maximum fat storage signaling, especially around the middle.

Fourth, cortisol promotes the breakdown of muscle to use for energy stores. Cortisol is catabolic, which means it breaks down protein and muscle tissue into amino acids to use as fuel through a process called gluconeogenesis. This further drops metabolic rate because, as we discussed, muscle burns more calories than fat. This shifts body composition to burn fewer calories, even if the number on the scale stays the same.

Fifth, as we discussed, cortisol dysregulation impairs sleep. And sleep deprivation sets off a whole cascade of issues that lead to dysregulated hunger hormones (increased ghrelin, decreased leptin), impaired glucose metabolism worsening insulin resistance, and decreased growth hormone release, which means the body can't regenerate and heal itself at night. (In Part II, we'll go over protein in detail—how it's broken into amino acids and why fueling your body with adequate protein allows you to build hormones and maintain muscle mass.)

Sixth, elevated cortisol impairs thyroid function, which we'll discuss in the next chapter. This further slows metabolism.

Poor Memory and Brain Shrinkage

This is one of the most disturbing effects of chronic cortisol elevation, and it's extensively documented in research. Chronic elevated cortisol literally damages the neurons in your hippocampus—your brain's primary memory center. It doesn't just impair function; it actually reduces hippocampal volume. We're talking about actual measurable shrinkage visible on MRI imaging. This damage impairs both memory consolidation—your ability to form new memories—and memory retrieval, making it difficult to recall existing ones. Cortisol interferes with neurogenesis, the formation of new brain cells that should be happening throughout your life. And chronic elevation is associated with cognitive decline and increased risk for dementia.

If you've noticed that your memory isn't what it used to be—forgetting names of people you've known for years, losing your train of thought mid-sentence, walking into a room and completely forgetting why you're there—chronic cortisol elevation may be contributing. It's not early dementia, it's not "just getting older," and you're not losing your mind. It's a physiological consequence of chronic stress affecting brain structure and function.

The somewhat reassuring news is that research suggests when cortisol levels normalize, some of this damage can be reversed, and cognitive function can improve. Your brain has more plasticity and regenerative capacity than we once thought. The damage isn't necessarily permanent if you address it.

Muscle Tension, Aches, Pain, and Headaches

Chronic stress causes sustained muscle contraction, particularly in your neck, shoulders, jaw, and back. You might not even realize you're doing it—your shoulders creep up toward your ears, your jaw clenches, your neck muscles stay tight. Over time, this persistent tension creates a cascade of pain problems. You develop tension-type headaches from the sustained contraction in your neck and scalp muscles. The pain can be debilitating, wrapping around your head like a vise. You develop temporomandibular joint problems—TMJ dysfunction—from jaw clenching that often happens unconsciously, especially during sleep. You might wake up with a sore jaw and not understand why. Chronic neck and shoulder pain becomes your constant companion from those elevated, tight shoulders you've been holding for months or years. Back pain develops and worsens, and your injury risk increases because muscles that are constantly contracted lose flexibility and proper function. And perhaps most frustrating, everything hurts more when you're chronically stressed—a phenomenon called stress-induced hyperalgesia where your pain threshold actually decreases.

Many women don't realize their chronic pain is stress-related until they address cortisol dysregulation and suddenly notice their pain has decreased or disappeared entirely. The connection seems obvious in retrospect, but when you're in it, it's hard to see. You assume the pain is structural: a pinched nerve, arthritis, a disc problem. Sometimes those things contribute, but often the primary driver is chronic muscle tension from unrelenting stress.

Chapter 2: Cortisol Dysregulation and Adrenal Fatigue—The Burnout Metabolizer

Mental Health Problems

The relationship between chronic cortisol elevation and mental health disorders is extensively documented and, importantly, bidirectional—chronic stress contributes to mental health problems, and mental health problems perpetuate stress and HPA axis dysregulation. The cycle feeds itself in ways that can feel impossible to break.

Chronic cortisol elevation is directly linked to anxiety disorders, including generalized anxiety disorder where you worry constantly about everything and panic disorder where you experience sudden, intense episodes of fear and physical symptoms. It's linked to major depressive disorder—in fact, many people with depression have elevated cortisol and HPA axis dysfunction that's driving or worsening their depression. You experience persistent irritability and emotional dysregulation, finding it increasingly difficult to control your emotional responses. Mood swings become more frequent and intense. Some people describe feeling emotionally numb or disconnected from their feelings and experiences, like they're going through life behind a pane of glass. And your stress resilience—your ability to handle challenges and bounce back from difficulties—becomes profoundly reduced. Things that wouldn't normally bother you suddenly feel completely overwhelming.

The mechanism involves altered neurotransmitter function, particularly changes in serotonin, dopamine, and GABA, the brain chemicals that regulate mood, motivation, and your ability to feel calm. There are structural changes in brain connectivity. And chronic inflammation affects brain function, contributing to what researchers sometimes call "inflammatory depression."

Hypertension

Chronic stress and elevated cortisol contribute to hypertension—high blood pressure. Over time, elevated blood pressure damages the delicate blood vessels in your body.

Skin Problems

Chronic stress and cortisol elevation increase systemic inflammation throughout your body, and your skin tells that story clearly. You might notice acne breakouts or worsening of existing acne. Psoriasis flares if you're prone to it. Eczema patches appear or worsen. Rosacea becomes more pronounced. Your skin barrier function becomes impaired, leading to dryness, sensitivity, and reactivity to products that never bothered you before. Collagen production slows, causing premature aging, fine lines, and wrinkles that seem to appear overnight. Wounds heal more slowly. And stress often triggers unconscious behaviors like skin picking or nail biting that create additional damage.

Many women notice their skin looks dull, aged, or problematic during high-stress periods. This isn't vanity; it's the direct effect of cortisol and inflammation on skin health.

Immune Suppression and Increased Illness

Remember that cortisol suppresses immune function as part of the acute stress response. Your body conserves energy by temporarily reducing immune activity during a crisis. When cortisol is chronically elevated, this immune suppression becomes ongoing, leaving you vulnerable in ways you've probably noticed. You catch every cold that goes around the office. You get frequent infections—respiratory infections, urinary tract infections, whatever's circulating. When you do get sick, recovery takes forever. That cold lingers for weeks. Infections keep returning just when you think you've finally kicked them. Latent viruses like herpes simplex reactivate, causing cold sores you haven't had in years. Wounds heal slowly. You're more susceptible to infections overall. And if you have an autoimmune condition, you might notice more frequent flares—paradoxically, chronic stress can both suppress and dysregulate immune function.

This is why highly stressed people often say they're "always sick" or "can't shake this cold." It's not bad luck or a weak constitution—it's cortisol-mediated immune suppression.

Chapter 2: Cortisol Dysregulation and Adrenal Fatigue—The Burnout Metabolizer

Interestingly, this is exactly why synthetic corticosteroids—medications that mimic cortisol—are used in medicine to suppress immune function in autoimmune diseases and after organ transplants. The immune-suppressing effect of cortisol is powerful, well-established, and clinically utilized. When that suppression is unintended and chronic from stress, it leaves you vulnerable and depleted.

Sleep Disruption

We've mentioned sleep disruption repeatedly throughout this chapter, but it deserves its own detailed section because sleep disruption is both a consequence of cortisol dysregulation and a perpetuating factor that worsens it. It's one of the most vicious cycles in the entire stress-hormone relationship.

Cortisol should follow a specific daily pattern called the diurnal rhythm. It should be high in the morning, peaking around eight or nine a.m. to help you wake up and feel alert and ready for the day. Then it should gradually decline throughout the day as evening approaches. By around midnight, it should be at its lowest point to allow your body to sleep deeply and restoratively.

When this pattern is disrupted by chronic stress, several dysfunctional patterns emerge, and you might recognize yourself in one or more of these. Some women experience elevated evening cortisol, where cortisol remains high when it should be dropping. You feel what people describe as "tired but wired," physically exhausted but mentally alert and unable to settle down. You have difficulty falling asleep despite feeling exhausted. Your mind starts racing the moment your head hits the pillow, cycling through worries, to-do lists, conversations from the day, things you need to remember for tomorrow.

Other women experience a middle-of-night cortisol spike. You fall asleep normally, often quickly because you're genuinely exhausted. But then you wake abruptly at two or three a.m. with your mind suddenly racing. You're wide awake, often anxious or worried, unable to fall back asleep for hours. Sometimes you lie there until four or five a.m., finally drifting off right before your alarm goes off. This pattern is particularly frustrating because you're getting some sleep, but it's so fragmented that you never feel rested.

Part I: Understanding Why You Are Struggling With The Scale

Some women experience early morning awakening, waking at four or five a.m. and being unable to return to sleep at all. You feel anxious or alert despite not being rested. Your brain is already spinning with the day's concerns even though it's still dark outside.

And some women develop what's called a flattened curve, where cortisol doesn't rise adequately in the morning, which means you feel absolutely terrible waking up, like you're pushing through cement to get out of bed, and it doesn't drop adequately at night, which means poor sleep quality even when you do sleep. It's an overall low but dysregulated pattern where your cortisol rhythm has lost its normal variation.

Each of these patterns disrupts restorative sleep in significant ways. And poor sleep further elevates cortisol, creating a vicious cycle that's difficult to break without targeted intervention. You're tired, so your body is stressed. Stress elevates cortisol. Elevated cortisol disrupts sleep. Poor sleep creates more stress. And around and around you go.

Digestive Issues

The stress response suppresses digestive function because digestion isn't a priority when you're running from a tiger. When stress becomes chronic, this suppression becomes ongoing, and your digestive system suffers. You might experience nausea, particularly during high-stress periods or when you're feeling especially overwhelmed. Chronic constipation develops from slowed gut motility—your intestines literally move more slowly under stress. Or you might have the opposite problem: diarrhea from stress-induced changes in gut transit time. Many women experience alternating constipation and diarrhea, a pattern that's particularly common in stress-related irritable bowel syndrome. Abdominal pain and cramping become constant companions. Bloating and gas make you uncomfortable. Your stomach produces less acid, impairing protein digestion and nutrient absorption. The composition of your gut microbiome changes, leading to dysbiosis, an imbalance of good and bad bacteria. And intestinal permeability increases, the phenomenon sometimes called "leaky gut" where the intestinal barrier becomes compromised.

Chapter 2: Cortisol Dysregulation and Adrenal Fatigue—The Burnout Metabolizer

The gut-brain axis—the bidirectional communication between your digestive system and brain—is profoundly affected by chronic stress. This is why stress management is considered a cornerstone of treating functional gastrointestinal disorders like IBS.

Many women are genuinely surprised to discover that their chronic digestive issues improve dramatically when they address cortisol dysregulation, even without changing their diet at all. The problem wasn't what they were eating; it was how stress was affecting their gut function. (We'll talk more about gut health and its connection to hormones in Part II.)

What Cortisol Dysregulation Feels Like Every Day

Now that we understand the mechanisms, let's look at what cortisol dysregulation actually feels like in daily life, because recognizing the pattern is crucial for identifying whether this is affecting you.

The Energy Pattern

Unlike the consistent fatigue of hypothyroidism (which we'll discuss in the next chapter), cortisol dysregulation creates a specific, recognizable energy pattern:

Morning: You wake up exhausted, despite adequate sleep hours. Getting out of bed feels like a monumental task. You need coffee immediately just to function. You may feel somewhat better mid-morning after your first or second cup of coffee, but you're running on stimulants and willpower, not genuine energy.

Afternoon: Around 2-3 p.m., you crash hard. This isn't just "afternoon sleepiness"; it's profound fatigue that makes it difficult to concentrate, think clearly, or complete tasks. You may reach for sugar, caffeine, or both just to get through the afternoon.

Evening: Paradoxically, you may feel a second wind in the evening. Just when you should be winding down, you feel more alert and energized. This makes it difficult to fall asleep at an appropriate time.

Night: One of two patterns emerges:

- You try to fall asleep, but your mind starts racing. You're exhausted but simultaneously wired. You lie awake for hours despite being tired.
- You fall asleep easily (you're genuinely exhausted), but wake at 2-3 a.m. with your mind racing, suddenly wide awake, often anxious or worried, unable to fall back asleep for hours.

The next morning, the cycle repeats. You wake exhausted, and the pattern continues.

The Emotional Pattern

Cortisol dysregulation profoundly affects mood and emotional regulation:

- **Irritability:** You're short-tempered, easily annoyed by minor inconveniences, quick to snap at family members or colleagues
- **Anxiety:** Persistent worry, feeling on edge, difficulty relaxing, racing thoughts
- **Feeling overwhelmed:** Tasks that should be manageable feel impossible; your stress tolerance is dramatically reduced
- **Emotional reactivity:** Crying easily, overreacting to situations, difficulty controlling emotional responses
- **Burnout and apathy:** Feeling emotionally depleted, detached, like you have nothing left to give

Many women describe feeling like they're not themselves—more reactive, more anxious, more depleted than they've ever felt.

The Physical Pattern

Beyond the energy and mood effects:

- Persistent tension in shoulders, neck, jaw
- Frequent headaches

- Digestive problems that come and go with stress
- Getting sick frequently and taking longer to recover
- Weight gain around the middle despite efforts to control it
- Cravings for comfort foods, particularly in the evening
- Feeling "wired and tired" simultaneously

The Cognitive Pattern

- Brain fog and difficulty concentrating
- Memory problems—forgetting names, losing your train of thought, walking into rooms and forgetting why
- Difficulty making decisions, even simple ones
- Reduced productivity despite working longer hours

Women often describe feeling like they're moving through molasses mentally—thoughts are slow, focus is difficult, and nothing feels sharp or clear.

Testing for Cortisol: What Actually Helps

Unlike insulin resistance, where we have clear, accessible lab markers that are well-accepted in both traditional and functional medicine, cortisol testing is more nuanced and frankly controversial. Let us walk you through the landscape so you understand what's available, what's useful, and what approach we take.

Traditional Medicine Approach

In traditional endocrinology, cortisol testing is used specifically to diagnose disease states—conditions where cortisol is so abnormally high or low that it meets criteria for a named disease:

- Cushing's syndrome (pathological cortisol excess)
- Addison's disease (adrenal insufficiency—the adrenal glands have failed)

Tests used:
- 24-hour urinary free cortisol collection
- Late-night salivary cortisol
- Dexamethasone suppression test

However, these tests are designed to identify frank disease—severe, pathological dysfunction. They're not at all sensitive to the subclinical dysfunction that most perimenopausal women experience.

The "Adrenal Fatigue" Controversy

It's important to acknowledge: "Adrenal fatigue" is not recognized as a diagnosis in traditional medicine. There's no ICD-10 code for it. The Endocrine Society has stated there's insufficient evidence for "adrenal fatigue" as a distinct medical condition.

However—and this is crucial—what IS extensively documented and well-accepted in research includes:
- HPA axis dysregulation associated with chronic stress
- Altered cortisol patterns in burnout, chronic fatigue, PTSD
- Altered cortisol awakening response (validated biomarker)
- Flattened diurnal cortisol slope associated with numerous adverse health outcomes
- Hypocortisolism in chronic stress states

So while the terminology differs, the physiological phenomenon—chronic stress altering cortisol patterns and causing significant symptoms—is absolutely real and well-established in scientific literature.

Functional Medicine Testing Options

1. Salivary Cortisol (4-5 point collection over twenty-four hours)
Collection times:
- Upon waking (should be highest)
- Mid-morning
- Afternoon

Chapter 2: Cortisol Dysregulation and Adrenal Fatigue—The Burnout Metabolizer

- Evening
- Bedtime (should be lowest)

Can identify patterns like:
- Elevated morning cortisol
- Flattened curve (insufficient variation)
- Reversed pattern (low morning, high evening)
- Overall elevated production
- Overall low production (burnout pattern)

Advantages: Shows pattern, not just snapshot; relatively non-invasive

Limitations: Not typically covered by insurance; requires specialty lab; relatively expensive ($150-300)

2. DUTCH Test (Dried Urine Test for Comprehensive Hormones)

Measures:
- Cortisol and cortisol metabolites throughout the day
- Cortisone (inactive form)
- DHEA and metabolites
- Melatonin (cortisol-melatonin relationship)
- Sex hormones and their metabolites

Advantages: Most comprehensive picture available

Limitations: Expensive ($300-400); not covered by insurance; may provide more information than necessary for initial assessment

3. Serum (Blood) Morning Cortisol

Single blood draw, typically 7-9 a.m.

Advantages:
- Cheap and accessible
- Can be ordered through standard labs
- Typically covered by insurance
- Widely available

Limitations:
- Only a snapshot; doesn't show daily pattern

Part I: Understanding Why You Are Struggling With The Scale

- Doesn't capture evening cortisol
- Can miss dysfunction if timing is off
- Affected by stress of blood draw itself
- Many women with significant dysfunction have "normal" morning cortisol

Our Approach: Symptom-Based Diagnosis with Accessible Screening

Given the limitations and costs of various testing approaches, we use a practical method:

1. **Primary assessment:** Comprehensive symptom evaluation using the quiz at the end of this chapter
2. **Screening lab:** Morning serum cortisol through standard insurance-covered labs

Rationale:
- Cortisol patterns vary significantly; single value may not capture dysfunction
- Symptom correlation is often more clinically relevant than lab values in subclinical states
- Treatment focuses on stress management, lifestyle, and adrenal support regardless of exact cortisol level
- This approach is accessible and affordable for most patients

If symptoms are severe and we need more detailed information, we may order salivary cortisol or DUTCH testing, but for most women, symptom-based assessment with basic screening labs provides adequate information to guide treatment.

The Reality: Whether your morning cortisol is 10 or 15 mcg/dL matters less than how you're actually feeling and functioning. If you have the symptom constellation of cortisol dysregulation—disrupted sleep, afternoon crashes, difficulty handling stress, anxiety, belly weight gain, frequent illness—those symptoms warrant treatment regardless of what a single cortisol measurement shows.

Cortisol Dysregulation Symptom Quiz

Cortisol dysregulation doesn't mean your body is "failing." It often reflects a stress response that has been active for too long—something that is extremely common in midlife women. Use the checklist below to identify symptoms that may suggest altered cortisol signaling or rhythm.

Energy & Fatigue Patterns:

- ☐ Chronic fatigue and constant tiredness throughout the day
- ☐ Difficulty waking up in the morning despite adequate sleep
- ☐ Morning fatigue—feeling worst when you first wake up
- ☐ Afternoon or evening energy crash (typically 2-4 p.m.)
- ☐ Increased effort required to perform even simple daily tasks
- ☐ Feeling "tired but wired"—exhausted but unable to relax

Sleep Disturbances:

- ☐ Difficulty falling asleep despite being tired
- ☐ Waking at 2-3 a.m. with mind racing, unable to fall back asleep
- ☐ Early morning awakening (4-5 a.m.) and can't return to sleep
- ☐ Insomnia or consistently poor sleep quality
- ☐ Non-restorative sleep—waking unrefreshed even after adequate hours

Stress & Mental Health:

- ☐ Decreased ability to handle stress—minor stressors feel overwhelming
- ☐ Feeling constantly "on edge" or anxious
- ☐ Depression or persistent low mood
- ☐ Irritability—quick to snap or lose patience
- ☐ Feeling emotionally overwhelmed or burnt out

Physical Symptoms:

- ☐ Muscle aches and pains, particularly in neck, shoulders, back
- ☐ Frequent headaches or tension headaches

- ☐ Weight gain, particularly around the midsection/belly
- ☐ Difficulty losing weight despite appropriate diet and exercise
- ☐ Salt or sugar cravings, particularly for "comfort foods"
- ☐ Frequent illnesses or infections
- ☐ Slow recovery from illness
- ☐ Poor immune function—"always getting sick"

Other Symptoms & Risk Factors:

- ☐ Allergies or worsening of existing allergies
- ☐ History of autoimmune disease or autoimmune flares
- ☐ Bone loss or osteopenia/osteoporosis
- ☐ Chronic health problems that don't resolve
- ☐ History of chronic stress or high-stress lifestyle
- ☐ History of corticosteroid medication use (prednisone, etc.)
- ☐ Diabetes, prediabetes, or difficulty managing blood sugar
- ☐ Low blood sugar episodes (hypoglycemia)

Scoring: Count your total checked items: ___________

Interpreting Your Results:

0-3 symptoms: Low likelihood of significant cortisol dysregulation, though some stress management is beneficial for everyone

4-7 symptoms: Moderate likelihood of cortisol dysregulation; stress management and adrenal support recommended

8-12 symptoms: High likelihood of significant cortisol dysregulation; comprehensive stress management, lifestyle modification, and possible adrenal support are strongly recommended

13+ symptoms: Very high likelihood of severe cortisol dysregulation and potential adrenal burnout; immediate intervention with comprehensive stress management, adrenal support, and lifestyle modification is critical

- This quiz is a screening tool to identify likely cortisol dysregulation, not a diagnostic test
- Cortisol dysregulation is extremely common in perimenopausal women due to the convergence of life stressors and hormonal changes
- Symptom patterns are often more clinically relevant than lab values for assessing cortisol dysfunction
- Even if lab values appear "normal," if you have significant symptoms, treatment is warranted
- Addressing cortisol dysregulation is essential for optimizing sex hormone production and overall health during perimenopause

Chapter Summary

If there's one thing to understand about cortisol dysregulation and adrenal fatigue—about being a Burnout Metabolizer—it's this: High-performing women can't necessarily escape their demanding, high-stress lives, but they CAN change how stress impacts their bodies. Once you learn how to do this, damage can be reversed, symptoms can disappear, and your adrenal glands can start producing sex hormones (and other hormones) the way they were meant to.

Being a Burnout Metabolizer means your metabolism itself has experienced burnout. Your adrenal glands are depleted. Your body is breaking down muscle tissue while storing fat. You're running on empty but can't rest. This isn't a personal failing or a sign of weakness. It's a physiological consequence of chronic stress in a body that was designed to handle only acute, temporary stressors.

Cortisol dysregulation isn't a personal failing or a sign of weakness. It's a physiological consequence of chronic stress in a body that was designed to handle only acute, temporary stressors. When you've been functioning in a state of chronic stress for years or decades, and then perimenopause adds additional hormonal and life stressors to the mix, cortisol dysregulation becomes almost inevitable.

The empowering truth: You have control here. While you may not be able to eliminate all stress from your life (and honestly, some stress is beneficial and motivating), you can dramatically change how your body responds to stress through:

- Evidence-based stress management techniques
- Strategic nutritional support for adrenal function
- Lifestyle modifications that support healthy cortisol patterns
- Sleep optimization
- Appropriate supplementation and, when needed, medication
- Reframing your relationship with stress

When cortisol patterns normalize, a cascade of positive changes occurs:
- Energy returns and stabilizes throughout the day
- Sleep becomes restorative
- Weight loss becomes possible as the metabolic trap is released
- Mood stabilizes—anxiety decreases, irritability resolves
- Immune function recovers
- Mental clarity improves
- Your adrenal glands can finally shift resources toward producing adequate sex hormones
- All perimenopausal symptoms improve

But you cannot optimize sex hormones without addressing cortisol first. If your adrenal glands are depleted and overwhelmed with cortisol production, they cannot adequately produce progesterone, estrogen, or testosterone—regardless of whether you use hormone replacement therapy or not.

This is why cortisol management is not optional during perimenopause. It's foundational.

Chapter 2: Cortisol Dysregulation and Adrenal Fatigue—The Burnout Metabolizer

Looking Ahead

In the next chapter, we'll explore the third hormone imbalance that commonly affects women during perimenopause: thyroid dysfunction. You'll discover why your thyroid—your body's metabolic master regulator—can be suboptimal even when your labs are "normal," how thyroid dysfunction creates a specific pattern of symptoms distinct from cortisol dysregulation or insulin resistance, and why optimizing thyroid function is essential for metabolic health, energy, and weight management.

You'll also learn how cortisol dysregulation (Chapter 2), insulin resistance (Chapter 1), and thyroid dysfunction (Chapter 3) interact and compound each other's effects—creating a complex web of metabolic dysfunction that requires comprehensive treatment not single-hormone focus.

Thyroid Dysfunction— The Slow Burner Metabolizer

When you walk into your doctor's office complaining about unexplained weight gain, fatigue, or difficulty losing weight despite your best efforts, one of the first tests ordered is almost always TSH—thyroid stimulating hormone. It's the standard screening for thyroid function, and for good reason. Your thyroid is your body's metabolic master regulator, and when it's not working properly, weight gain and crushing fatigue are hallmark symptoms.

Maybe your TSH came back elevated and your doctor prescribed levothyroxine (Synthroid). You've been taking it faithfully every morning. Your follow-up labs show your TSH is now "normal." Your doctor says your thyroid is controlled.

Or maybe your TSH came back "within normal range" and your doctor told you your thyroid is fine—nothing to worry about.

Either way, you still feel terrible.

The exhaustion is unrelenting. The weight keeps creeping up or won't budge despite eating carefully and exercising. Your brain feels foggy. Your hair is thinning. You're cold all the time. You feel like you're barely functioning, yet you've been told your thyroid is "fine" or "controlled."

Here's what you need to understand: Being told your thyroid is normal—or being on thyroid medication with a normalized TSH—doesn't mean your thyroid function is actually optimized. There are critical pieces of information that standard testing doesn't capture, and these missing pieces explain why you still feel awful.

This is why we call this pattern "The Slow Burner Metabolizer." When your thyroid isn't functioning optimally, your entire metabolism slows down—you're burning fuel at a crawl rather than at the rate you should be. Your cells can't produce energy efficiently. Your body temperature drops. Your metabolic rate plummets. Everything feels sluggish and heavy because your metabolic fire has been reduced to barely smoldering embers. You're a Slow Burner, and no amount of effort can compensate for a metabolism that's fundamentally running too slowly.

This isn't in your head. You're not being dramatic. You're not just "getting older" or "not trying hard enough." There is a physiological reason you still feel terrible—and it's discoverable and fixable.

In this chapter, you'll discover what standard thyroid testing is missing, why the conventional approach leaves so many women suffering despite treatment, and why perimenopause creates the perfect storm for thyroid dysfunction. Most importantly, you'll learn what comprehensive evaluation looks like and what it means to truly optimize your thyroid function—not just get your TSH "within range."

When the missing pieces are finally identified and properly addressed, women don't just see their lab numbers improve—they feel like themselves again. Energy returns. Brain fog lifts. Weight becomes manageable. The transformation is real, and it starts with understanding what's actually happening in your body.

Let's dive in.

What Is Your Thyroid and Why Does It Matter?

Your thyroid is a small, butterfly-shaped gland located at the base of your neck, just below your Adam's apple. Don't let its size fool you—this tiny gland is your body's master metabolic regulator, controlling the speed at which virtually every cell in your body operates.

Think of your thyroid as the gas pedal for your metabolism. When it's functioning optimally, everything hums along smoothly—your energy is good, your weight is stable, your thinking is clear, your mood is balanced. But when thyroid function declines, it's like someone's pressing the brake pedal on your entire system.

Your thyroid produces two main hormones: T4 (thyroxine) and T3 (triiodothyronine). Here's what you need to understand about each:

T4—The Storage Form

Your thyroid produces mostly T4—about 80-90 percent of your total thyroid hormone output. But here's the critical thing to understand: T4 is the inactive, storage form of thyroid hormone. It's like having money in a savings account. You have it, but you can't spend it yet.

T4 must be converted into T3—the active form—before your cells can actually use it.

T3—The Active Form

T3 is the metabolically active thyroid hormone—the form that actually binds to receptors in your cells and regulates metabolism. Your thyroid produces only about 10-20 percent of your body's T3 directly. The rest must be created through conversion of T4 to T3, which happens primarily in three places:

- Liver (about sixty percent of conversion)
- Kidneys (about twenty percent of conversion)
- Other tissues including the gut, brain, and muscles (about twenty percent of conversion)

T3 is approximately 3-4 times more potent than T4 in regulating your metabolism. This is why proper conversion from T4 to T3 is absolutely critical—and why testing only TSH completely misses a huge piece of the puzzle.

The Feedback Loop: How Your Thyroid System Works

Your thyroid doesn't operate in isolation. It's part of an elegant feedback system:

1. Your hypothalamus (in your brain) produces TRH (Thyrotropin-Releasing Hormone)
2. TRH signals your pituitary gland to produce TSH (Thyroid Stimulating Hormone)
3. TSH travels to your thyroid gland and tells it to produce T4 and T3
4. When adequate T4 and T3 are circulating in your bloodstream, they send a signal back to your pituitary and hypothalamus that says "we have enough"—and TSH production decreases
5. When T4 and T3 levels are low, the pituitary produces more TSH to stimulate the thyroid to make more hormone

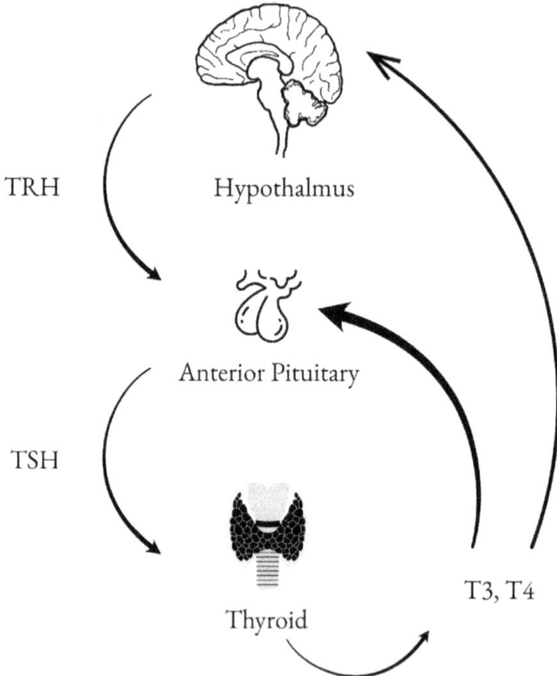

But this simplistic approach misses critical problems.

The Problem: Two Root Causes Traditional Medicine Misses

TSH can be elevated for two very different reasons, but standard treatment doesn't address the underlying cause; it just replaces the hormone. This is why so many women on thyroid medication still feel terrible.

ROOT CAUSE #1: Conversion Issues

Multiple factors can block or impair the conversion of T4 (inactive) to T3 (active). This means you can have plenty of T4 in your system, either from your own thyroid or from medication, but your cells aren't getting the active T3 they need to function properly.

What blocks T4 to T3 conversion? Elevated cortisol from chronic stress (as we discussed in Chapter 2), chronic inflammation, nutrient deficiencies (particularly selenium, zinc, iron, vitamin D), liver dysfunction, certain medications (beta-blockers, birth control, corticosteroids), aging, insulin resistance (remember Chapter 1?), chronic alcohol consumption, and severe caloric restriction or yo-yo dieting.

There's also a genetic component that significantly affects conversion:

MTHFR Gene Mutation

Between 40-60 percent of the population carries a mutation in the MTHFR gene (methylenetetrahydrofolate reductase—thankfully abbreviated). This gene is responsible for a process called methylation, which is critical for:

- T4 to T3 conversion
- Detoxification pathways
- DNA repair
- Neurotransmitter production
- Inflammation reduction

When you have an MTHFR mutation, methylation is impaired, which means:

- Your T4 to T3 conversion is significantly reduced

- You're at increased risk for autoimmune conditions (including Hashimoto's)
- You have higher levels of inflammation
- You're more susceptible to hormone imbalances

This is why it's entirely possible to take levothyroxine (Synthroid)—which is synthetic T4—and see your TSH normalize while feeling absolutely no better. Your body can't efficiently convert that T4 into the T3 your cells actually need.

ROOT CAUSE #2: Hashimoto's Thyroiditis (Autoimmune Thyroid Disease)

Hashimoto's thyroiditis is an autoimmune condition where your immune system mistakenly attacks your thyroid gland. It's the number one cause of hypothyroidism in developed countries—yet it's rarely tested for in conventional medicine.

In Hashimoto's, your body produces antibodies against proteins essential for thyroid function:

- **TPO antibodies (thyroid peroxidase antibodies)** attack the enzyme needed to produce thyroid hormone. When this enzyme is damaged, your thyroid can't manufacture T4 and T3 efficiently.
- **TG antibodies (thyroglobulin antibodies)** attack thyroglobulin, a protein that's essential for storing and releasing thyroid hormones.

Over time, this autoimmune attack causes progressive damage to the thyroid gland, reducing its ability to produce hormones. This is why your TSH rises—your pituitary is sending increasingly desperate signals trying to get your damaged thyroid to produce more hormone.

Here's what makes Hashimoto's particularly insidious:

- **It often exists for years before causing obvious hypothyroidism.** You can have significantly elevated antibodies—meaning active autoimmune attack on your thyroid—while your TSH is still "normal." Most doctors only check TSH, so they completely miss the ongoing destruction happening in your thyroid gland.

- **Symptoms often appear long before TSH becomes abnormal.** You might have fatigue, weight gain, brain fog, hair loss, cold intolerance—classic hypothyroid symptoms—but your TSH is still within the reference range. Your doctor tells you your thyroid is "fine," yet you feel terrible. The reality? Your antibodies have been attacking your thyroid for months or years, damaging it progressively but not enough yet to make your TSH rise above the laboratory cutoff.

- **The damage is progressive and very difficult to reverse.** While thyroid tissue does have some regenerative capacity, and approximately twenty percent of patients experience spontaneous return to normal thyroid function, this regeneration is unpredictable and cannot be directly stimulated through current medical interventions. The destroyed thyroid tissue typically does not regenerate sufficiently to restore full function, which is why early diagnosis is crucial. If you can identify and address the root causes of the autoimmune process early—before significant damage has accumulated—you may be able to slow, halt, or even reverse the antibody production and prevent further destruction. However, once substantial thyroid tissue has been destroyed, most patients require lifelong thyroid hormone replacement.

- **Many women with Hashimoto's experience a "Hashitoxic" phase.** In the early stages of the disease, as antibodies attack and damage thyroid tissue, thyroid hormone stored in that damaged tissue gets dumped into your bloodstream all at once. This creates temporary hyperthyroid symptoms—heart palpitations, anxiety, insomnia, sweating, weight loss—even though you have an autoimmune condition that will eventually cause hypothyroidism. This confusing pattern often leads to misdiagnosis or missed diagnosis entirely.

- **Hashimoto's doesn't just affect your thyroid.** As with all autoimmune conditions, having one increases your risk for developing others. Women with Hashimoto's have higher rates of celiac disease, rheumatoid arthritis, lupus, and other autoimmune conditions. The underlying immune dysregulation affects multiple body systems.

Here's what's most frustrating: even if Hashimoto's is diagnosed, conventional treatment is the same as non-autoimmune hypothyroidism—just thyroid hormone replacement. But replacing the hormone doesn't address the underlying autoimmune process. Your immune system continues attacking your thyroid. The inflammation continues. And you continue feeling suboptimal, even with "normal" TSH on medication.

Addressing Hashimoto's comprehensively requires more than just thyroid hormone replacement. It requires:

- Identifying and addressing triggers that activate the immune system (food sensitivities, gut dysbiosis, chronic infections, environmental toxins, chronic stress)
- Reducing systemic inflammation through nutrition, lifestyle, and targeted supplementation
- Supporting gut health (since seventy percent of your immune system is in your gut)
- Managing stress and supporting adrenal function
- Optimizing vitamin D, selenium, and other nutrients critical for immune and thyroid function
- In some cases, using medications that modulate immune response

Finding and treating Hashimoto's early can change the entire trajectory of the disease. (We will go over our specific treatment protocols in Part III)

Why Comprehensive Thyroid Testing Matters

This is where comprehensive thyroid evaluation becomes essential. Testing TSH alone—or even TSH and Free T4—doesn't capture conversion problems or autoimmune thyroid disease.

Here's what comprehensive thyroid testing includes and what each marker tells you:

TSH (Thyroid Stimulating Hormone)

What it measures: The signal from your pituitary telling your thyroid to produce more hormone.

What it reveals: Whether your pituitary senses adequate thyroid hormone in your bloodstream.

What it misses: Everything else. TSH can be "normal" while you have significant conversion problems, autoimmune disease, or inadequate Free T3 levels. It's a screening tool, not a complete picture.

Free T4 (Free Thyroxine)

What it measures: The amount of unbound, active T4 circulating in your bloodstream (as opposed to T4 that's bound to proteins and unavailable for use).

What it reveals: Whether your thyroid is producing adequate amounts of T4, the storage form of thyroid hormone.

Why it matters: If Free T4 is low despite normal or elevated TSH, it suggests your thyroid itself isn't responding adequately to stimulation. If Free T4 is normal or high but you have symptoms, it suggests a conversion problem—plenty of storage hormone, but it's not being converted to active T3.

Free T3 (Free Triiodothyronine)

What it measures: The amount of unbound, metabolically active thyroid hormone available to your cells.

What it reveals: Whether you have adequate active thyroid hormone regardless of your TSH or T4 levels.

Why it's critical: This is the hormone that actually matters for metabolism. You can have "normal" TSH and "normal" Free T4 but low Free T3—meaning your cells aren't getting the active hormone they need to function. This is conversion failure, and it's epidemic in stressed, perimenopausal women.

Reverse T3 (rT3)

What it measures: An inactive form of T3 that your body produces when it wants to slow metabolism (as a protective mechanism during illness, severe stress, or caloric restriction).

What it reveals: Whether your body is shunting T4 away from active T3 production and toward inactive Reverse T3 instead.

Why it matters: Elevated Reverse T3 suggests your body is in "conservation mode"—trying to slow metabolism to conserve energy. This happens during chronic stress, severe caloric restriction, chronic illness, or significant inflammation. High Reverse T3 can also compete with Free T3 at cellular receptors, blocking the action of active thyroid hormone even when Free T3 levels look adequate.

When to test it: If you have normal TSH, normal or low-normal Free T3 but persistent hypothyroid symptoms, Reverse T3 testing helps identify whether your body is producing the wrong form of T3.

TPO Antibodies (Thyroid Peroxidase Antibodies)

What it measures: Antibodies attacking thyroid peroxidase, the enzyme essential for making thyroid hormone.

What it reveals: Whether you have Hashimoto's thyroiditis (autoimmune thyroid disease).

Why it's critical: TPO antibodies indicate active autoimmune attack on your thyroid. Elevated antibodies mean your immune system is progressively damaging your thyroid gland, even if your TSH is currently normal. Catching this early allows intervention to slow the autoimmune process.

TG Antibodies (Thyroglobulin Antibodies)

What it measures: Antibodies attacking thyroglobulin, a protein essential for storing and releasing thyroid hormones.

What it reveals: Additional evidence of Hashimoto's. About 10-20 percent of people with Hashimoto's have elevated TG antibodies but negative TPO antibodies, so testing both increases diagnostic accuracy.

Why it matters: If TPO antibodies are negative but you have symptoms and elevated TG antibodies, you may still have Hashimoto's that would be missed if only TPO was checked.

The Bottom Line on Testing

Comprehensive thyroid testing—including TSH, Free T4, Free T3, and TPO antibodies at minimum—is essential for accurate diagnosis and effective treatment. If you have persistent symptoms despite "normal" TSH, request Reverse T3 testing as well. If you have Hashimoto's diagnosed by TPO antibodies, adding TG antibodies helps monitor disease activity and treatment response.

Working with a provider who understands these nuances makes the difference between continuing to suffer with "treated" hypothyroidism and actually feeling well again.

Testing Logistics: What You Need to Know

You can have thyroid labs drawn at any time of day. However, morning testing is often most convenient—particularly if your provider is ordering a comprehensive hormone panel that includes cortisol and insulin, which should be drawn in the morning. If you take thyroid medication, check with your provider about whether to take it before your blood draw. Most providers want you to communicate clearly what medication you take, the dose, whether you took it before the draw, and what time your blood was drawn versus when you took your medication.

Sex Hormones and Thyroid: Understanding the Connection

As we'll explore in detail in Chapter 4, perimenopause creates dramatic sex hormone shifts. Here's how those changes directly impact your thyroid function:

Estrogen's Effects on Thyroid Function

Estrogen affects thyroid labs and thyroid symptoms mainly by changing how thyroid hormone is carried in the bloodstream. Estrogen increases production of thyroid-binding globulin (TBG), a transport protein made in the liver that binds thyroid hormone and carries it through circulation.

Here's why that matters: Thyroid hormone exists in two forms in the blood—bound (attached to proteins like TBG) and free (unbound). Only the free portion can enter cells and do its job. When TBG rises, more thyroid hormone becomes bound, and lab results can look "normal" or even "high" on Total T4/Total T3, while the free, active fraction may not reflect what your tissues are actually experiencing, especially in people who already have limited thyroid reserve or are on thyroid medication.

During perimenopause, estrogen levels fluctuate wildly. In the early stages, you might have estrogen surges that dramatically increase TBG. Suddenly, despite having adequate total thyroid hormone, your free levels plummet. You feel hypothyroid—exhausted, brain foggy, cold, unable to lose weight—even though your thyroid hormone production itself hasn't changed. The estrogen surge has simply bound up more of your thyroid hormone, leaving less available for cellular use.

As perimenopause progresses and estrogen begins its overall decline, this problem evolves differently. Lower estrogen means less TBG, which theoretically should increase free thyroid hormone. But declining estrogen also reduces cellular sensitivity to thyroid hormone, meaning your cells don't respond as well to the thyroid hormone that is available. It's like turning down the volume on the thyroid hormone signal, even when the signal is present.

This shifting dynamic—sometimes too much TBG binding up hormone, sometimes reduced cellular sensitivity—is one reason why thyroid function can feel so erratic during perimenopause and why optimizing sex hormones often improves thyroid symptoms even without changing thyroid medication.

Progesterone's Role in Thyroid Support

Progesterone supports thyroid function in several critical ways:

- It enhances the sensitivity of thyroid receptors, meaning your cells respond more effectively to the thyroid hormone that's present. Even if your Free T3 is only moderately available, adequate progesterone helps your cells use that T3 more efficiently.

- Progesterone also supports T4 to T3 conversion—the process we discussed earlier where inactive storage hormone becomes active metabolic hormone. When progesterone is adequate, conversion happens more readily.

During perimenopause, progesterone typically drops first and can plummet dramatically, often falling to nearly undetectable levels while estrogen remains relatively high. This creates what we call estrogen dominance, but it also removes critical thyroid support.

Without adequate progesterone:

- Thyroid receptors become less sensitive (so even adequate Free T3 doesn't work as effectively)

- T4 to T3 conversion slows (so you have plenty of storage hormone but can't convert it to active form)

- Your cells essentially become more resistant to thyroid hormone, similar to how insulin resistance makes cells less responsive to insulin

This is one reason why women often need thyroid medication adjustments during perimenopause—not necessarily because their thyroid gland is suddenly producing less hormone but because the declining progesterone has made their existing thyroid hormone less effective.

Perimenopause Creates the Perfect Storm for Thyroid Dysfunction

Now you can see why thyroid issues are epidemic in women over forty. It's not just one factor—it's the convergence of multiple physiological changes:

- **Natural thyroid atrophy with aging:** Your thyroid gland naturally becomes less efficient as you age. This happens to everyone but becomes more clinically significant during perimenopause when other factors compound the effect

- **Increased inflammation:** As estrogen declines, the natural anti-inflammatory protection estrogen provides diminishes. Gut permeability increases, food sensitivities become more common, systemic inflammation rises. Chronic inflammation impairs T4 to T3 conversion and can trigger or worsen autoimmune conditions like Hashimoto's

- **Sex hormone changes impairing conversion and cellular response:** As we just discussed, erratic estrogen and plummeting progesterone impairs how your thyroid hormone works—independent of how much your thyroid itself is producing

- **Chronic stress and cortisol dysregulation:** As we covered in Chapter 2, chronic stress and elevated cortisol directly impair T4 to T3 conversion. Stressed, busy women in perimenopause often have the worst conversion because their cortisol is chronically elevated, their adrenal glands are depleted, and their bodies are stuck in survival mode

- **Potential autoimmune activation:** Perimenopause is a time when previously silent autoimmune conditions often become active. The immune system changes during this transition, inflammation increases, gut health often deteriorates, and Hashimoto's can develop or worsen rapidly

- **Accumulation of metabolic dysfunction:** By midlife, many women have developed some degree of insulin resistance (Chapter 1), which also impairs thyroid function. The combination of insulin resistance, cortisol dysregulation, sex hormone imbalance, and thyroid dysfunction creates a metabolic perfect storm

All of these factors converge during perimenopause, making thyroid dysfunction incredibly common and often quite severe—yet completely missed by conventional testing that only checks TSH.

The Empowering Truth: Optimization Is Possible

Even without diagnosed thyroid pathology, as you age, your thyroid needs support. Optimizing thyroid function through targeted nutrition, specific supplements, stress management, addressing gut health and inflammation, and optimizing sex hormones helps you age with vitality and metabolic health.

Your thyroid is more than just a TSH number. It's a complex system influenced by your sex hormones, stress levels, gut health, inflammation, nutritional status, and overall metabolic function.

If you're on medication but still struggling with symptoms, you deserve comprehensive evaluation that looks beyond a single TSH number. Investigating root causes—whether that's conversion issues, Hashimoto's, nutrient deficiencies, chronic stress, gut inflammation, or other factors—not only supports optimal thyroid function but makes traditional medical treatments more effective.

Women who suffered for years with "treated" hypothyroidism finally get comprehensive evaluation, the missed diagnosis is discovered, root cause is addressed, and suddenly they start feeling like themselves again. Energy returns. Weight starts coming off. Brain fog lifts. Mood stabilizes. Hair stops falling out.

Many women actually need less thyroid medication once the underlying dysfunction is addressed because their thyroid glands start functioning better when the obstacles (inflammation, autoimmunity, nutrient deficiencies, conversion blocks) are removed.

You deserve to feel well, not just have "normal" labs. You deserve treatment that addresses root causes, not just replaces hormones. This isn't about accepting a diminished quality of life as you age. It's about getting proper answers and proper treatment so you can thrive—not just survive—through perimenopause, menopause, and beyond.

Thyroid Dysfunction Symptom Quiz

Many women are told their thyroid is "fine" simply because TSH falls within range—yet their symptoms persist. As you've learned in this chapter, thyroid function during perimenopause is influenced by far more than a single lab value. Check any symptoms that are present, problematic, or persist over time:

- ☐ Fatigue and low energy levels
- ☐ Depression
- ☐ Anxiety
- ☐ Difficulty concentrating or foggy thinking
- ☐ Dry skin
- ☐ Brittle hair and nails
- ☐ Thinning hair or hair loss
- ☐ Heart palpitations
- ☐ Excessive sweating
- ☐ Weight gain or difficulty losing weight
- ☐ Inability to lose weight despite diet and exercise
- ☐ Thermodysregulation (feeling too cold or too hot)
- ☐ Feeling cold all the time
- ☐ Cold hands and feet
- ☐ Elevated cholesterol
- ☐ Constipation
- ☐ Sleep disturbances or insomnia
- ☐ Headaches
- ☐ Low libido or decreased sexual function

☐ Menstrual irregularities

☐ Infertility or history of miscarriages

☐ Aches and pains

☐ General hormone imbalance

Interpreting Your Results:

- If you checked **five or more symptoms**, thyroid dysfunction is likely contributing to how you feel—even if you've been told your thyroid is "fine" based on TSH alone.

- If you're already on thyroid medication but still experiencing symptoms, you may have an undiagnosed conversion issue or Hashimoto's that requires additional evaluation and treatment.

Use this quiz as documentation when advocating for comprehensive thyroid testing with your healthcare provider.

Chapter Summary

Your thyroid is your body's metabolic master regulator—controlling energy, weight, temperature, mood, cognition, and countless other functions. When thyroid function is compromised, every system in your body suffers. When you're a Slow Burner Metabolizer, your entire metabolism operates at a crawl, making weight loss nearly impossible and leaving you exhausted no matter how much you rest. Here's what you need to remember:

- **Being on thyroid medication with "normal" TSH doesn't mean your thyroid is optimized.** Standard treatment replaces the hormone but doesn't address underlying dysfunction. If you're on medication but still struggling, there's a reason—and it's not in your head.

- **Two root causes are commonly missed:** conversion issues (inability to convert T4 to active T3) and Hashimoto's thyroiditis (autoimmune thyroid disease). Both require specific evaluation and treatment approaches that go beyond standard thyroid hormone replacement.

- **Sex hormone changes during perimenopause directly impact thyroid function.** Erratic estrogen increases thyroid binding globulin (reducing free active hormone), while plummeting progesterone removes critical thyroid support. Declining estrogen over time reduces cellular sensitivity to thyroid hormone. This is why thyroid evaluation must be part of comprehensive perimenopause care.

- **Perimenopause creates a perfect storm for thyroid dysfunction:** natural thyroid atrophy with aging, dramatic increase in inflammation from gut permeability, hormonal changes impairing conversion and cellular response, and potential autoimmune activation. No wonder thyroid issues are epidemic in women over forty.

- **Comprehensive testing is essential—TSH alone is insufficient.** You need TSH, Free T4, Free T3, and TPO antibodies at minimum to accurately assess thyroid function. Without this complete picture, conversion issues and Hashimoto's go undiagnosed, leaving women suffering despite "treatment."

- **Optimizing thyroid function even without diagnosed pathology is important.** As you age, your thyroid needs support. Optimizing through targeted nutrition, specific supplements, stress management, addressing gut health and inflammation—helps you age with vitality and metabolic health.

Looking Ahead

We've now covered three of the five hormone imbalances that sabotage women's health during perimenopause:

- **Chapter 1: Insulin Resistance (The Locked Metabolizer)**—the metabolic dysfunction that makes weight loss nearly impossible

- **Chapter 2: Cortisol Dysregulation and Adrenal Fatigue (The Burnout Metabolizer)**—the stress hormone chaos driving exhaustion and belly fat

- **Chapter 3: Thyroid Dysfunction (The Slow Burner Metaboliz-er)**—the commonly missed diagnoses keeping you stuck despite "treatment"

In the next chapter, we'll explore the hormonal shifts that define perimenopause and menopause: sex hormone imbalance. You'll discover exactly what's happening to your estrogen, progesterone, and testosterone levels, and why these changes create the cascade of symptoms that brought you to this book.

You'll learn why hot flashes and night sweats are just the tip of the iceberg, how declining hormones affect your brain, bones, heart, and metabolism, and most importantly, what you can do to optimize your sex hormones and reclaim your body.

Let's continue.

Sex Hormone Imbalance—The Hormonally Hijacked Metabolizer

Maybe you're the woman who has been bleeding heavily for years—soaking through super tampons in an hour, passing clots the size of golf balls, feeling utterly exhausted from the blood loss. Your periods last seven, eight, or even nine days. The week before your period, your breasts are so tender you can't hug your kids. You're irritable, anxious, can't sleep. Your doctor ran some tests, told you everything was "normal," and put you on synthetic progesterone to try to control the bleeding. When that didn't work well enough, she suggested a hysterectomy. You're in your early forties, still having periods, but you feel like your body has turned against you.

Or maybe you're the woman waking up drenched in sweat at three a.m., having to change your pajamas and sheets. Hot flashes wash over you without warning—in meetings, at dinner, in the grocery store—leaving you flushed, sweating, and mortified. Your libido has vanished. Sex is painful because of vaginal dryness. You forget words mid-sentence, can't remember why you walked into a room, and feel like your brain is failing you. You're exhausted but can't sleep through the night. When you asked your doctor about hormone testing, she said, "We don't test hormones—they fluctuate too much," and "Hormones are dangerous. You'll just have to get through this." So you're suffering, told this is just what happens to women, that you need to accept it.

Or maybe you've struggled with hormones your entire adult life. Irregular periods, terrible acne, unwanted facial hair. Maybe you were diagnosed with PCOS. Maybe you had fertility struggles. Your doctor put you on birth control pills in your teens or twenties to "regulate" your cycles and control symptoms, and you've been on them for years—maybe decades. You've battled your weight the whole time, and now as you're approaching or going through perimenopause, everything is worse. The weight is even harder to manage. Your symptoms are more severe. You feel trapped in a body you can't control, and no one seems to understand that this isn't just about willpower or trying harder.

If any of these scenarios describes your experience, you're dealing with sex hormone imbalance—the fourth of the five critical hormone imbalances that sabotage women's health during perimenopause and menopause. You're what we call a Hormonally Hijacked Metabolizer.

The term "Hormonally Hijacked Metabolizer" captures exactly what's happening in your body. Your sex hormones—estrogen, progesterone, and testosterone—have been hijacked by the hormonal chaos of perimenopause. They're fluctuating wildly, plummeting unpredictably, or have been suppressed for years by birth control pills. Your metabolism has been hijacked by these erratic hormone patterns, leaving you unable to control your weight, your energy, your mood, or your body's responses. You've literally been hijacked—taken hostage by hormonal forces beyond your control. Your body is no longer responding to your efforts because the hormonal signals governing everything have been commandeered.

These aren't three different diseases. They're three different patterns of the same fundamental problem: Your sex hormones—estrogen, progesterone, and testosterone—are out of balance, and that imbalance is creating symptoms that profoundly affect your quality of life, your weight, your energy, your mental clarity, your relationships, and your sense of self.

And here's what makes this particularly frustrating: Traditional medicine either dismisses these symptoms as "normal aging" that you should accept, warns you that hormone replacement therapy is dangerous and you shouldn't use it, or treats your symptoms with synthetic medications or surgery without ever addressing the underlying hormonal imbalance.

Chapter 4: Sex Hormone Imbalance—The Hormonally Hijacked Metabolizer

The result? Millions of women suffering unnecessarily, told their symptoms don't matter, that hormones are too dangerous to consider, or that removing organs is the solution to a hormonal problem.

There is a better way.

In this chapter, you'll learn exactly what estrogen, progesterone, and testosterone do in your body, why they become imbalanced during perimenopause, the three distinct patterns of sex hormone imbalance and which one you're experiencing, and what comprehensive testing and treatment actually look like. You'll understand why your symptoms aren't "all in your head" or "just part of aging"; they're the result of specific, measurable hormonal changes that can be identified and addressed.

When sex hormones are properly evaluated and balanced—whether through lifestyle interventions, bioidentical hormone replacement, or other therapeutic approaches—women don't just see symptom improvement. They start feeling like themselves again. Energy returns. Weight becomes manageable. Brain fog lifts. Sleep improves. Mood stabilizes. Libido returns. The transformation is real, and it starts with understanding what's actually happening in your body and refusing to accept that suffering is inevitable.

Let's dive in.

SECTION 1: What Are Sex Hormones And What Do They Do?

When most people think about sex hormones, they think exclusively about reproduction—fertility, menstruation, pregnancy, libido. And while those functions are certainly important, they represent only a fraction of what these hormones actually do in your body.

Estrogen, progesterone, and testosterone are profoundly metabolic hormones. They regulate fat storage and distribution, influence insulin sensitivity, affect thyroid function, modulate inflammation, impact bone density, influence cardiovascular health, and even affect brain function and mood.

Understanding this broader picture is essential because it explains why hormonal changes during perimenopause create such widespread dysfunction beyond just hot flashes and missed periods.

The Trio Working Together: Estrogen, Progesterone, and Testosterone

These three hormones don't work in isolation. They function as an interconnected system where the ratio and balance between them matters as much as—or more than—their absolute levels. Think of them as three instruments in a jazz trio. Each can play beautifully solo, but the magic happens when they're properly balanced and harmonizing together.

Throughout your reproductive years (roughly ages 20-35), these hormones maintain relatively consistent ratios to each other, even though absolute levels fluctuate throughout your menstrual cycle. Your estrogen rises in the first half of your cycle, progesterone surges after ovulation in the second half, and testosterone remains relatively steady with a small mid-cycle peak around ovulation.

During perimenopause (typically starting around age 35-40), these ratios begin to shift—sometimes dramatically, sometimes erratically—and it's these shifting ratios that create many of the symptoms women experience. You might have perfectly "normal" estrogen levels by laboratory standards, but if your progesterone has dropped to nearly nothing, you're experiencing estrogen dominance even though your estrogen itself isn't elevated.

This is why we focus on ratios and balance rather than just looking at whether individual hormone levels fall within reference ranges.

DHEA and Hormone Precursors: The Starting Materials

Before looking at individual hormones, it's important to understand how your body actually *makes* them because this production process becomes especially relevant during perimenopause and menopause, when hormone demand increases and reserve capacity declines.

Chapter 4: Sex Hormone Imbalance—The Hormonally Hijacked Metabolizer

All steroid hormones including cortisol, estrogen, progesterone, testosterone, and DHEA (dehydroepiandrosterone), are synthesized from cholesterol. Cholesterol is not the enemy of your hormone system; it is the raw material from which hormones are made. Extremely low cholesterol levels can impair steroid hormone production, particularly in midlife.

The first and most important step in this process is the conversion of cholesterol into pregnenolone. Pregnenolone is often referred to as the "parent" or "starter" hormone because it sits at the top of the steroid hormone pathway.

From pregnenolone, hormone production branches into multiple pathways:

- One pathway supports stress hormones, ultimately producing cortisol:
  Pregnenolone → Progesterone → Cortisol (via multiple steps)

- Other pathways support sex hormones, including progesterone, DHEA, estrogen, and testosterone
  Pregnenolone → DHEA → Testosterone and Estrogen

Pregnenolone: The Master Hormone Precursor

Pregnenolone	⟶	DHEA
Pregnenolone	⟶	Estradiol
Pregnenolone	⟶	Estrone
Pregnenolone	⟶	Testosterone
Pregnenolone	⟶	Progesterone
Pregnenolone	⟶	Cortisol
Pregnenolone	⟶	Aldosterone

Part I: Understanding Why You Are Struggling With The Scale

Pregnenolone itself is not stored in large amounts. At any given time, your body must decide how to allocate it based on perceived needs. Under conditions of chronic stress, inflammation, illness, or sleep deprivation, the body prioritizes cortisol production because cortisol is essential for short-term survival.

This concept is sometimes referred to clinically as "pregnenolone steal" or "cortisol dominance." While not a literal stealing of pregnenolone, it describes a stress-driven shift in hormone production, where cortisol synthesis is prioritized at the expense of downstream sex hormones.

Over time, this pattern can contribute to:

- Elevated or dysregulated cortisol
- Declining progesterone
- Reduced DHEA
- Secondary reductions in estrogen and testosterone
- Worsening perimenopausal symptoms

The Role of DHEA in Midlife Hormone Balance

DHEA (dehydroepiandrosterone) is a key hormone produced primarily by the adrenal glands. It serves as a precursor to both testosterone and estrogen in peripheral tissues such as fat, muscle, bone, and skin. DHEA also has important independent effects—it supports muscle mass, bone density, immune function, insulin sensitivity, and overall metabolic health.

Unlike estrogen and progesterone, which are primarily produced by the ovaries during reproductive years, DHEA production gradually declines with age, often beginning in the thirties and accelerating through perimenopause and menopause.

As ovarian hormone production becomes more erratic and eventually declines, the body becomes increasingly reliant on adrenal and peripheral conversion of DHEA to help maintain androgen and estrogen balance. When DHEA levels are low, this compensatory mechanism is weakened.

Chronic stress compounds the problem. When adrenal resources are heavily directed toward cortisol production, DHEA output may decline further. The result is a pattern commonly seen in midlife women:

Chapter 4: Sex Hormone Imbalance—The Hormonally Hijacked Metabolizer

- High or unstable cortisol
- Low DHEA
- Worsening fatigue, muscle loss, mood changes, sleep disruption, and metabolic resistance
- Reduced support for estrogen and testosterone signaling

This is why cortisol regulation and adrenal health are foundational—not optional—when addressing hormone balance in perimenopause and menopause. You cannot effectively optimize sex hormones without also addressing stress physiology. The pathways are interconnected, and ignoring cortisol undermines every downstream hormone.

Estrogen: "The Exciting Hormone"

Estrogen is often called the "exciting hormone" because of its stimulating, growth-promoting effects throughout your body. But "estrogen" isn't just one hormone; it's actually a family of three related hormones:

- **Estradiol (E2)**—The most potent form, produced primarily by the ovaries during reproductive years
- **Estrone (E1)**—Weaker form, produced in fat tissue, becomes dominant after menopause
- **Estriol (E3)**—Weakest form, produced in large amounts during pregnancy

When we test "estrogen" clinically, we're typically measuring estradiol (E2), as it's the most metabolically active form during the reproductive and perimenopausal years.

Here's what estrogen actually does:

1. **Metabolism and Energy Production**
   Estrogen enhances your metabolic rate—the number of calories your body burns at rest. It does this by regulating the activity of thyroid hormone in your cells and by promoting the formation of new mitochondria (your cellular energy factories). When estrogen declines during perimenopause, metabolic rate slows, which is one

reason women often gain weight even when eating the same amount they always have.

2. **Fat Distribution and Storage**

Estrogen influences where your body stores fat. Higher estrogen levels promote subcutaneous fat storage (the relatively benign fat under your skin, particularly in hips, thighs, and breasts) rather than visceral fat storage (the dangerous belly fat that accumulates around your organs and drives metabolic dysfunction).

When estrogen declines, fat distribution shifts. Even without weight gain, you'll notice fat accumulating around your midsection rather than your hips and thighs. This isn't just aesthetic; visceral fat is metabolically active tissue that promotes insulin resistance, inflammation, and cardiovascular disease.

3. **Insulin Sensitivity**

Estrogen improves insulin sensitivity, helping your cells respond appropriately to insulin's signal to take up glucose. When estrogen is adequate, your pancreas doesn't have to produce as much insulin to achieve the same glucose control. When estrogen declines, insulin sensitivity decreases, which means your pancreas must produce more insulin to manage blood sugar. Over time, this can progress to full insulin resistance. This is one reason why the prevalence of type 2 diabetes increases dramatically in women after menopause.

4. **Brain Function and Mood**

Estrogen has profound effects on brain function. It enhances the production and function of neurotransmitters including serotonin, dopamine, and acetylcholine. It promotes the formation of new neural connections (neuroplasticity) and protects brain cells from damage. Estrogen also increases blood flow to the brain and enhances energy production in brain cells.

This is why declining estrogen creates the brain fog, memory problems, and difficulty concentrating that so many perimenopausal

Chapter 4: Sex Hormone Imbalance—The Hormonally Hijacked Metabolizer

women experience. It's not "just stress" or "getting older"—it's the direct result of decreased estrogen's effects on brain function.

Estrogen also regulates mood by influencing neurotransmitter systems. When estrogen is adequate, mood tends to be more stable. When estrogen fluctuates wildly (as in early perimenopause) or declines significantly (as in late perimenopause), mood instability, anxiety, and depression become common.

5. **Bone Density**

Estrogen is critical for maintaining bone strength. It inhibits osteoclasts (cells that break down bone) and supports osteoblasts (cells that build new bone). When estrogen declines after menopause, bone loss accelerates dramatically. Women can lose up to twenty percent of their bone density in the first five years after menopause, significantly increasing fracture risk.

This is one reason why bioidentical hormone replacement therapy with estrogen is so protective for long-term health: It helps preserve bone density and reduces osteoporosis risk.

6. **Cardiovascular Health**

Estrogen supports cardiovascular health in multiple ways. It helps maintain flexible, healthy blood vessels, promotes healthy cholesterol profiles (higher HDL, lower LDL), and reduces inflammation in blood vessel walls. This is why heart disease risk increases dramatically for women after menopause—the loss of estrogen's protective effects leaves women more vulnerable to cardiovascular disease.

7. **Skin, Hair, and Connective Tissue**

Estrogen supports collagen production, helping maintain skin elasticity and thickness. It also supports hair growth and health. When estrogen declines, skin becomes thinner and less elastic, wrinkles deepen, and hair may thin or become more brittle.

Summary: What Happens When Estrogen Declines

When estrogen drops during perimenopause and menopause, you experience:

Part I: Understanding Why You Are Struggling With The Scale

- Slower metabolism and easier weight gain
- Shift toward visceral belly fat accumulation
- Decreased insulin sensitivity (promoting insulin resistance)
- Brain fog, memory problems, difficulty concentrating
- Mood instability, anxiety, depression
- Accelerated bone loss
- Increased cardiovascular disease risk
- Hot flashes and night sweats
- Vaginal dryness and painful intercourse
- Thinning skin and hair
- Loss of energy and generally "not feeling like yourself"

Progesterone: "The Calming Hormone"

If estrogen is the stimulating, activating hormone, progesterone is its stabilizing counterpart. Throughout the body—especially in the brain and reproductive tissues—progesterone helps balance estrogen's effects and promotes a sense of calm, safety, and physiological resilience.

Progesterone's influence extends far beyond reproduction. It plays a critical role in mood regulation, sleep quality, fluid balance, metabolic signaling, and how tissues respond to estrogen.

Here's what progesterone does:

1. **Mood and Anxiety Regulation**

   Progesterone has a calming, anti-anxiety effect on the brain. One of its key metabolites, allopregnanolone, enhances the activity of GABA (gamma-aminobutyric acid). This is the brain's primary calming neurotransmitter.

   When progesterone levels drop, one of the first things you may notice is an increase in anxiety and irritability, even though nothing in your external life has changed to cause this.

2. **Sleep Quality**

   Progesterone promotes deep, restorative sleep. It has sedative effects that help you fall asleep and stay asleep. Many women notice that

Chapter 4: Sex Hormone Imbalance—The Hormonally Hijacked Metabolizer

their sleep quality declines precipitously during perimenopause. This is often due to dropping progesterone rather than just stress or aging.

3. **Balancing Estrogen's Effects**

   Throughout your body, progesterone moderates estrogen's growth-promoting effects. This balance is most clearly established in the uterine lining, where estrogen thickens the endometrium each month and progesterone stabilizes it, preventing excessive growth. Without sufficient progesterone, estrogen's proliferative effects can become excessive, leading to heavy menstrual bleeding, prolonged periods, and large clots.

   In breast tissue, estrogen promotes ductal growth and fluid retention while progesterone helps regulate this process. When progesterone is low, estrogen's effects feel amplified—contributing to breast tenderness, swelling, and fibrocystic changes.

   When progesterone drops but estrogen remains relatively high, we refer to this as *estrogen dominance*. Estrogen dominance simply means progesterone is insufficient to balance estrogen's effects, not one where estrogen is necessarily elevated. When progesterone declines, estrogen's stimulatory influence becomes more pronounced, leading to symptoms such as heavy bleeding, PMS, breast tenderness, fibrocystic changes, and increased risk for estrogen-sensitive conditions including fibroids and endometriosis.

4. **Fluid Balance and Bloating**

   Progesterone has a natural diuretic effect, helping reduce water retention. When progesterone is low, you're more likely to experience bloating and fluid retention, particularly before your period.

5. **Metabolic Support**

   Progesterone supports healthy metabolism and helps prevent insulin resistance. It also supports thyroid function (as we discussed in Chapter 3) by enhancing thyroid hormone receptor sensitivity.

Summary: What Happens When Progesterone Declines

When progesterone drops during perimenopause, you experience:
- Increased anxiety and irritability
- Sleep disruption (difficulty falling asleep, waking during night)
- Heavy menstrual bleeding
- Severe PMS symptoms
- Breast tenderness and fibrocystic breasts
- Bloating and water retention
- Worsening metabolism
- Increased risk for fibroids and endometriosis

Testosterone: "The Vitality Hormone"

While we typically think of testosterone as a male hormone, women also produce testosterone (in smaller amounts than men), and it plays crucial roles in female health and metabolism.

Testosterone levels in women are typically 10-20 times lower than in men, but that doesn't mean it's unimportant—even small declines create significant symptoms. Women's testosterone is produced partly by the ovaries and partly by the adrenal glands through conversion of DHEA.

Here's what testosterone does in women:

1. **Libido and Sexual Function**

   Testosterone is the primary driver of sexual desire in both men and women. When testosterone is adequate, libido is healthy. When testosterone declines, sexual desire often vanishes entirely—one of the most frustrating symptoms many perimenopausal women experience.

2. **Muscle Mass and Strength**

   Testosterone supports muscle growth, strength, and maintenance. It promotes protein synthesis and helps prevent muscle breakdown. When testosterone declines, maintaining muscle mass becomes significantly more difficult, even with consistent strength training.

We will discuss this more in depth in Part II, but take note of this key point: Muscle is metabolically active tissue. As you lose muscle and replace it with fat, your metabolic rate drops, making weight gain easier and weight loss harder.

3. **Energy and Vitality**

Testosterone contributes to overall energy, motivation, drive, and sense of vitality. When testosterone is adequate, you feel energized and motivated to tackle challenges. When it's low, you may feel flat, unmotivated, lacking your usual drive and zest for life.

4. **Cognitive Function**

Testosterone supports cognitive function, particularly mental clarity, focus, and decisiveness. Low testosterone can contribute to brain fog and difficulty making decisions.

5. **Bone Density**

Like estrogen, testosterone supports bone health and helps prevent osteoporosis. This is one reason why women with very low testosterone levels are at increased risk for fractures.

6. **Metabolic Function**

Testosterone helps maintain healthy body composition by supporting muscle mass and preventing excessive fat accumulation, particularly abdominal fat. It also supports healthy insulin sensitivity.

Summary: What Happens When Testosterone Declines

When testosterone drops during perimenopause and menopause, you experience:

- Loss of libido and sexual desire
- Difficulty building or maintaining muscle mass
- Increased fat accumulation (particularly abdominal)
- Decreased energy and motivation
- Reduced mental clarity and decisiveness

- Declining bone density
- Loss of vitality and drive

SECTION 2: The Three Patterns of Sex Hormone Imbalance

Now that you understand what each hormone does, let's explore the three distinct patterns of sex hormone imbalance women experience during perimenopause. Understanding which pattern you're experiencing helps guide testing and treatment, though comprehensive evaluation of all three hormones is always necessary.

Pattern 1: Estrogen Dominance (Early Perimenopause)

What's Happening:

Progesterone drops dramatically—often to nearly undetectable levels—while estrogen remains normal or even elevated. This creates an imbalanced ratio where estrogen's effects are unopposed and exaggerated.

Typical Timeline:

This pattern is most common in early to mid-perimenopause, typically ages 35-45, when ovulation becomes irregular or absent. When you don't ovulate, your body doesn't produce the progesterone surge that normally occurs after ovulation in the second half of your cycle. This leads to progesterone deficiency while estrogen continues being produced in relatively normal amounts.

Women with cortisol dysregulation (chronic stress, high performing women) are at the highest risk for developing estrogen dominance (as we discussed in Chapter 2) due to the "pregnenolone steal" and demand for chronic cortisol production.

Characteristic Symptoms:

- **Heavy menstrual bleeding:** Soaking through pads or tampons hourly, periods lasting 7+ days, passing large clots
- **Severe PMS:** Irritability, anxiety, mood swings in the week or two before your period
- **Breast tenderness:** Particularly severe before periods, sometimes lasting weeks
- Bloating and water retention
- **Difficulty sleeping:** Particularly premenstrually
- Anxiety and emotional volatility
- Weight gain, particularly around hips and thighs initially
- Fibrocystic breasts, fibroids, or endometriosis worsening

Why This Pattern Creates Problems:

Without adequate progesterone to balance estrogen, estrogen's growth-promoting effects go unchecked. In the uterine lining, this creates excessive tissue growth, leading to heavy bleeding. In breast tissue, it creates tenderness and potentially fibrocystic changes. The lack of progesterone's calming effects creates anxiety, sleep disruption, and mood instability.

Many women with this pattern are told their hormones are "fine" based solely on normal FSH levels or dismissed entirely without any hormone testing. Here's the frustrating reality: most conventional providers don't routinely check sex hormone levels at all during perimenopause.

The rationale behind not testing sex hormones is that they fluctuate throughout a normal menstrual cycle, making it challenging to establish "standard" reference ranges. In a regular 28-day cycle, estrogen rises and falls twice, peaking at ovulation and again in the luteal phase, while progesterone surges after ovulation and drops before menstruation. This variability makes providers hesitant to order testing, arguing that a single snapshot might not be meaningful.

But here's what that reasoning misses: Even with normal hormonal fluctuation, the ratio between estrogen and progesterone at any given point in time tells us something important about how these hormones are working together in your body. You can have perfectly "normal" estrogen levels and still have estrogen dominance if your progesterone has dropped significantly. Two hormones measured on the same day, at the same time, reveal their relationship to each other—and that balance is what determines how you feel and function.

In perimenopause, this becomes even more relevant because the "normal fluctuation" argument falls apart. Your cycles aren't predictably following a twenty-eight-day pattern anymore. Ovulation may be sporadic or absent. The hormonal chaos of perimenopause means we're not dealing with textbook cyclical variation—we're dealing with erratic, unpredictable patterns that absolutely warrant investigation. Yet this critical balance between estrogen and progesterone is almost never assessed in conventional medicine, leaving women suffering without answers.

Pattern 2: Overall Low Sex Hormones (Late Perimenopause/Menopause)

What's Happening:

Both estrogen and progesterone decline significantly. This is the pattern most people associate with menopause—the classic "low hormone" state. However, the symptoms are so much more than just "hot flashes and night sweats." There are estrogen receptors almost everywhere within the body, and they affect both quality of life and lifelong health risks.

Typical Timeline:

This pattern emerges in late perimenopause (typically ages 45-55) and continues after menopause. As ovarian function winds down, production of both estrogen and progesterone declines. Your body should compensate somewhat through adrenal production of DHEA (which converts to estrogen and testosterone), but if adrenal function is compromised by stress, this compensation fails.

Chapter 4: Sex Hormone Imbalance—The Hormonally Hijacked Metabolizer

Common Symptoms:

- **Hot flashes:** Sudden intense waves of heat, often multiple times per day
- **Night sweats:** Waking drenched in sweat, having to change pajamas/sheets
- **Sleep disruption:** Difficulty falling asleep, frequent waking, unrefreshing sleep
- **Brain fog:** Difficulty concentrating, memory problems, word-finding difficulties
- **Mood changes:** Depression, anxiety, emotional flatness
- **Vaginal dryness:** Painful intercourse, increased UTI risk
- **Loss of libido:** Complete loss of sexual desire
- Thinning hair and dry skin
- Weight gain, particularly abdominal/belly fat
- Joint pain and stiffness
- Fatigue and low energy
- Bone density loss
- Dry eyes, itchy ears, tinnitus (ringing in the ears)

Why This Pattern Creates Problems:

When both estrogen and progesterone are deficient, you lose the protective and regulatory effects these hormones provide throughout your body. Metabolism slows, insulin resistance develops, visceral fat accumulates, bone density declines, cardiovascular risk increases, brain function suffers, and overall health diminishes.

This is also when the cascade effect becomes most pronounced—low sex hormones trigger insulin resistance, thyroid dysfunction, worsening cortisol patterns, and accelerated muscle loss.

Pattern 3: Lifelong Hormone Disruptions—When Perimenopause Amplifies Existing Imbalances

What's Happening:

This pattern is fundamentally different from the first two. Rather than being caused by perimenopause, these are lifelong hormonal imbalances that have existed since adolescence or young adulthood and become significantly worse during the perimenopausal transition.

The most common condition in this category is PCOS (Polycystic Ovary Syndrome), affecting up to thirteen percent of women of reproductive age. But this pattern also includes other lifelong hormone disruptions such as premature ovarian insufficiency, hypothalamic amenorrhea (from chronic stress, under-eating, or over-exercising), endometriosis, and other conditions that impacted fertility or menstrual regularity throughout your reproductive years.

What these conditions share is that they were often masked by birth control pills for years or decades—the pill suppressed symptoms but never addressed the underlying hormone dysfunction. When women discontinue the pill (whether trying to conceive or entering perimenopause), symptoms return, often more intensely than before.

PCOS: The Most Common Lifelong Hormone Disruption

Because PCOS is by far the most prevalent condition in this category, we'll focus primarily on it, but the principles of addressing root causes rather than just suppressing symptoms apply to all lifelong hormone disruptions.

PCOS is characterized by elevated androgens (male hormones, particularly testosterone and DHEA-S), insulin resistance, and irregular or absent ovulation. The fundamental problem is insulin resistance, which triggers the ovaries to overproduce androgens. This creates a cascade of hormonal disruption that affects everything from menstrual cycles to metabolism to fertility.

Chapter 4: Sex Hormone Imbalance—The Hormonally Hijacked Metabolizer

Typical Timeline:

Symptoms often begin in adolescence or the early twenties: irregular periods (cycles longer than thirty-five days or completely absent), acne, unwanted hair growth, difficulty losing weight despite reasonable diet and exercise efforts. Many women are placed on birth control pills to "regulate" their cycles and control symptoms like acne and excess hair growth.

The pill effectively masks PCOS symptoms by artificially regulating cycles and lowering androgen levels, but it doesn't address the underlying insulin resistance driving the condition. When women discontinue the pill—whether trying to conceive or reaching perimenopause—symptoms return, often worse than before because the metabolic dysfunction has progressed untreated for years or decades.

During perimenopause, as estrogen and progesterone naturally decline, the relative androgen dominance becomes even more pronounced. Women face a "perfect storm" of worsening PCOS symptoms overlaid with typical perimenopausal changes, creating an intensely challenging experience.

Characteristic Symptoms:

- **Menstrual irregularity:** Cycles longer than thirty-five days or absent periods for months at a time
- **Heavy, unpredictable bleeding:** When periods do occur, they're often very heavy due to prolonged estrogen stimulation without regular progesterone opposition
- **Weight struggles:** Extreme difficulty losing weight despite good compliance with diet and exercise; weight gain that seems disproportionate to caloric intake
- **Central obesity:** Weight concentrated around the abdomen rather than hips and thighs
- **Persistent acne:** Particularly along the jawline, chin, and chest—often cystic and resistant to typical treatments
- **Excess hair growth (hirsutism):** Dark, coarse hair on the face (chin, upper lip, sideburns), chest, abdomen, back, or inner thighs

- **Thinning scalp hair:** Widening part, receding hairline, or male-pattern hair loss
- **Acanthosis nigricans:** Dark, velvety skin patches on the neck, armpits, or groin—a visible sign of insulin resistance
- **Skin tags:** Small, benign skin growths, typically in skin folds
- **Fertility challenges:** Difficulty conceiving due to irregular or absent ovulation
- **Recurrent pregnancy loss:** Multiple miscarriages, often in the first trimester
- **Mood symptoms:** Anxiety, depression, and emotional dysregulation—worsened by the hormonal instability

Why This Pattern Creates Problems:

PCOS is fundamentally driven by insulin resistance. When cells become resistant to insulin's signals, the pancreas compensates by producing more insulin. These chronically elevated insulin levels signal the ovaries to produce excess androgens. The elevated androgens disrupt the normal feedback loops that regulate ovulation, creating irregular or absent cycles and significant fertility challenges.

The insulin resistance itself makes weight loss extraordinarily difficult—it promotes fat storage (particularly in the abdomen) and makes it nearly impossible to access stored fat for energy. This creates a vicious cycle: Excess body fat worsens insulin resistance, which further elevates insulin and androgens, making weight loss even harder.

When perimenopause begins and estrogen and progesterone naturally decline, the androgen dominance becomes even more pronounced relative to other sex hormones. Women experience worsening of all their PCOS symptoms—more weight gain, more unwanted hair growth, worsening acne, more irregular bleeding—plus all the typical perimenopausal symptoms like hot flashes, mood changes, brain fog, and sleep disruption. It's layering one hormone crisis on top of another.

Many women with PCOS were never properly diagnosed. They were simply told they had "irregular periods" and prescribed birth control pills.

Chapter 4: Sex Hormone Imbalance—The Hormonally Hijacked Metabolizer

Decades later, when they reach perimenopause and discontinue the pill (or it becomes less effective as they age), they struggle intensely with weight, metabolic dysfunction, and severe symptoms without understanding that an undiagnosed and untreated condition has been progressing beneath the surface for years.

Critical Understanding:

PCOS is fundamentally a metabolic disorder—specifically insulin resistance—that manifests as a hormone imbalance. Birth control pills can effectively suppress symptoms by artificially lowering androgens and regulating cycles, but they don't address the insulin resistance driving the condition. When women stop the pill, symptoms return because the underlying metabolic dysfunction was never treated.

This is also why women with PCOS often struggle more intensely during perimenopause than women without it. They're entering perimenopause with already-compromised metabolic function and existing insulin resistance. When the natural hormonal decline of perimenopause occurs, it amplifies metabolic dysfunction and makes all symptoms worse.

Successfully addressing PCOS—and navigating perimenopause with PCOS—requires treating the insulin resistance (as we discussed in Chapter 1) while simultaneously supporting hormonal balance and addressing the other hormone imbalances that inevitably develop. This is why women with PCOS often experience dramatic, life-changing improvement when they address all five hormone imbalances comprehensively through The Matrix Method rather than just taking medications that suppress symptoms without fixing root causes.

If you struggled with irregular periods, fertility challenges, or were diagnosed with PCOS earlier in life, understanding this pattern is crucial. Your perimenopausal experience will be different—likely more challenging—than women without these underlying conditions. But with the right approach addressing root causes rather than just managing symptoms, you can absolutely achieve the transformation you're seeking.

SECTION 3: The Cascade Effect—How Sex Hormone Decline Triggers the Other Four Imbalances

Now that you understand the three distinct patterns of sex hormone imbalance during perimenopause, let's explore exactly how these changes create the domino effect we've been referencing. You know that sex hormone decline doesn't happen in isolation—but what does that actually look like physiologically? How does dropping progesterone trigger insulin resistance? Why does estrogen decline worsen thyroid function? What's the mechanism connecting cortisol dysregulation to accelerated muscle loss?

Understanding these specific pathways is critical because it explains why addressing sex hormones alone, whether through hormone replacement therapy or any single intervention, rarely solves the weight problem. The damage has already cascaded. Once sex hormone decline has triggered the other four imbalances, each system must be addressed individually to restore optimal function.

The Timeline of Decline

Before we explore the cascade, let's understand the typical timeline of sex hormone decline during perimenopause. This helps explain why symptoms evolve and worsen over time.

Age 35-40 (Early Perimenopause):

Progesterone begins declining first and most dramatically. You may still have regular periods, but ovulation becomes irregular or absent. When you don't ovulate, your body doesn't produce the normal progesterone surge. This creates early estrogen dominance—progesterone has dropped significantly while estrogen remains relatively normal.

Age 40-45 (Mid-Perimenopause):

Estrogen levels begin fluctuating wildly—some months high, some months low, creating erratic symptoms. Progesterone continues declining. Testosterone starts its gradual decline. DHEA production from adrenal glands begins dropping (DHEA naturally declines about two percent per year starting in your thirties). The ratios between hormones become increasingly imbalanced.

Age 45-50 (Late Perimenopause):

Estrogen decline accelerates. Both estrogen and progesterone are now significantly lower than baseline. Testosterone continues declining. DHEA depletion worsens, particularly if you're under chronic stress. Periods become irregular—sometimes skipped, sometimes heavy. Classic menopausal symptoms (hot flashes, night sweats, vaginal dryness) emerge or intensify.

Age 50-55 (Approaching/Reaching Menopause):

Most women reach menopause (defined as twelve consecutive months without a period). Estrogen and progesterone from the ovaries are minimal. Your body is supposed to compensate by increasing production from other sources—particularly DHEA from the adrenal glands converting to estrogen and testosterone—but if adrenal function is compromised by stress, this compensation fails.

By the numbers:
- Estrogen drops approximately 40-50 percent from peak reproductive levels
- Progesterone drops approximately 90-99 percent from peak reproductive levels (often to near-zero)
- Testosterone drops approximately fifty percent from peak levels
- DHEA declines steadily, approximately two percent per year starting in your thirties

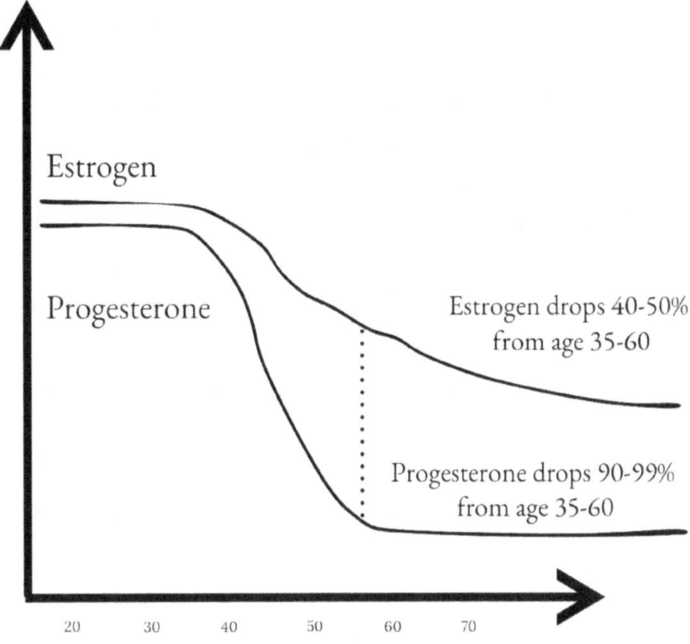

Hormone changes from age 35-60

Now let's explore how these declining sex hormones trigger the other four imbalances:

Sex Hormones → Insulin Resistance

Remember from Chapter 1 that estrogen enhances insulin sensitivity. When estrogen is adequate, your cells respond appropriately to insulin, and your pancreas doesn't have to produce excessive amounts to manage blood sugar. When estrogen declines, insulin sensitivity decreases.

The result: Your pancreas must produce more insulin to achieve the same glucose control. Over time, this leads to hyperinsulinemia (chronically elevated insulin), which then progresses to full insulin resistance. The declining estrogen of perimenopause is one reason why insulin resistance becomes so common in women over forty, even in women who were previously metabolically healthy.

And as we covered in Chapter 1, insulin resistance directly promotes weight gain—particularly visceral fat accumulation—and makes fat loss nearly impossible. So the sex hormone decline creates insulin resistance, which then blocks your ability to lose weight.

Sex Hormones → Thyroid Dysfunction

As we discussed in detail in Chapter 3, the relationship between sex hormones and thyroid function is complex and bidirectional:

Estrogen increases thyroid binding globulin (TBG), which binds up thyroid hormone and reduces the amount of free, active hormone available to your cells. When estrogen fluctuates wildly (estrogen dominance in early perimenopause), you can develop functional hypothyroidism even with normal TSH. When estrogen declines too low (late perimenopause), thyroid tissue can atrophy and thyroid function declines.

Progesterone supports thyroid function by enhancing thyroid hormone receptor sensitivity and supporting T4 to T3 conversion. When progesterone plummets during perimenopause, this supportive effect is lost. Your cells become less responsive to thyroid hormone, and conversion of inactive T4 to active T3 slows.

The combination of erratic estrogen and very low progesterone creates thyroid dysfunction in many women. You may have "normal" TSH but feel terrible because your free T3 is inadequate, or you may develop subclinical or overt hypothyroidism during perimenopause. And as we covered in Chapter 3, thyroid dysfunction directly impairs metabolism, making weight loss difficult and weight gain easy.

Sex Hormones → Cortisol Dysregulation

The relationship between sex hormones and cortisol is bidirectional and complex. As we discussed earlier in this chapter and in Chapter 2, chronic stress and elevated cortisol steal pregnenolone away from sex hormone production (the pregnenolone steal), leaving you with high cortisol and low progesterone.

But the reverse is also true: Declining sex hormones worsen your stress response and cortisol regulation. Estrogen and progesterone both modulate the HPA axis (hypothalamic-pituitary-adrenal axis) that controls cortisol production. When these hormones are adequate, your stress response is well-regulated. When they decline, your HPA axis becomes dysregulated, often leading to exaggerated cortisol responses to stress or flattened cortisol curves with disrupted diurnal rhythm.

The result: worsening sleep, increased anxiety, difficulty managing stress, and the cortisol-driven belly fat accumulation we discussed in Chapter 2. And remember, elevated cortisol directly promotes insulin resistance and blocks thyroid hormone conversion, creating multiple vicious cycles.

Sex Hormones → Accelerated Muscle Loss (Sarcopenia)

As we will discuss further in Part II, women naturally lose approximately 3.5 percent of muscle mass per decade after age thirty through a process called sarcopenia. But declining sex hormones—particularly estrogen and testosterone—dramatically accelerate this process.

Estrogen supports muscle strength and helps prevent muscle breakdown. Testosterone promotes muscle growth and protein synthesis. When both decline during perimenopause, maintaining muscle mass becomes significantly more difficult. Even women who continue exercising regularly often notice they're losing muscle and gaining fat despite consistent effort.

Muscle is metabolically active tissue. One pound of muscle burns approximately nine calories per day at rest, while one pound of fat burns only about five calories per day. As you lose muscle and replace it with fat, your metabolic rate drops, sometimes by hundreds of calories per day. This makes weight maintenance increasingly difficult and weight loss seem nearly impossible.

Why Weight Loss Becomes Impossible: The Biology of a Stressed Body

Here's what you need to understand: When your body is in a state of hormonal chaos—low sex hormones, insulin resistance, thyroid dysfunction, cortisol dysregulation, and declining muscle mass—it interprets this as a state of threat. From an evolutionary perspective, hormonal decline signals aging and reduced resources. Your body's biological imperative becomes resource conservation.

What does resource conservation look like physiologically?

- **Slower metabolism:** Your body reduces energy expenditure to conserve resources
- **Enhanced fat storage:** Your body prioritizes storing any excess energy as fat rather than using it
- **Reduced fat mobilization:** Your body becomes reluctant to release stored fat for energy
- **Increased hunger signaling:** Your body increases appetite to encourage food intake
- **Decreased satiety signaling:** You don't feel full as easily, leading to overeating
- **Preferential muscle loss over fat loss:** When in caloric deficit, your body breaks down muscle for energy while protecting fat stores

This is why "eat less, exercise more" stops working during perimenopause. You're not battling a lack of willpower or discipline. You're battling your own biology.

Your body is hormonally programmed to hold on to weight when it perceives threat, and the combination of declining sex hormones plus the other four imbalances creates precisely that perception of threat. You can restrict calories severely, you can exercise for hours daily, but if the underlying hormone imbalances aren't addressed, your body will fight you every step of the way.

Women often describe feeling like they're "gaining weight on 1200 calories a day" or "exercising two hours daily and not losing a pound."

They're not exaggerating. They're experiencing the metabolic consequences of multiple hormone imbalances, creating a perfect storm that makes weight loss physiologically very difficult—sometimes nearly impossible—until the underlying dysfunction is corrected.

Why "Eat Less, Exercise More" Doesn't Work

Let's be very clear about this: The traditional weight loss advice of "create a caloric deficit through reducing food intake and increasing exercise" is based on a fundamental misunderstanding of how metabolism actually works—particularly in women during perimenopause.

The "calories in, calories out" model assumes your metabolism is a fixed, unchanging furnace that burns a consistent number of calories regardless of what you do. This is false. Your metabolism is dynamic and adaptive. It responds to your food intake, your activity level, your stress levels, your sleep quality, and most importantly, your hormonal status.

Here's what actually happens when a hormonally-imbalanced woman restricts calories and increases exercise:

Phase 1: Initial Success

You create a caloric deficit. The scale drops. You lose 5-10 pounds in the first few weeks. You feel encouraged. It's working!

Phase 2: Metabolic Adaptation

Your body perceives the caloric restriction as a threat—especially when hormones are already signaling resource scarcity. Your metabolism down-regulates. You start burning fewer calories at rest. Your thyroid function decreases (lower T3 production). Your hunger hormones increase (elevated ghrelin, decreased leptin). You feel hungrier and less satisfied after meals.

Phase 3: Plateau

Weight loss stalls despite continued restriction and exercise. The scale won't budge. You get frustrated. You restrict calories even more. You add more exercise. Nothing changes.

Chapter 4: Sex Hormone Imbalance—The Hormonally Hijacked Metabolizer

Phase 4: The Breakdown

You're exhausted. You're irritable. You're hungry all the time. Your sleep is disrupted. Your workouts feel terrible. Your performance suffers. Eventually, you can't sustain the restriction anymore. You start eating normally again—or you binge because you're so hungry and deprived.

Phase 5: Rapid Regain

The weight comes back quickly—often faster than it came off. And it brings friends. You end up heavier than when you started. Your metabolism is now slower than before because you've lost muscle mass during the restriction phase and you've downregulated your metabolic rate through chronic caloric deprivation.

This cycle—often called "yo-yo dieting" or "weight cycling"—is incredibly common among perimenopausal women. And it's not a failure of willpower. It's a predictable physiological response to caloric restriction in a hormonally-compromised body.

The solution isn't more restriction or more exercise. The solution is addressing the underlying hormone imbalances so your body can respond appropriately to nutrition and movement interventions.

SECTION 4: How to Test Sex Hormones— Getting the Answers You Need

Understanding what's happening is the first step. The second step is getting objective data that confirms which hormones are out of balance and by how much. You cannot treat what you don't measure, and you cannot optimize hormones based on symptoms alone.

The Standard Approach (Blood Testing)

Blood testing is the gold standard for sex hormone evaluation. Despite what you may have heard about saliva or urine testing being "better," blood testing provides adequate, reproducible, standardized results for sex hormones in perimenopausal women. Here are the specific tests that should be ordered:

Estradiol (E2)

What it measures: The most potent and metabolically active form of estrogen during reproductive years and perimenopause.

Why it matters: This tells you whether your estrogen levels are adequate, elevated, or deficient. In perimenopause, estradiol often fluctuates dramatically from cycle to cycle, which is why testing multiple times can be valuable if symptoms are erratic.

Progesterone

What it measures: The calming, balancing hormone produced after ovulation in the second half of your cycle.

Why it matters: Low progesterone creates estrogen dominance even when estrogen itself is normal. In perimenopause, progesterone often drops precipitously while estrogen remains relatively normal, creating the heavy bleeding, anxiety, and sleep disruption characteristic of Pattern 1.

When to test: Although standard recommendations are to test Progesterone on day 19-21 of your cycle (about one week after ovulation), we know that hormones are unpredictable and erratic during perimenopause. In our practice, we test at any time—and ask that you communicate specifics about your cycle at the time of interpretation.

Testosterone (Total and Free)

What it measures: Your levels of the hormone that supports libido, muscle mass, energy, and motivation.

Why it matters: Testosterone declines gradually during perimenopause, but the decline can be significant. Low testosterone creates loss of libido, difficulty maintaining muscle, decreased energy, and loss of drive—symptoms that profoundly impact quality of life.

Why both total and free: Total testosterone tells you how much testosterone you have overall. Free testosterone tells you how much is unbound and biologically active. If your SHBG (see below) is high, your total testosterone might look adequate but your free testosterone could be very low—meaning you have the hormone, but it's bound up and unavailable for use.

DHEA-S (DHEA-Sulfate)

What it measures: Your adrenal production of DHEA, the precursor hormone that converts to both estrogen and testosterone.

Why it matters: DHEA production should increase during perimenopause to help compensate for declining ovarian production of sex hormones. But if your adrenal glands are depleted from chronic stress (as we discussed in Chapter 2), DHEA production is often low. This means you lose the compensatory mechanism that should help maintain sex hormone levels as ovarian production declines.

Additional Testing Options: SHBG, FSH, and LH

Beyond the core hormone panel (Estradiol, Progesterone, Testosterone, and DHEA-S), there are additional tests that some practitioners find helpful for specific clinical scenarios. Whether these tests are necessary depends on your provider's approach and your individual situation.

SHBG (Sex Hormone Binding Globulin)

What it measures: The protein that binds and transports sex hormones through your bloodstream.

When it might be useful: SHBG testing can provide additional insight when troubleshooting persistent low libido or when free testosterone results seem inconsistent with symptoms. SHBG binds to estrogen, progesterone, and testosterone, making them unavailable for use by your cells.

Our approach: In our practice, we typically rely on free testosterone levels and symptom correlation rather than routinely checking SHBG. If free testosterone is low and libido symptoms are significant, we have the information we need to guide treatment. However, SHBG can be a useful additional data point for some providers and certain clinical situations.

FSH (Follicle Stimulating Hormone)

What it measures: The signal from your pituitary gland telling your ovaries to produce more hormones.

When it might be useful: FSH rises as your ovaries become less responsive during perimenopause. Consistently elevated FSH (above 30-40 mIU/mL combined with very low estradiol) can confirm menopausal status—which is particularly helpful for women who've had a hysterectomy and therefore don't have periods to track. However, FSH fluctuates significantly during perimenopause—it may be elevated one month and normal the next—so it's not always reliable until you're very close to menopause.

Our approach: We don't routinely check FSH because knowing exactly where you are in the perimenopause-to-menopause journey doesn't change our treatment approach. Whether you're in early perimenopause, late perimenopause, or post-menopause, we meet you where you are, assess your current hormone levels and symptoms, and optimize accordingly. If you're experiencing symptoms, we address them regardless of your "menopausal status." That said, some women find it psychologically helpful to confirm they've reached menopause, and some providers prefer this marker for documentation purposes.

LH (Luteinizing Hormone)

What it measures: Another pituitary signal that triggers ovulation.

When it might be useful: LH is primarily useful for women with suspected PCOS. In PCOS, the LH to FSH ratio is often elevated (greater than 2:1 or 3:1), though this is not diagnostic by itself. Outside of PCOS evaluation, LH provides limited additional information beyond what we get from the core hormone panel.

Our approach: We check LH only when PCOS is suspected based on clinical presentation (irregular cycles, androgen excess symptoms, difficulty losing weight, insulin resistance). For most perimenopausal women, LH doesn't meaningfully change our treatment decisions.

Chapter 4: Sex Hormone Imbalance—The Hormonally Hijacked Metabolizer

When and How to Test

Our Philosophy on Timing:

Different providers have different approaches to timing hormone testing, and both approaches have merit. Some practitioners prefer cycle-specific timing to capture hormones at particular phases. In our practice, we take a different approach: We test whenever you're ready for answers, regardless of where you are in your cycle. Here's why:

1. **We focus on ratios and symptom correlation.** What matters most isn't whether your estradiol is 150 pg/mL on day three versus day twenty-one—what matters is the ratio of estrogen to progesterone and how those levels correlate with your symptoms. If your estrogen is relatively normal but your progesterone is nearly undetectable, you have estrogen dominance creating symptoms—regardless of cycle day.

2. **Hormones are erratic during perimenopause.** Many women no longer have predictable cycles. Waiting to test on "day three" or "day twenty-one" can mean waiting weeks or months if cycles are irregular or absent. We want to get you answers and start treatment as soon as possible.

3. **We meet you where you are right now.** Our goal is to assess your current hormonal state and optimize it. If things change and symptoms return, we simply retest and adjust the treatment plan. We're not trying to fit you into a textbook pattern of what perimenopause "should" look like. We're addressing what's actually happening in your body right now.

4. **For women who aren't cycling or have irregular cycles,** timing is impossible anyway—and that's fine. Your current hormone levels, regardless of when they're drawn, tell us what we need to know.

Alternative Timing Approach:

That said, some providers prefer cycle-specific timing for women who still have relatively regular periods, as it can provide additional context:

- **Estradiol and FSH:** Can be tested on day 3-5 of your cycle (where day one = first day of bleeding) to assess baseline levels
- **Progesterone:** Can be tested on day 19-21 (or about one week after suspected ovulation) to confirm ovulation occurred and assess progesterone production
- **Testosterone and DHEA-S:** Can be tested any time—they don't fluctuate significantly with cycle

Some practitioners order labs twice in one cycle—once on day 3-5 and once on day 19-21—to capture both the follicular phase and luteal phase. This provides the most detailed picture of cyclical hormone patterns.

Which approach is right for you? Both are valid. If your cycles are regular and your provider prefers cycle-specific timing, that's perfectly reasonable. If you want answers immediately and your provider is comfortable testing at any point (as we are), that works too. The most important thing is getting comprehensive testing done—the specific timing is less critical than ensuring all the right markers are checked.

Morning Testing:

Most sex hormone testing can be done at any time of day, but morning testing is often most convenient because comprehensive hormone evaluation typically includes cortisol and insulin testing (covered in Chapters 1 and 2), which must be done in the morning. It's simpler to have all labs drawn together.

Fasting:

You don't need to fast for sex hormone testing specifically. However, since comprehensive hormone evaluation includes fasting insulin and possibly fasting glucose, you'll likely be fasting anyway for the complete panel.

Chapter 4: Sex Hormone Imbalance—The Hormonally Hijacked Metabolizer

Alternative Testing: DUTCH Complete (Optional)

Some practitioners offer DUTCH Complete testing (Dried Urine Test for Comprehensive Hormones), which measures hormone metabolites in dried urine samples collected over twenty-four hours.

What DUTCH adds:

- Estrogen metabolites (the breakdown products showing which pathways your body uses to metabolize estrogen)
- Cortisol and cortisone patterns throughout the day (the adrenal assessment we discussed in Chapter 2)
- Melatonin metabolites (sleep hormone assessment)
- Organic acids that reflect nutritional status and neurotransmitter production

When DUTCH might be useful:

The estrogen metabolite information can be particularly valuable for women with:
- Personal or family history of estrogen-sensitive cancers (breast, ovarian, uterine)
- Concerns about estrogen metabolism and cancer risk
- Unexplained symptoms despite apparently normal hormone levels

The reality about DUTCH:

However, DUTCH testing is expensive (typically $300-500), not covered by insurance, and requires interpretation by a provider trained in functional medicine. It provides interesting and sometimes useful information, but it's not essential for the vast majority of women. Standard blood testing gives us the information needed to create effective treatment plans.

Consider DUTCH as an option if you want deeper investigation, but don't feel it's necessary for successful treatment. The choice is yours.

Once you have baseline hormone testing (along with testing for the other four hormone systems—insulin resistance, cortisol, thyroid, and vitamin D), a comprehensive treatment plan can be created that addresses all identified imbalances simultaneously.

That plan should be implemented for ninety days, giving your body time to respond to interventions, and then retesting occurs. This allows assessment of:

- Whether hormone levels have improved and optimized
- Whether the ratios between hormones are now balanced
- Whether symptoms have improved (which matters more than numbers)
- Whether any adjustments to treatment are needed

This test-treat-retest cycle continues until optimal balance is achieved, symptoms resolve, and results are sustainable. This isn't guessing. This isn't treating blindly. This is using objective data to guide personalized treatment and tracking response systematically.

The testing approach outlined here, along with testing for the other four imbalances, provides the comprehensive picture needed. In Part III, we'll show you exactly what optimal ranges look like for each hormone, how to interpret results, and the specific treatment protocols used to restore balance and reverse symptoms.

SECTION 6: Sex Hormone Imbalance Symptom Quiz

Review the symptoms below and check any that apply to you. This quiz combines symptoms from all three patterns of sex hormone imbalance. Your symptom pattern will help guide testing and treatment, but remember, you cannot diagnose based on symptoms alone. Comprehensive testing of all five hormone systems is essential for accurate diagnosis and effective treatment.

☐ Heavy menstrual bleeding (soaking through pads/tampons hourly)
☐ Prolonged periods (lasting 7+ days)
☐ Passing large blood clots during menstruation
☐ Irregular menstrual cycles (unpredictable timing)
☐ Absent or very infrequent periods (35+ days between cycles)
☐ Severe menstrual cramps
☐ Premenstrual syndrome (PMS) symptoms worsening
☐ Uterine fibroids
☐ Endometriosis
☐ Polycystic ovaries (PCOS) diagnosis
☐ Fertility difficulties
☐ Recurrent miscarriages
☐ Hot flashes (sudden intense heat)
☐ Night sweats (waking drenched in sweat)
☐ Feeling unusually cold or having cold hands/feet
☐ Increased sweating throughout the day
☐ Flushing or reddening of skin
☐ Difficulty falling asleep
☐ Waking frequently during the night
☐ Waking at 2-3 a.m. unable to return to sleep
☐ Night sweats disrupting sleep
☐ Unrefreshing sleep (waking tired despite adequate hours)
☐ Racing mind preventing sleep
☐ Anxiety or increased nervousness
☐ Irritability or mood swings
☐ Depression or persistent low mood
☐ Brain fog or difficulty concentrating
☐ Memory problems (forgetting words, names, tasks)
☐ Difficulty making decisions
☐ Decreased motivation or sense of drive
☐ Feeling unlike yourself
☐ Crying easily or feeling emotionally fragile
☐ Decreased confidence or assertiveness

Part I: Understanding Why You Are Struggling With The Scale

- ☐ Weight gain, particularly around midsection/belly
- ☐ Weight gain despite no change in diet or exercise
- ☐ Difficulty losing weight despite efforts
- ☐ Fat distribution changing (more belly fat, less hip/thigh fat)
- ☐ Bloating or water retention
- ☐ Breast tenderness (particularly premenstrually)
- ☐ Fibrocystic breasts (lumpy, tender breast tissue)
- ☐ Decreased muscle mass or strength
- ☐ Increased body fat percentage
- ☐ Acne (particularly jawline, chin, or chest)
- ☐ Increased facial hair growth
- ☐ Unwanted hair growth on body (chest, abdomen, back)
- ☐ Thinning hair on scalp or hair loss
- ☐ Dry skin
- ☐ Dark skin patches (neck, armpits, groin)
- ☐ Skin tags
- ☐ Rashes or skin sensitivity
- ☐ Chronic fatigue or low energy
- ☐ Afternoon energy crashes
- ☐ Difficulty completing daily tasks due to exhaustion
- ☐ Loss of vitality or "spark"
- ☐ Decreased endurance or stamina
- ☐ Decreased libido or loss of sex drive
- ☐ Complete absence of sexual desire
- ☐ Vaginal dryness
- ☐ Painful intercourse
- ☐ Decreased arousal or difficulty achieving orgasm
- ☐ Changes in sexual satisfaction
- ☐ Joint pain or stiffness
- ☐ Muscle aches
- ☐ Decreased bone density or osteopenia/osteoporosis
- ☐ Increased susceptibility to injuries
- ☐ Slower recovery from exercise

Chapter 4: Sex Hormone Imbalance—The Hormonally Hijacked Metabolizer

☐ Increased hunger or cravings
☐ Difficulty feeling full or satisfied after eating
☐ Sugar or carbohydrate cravings
☐ Salt cravings
☐ Blood sugar fluctuations
☐ Elevated cholesterol (particularly increased LDL or decreased HDL)
☐ High blood pressure
☐ Poor gut health or digestive issues
☐ Headaches or migraines (particularly cyclical with periods)
☐ Heart palpitations
☐ Dizziness
☐ Urinary incontinence or urgency
☐ Frequent urinary tract infections
☐ Autoimmune condition diagnosed during perimenopause
☐ Worsening of existing autoimmune condition

Interpreting Your Results:

High number of symptoms checked (15+): You very likely have significant sex hormone imbalance, and based on the severity and number of symptoms, it's probable that multiple hormone systems are affected. Comprehensive testing of all five hormone imbalances is essential.

Moderate number of symptoms (8-14): Sex hormone imbalance is likely contributing to your symptoms, though you may have one or two of the five imbalances rather than all five. Testing will clarify which systems need support.

Lower number of symptoms (1-7): You may have early or mild sex hormone imbalance, or your primary issues may be in one of the other hormone systems. Testing all five systems will identify where your imbalances lie.

Remember: Symptoms overlap significantly between different hormone imbalances. You cannot determine based on symptoms alone whether your issues stem primarily from sex hormone imbalance, insulin resistance, thyroid dysfunction, cortisol dysregulation, or vitamin D deficiency. Many symptoms (fatigue, weight gain, mood changes, brain fog) appear in all five imbalances.

This is why comprehensive testing is essential rather than guessing based on symptoms. The quiz helps you document your experience and advocate for appropriate testing, but the lab work provides the definitive answers about what's actually happening in your body.

Chapter Summary

Sex hormones—estrogen, progesterone, and testosterone—are far more than reproductive hormones. They are profoundly metabolic hormones that regulate fat storage and distribution, insulin sensitivity, thyroid function, inflammation, bone density, cardiovascular health, brain function, and mood. When these hormones become imbalanced during perimenopause, the effects ripple through every system in your body. This is what it means to be a Hormonally Hijacked Metabolizer—your metabolism has been taken hostage by hormonal chaos, leaving you unable to control your weight, energy, or well-being through willpower alone. The three patterns of sex hormone imbalance are:

- **Pattern 1: Estrogen Dominance**—Progesterone drops dramatically while estrogen remains normal or elevated, creating an imbalanced ratio. This typically occurs in early perimenopause (ages 35-45) and creates heavy bleeding, severe PMS, breast tenderness, anxiety, and difficulty sleeping.

- **Pattern 2: Overall Low Sex Hormones**—Both estrogen and progesterone decline significantly, creating the classic menopausal symptoms of hot flashes, night sweats, vaginal dryness, brain fog, and mood changes. This pattern typically emerges in late perimenopause and continues after menopause.

- **Pattern 3: Lifelong Hormone Disruptions**—Pre-existing hormone imbalances (most commonly PCOS) that have existed since adolescence and worsen during perimenopause. PCOS is characterized by androgen dominance, irregular periods, difficulty losing weight, acne, and excess hair growth. Birth control pills masked symptoms

Chapter 4: Sex Hormone Imbalance—The Hormonally Hijacked Metabolizer

for years but never addressed the underlying insulin resistance driving the condition. When perimenopause begins, these women face amplified symptoms from both their pre-existing condition and natural hormonal decline.

The cascade is what makes perimenopause so challenging: Sex hormone decline doesn't just create hot flashes and mood swings. It directly triggers the other four hormone imbalances—insulin resistance, thyroid dysfunction, cortisol dysregulation, and accelerated muscle loss. Each of these imbalances then worsens the others, creating a downward spiral that makes weight loss feel impossible and leaves you feeling like your body has betrayed you. By the time you're in full perimenopause:

- Estrogen has dropped 40-50 percent
- Progesterone has dropped 90-99 percent
- Testosterone has dropped approximately fifty percent
- Your metabolism has slowed significantly
- You've lost substantial muscle mass
- Insulin resistance has developed or worsened
- Thyroid function has declined
- Cortisol patterns have become dysregulated
- Chronic inflammation has increased

Your body interprets this hormonal chaos as threat and activates resource conservation mode—slower metabolism, enhanced fat storage, increased hunger, resistance to releasing stored fat. This is why "eat less, exercise more" stops working. You're not battling a lack of willpower. You're battling your biology. You've been hormonally hijacked.

Sex hormones are critically important, but they're just one piece of the puzzle. This is the key message you need to understand.

Hormone replacement therapy (HRT) with bioidentical estrogen and progesterone can be incredibly effective for alleviating hot flashes, night sweats, mood symptoms, brain fog, vaginal dryness, and sleep disturbances. It can protect your bones, support cardiovascular health, and improve quality of life dramatically. These benefits are real and significant.

But HRT alone often doesn't result in substantial weight loss because by the time most women start HRT, the cascade has already occurred. You've already developed insulin resistance. Your thyroid function has already declined. You've already lost significant muscle mass. Your cortisol patterns are already disrupted.

Replacing sex hormones addresses one foundational piece, but it doesn't reverse the insulin resistance, fix thyroid conversion issues, rebuild lost muscle, or correct flattened cortisol curves. This is why comprehensive treatment of all five hormone imbalances is essential. When you address sex hormones AND insulin resistance AND thyroid function AND cortisol AND preserve muscle mass through proper nutrition and resistance training—that's when you see dramatic, sustainable results.

Even if you've been told you can't take HRT—whether due to personal health history, family history of hormone-sensitive cancers, blood clotting disorders, or other contraindications—healing is still possible. When you address the other four hormone imbalances (insulin resistance, thyroid, cortisol, vitamin D), you create the physiological environment that allows your body to produce and utilize its own sex hormones more effectively. Your adrenal glands can better compensate through DHEA production. Your body can convert DHEA to estrogen and testosterone more efficiently. The pregnenolone steal reverses, allowing more progesterone production.

Women who cannot use HRT can still achieve remarkable results—weight loss, symptom reversal, improved energy, better sleep, stabilized mood—by comprehensively addressing the interconnected hormone systems. Sex hormones are important, but the other four systems matter tremendously. You have options and pathways to healing regardless of whether HRT is appropriate for you.

You are not broken. You are not failing. You are not lacking willpower or discipline. You are experiencing the predictable physiological consequences of hormonal changes that happen to a hundred percent of women during perimenopause—changes that traditional medicine has failed to address adequately.

Chapter 4: Sex Hormone Imbalance—The Hormonally Hijacked Metabolizer

But now you understand what's actually happening in your body. You understand the cascade. You understand why isolated interventions haven't worked. And you understand that comprehensive treatment addressing all five hormone imbalances is what creates transformation.

Looking Ahead

We've now completed our exploration of four of the five hormone imbalances that sabotage women's health during perimenopause:

Chapter 1: Insulin Resistance (The Locked Metabolizer)—The metabolic dysfunction that makes weight loss nearly impossible and drives visceral fat accumulation

Chapter 2: Cortisol Dysregulation and Adrenal Fatigue (The Burnout Metabolizer)—The stress hormone chaos driving exhaustion, anxiety, and belly fat

Chapter 3: Thyroid Dysfunction (The Slow Burner Metabolizer)—The commonly missed diagnoses (conversion issues and Hashimoto's) keeping you stuck despite "treatment"

Chapter 4: Sex Hormone Imbalance (The Hormonally Hijacked Metabolizer)—The foundation of perimenopause that triggers the cascade affecting all other systems

There is one more hormone we need to address—one that most people don't even realize is a hormone, yet it regulates the function of all the other hormones we've covered. In Chapter 5, we'll explore the "shadow hormone" and why this critical hormone is essential for metabolic health, immune function, mood stability, and successful aging.

But before we move to Chapter 5, let's acknowledge where you are right now. You've just absorbed a tremendous amount of information about complex physiological processes. You understand what's happening in your body in a way that most women—and frankly, most healthcare providers—never do.

This knowledge is power. This understanding allows you to advocate for yourself, to insist on appropriate testing, to recognize that your symptoms are real and valid and measurable. You're not crazy. You're not weak. You're not failing. Your body is responding exactly as it should to profound hormonal changes—changes that can be identified, measured, and addressed.

In Part II, we'll give you the foundational lifestyle interventions you can implement immediately—before you even have your lab results back. These foundations (nutrition, movement, stress management, sleep optimization) make everything else more effective and begin shifting your physiology in the right direction.

In Part III, we'll provide the specific treatment protocols for optimizing sex hormones (and the other four systems), show you what optimal ranges look like, explain medication options including bioidentical hormone replacement therapy, and teach you exactly how to work with providers to get the comprehensive care you deserve.

You've taken the first crucial step—understanding what's wrong. Now we're going to show you how to fix it.

But first—Chapter 5: The Shadow Metabolizer. Let's continue.

Chapter 4: Sex Hormone Imbalance—The Hormonally Hijacked Metabolizer

Vitamin D Deficiency—The Shadow Metabolizer

You wake up stiff every morning. Your joints ache—your knees, your hips, your lower back. Getting out of bed requires a mental pep talk. Standing up from a chair makes you groan "ughhh" involuntarily, like someone twice your age.

The fatigue is constant, but it's different from the exhaustion you felt from cortisol dysregulation. This feels heavier, harder to shake—especially in winter. The dark, gray days make everything worse. Your mood is flat, your energy nonexistent.

You catch every cold that goes around. That strange rash on your arms won't go away. Your migraines have gotten worse. But these symptoms seem random, unconnected, too vague to mention to your doctor.

If this sounds familiar, you're dealing with the fifth and final hormone imbalance—the one we call the "shadow imbalance" because it works quietly in the background, making every other hormone imbalance worse while creating its own constellation of vague, easily-dismissed symptoms. You're what we call a Shadow Metabolizer.

The term "Shadow Metabolizer" captures exactly what's happening in your body. This hormone deficiency operates in the shadows—lurking behind all your other symptoms, amplifying every other imbalance, making everything harder to fix. You can't see it directly, but its effects cast a dark shadow over everything. It makes your insulin resistance worse. It slows your thyroid function even more. It depletes your sex hormones. It dysregulates your cortisol. Like a shadow that darkens everything it touches, this deficiency makes every other metabolic problem more severe. You're metabolizing in the shadows, struggling in ways you can't quite identify, while this hidden deficiency sabotages every attempt at healing.

We're talking about Vitamin D deficiency.

Here's what makes this particularly insidious: Vitamin D isn't actually a vitamin at all. It's actually a major hormone regulator—it helps your body build and utilize all the other hormones we've discussed in the previous four chapters. It regulates inflammation throughout your body. It protects against heart attack, stroke, and osteoporosis. It supports immune function, bone health, muscle function, and mood. And it contributes to your ability to control the number on the scale.

Vitamin D deficiency is the shadow that makes everything else darker. And correcting it—getting your levels truly optimal, not just "in range"— is often the key that allows all the other interventions to finally work the way they should. Optimizing Vitamin D will shorten your timeline to feeling better.

In this chapter, you'll learn why Vitamin D is actually a hormone (not a vitamin), how deficiency develops and why it's epidemic in perimenopausal women, the specific symptoms to watch for, how Vitamin D regulates the other four hormone systems, and how to test for deficiency easily.

By the end of this chapter, you'll understand why addressing all five hormone imbalances—including this often-overlooked shadow imbalance—is essential for complete healing, longevity, and controlling the number on the scale for good.

Let's dive in.

Section 1: Why Vitamin D Is Actually a Hormone (Not a Vitamin)

Let's start by clearing up a fundamental misunderstanding that has profound implications for your health.

In order for something to be considered a "vitamin," it cannot be synthesized by the body and therefore must be obtained only through diet.

Chapter 5: Vitamin D Deficiency—The Shadow Metabolizer

Vitamin D doesn't meet this definition. It's actually a steroid hormone that can be synthesized through UV exposure of the skin. Only about ten percent of vitamin D comes from dietary sources—the remaining ninety percent is made by your body when your skin is exposed to sunlight.

This distinction matters far more than semantics. Understanding that vitamin D is a hormone—not a vitamin—helps explain why deficiency creates such widespread, seemingly unrelated symptoms and why optimizing your levels is so critical for healing the other four hormone imbalances we've discussed.

Vitamin D: The Hormone Regulator

Here's what makes vitamin D truly remarkable: It's not just another hormone in your body. It's a hormone regulator that contributes to the function of all your other hormones.

Let's walk through how vitamin D supports each of the hormone systems we've covered in the previous chapters:

Insulin and Metabolic Function

Vitamin D is needed for the production of insulin. It also helps determine how sensitive your cells are to insulin itself. Remember from Chapter 1 how insulin resistance develops when cells stop responding properly to insulin's signal? Vitamin D deficiency makes that problem worse. When vitamin D levels are low, not enough insulin is secreted, and the cells that should be responding to insulin become even more resistant to its message. This creates a vicious cycle—deficient vitamin D worsens insulin resistance, which drives weight gain and metabolic dysfunction, which further depletes vitamin D.

Thyroid Function

Vitamin D deficiency is associated with decreased sensitivity to thyroid hormones by more than fifty percent. Think about what we discussed in

Chapter 3—you can be taking thyroid medication, your TSH can be "normal," and you can still feel terrible if your cells aren't responding to thyroid hormone properly. Vitamin D is part of that cellular response system. Conversely, vitamin D replacement improves thyroid function AND decreases circulating thyroid antibodies, making it absolutely crucial for anyone with Hashimoto's thyroiditis. If you're dealing with autoimmune thyroid disease and you haven't optimized your vitamin D levels, you're missing a foundational piece of your treatment.

Cortisol and Adrenal Function

Supplementing with vitamin D reduces the body's production of cortisol, allowing the adrenal glands to heal and function properly. Remember from Chapter 2 how chronic stress and elevated cortisol create that exhausted-but-wired feeling, disrupt sleep, and steal the raw materials needed to make sex hormones? When vitamin D levels are adequate, cortisol demands decrease. This gives your adrenal glands the opportunity to shift resources back toward producing sex hormones instead of being stuck in survival mode, constantly churning out cortisol.

Sex Hormones

The active metabolite of vitamin D—1,25-dihydroxyvitamin D—directly regulates sex hormone production and signaling. It aids in the conversion of androgens into estrogens and can stimulate estrogen and progesterone production in ovarian cells. Lower levels of vitamin D have been associated with lower SHBG levels (the protein that carries sex hormones through your bloodstream) and lower estradiol levels. During perimenopause, when your ovaries are already producing less estrogen and progesterone, vitamin D deficiency compounds the problem, worsening all those perimenopausal symptoms we discussed in Chapter 4.

Weight and Metabolism

Beyond supporting the other four hormone systems, vitamin D has direct effects on weight and body composition.

Adequate levels of vitamin D help alter the storage and formation of fat cells. They also increase levels of serotonin and testosterone—both of which influence metabolism and body composition. All of these effects work together to boost your metabolism, increase the calories you burn after eating, and may even block the formation of new fat cells.

This is why women with vitamin D deficiency often struggle to lose weight even when they're doing everything else right. It's not just about calories in and calories out. If vitamin D is deficient, your body's ability to mobilize and burn fat is compromised at the cellular level.

Mood Regulation

Perhaps one of the most profound effects of vitamin D—and one that often gets overlooked—is its role in mood and mental health.

Vitamin D is crucial for the brain's synthesis of serotonin, one of the "feel-good" neurotransmitters that regulates mood, sleep, and appetite. It not only helps your brain produce serotonin but also helps serotonin remain in the body for longer periods of time—essentially doing the same job that antidepressant medications (SSRIs) are designed to do but through a natural, hormonal mechanism.

Low vitamin D has been directly associated with depression, and supplementation can significantly improve depressive symptoms when treated properly. If you've been struggling with that flat, heavy mood—especially during winter months—vitamin D deficiency may be a significant contributing factor.

The Gene Regulation Powerhouse

Here's where vitamin D's role becomes even more impressive: When vitamin D binds to vitamin D receptors—which exist in nearly every cell in your body—it functions as a transcription factor, directly regulating gene expression.

In practical terms, this means vitamin D influences which genes get turned on or off in your cells. These aren't just a handful of genes—vitamin D regulates the expression of over 2,000 genes throughout your body, many of which are involved in hormone production, immune function, inflammation control, and metabolic processes.

This widespread genetic influence explains why vitamin D deficiency creates such diverse symptoms and why it's been linked to so many different health conditions—from autoimmune disease to cardiovascular problems to cancer risk. When this master regulatory hormone is deficient, the effects cascade through multiple systems simultaneously.

Why Understanding This Distinction Matters

When you think of vitamin D as just another vitamin—something you might take if you remember, something that's "nice to have" but not critical—you underestimate its importance.

But when you understand that vitamin D is actually a steroid hormone that regulates thousands of genes, supports the production and function of your other hormones, influences your metabolism and body composition, and affects your brain's ability to produce mood-stabilizing neurotransmitters, the picture changes completely.

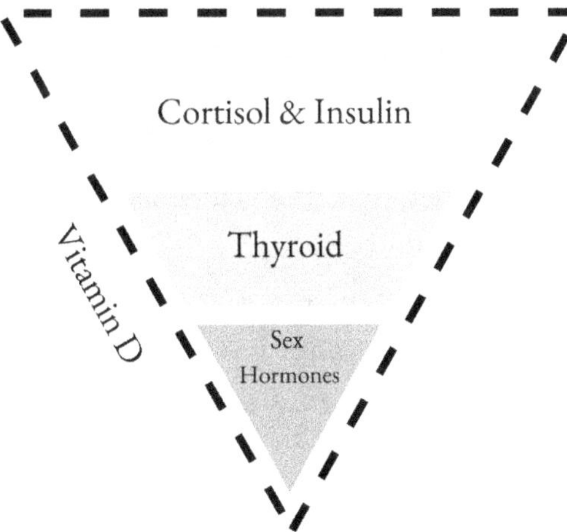

Chapter 5: Vitamin D Deficiency—The Shadow Metabolizer

Optimizing vitamin D isn't optional. It's foundational. It's the hormone that helps all your other hormones work properly. Without adequate vitamin D, you can address insulin resistance, support your thyroid, balance your cortisol, and even take bioidentical hormone replacement—and still not feel your best because the foundational regulatory system isn't functioning optimally.

This is why we call vitamin D the "shadow imbalance." It's working quietly in the background, influencing every other system. When it's deficient, it makes everything else worse. When it's optimized, it accelerates healing across all five hormone systems. When you're a Shadow Metabolizer, you're struggling in ways that are hard to identify because the deficiency operates behind the scenes, casting its dark influence over everything.

Section 2: How Vitamin D Deficiency Develops and Why It's Epidemic in Women Over Forty

Vitamin D deficiency can happen for a variety of reasons. There are seasonal and geographic components, aging and skin synthesis decline, obesity and body composition changes, and menopause-specific factors.

Geography and Season

Geographically and seasonally, the further north you go, the less UVB radiation is available for vitamin D synthesis in the skin, with sunlight being the main contributor. Thankfully the body is able to store vitamin D, and spring and summer provide over eighty percent of total annual intake.

So what does "sun exposure" actually look like? In spring and summer, with twenty-five percent of the body exposed (hands, face, neck, and arms), about 8-10 minutes of midday sun exposure without sunscreen, 2-3 times per week, produces the recommended amount of vitamin D for lighter skin, and 25-40 minutes per day for darker skin. This is much harder to accomplish in colder weather at higher latitudes, which is why testing and supplementation is often necessary.

The Impact of Aging

In general, vitamin D production decreases by thirteen percent each decade of life due to decreasing collagen within the skin, reducing its ability to synthesize vitamin D. By the time you're seventy, your skin produces less than half the vitamin D it did when you were in your twenties—even with the same amount of sun exposure.

In women specifically, declining estrogen levels accelerate that decrease. Your skin becomes thinner during perimenopause and menopause, further impairing its ability to produce vitamin D from sunlight. This is one of the reasons why vitamin D deficiency is so prevalent among menopausal women—accounting for 50-80 percent of all women going through this transition.

Body Composition and Weight

When you consider body composition as well, vitamin D is stored in adipose tissue, making it less bioavailable to the body. This is why women who are struggling with weight gain during perimenopause face a double challenge: Their expanding fat tissue essentially "traps" vitamin D, sequestering it away from circulation where it's needed.

Research shows that obese individuals have greater total body stores of vitamin D but lower levels circulating in the bloodstream. The vitamin gets diluted in the larger volume of fat, blood, muscle, and liver tissue. And here's the vicious cycle: Low vitamin D makes it harder to lose weight, and carrying excess weight worsens vitamin D deficiency.

Race and Ethnicity

Dark-skinned individuals have a 15-20-fold higher prevalence of severe vitamin D deficiency when compared with lighter-skinned individuals. This is due to the melanin in the skin blocking UVB exposure needed in order to produce vitamin D. They can require six times more sun exposure—ninety minutes three times per week—than lighter-skinned individuals who need only fifteen minutes three times per week.

Moreover, dark-skinned individuals living in the US have substantially lower levels of vitamin D when compared with those living at lower latitudes closer to the equator. The prevalence of vitamin D deficiency in African American people living within the US is 82.1 percent compared with the national average of 41.9 percent. This "latitude-skin color mismatch" creates significant health disparities, as dark skin that's perfectly adapted to equatorial sun exposure struggles to produce adequate vitamin D in northern climates.

The Perfect Storm

Bottom line: aging, menopause, being overweight, having darker skin, and living at higher latitudes all contribute to the decline of the body's ability to produce vitamin D.

For perimenopausal women over forty, these factors often converge simultaneously. You're aging (thirteen percent decrease per decade). Your estrogen is declining (accelerating skin changes). You are gaining weight (sequestering vitamin D in expanding fat tissue). If you have darker skin and live in a northern climate, you're facing even steeper odds.

And in our clinical practice? More than ninety percent of women we treat have vitamin D deficiency, many being critically low. These women struggle with most (if not all) of the other four hormone imbalances, suffer from depressed mood, and battle weight and inflammation even when they're doing "everything" right.

As we mentioned in the opening, vitamin D deficiency is simply a carryover that amplifies the symptoms of the other hormone imbalances, making those symptoms more intense and more difficult to balance.

Testing for Vitamin D Deficiency

The only way to know if you're vitamin D deficient is through a blood test. Not a symptom quiz, not a guess based on how much time you spend outdoors—an actual lab test.

The test you need is called **25-hydroxyvitamin D**, also written as **25(OH)D**. This is the storage form of vitamin D in your bloodstream and the most accurate marker of your vitamin D status. Some labs may call it "Vitamin D, 25-Hydroxy" or simply "Vitamin D." Make sure they're testing the 25-hydroxy form, not the active 1,25-dihydroxyvitamin D, which is a different test that doesn't accurately reflect your body's vitamin D stores.

What Happens Next

Once you know your vitamin D level, you'll understand where you stand. If you're deficient—and statistically, there's a ninety percent chance you are if you haven't been supplementing—you'll need a treatment plan to bring your levels up to the optimal range.

We'll cover exactly how to optimize your vitamin D levels—including supplementation protocols, dosing strategies, co-factors you need, and re-testing timelines—in Part III of this book when we discuss comprehensive treatment approaches.

For now, the most important action you can take is to get tested. Know your number. And understand that "normal" isn't good enough when you're trying to heal from multiple hormone imbalances and reclaim your health.

Vitamin D Deficiency Symptom Quiz

Check any symptoms that are present, problematic, or persist over time:

- ☐ Fatigue and low energy levels
- ☐ Mood swings or depression
- ☐ Muscle weakness

☐ Joint pain (knees, hips, lower back)

☐ Bone pain or aching bones

☐ Groaning or stiffness when getting up from a chair or bed

☐ Increased risk of bone loss or fractures

☐ Frequent illness or catching every cold that goes around

☐ Poor immune function or slow wound healing

☐ Difficulty losing weight despite diet and exercise

☐ Chronic inflammation or body aches

☐ Elevated blood pressure

☐ Hair loss or thinning hair

☐ Muscle pain or generalized body aches

☐ Feeling significantly worse during winter months or on gray days

☐ Difficulty concentrating or brain fog

☐ Anxiety

☐ Sleep disturbances or poor sleep quality

☐ Rashes or skin problems that won't resolve

☐ Headaches or worsening migraines

Total Symptoms Checked: _____________

Interpreting Your Results:

- If you checked **five or more symptoms**, vitamin D deficiency is likely contributing to how you feel—and more importantly, it's amplifying all the other hormone imbalances you're dealing with. This is the "shadow imbalance" that makes everything else harder to fix.
- If you checked **ten or more symptoms**, you almost certainly have significant vitamin D deficiency that's actively sabotaging your health, your metabolism, and your ability to heal. Your levels may be critically low (under 20 ng/mL, possibly even in the teens).

Critical Reminder: More than ninety percent of the women we treat have vitamin D deficiency, many with critically low levels. You can have severe deficiency without obvious standalone symptoms because vitamin D works quietly in the background, making your

Part I: Understanding Why You Are Struggling With The Scale

other hormone imbalances worse. The only way to know your true vitamin D status is through a 25-hydroxyvitamin D blood test.

If you scored moderate to high on this quiz AND on the quizzes in Chapters 1-4, pay particular attention. You're experiencing the cascade effect of multiple hormone imbalances, with vitamin D deficiency amplifying everything else.

Use this quiz as documentation when requesting vitamin D testing from your healthcare provider. And remember: if your level comes back at 32 or 35 ng/mL and you're told it's "fine," it's not optimal. Push for levels between 60-80 ng/mL—the range where you'll actually get the full health benefits vitamin D provides.

Transition to Part I Conclusion

You've now learned about all five hormone imbalances that sabotage your health, your weight, and your vitality during perimenopause and beyond:

- **Insulin Resistance (The Locked Metabolizer)**—driving weight gain, inflammation, and metabolic dysfunction
- **Cortisol Dysregulation (The Burnout Metabolizer)**—stealing your sleep, energy, and sex hormones
- **Thyroid Dysfunction (The Slow Burner Metabolizer)**—slowing your metabolism and leaving you exhausted
- **Sex Hormone Imbalance (The Hormonally Hijacked Metabolizer)**—creating the classic perimenopausal symptoms everyone recognizes
- **Vitamin D Deficiency (The Shadow Metabolizer)**—the shadow imbalance making everything else worse

Each of these imbalances creates its own constellation of symptoms. But more importantly, they don't exist in isolation. They interact, amplify, and cascade into each other, creating the complex picture of suffering that brought you to this book in the first place.

The fatigue you're feeling isn't just from one thing—it's from disrupted cortisol, sluggish thyroid, low vitamin D, and insulin resistance all working together to drain your energy. The weight you can't lose isn't just about calories—it's about insulin resistance making your cells store fat, cortisol breaking down muscle, thyroid slowing your metabolism, estrogen dominance driving visceral fat accumulation, and vitamin D deficiency impairing fat mobilization.

This is why single interventions—taking just thyroid medication, or just trying to eat less and exercise more, or just going on hormone replacement—so often fail to deliver the results women desperately need.

You can't fix a five-alarm fire by addressing one flame.

But here's the powerful truth: When you understand what's actually happening in your body, when you can identify which systems are out of balance, and when you address all five imbalances systematically, healing becomes possible.

More than possible—it becomes inevitable.

Understanding Your Body's Truth

You've now completed Part I of your journey. You've learned about all five hormone imbalances that have been sabotaging your health, your weight, and your vitality:

- **Insulin Resistance**—driving weight gain, inflammation, and metabolic dysfunction
- **Cortisol Dysregulation**—stealing your sleep, energy, and sex hormones
- **Thyroid Dysfunction**—slowing your metabolism and leaving you exhausted
- **Sex Hormone Imbalance**—creating the classic perimenopausal symptoms everyone recognizes
- **Vitamin D Deficiency**—the shadow imbalance making everything else worse

If you're like most women who find their way to us, you probably recognized yourself in multiple chapters. Maybe you saw yourself in all five. And that recognition—that validation that what you're experiencing is real, explainable, and fixable—may be the first relief you've felt in years.

This Is Why You've Been Struggling

Here's what you need to understand: These five hormone imbalances don't exist in isolation. They interact with each other. They amplify each other. They cascade into each other, creating a complex web of dysfunction that becomes increasingly difficult to untangle the longer it goes unaddressed.

The fatigue you're feeling isn't just from one thing. It's from disrupted cortisol stealing your sleep and energy, sluggish thyroid slowing every metabolic process, low vitamin D depleting your cellular function, insulin resistance preventing your cells from accessing fuel efficiently, and declining sex hormones affecting your motivation and vitality. All of these work together to drain you completely.

The weight you can't lose isn't just about calories or willpower. It's about insulin resistance making your cells store every calorie as fat, elevated cortisol breaking down your precious muscle tissue while depositing fat around your midsection, sluggish thyroid dramatically slowing your metabolic rate, estrogen dominance driving visceral fat accumulation, and vitamin D deficiency impairing your body's ability to mobilize and burn stored fat. Every single one of these imbalances is actively working against your weight loss efforts.

The brain fog, the mood swings, the anxiety, the sleep problems, the joint pain, the digestive issues, the loss of libido—none of these symptoms exist in a vacuum. They're all interconnected pieces of the same puzzle. They're all manifestations of these five fundamental hormone imbalances.

This is why you've been struggling. This is why eating less and exercising more didn't work. This is why the thyroid medication alone didn't fix everything. This is why losing ten pounds and gaining back fifteen has been your frustrating reality.

You weren't failing. The approach was failing you.

Let's start to fix things naturally using the strategies in Part 2.

Nutrition, Foundations & Lifestyle

Finding Freedom with Food and Rebuilding Trust with Your Body

The Truth About Why Diets Fail

If you're reading this section, I'm going to make a few educated guesses about where you are right now.

You're frustrated—deeply, bone-achingly frustrated. You've been dieting for years, maybe even decades. And your lack of results isn't from a lack of effort. This isn't about sitting on the couch eating Doritos and wondering why your jeans don't fit.

You've tried intermittent fasting, keto, tracking every macro, cutting carbs to nearly nothing, and whatever new "miracle plan" your trainer or favorite influencer promised would finally unlock your metabolism. You've hired coaches who promised results. You've signed up for challenges that guarantee transformation. You've bought the supplements, downloaded the apps, followed the meal plans that swore this time would be different. And you started out hopeful every single time.

But then the scale stopped moving—or worse, it crept up. Not just a pound or two of normal fluctuation. Week after week, the number climbed or stubbornly refused to budge. And that's when the real frustration hit—the kind that makes you want to throw the scale out the window and never look at a vegetable again.

You're not asking for perfection. You're not chasing some magazine cover ideal or trying to look like you did at twenty-five. You just want to feel confident in your own skin again. You want to be able to open your closet and actually WANT to wear what's inside instead of reaching for the same three "safe" outfits that hide your midsection. You want to feel desirable—not just to others but to yourself.

You want to wake up feeling strong instead of swollen. You want to stop thinking about food all the time—the constant mental calculation of "Can I eat that? Should I eat that? What will happen if I eat that?"

But instead, every morning you step on that scale, and it feels like it's mocking you. That little number has become a daily verdict on whether you're being "good" or "bad." You've tried to make peace with it, tried to tell yourself it doesn't matter, but every time it doesn't move the way you expect—or moves in the wrong direction despite your best efforts—your heart sinks a little more.

You're not lazy or unmotivated. You're fighting biology with the wrong weapons. You've been conditioned to believe that the answer is always LESS: fewer calories, less food, less pleasure, less rest. You're exhausted from trying to "earn" your worth one salad and spin class at a time.

We get it because we've worked with thousands of women who've been right here—women who have white-knuckled their way through 1,200-calorie diets, intermittent fasting windows, and every "clean eating" plan imaginable. What no one told them was that eating less and stressing more is the exact hormonal storm that locks their bodies into fat storage mode.

In part 1 we talked about the different hormone imbalances that are creating roadblocks to your weight loss. Let's tie this in with constantly under-eating, skipping meals, and over-exercising. Here's what happens on the inside:

Cortisol, your stress hormone, goes up. Every time you restrict food, skip meals, or push through exhaustion to complete another workout your body isn't ready for, cortisol rises. This isn't just a minor inconvenience—elevated cortisol directly signals your body to store fat, particularly around your midsection. It also breaks down muscle tissue to convert protein into glucose, further slowing your metabolism.

Insulin sensitivity goes down, meaning your body is more likely to store fat. When cortisol is chronically elevated, it interferes with insulin signaling at the cellular level. Your cells become resistant to insulin's message, glucose can't enter efficiently, and your body converts that excess circulating glucose into stored fat. This is why you can be eating "perfectly" and still gaining

Introduction: The Truth About Why Diets Fail

weight—your hormones are literally blocking fat burning and promoting fat storage.

Thyroid function slows, lowering your metabolic rate. Your thyroid is exquisitely sensitive to caloric intake and stress levels. When you eat too little or stress too much, your body downregulates thyroid hormone production and conversion. Specifically, it reduces the conversion of T4 (inactive thyroid hormone) to T3 (active thyroid hormone). Less T3 means slower metabolism, more fatigue, more difficulty losing weight, and often weight gain even with minimal food intake.

Sex hormones like estrogen and progesterone become imbalanced, leading to cravings, fatigue, mood changes, and water retention. Chronic stress and undereating disrupt the hypothalamic-pituitary-ovarian axis. Your brain starts prioritizing survival over reproduction, which means hormone production gets deprioritized. This leads to irregular cycles, PMS, worsening perimenopausal symptoms, and that characteristic hormone-driven weight gain that seems impossible to budge.

That's why eating less, working out more, and pushing through exhaustion doesn't work long-term—because those strategies push your body deeper into survival mode.

The Vicious Cycle of Yo-Yo Dieting

If you've ever done a restrictive diet, lost weight quickly, and then gained it all back (plus some), you've already felt the effects of what's known as yo-yo dieting. Here's the physiological truth behind that: When you lose weight rapidly, your body doesn't just lose fat—it loses muscle. Muscle is metabolically active tissue; it's what helps you burn calories even at rest.

Research shows that up to thirty percent of the weight lost in a crash diet comes from muscle, not fat. Let us repeat that because it's crucial: When you lose twenty pounds through restrictive dieting, approximately six pounds of that is MUSCLE and only fourteen pounds is fat.

Then when you regain the weight (because no one can live on less than 1,200 calories forever), your body stores that regained weight primarily as fat. Your body doesn't rebuild the muscle you lost.

Over time, this means your metabolism slows (because you have less muscle), your body composition shifts (more fat, less muscle), and you end up at the same weight but with a fundamentally different—and metabolically less healthy—body composition.

That's why, even when you're eating less than ever, it can feel impossible to lose weight again. Your metabolism has learned to survive on less. It's not broken; it's adaptive.

The math is devastating. Let's walk through a typical yo-yo dieting cycle:

Starting point: 180 pounds, 30 percent body fat (54 pounds fat, 126 pounds lean mass)

Diet #1: Lose twenty pounds rapidly (fourteen pounds fat, six pounds muscle)

New composition: 160 pounds, 31 percent body fat (50 pounds fat, 110 pounds lean mass)

Your scale weight looks better, but you've lost muscle and your body fat percentage actually went UP slightly.

Regain: Gain back twenty pounds (nineteen pounds fat, one pound muscle)

New composition: 180 pounds, 38 percent body fat (69 pounds fat, 111 pounds lean mass)

You're back at your starting WEIGHT, but now you have fifteen more pounds of fat and fifteen fewer pounds of muscle than when you started.

After just ONE diet-regain cycle, you're metabolically worse off than before you started. Your metabolism is slower because you have less muscle. Your body fat percentage is higher. Your insulin sensitivity is likely worse. Your hormones are more dysregulated.

And if you've been dieting for years or decades? If you've done this cycle five, ten, or twenty times? The cumulative damage is staggering. This is why women in their forties and fifties often say, "I used to be able to lose weight easily, but now nothing works." It's not just age and hormones; it's the accumulated metabolic adaptation from years of yo-yo dieting.

Even if you haven't been dieting and you used to be able to maintain weight easily until you hit your forties, everyone—male and female—experiences age-related muscle loss called sarcopenia. But here again, women get the short end of the biological stick.

Men experience sarcopenia at a rate of approximately 1.5 percent per decade after age thirty. Women lose muscle mass at a rate of 3.5 percent per decade—more than twice as fast.

This might not sound significant until you understand the metabolic implications. Let's look at a real example that makes this devastatingly clear.

Kathy's Story: The Math That Explains Everything

Meet Kathy. At age twenty-five, Kathy is 5'6" and weighs 160 pounds. Using a simple basal metabolic rate (BMR) calculator—a tool that estimates how many calories your body burns just to maintain basic physiological functions, regardless of any physical activity—we can see that Kathy burns approximately 1,487 calories per day simply existing.

This is the energy her body uses for breathing, circulating blood, maintaining body temperature, growing and repairing cells, and keeping all her organs functioning. She hasn't done a single workout, taken a single step, or moved from the couch. This is just what her body requires to stay alive.

Now let's advance Kathy's age by twenty years.

At age forty-five, Kathy is still 5'6" and still weighs 160 pounds. She hasn't changed anything about her lifestyle. She eats the same foods in the same quantities. She exercises the same amount. Her activity level is identical.

But now her BMR is 1,387 calories per day.

That's a hundred fewer calories burned per day simply because she aged twenty years—even though her weight stayed exactly the same.

Let's do the math on what this means:

    100 fewer calories burned per day

    × 365 days per year

    = 36,500 fewer calories burned annually

We know that 3,500 excess calories result in approximately one pound of weight gain. So:

36,500 ÷ 3,500 = 10.4 pounds of potential weight gain per year

Read that again: If Kathy eats exactly the same and moves exactly the same, she can expect to gain more than ten pounds per year simply due to the metabolic slowdown associated with aging.

This isn't theoretical. This is basic thermodynamics. If energy intake remains constant but energy expenditure decreases, the excess energy must go somewhere—and it goes into fat storage.

But wait—it gets worse.

This calculation assumes that Kathy maintained her weight at 160 pounds across those twenty years, which, as we just established, would have been nearly impossible without making changes. In reality, most women have gained weight during this timeframe, which means their BMR calculations look even more discouraging.

Furthermore, this BMR calculation doesn't fully capture the body composition changes happening beneath the surface. Remember that 3.5 percent muscle loss per decade we discussed? Over twenty years, Kathy has likely lost seven percent of her muscle mass—and if she wasn't actively strength training, that lost muscle has been replaced with fat.

One pound of muscle burns approximately nine calories per day at rest. One pound of fat burns only five calories per day—nearly half as much.

So not only has her baseline metabolic rate declined due to aging, but the composition of her body has shifted toward less metabolically active tissue, further reducing her caloric burn.

When you factor in additional age-related metabolic changes—decreased thyroid function, reduced mitochondrial efficiency, declining growth hormone, hormonal shifts during perimenopause—the cumulative effect is profound.

Now you can see why the standard advice is so inadequate and why it feels impossible to follow.

To simply maintain the same weight she was at twenty-five, Kathy would need to either:

- **Option 1**: Reduce her caloric intake by 100+ calories per day every single day for the rest of her life.

  But chronic caloric restriction triggers metabolic adaptation—her body will further reduce energy expenditure to match the lower intake, requiring even more restriction to maintain weight. Plus, undereating creates its own hormonal disruptions: decreased thyroid function, elevated cortisol, reduced sex hormone production, and increased hunger hormones that make the restriction increasingly unsustainable.

- **Option 2**: Increase her activity level to burn an additional 100+ calories per day consistently.

  One hundred calories is approximately equivalent to a twenty-minute brisk walk or fifteen minutes of moderate-intensity cardio. Every single day. On top of whatever she's already doing. Most women, juggling careers, families, and the demands of daily life, cannot sustain adding this much additional activity indefinitely. And for women already exercising regularly, adding more activity without adequate recovery can backfire, increasing cortisol and creating additional metabolic stress.

Neither option is sustainable long-term. And remember—these calculations are just to maintain weight, not to lose it.

To actually lose weight, Kathy would need an even greater caloric deficit—typically 500 calories per day to lose one pound per week. For a woman burning only 1,387 calories at rest, creating a 500-calorie deficit through diet and exercise while still consuming enough to support basic health and hormonal function becomes a nearly impossible balancing act.

Now if you're feeling a little hopeless after that breakdown and you're thinking, *I don't think anything will ever work for me again*, we hear you. Not only have we walked with thousands of women through that exact sentence, we've said versions of it ourselves when life was loud and our bodies felt like a stranger. So let's say this clearly: Your body isn't broken, and your lack of results is not a reflection of your effort—it's a reflection of a system that was never designed for you.

Your body's entire design is to protect you, not punish you. You are uniquely and divinely made. Nothing about your design is a mistake. But we do live in a world that works against your hormonal balance every single day. Toxins in skincare and household products. Pesticides on foods. Ultra-processed "health" products engineered to be addictive and to short-circuit your fullness signals.

We have been taught to treat symptoms with willpower instead of healing the systems that drive our results. We've been told to make ourselves smaller by eating less and moving more without ever being taught how hormones, stress, sleep, and nourishment shape our biology—especially in perimenopause. It's time to stop following plans made for men. When we balance hormones, fuel our female biology, and make peace with food, our body finally feels safe enough to start releasing fat.

If you're tired of starting over, of doing "everything right" and still feeling like nothing works, we want you to know there's a better way. You don't need to starve your body or out-exercise your hormones. You need to rebuild trust with your body.

We're going to teach you a simple and sustainable foundation that makes everything else possible. It's not another diet or set of rules—it's a way to reestablish safety in your metabolism. Because when your body feels safe, it finally releases what it's been holding on to.

We're going to teach you four science-backed habits that move the needle most and how to build your foundation while we are waiting to layer in advanced strategies from your lab testing results. For now, take a deep breath and have an open mind. These are not new, sexy ideas, but they absolutely will bring you sexy and sustainable results when you put it all together.

Introduction: The Truth About Why Diets Fail

Home Base

Your Foundation for Losing Weight and Maintaining It for Life

We named this chapter and this core concept of our nutrition philosophy "Home Base" because we want you to know you can always come back. No matter how far you've wandered into diet culture, no matter how many times you've quit, no matter what last night looked like—you are never too far from where you need to be.

Home Base is not a punishment; it's a place of peace. It has four simple, powerful habits that never go out of style and always move the needle:

- More Water
- More Vegetables
- More Sleep
- More Movement

Yes, we will talk about supplements, labs, medications, and advanced strategies in later sections. Those can be wonderful and necessary for many women. But if we skip the basics, we blunt the impact of everything else. We don't need to pile on the sexy biohacks if the foundations aren't solid. Follow Home Base, and you will get ten times the results of every advanced tool that comes later.

Home Base also represents the mindset we teach: addition, not subtraction. Dieting asks, "What do I need to remove?" Home Base asks, "What does my body need more of?" When we add the things your body is starved for—veggies, sleep, water, movement—we turn off the internal alarm bells (hello, cortisol) and help insulin behave. In plain English: your body feels safe again, which is the only environment where sustainable fat loss actually happens.

The Philosophy of Addition vs. Subtraction

Let us explain why this distinction matters so profoundly. Diet culture has conditioned you to think in terms of restriction: what you need to eliminate, avoid, or reduce. This creates a scarcity mindset that triggers stress responses in your body and your brain.

When you think *I can't have carbs* or *I need to avoid sugar* or *I shouldn't eat after six p.m.,* your brain interprets these as threats to your survival. Remember, your subconscious brain doesn't distinguish between voluntary restriction and famine—it just knows resources are being limited. This perception of scarcity:

1. Elevates cortisol (stress hormone), which promotes fat storage
2. Increases ghrelin (hunger hormone), making you ravenously hungry
3. Decreases leptin sensitivity (your "I'm full" signal), so you never feel satisfied
4. Triggers psychological rebellion (you want what you can't have even MORE)
5. Creates shame and guilt when you inevitably "break" the rules

In contrast, the "addition mindset" asks: "What does my body NEED that it's not getting?" This reframe is psychologically and physiologically different. When you focus on adding water, vegetables, sleep, and movement, you're:

1. Signaling abundance and safety to your body
2. Providing the raw materials your hormones need to function
3. Crowding out less helpful foods naturally (without restriction)
4. Creating positive momentum and self-efficacy
5. Building habits that feel good rather than punitive

Women we've worked with report that this single shift—from "what should I remove" to "what should I add"—transforms their entire relationship with food and their bodies.

The Pink Elephant—Psychology And Neuroscience Of Restriction

Let's talk about the pink elephant. If we tell you, "Think about anything you want today, just don't think about a pink elephant," what image keeps popping up? That elephant, bright as ever.

Restriction does the same thing in your brain. When you make a food "off limits," your brain checks in on it repeatedly—"Are we still avoiding it? Are we sure?"—and the forbidden thing takes up more mental real estate, not less. That mental tug-of-war raises stress, which raises cortisol, which makes you more insulin-resistant, which pushes your body toward fat storage.

This phenomenon—where trying NOT to think about something makes you think about it more—is called Ironic Process Theory and was first documented by psychologist Daniel Wegner in the 1980s.

Here's what happens in your brain. When you try to suppress a thought ("Don't think about cookies"), two mental processes activate simultaneously:

1. The operating process: actively tries to keep the forbidden thought out of consciousness
2. The monitoring process: constantly scans your consciousness to check whether the forbidden thought has appeared (ironically, this requires thinking about the very thing you're trying to avoid)

The monitoring process runs in the background, constantly checking: "Am I thinking about cookies? No? Good. Wait, am I thinking about cookies now? Still no? Okay, how about now?" Each check is, by definition, thinking about cookies.

Worse, the operating process (active suppression) requires mental resources—willpower, attention, cognitive capacity. When you're stressed, tired, distracted, or cognitively taxed (which describes most women in perimenopause), the operating process weakens, but the monitoring process continues. Result: the forbidden thought becomes EVEN MORE intrusive.

This doesn't just create mental obsession—it creates behavioral rebound effects. Research shows that people who attempt to suppress thoughts about a specific food subsequently:

- Think about that food more frequently
- Experience more intense cravings for that food
- Consume MORE of that food when they do eat it
- Feel less satisfied after eating it (because it's tangled up with guilt and shame)

And here's where it gets truly problematic: Once you "break" your diet rule by eating the forbidden food, you experience what psychologists call the "abstinence violation effect"—a cascade of negative thoughts and emotions:

"I've already ruined it"

"I have no willpower"

"I might as well keep eating since the day is shot anyway"

"I'll start over tomorrow/Monday/next month"

These thoughts trigger more overeating, not because you're weak but because it activates the restriction-rebellion cycle. The solution isn't more willpower or stricter rules. The solution is removing the restriction that creates the psychological pressure in the first place.

Removing foods from an already nutrient-depleted diet further disrupts your hormones and sets you up to regain weight. Restricting can feel virtuous for a few weeks, but almost everyone hits a breaking point—a birthday, a trip, a bad day—and the pendulum swings to a binge. It's not a character flaw; it's biology plus psychology. The Home Base Way fixes this by nourishing your body and quieting the alarm system.

When you follow the Home Base way, you're not "being good." You're finally giving your body the materials to do what it's designed to do: regulate, repair, and release.

In the next chapter, we will explore the four habits of Home Base, why it works, and practical strategies to make it work for you.

The Four Habits Of Home Base

In Chapter 6, we introduced you to the Home Base way. In this chapter, we'll explore each of the four habits of Home Base.

Home Base Habit #1: More Vegetables

Start here. Not because vegetables are morally superior (they're not) but because they deliver volume, fiber, water, vitamins, and minerals for very few calories. Our main reason is biology, not math. Those micronutrients are cofactors for almost every process your body uses to regulate hormones, stabilize blood sugar, and burn fat efficiently.

First goal: one serving of vegetables on your plate at lunch and dinner. If you're already doing that, move toward two.

Final Target: Half your plate at lunch and dinner; once that's easy, add a serving at breakfast.

Why it works (science, simply):

- **Volume** crowds out less helpful foods without "rules"
- **Fiber + water** create fullness and reduce blood sugar spikes
- **Micronutrients** provide cofactors for metabolic pathways

1. VOLUME: The Science of Feeling Full

Vegetables are high-volume, low-calorie foods. A huge serving of vegetables might be 50-100 calories but take up significant space in your stomach. This triggers mechanical stretch receptors that send "I'm full" signals to your brain.

Compare: two cups of broccoli equal about sixty calories, massive volume, and high satisfaction. Meanwhile, two tablespoons of peanut butter equal 200 calories, small volume, and less satisfaction. Both are nutritious, but vegetables allow you to feel physically full and satisfied while consuming fewer calories. This is how you "crowd out" less helpful foods without restriction—you're literally filling up on the good stuff first.

Volume Eating

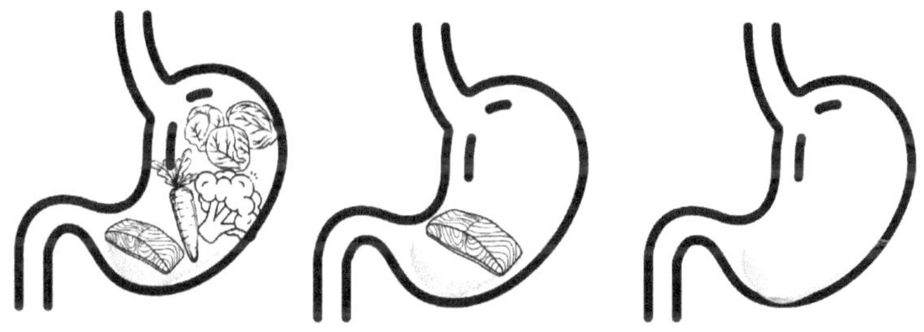

Vegetables take up more space on your plate and room in your stomach.

This is the "addition" mindset in action. We're not telling you what you can't eat. We're asking you to add more vegetables, which naturally creates less room for foods that don't serve your goals. No willpower required, no restriction, no deprivation—just strategic addition that works with your biology instead of against it.

2. FIBER + WATER: Blood Sugar Stability and Daily Elimination

The fiber in vegetables slows glucose absorption. Research shows that eating vegetables BEFORE carbohydrates—having a vegetable appetizer, then your main course—produces significantly lower post-meal glucose and insulin compared to eating the same foods in reverse order. In fact, studies demonstrate that eating vegetables first can reduce post-meal blood sugar spikes by 20-30 percent compared to eating carbohydrates first. Lower blood sugar spikes mean less insulin release, less fat storage, more stable energy, and fewer cravings.

But fiber does more than stabilize blood sugar. It's also essential for regular bowel movements—and if you're not eliminating daily, you're re-circulating hormones your body is trying to get rid of. Your liver packages used estrogen for elimination through your digestive tract. Without adequate fiber to bind to that estrogen and carry it out in stool, it gets reabsorbed back into your bloodstream, contributing to estrogen dominance and all the symptoms that come with it: weight gain, mood swings, heavy periods, and stubborn belly fat.

Fiber combined with adequate water creates the bulk and softness needed for easy, complete daily elimination. This is critical for hormone balance, not just digestive comfort.

Pro tip: Start each lunch and dinner with a few bites of vegetables before anything else hits your plate. This simple timing hack can dramatically improve your blood sugar response to the entire meal. But here's another reason this works: What you eat first sets the tone for your palate and influences what you'll crave more of during that meal. When you lead with vegetables, your taste buds and brain become primed to want more of them. You're literally training your body to crave the foods that serve you best.

This is the "addition" mindset again—we're not restricting anything; we're strategically adding vegetables first to naturally shift your appetite toward foods that support your goals. You can still have the pasta, the bread, the dessert—but by eating vegetables first, you'll naturally want less of those foods and feel more satisfied overall.

3. MICRONUTRIENTS & PHYTONUTRIENTS: Hormone Supports

Vegetables provide the micronutrients your body needs for hormone production and metabolism, plus thousands of beneficial plant compounds (phytonutrients) that influence gene expression, reduce inflammation, support detoxification, and even influence hormone receptor sensitivity.

Leafy greens (spinach, kale, arugula, collards) are rich in folate, magnesium, vitamin K, calcium, and iron. These support estrogen metabolism, bone health, and energy production.

Cruciferous vegetables (broccoli, cauliflower, Brussels sprouts, cabbage) contain compounds called indole-3-carbinol and sulforaphane that support healthy estrogen metabolism. They help your body convert estrogen into beneficial metabolites rather than harmful ones—critical for women in perimenopause dealing with estrogen dominance.

Colorful vegetables (peppers, tomatoes, carrots, beets) are high in antioxidants like carotenoids, lycopene, and anthocyanins that reduce inflammation and oxidative stress. The more colors on your plate, the more diverse phytonutrients you're getting.

Alliums (onions, garlic, leeks) contain sulfur compounds that support detoxification and liver function—helping your body process and eliminate used hormones efficiently.

These aren't just vitamins and minerals—they're bioactive compounds that provide health benefits beyond basic nutrition, influencing how your genes express themselves and how your hormones function at the cellular level.

HOW TO MAKE IT REAL: Practical Strategies

"I know I should eat more vegetables, but I don't like them / don't have time / they're boring."

Let us give you strategies that actually work:

STRATEGY 1: Batch Prep. Wash and chop vegetables when you bring them home from the store. Store them in clear containers at eye level in your fridge. You're far more likely to eat them if they're ready to grab.

STRATEGY 2: Roasting Is Magic. Toss vegetables with olive oil, salt, and pepper or a seasoning of your choice. Roast at 425°F until caramelized (20-30 minutes). Roasting brings out natural sweetness and creates delicious flavor. Game-changers: roasted Brussels sprouts, roasted cauliflower, roasted carrots.

STRATEGY 3: Hide Them. Add spinach or cauliflower rice to smoothies (you won't taste it). Use spiralized zucchini or spaghetti squash in place of pasta. Mix cauliflower rice into regular rice (50/50 blend). Add finely chopped vegetables to ground meat for meatballs, burgers, or tacos.

STRATEGY 4: Leverage Convenience. Frozen vegetables are just as nutritious as fresh. Pre-washed salad greens save time. Pre-cut vegetables are worth the upcharge if it means you'll actually eat them.

STRATEGY 5: Make Them Delicious. Stop eating sad, steamed vegetables with no seasoning. Use quality olive oil or grass-fed butter, fresh garlic and herbs, lemon juice, Parmesan cheese, balsamic glaze, everything bagel seasoning, or hot sauce. Your vegetables should taste GOOD. If they don't, you won't eat them consistently.

STRATEGY 6: The Salad Meal Formula
- **Base:** mixed greens or spinach (2-3 cups)
- **Protein:** chicken, salmon, steak, shrimp, eggs, chickpeas (palm-sized portion)
- **Healthy fat:** avocado, nuts, seeds, olive oil, cheese (thumb-sized portion)
- **Additional veggies:** tomatoes, cucumbers, peppers, onions, carrots, beets
- **Optional carb:** sweet potato, quinoa, fruit (if you tolerate carbs well)
- **Dressing:** olive oil + vinegar, or clean dressing without seed oils/sugar

This is a complete meal with vegetables as the foundation.

Make any meal work by adding vegetables:

- **Spaghetti:** Spaghetti squash, or regular pasta with LOTS of added veggies
- **Rice:** Mix riced cauliflower and rice together 50/50
- **Pizza:** Make it on a cauliflower crust or add a big salad on the side
- **Tacos:** Use lettuce wraps, make it a salad, or add tons of peppers, onions, tomatoes
- **Stir-fry:** Double or triple the vegetables, less rice

The goal isn't perfection. The goal is adding MORE than you're currently eating. If you currently eat one serving of vegetables daily, aim for two. Then three. Progress over perfection. This is the heart of the "addition mindset"—you're not taking anything away, you're simply adding more of what your body needs. When you do that consistently, everything else falls into place naturally.

You'll get full sooner, you'll have steadier energy, and—this is our favorite—you'll "crowd out" the foods that aren't serving your goals without declaring war on them. It's not that you can't eat them or won't eat them—you'll just eat less of them naturally. Eat the veggies first, then enjoy what you love. Remember that fiber also flattens your post-meal blood sugar spike, which is huge for insulin sensitivity, and supports daily bowel movements, which is critical for eliminating excess hormones.

Freedom in practice: There are no "bad" foods. Cookies don't build hormones, but enjoying one with a protein-and-vegetable meal is not sabotage. It's sanity. Our client Kara lost thirty pounds in ninety days and still kept her Friday pizza night tradition—with veggies first. Watch the scale drop while breaking up with dieting.

Chapter 7: The Four Habits Of Home Base

Goal — **Half your plate = non-starchy vegetables**

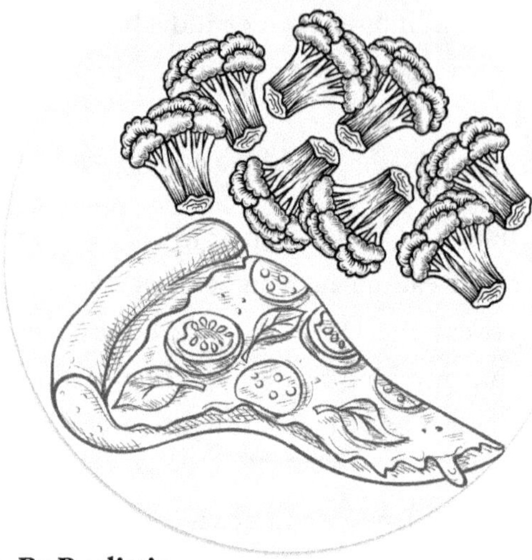

- ○ **Be Realistic**
    - ■ Sometimes you may eat pizza
    - ■ But can you still prioritize veggies?
    - ■ Why might you still be hungry? What is missing?

HOME BASE HABIT #2: More Water

You've probably heard "drink more water" a thousand times, but we want to help you understand WHY it matters so much—not just for your metabolism but for your skin, hormones, and even your energy and mood. Water is one of the simplest and most overlooked tools for transforming how your body looks and feels.

Goal: Minimum ≥ ½ your body weight (oz) daily, plus sixteen ounces for every thirty minutes of exercise. Most women do even better with more than half their body weight in ounces unless their doctor has told them otherwise due to a chronic kidney condition or medication.

Why it works (science, simply):

- **Cellular metabolism** requires water for every reaction in your body
- **Detoxification** depends on adequate hydration to flush waste
- **Appetite regulation** helps distinguish true hunger from thirst

THE SCIENCE EXPLAINED:
Why Water Is Essential

1. CELLULAR METABOLISM: Water Powers Every Body Function

Roughly sixty percent of your body is made up of water, and every system depends on it. Every single metabolic reaction in your body occurs in water. Your cells are like tiny factories, and water is the medium in which all production happens. When you're dehydrated, these reactions slow down. Your metabolism literally becomes less efficient at a cellular level.

Think about hormone production, fat burning, energy creation, muscle repair—none of these happen without adequate water. When you're even mildly dehydrated, your body has to work harder to do everything, which means you feel more tired, think less clearly, and burn fewer calories.

Even mild dehydration (just 1-2 percent of body weight) impairs concentration and focus, short-term memory, mood (increasing anxiety and irritability), and reaction time. If you've been blaming perimenopause brain fog entirely on hormones, hydration might be a significant contributing factor.

Your joints contain synovial fluid that cushions and lubricates. Your spinal discs are largely made of water. Your fascia (connective tissue) needs hydration to maintain elasticity. Without adequate hydration, you experience joint pain and stiffness, muscle cramps, reduced flexibility, and slower recovery from exercise.

Your skin is your largest organ, and it's about sixty-four percent water. Dehydration shows up as dryness and flaking, increased appearance of fine lines, loss of elasticity, dullness, and slower wound healing. While topical products help, true skin health starts from within. Adequate hydration plumps cells, improves elasticity, and gives your skin that healthy glow.

Research even shows that drinking water actually increases your metabolic rate temporarily—a phenomenon called water-induced thermogenesis. Drinking 500ml (about seventeen ounces) of water increases metabolic rate by approximately thirty percent for 30-40 minutes. Your body cannot efficiently metabolize stored fat without adequate water. The process of lipolysis (fat breakdown) requires water. If you're dehydrated, this process slows.

2. DETOXIFICATION: Your Body's Waste Removal System

Your kidneys filter approximately 120-150 quarts of blood daily, removing waste products and excess substances. This filtration requires adequate water volume. When you're chronically dehydrated, your kidneys cannot efficiently filter waste, toxins accumulate in your bloodstream, and ironically, your body retains water as a protective mechanism. You experience puffiness and edema—the opposite of what you want.

Adequate hydration allows your kidneys to function optimally, eliminating what your body doesn't need and reducing the water retention paradox. This is the "addition mindset" again—by adding more water, you actually reduce water retention and bloating.

Water is also essential for digestive health and hormone elimination. It's needed for producing saliva (digestion starts in your mouth), creating stomach acid (protein digestion), moving food through your intestines (peristalsis), and softening stool to prevent constipation. Remember: constipation means recirculating hormones. Adequate hydration supports daily bowel movements, which is crucial for hormone balance and eliminating the used estrogen your body is trying to get rid of.

Your lymphatic system removes waste and toxins from tissues, but unlike your cardiovascular system, it doesn't have a pump—it relies on muscle contraction and adequate fluid volume. Proper hydration supports lymphatic drainage, reducing puffiness and supporting immune function.

Your body maintains a precise internal temperature through sweating and evaporative cooling. When you're dehydrated, this system becomes less effective. You may feel overheated (perimenopausal hot flashes, anyone?), and your body has to work harder to maintain homeostasis.

3. APPETITE REGULATION: Stop Mistaking Thirst for Hunger

Here's something that surprises most people: Your brain's thirst and hunger centers are located close together in the hypothalamus, and the signals can be easily confused. If you've ever had an afternoon where you felt foggy, sluggish, or suddenly "hungry" for something, there's a good chance you weren't hungry at all; you were thirsty. Your body sends similar signals for both, which means dehydration often shows up as false hunger and cravings.

That's why one of the simplest things you can do to support weight loss is to drink water BEFORE meals. Start with 8-10 ounces before breakfast, lunch, and dinner. Not only does this help you reach your hydration goals, but research shows that drinking water before meals increases feelings of fullness, reduces calorie consumption by 75-90 calories per meal (without conscious effort), improves digestion, and helps distinguish true hunger from thirst.

We're not telling you to eat less or that you can't drink other beverages—we're asking you to drink water first. That simple addition naturally reduces your appetite and helps your body recognize when it's actually full. No restriction, no willpower, just strategic addition that works with your biology.

Pro tip: Keep a glass of water on your nightstand and drink 8-10 ounces first thing when you wake up—before coffee, before checking your phone, before anything else. You wake up already dehydrated after six to eight hours without fluid. Your liver and kidneys are most active overnight, busy processing and filtering toxins while you sleep. That morning glass acts like the "rinse cycle," helping your kidneys flush those toxins efficiently and rehydrating your cells before you even sip coffee or tea (which are diuretic and further dehydrating). Within a week, you'll notice a difference: your skin will look fresher, your digestion will feel smoother, and your energy will start to rise earlier in the day. Always think: Water first.

HOW TO MAKE IT REAL: Practical Strategies

Calculating Your Needs

Start with half your body weight in ounces. Example: A 180-pound woman needs a minimum of ninety ounces daily.

If your calculation exceeds 100 ounces to start, set your initial goal at 100 ounces and go from there. Over 100 ounces often requires electrolytes to properly hydrate.

Add more for:

- **Exercise:** +16oz for every thirty minutes (you lose fluid through sweat)
- **Caffeine:** +8-16oz for every caffeinated beverage (caffeine is a diuretic)
- Hot weather or dry climates
- Breastfeeding
- Illness or fighting infection

Be Reasonable: If you are not drinking anywhere close to your goal, start where you are and add. For example if you're only drinking one sixteen-ounce water bottle right now, can we try for two? We are reprogramming the all-or-nothing mindset and working on what we can give our body more of. Keep moving that goal up as you hit it consistently until you arrive at your target.

Signs You're Dehydrated:

Dark yellow urine, infrequent urination, dry mouth or lips, headaches, fatigue or sluggishness, difficulty concentrating, dizziness when standing, constipation, or dry skin are all signs of dehydration. Your urine should be pale yellow like diluted apple juice, and you should urinate every 2-4 hours.

Strategies to Drink More

- **Start your morning with water before coffee.** This one habit sets the tone for your entire day and jumpstarts your metabolism and detoxification.

- **Use a large bottle that you love** (thirty-two ounces or more means fewer refills). If you enjoy your water bottle, you'll use it more.

- **Drink through a straw** if that helps—many people drink significantly more water with a straw without even thinking about it.

- **Set "checkpoints" throughout the day:** before lunch, before dinner, mid-afternoon. Link water intake to existing routines.

- **Replace one daily beverage with water.** If you typically have three cups of coffee, make the third one water. If you have a soda every afternoon, swap it for sparkling water.

- **If taste is an issue,** infuse with lemon, cucumber, berries, or fresh herbs. Try a stevia or monk-fruit water enhancer (avoid artificial sweeteners). Herbal tea counts toward hydration.

- **Use a tracking app** if that motivates you, or create a visual system like rubber bands on your water bottle to track refills.

- **Link it to existing habits:** Drink water every time you use the bathroom, every time you check your phone, every time you stand up from your desk.

What About Electrolytes?

If you're drinking large amounts of water (over a hundred ounces daily) or sweating significantly through exercise, you need to replace electrolytes—primarily sodium, potassium, and magnesium. Without adequate electrolytes, you can drink tons of water and still feel dehydrated. The water passes right through without being absorbed into cells.

Add electrolytes through:

- A pinch of high-quality sea salt in your water
- Electrolyte powders (look for ones without sugar or artificial ingredients)
- Coconut water
- Bone broth
- Mineral-rich foods (leafy greens, avocados, nuts, seeds)

Chapter 7: The Four Habits Of Home Base

When Hydration Becomes Habit

You'll notice increased energy and mental clarity, better digestion and regular bowel movements, clearer skin with more elasticity and glow, reduced bloating and puffiness, fewer cravings and less false hunger, better temperature regulation and potentially fewer hot flashes, improved workout recovery and less joint pain, and naturally eating less at meals because you're properly hydrated and can distinguish real hunger from thirst.

The addition mindset in action: By adding more water, you naturally crowd out false hunger, support detoxification, and create an internal environment where your body feels safe enough to release stored fat. You're not restricting anything; you're giving your body what it desperately needs.

Client words you'll recognize: *"After just a week of changing my habits, my inflammation went down and my energy improved. My mantra now is, 'I will listen to my body and give it what it needs.'"* —**Brianne**

HOME BASE HABIT #3: More Sleep

Sleep isn't optional for fat loss; it's metabolic medicine. Less than seven hours a night raises cortisol and lowers insulin sensitivity. When you sleep, your body does the work you can't do while you're awake. It repairs, recalibrates, and restores the systems that keep you healthy, balanced, and metabolically active. It's not just rest—it's reconstruction.

You can eat perfectly, take all the supplements, and crush your workouts—but if you're sleeping five or six hours a night and running on caffeine, your results will stall. That's not because you're doing something wrong. It's because your biology runs on rhythm, and sleep is the master conductor.

Goal: 7–9 hours a night.

Your daily target: 7–9 hours between lights out and waking. If you need to wake at six a.m., be in bed by ten p.m. (accounting for time to fall asleep). Consistency matters more than perfection—go to bed and wake up at the same time every day, even weekends.

Why it works (science, simply):

- **Growth hormone release** during deep sleep burns fat and builds muscle
- **Cortisol regulation** keeps your stress hormones on a healthy rhythm
- **Hunger hormone balance** reduces cravings and appetite naturally

THE SCIENCE EXPLAINED:
Why Sleep Is Non-Negotiable

1. GROWTH HORMONE RELEASE: Your Body's Repair and Fat-Burning Mode

Human growth hormone (HGH) is released primarily during non-REM deep sleep. HGH is crucial for fat burning (lipolysis), muscle building and repair, cellular regeneration, bone density maintenance, and immune function.

When you don't get adequate deep sleep, HGH production plummets. Without sufficient HGH, your body struggles to burn fat and preserve muscle. This is why sleep-deprived people lose more muscle and less fat when dieting compared to well-rested people eating the same calories.

The research is striking: In one study, dieters who slept 8.5 hours lost fifty-five percent more fat and sixty percent less muscle compared to those who slept 5.5 hours—eating identical calories and following the same exercise program. Let that sink in: same food, same exercise, radically different body composition results based solely on sleep.

Sleep deprivation also reduces TSH (thyroid stimulating hormone) secretion and impairs the conversion of T4 to T3 (active thyroid hormone). The result is a sluggish metabolism, persistent fatigue, and difficulty losing weight. Your thyroid is exquisitely sensitive to stress and inadequate sleep. Many women who think they have a thyroid problem actually have a sleep problem that's suppressing thyroid function.

Sleep also matters for the production and balance of sex hormones. Testosterone production peaks during REM sleep, progesterone levels are influenced by sleep quality, and estrogen metabolism is affected by circadian rhythm disruption. Poor sleep worsens hormonal imbalances that are already problematic during perimenopause. If you're not sleeping well, hormone balance will be nearly impossible to achieve.

2. CORTISOL REGULATION: Keeping Your Stress Hormones in Check

Your cortisol follows a natural circadian rhythm. It should be highest in the morning (to wake you up and provide energy), gradually declining throughout the day, and lowest at night (allowing melatonin to rise and promote sleep).

When you don't get adequate sleep, this rhythm becomes dysregulated. Morning cortisol may be blunted (you wake up exhausted), evening cortisol remains elevated (you're tired but wired), and overall cortisol production increases.

Elevated cortisol, as we covered in Part 1, promotes fat storage (especially visceral fat), breaks down muscle tissue, increases insulin resistance, disrupts sex hormone production, increases appetite and cravings, and impairs immune function.

Less than seven hours of sleep is a stress signal to your body. That signal elevates cortisol, reduces insulin sensitivity, spikes cravings, slows thyroid conversion, and throws estrogen and progesterone off rhythm. We can't out-work a nervous system that thinks it's in danger.

Sleep deprivation also dramatically worsens insulin resistance. After just one night of poor sleep (4-5 hours), insulin sensitivity decreases by approximately thirty percent. After several nights of inadequate sleep, glucose metabolism resembles pre-diabetes—even in healthy, young individuals. This means that even if you're eating perfectly, inadequate sleep can prevent fat loss by locking your cells in storage mode.

During deep sleep, your brain's glymphatic system activates—essentially your brain's waste removal system. This system clears out metabolic waste products, including beta-amyloid (associated with Alzheimer's disease) and other toxins that accumulate during waking hours. Without adequate deep sleep, these waste products accumulate, contributing to brain fog, cognitive decline, and increased neuroinflammation. This is part of why sleep deprivation feels so mentally exhausting.

3. HUNGER HORMONE BALANCE: Why You Can't Stop Eating When You're Tired

Sleep deprivation directly affects appetite-regulating hormones in ways that make weight loss nearly impossible.

Ghrelin (the hunger hormone) increases by 15-30 percent after inadequate sleep. You feel hungrier, particularly craving calorie-dense, high-carbohydrate foods. Meanwhile, leptin (the satiety hormone) decreases by 15-20 percent after inadequate sleep. Your "I'm full" signal is blunted, so you never feel satisfied no matter how much you eat.

The result: you're significantly hungrier, less satisfied by the food you eat, and specifically crave calorie-dense junk food. This isn't a willpower issue—it's a biological response to sleep deprivation. Your body is desperately trying to get energy from somewhere, and when it can't get it from sleep, it demands it from food.

Studies show sleep-deprived people consume 300-500 additional calories daily compared to when they're well-rested, primarily from snacking and high-carbohydrate foods. That's 300-500 calories you're eating without even realizing you're doing it, simply because your hunger hormones are dysregulated from lack of sleep.

Sleep is also when your immune system does maintenance and repair. During sleep, T-cells are activated, cytokines are produced, immune memory is consolidated, and inflammation is regulated. Chronic sleep deprivation suppresses immune function, making you more susceptible to infections, slower to recover from illness, and more prone to chronic inflammation (which drives insulin resistance and weight gain).

This is why prioritizing sleep is actually the most powerful addition you can make to your routine. By adding adequate sleep, you naturally reduce hunger, increase satiety, improve insulin sensitivity, lower cortisol, optimize thyroid function, and support sex hormone production. Sleep isn't a luxury—it's the foundation that makes everything else work.

Instead of trying to force fat loss through more restriction, we're adding more sleep—the one thing your body desperately needs to heal, repair, and

Chapter 7: The Four Habits Of Home Base

function optimally. When you give your body adequate sleep, it can finally do the metabolic work it's been trying to do all along.

Pro tip: If you're waking up at five a.m. to work out but dragging all day, trade that hour for more sleep while we heal your hormones. Here's the truth: If you're sleep-deprived, that workout is causing more harm than good. When you exercise on insufficient sleep, cortisol is already elevated (exercise raises it further), recovery is impaired (you're not building muscle; you're breaking it down), immune function is suppressed (increasing injury and illness risk), energy is depleted (making you less active the rest of the day), and appetite increases (you eat more to compensate). If you're sleeping less than seven hours to exercise, STOP. Trade that workout for an extra hour of sleep. You will lose more fat, feel dramatically better, and when you do exercise, you'll perform better and recover faster. Once your sleep is consistently 7-9 hours, then add back structured exercise. Until then, stick with walks and gentle movement.

HOW TO MAKE IT REAL: Practical Strategies for Better Sleep

Many women tell us "I can't sleep" or "I have insomnia." While true sleep disorders exist and sometimes require medical intervention, most sleep problems in perimenopausal women are actually sleep hygiene issues combined with hormonal changes. Let's address both:

Sleep Hygiene Fundamentals

- **Consistent sleep schedule:** Go to bed and wake up at the same time every day—yes, even weekends. This entrains your circadian rhythm, making it easier to fall asleep and wake naturally. Your body craves consistency. When you go to bed at ten p.m. Monday through Friday but stay up until midnight on weekends, you're essentially giving yourself jet lag every week. This is called "social jet lag," and it wreaks havoc on your hormones. Target 7-9 hours between lights out and alarm. If you need to wake at six a.m., be in bed by ten p.m.

- **Dark, cool bedroom:** Temperature of 65-68°F is ideal. Your body temperature naturally drops as you fall asleep; a cool room facilitates this process. Many perimenopausal women need even cooler temperatures due to night sweats. Lower your thermostat at night, use a fan, try cooling sheets or a cooling mattress pad, sleep in minimal clothing, and keep a glass of ice water bedside. For darkness, light exposure suppresses melatonin production. Even small amounts of light from electronics, street lights, or hallway lights can disrupt sleep quality. Use blackout curtains, remove all electronics with lights (or cover with tape), use an eye mask if complete darkness isn't possible, and don't check your phone if you wake at night.

- **Remove technology:** Your bedroom should be for sleep and intimacy only—not work, social media, or TV. Blue light from screens suppresses melatonin production for 2-3 hours after exposure. Scrolling your phone in bed makes it biochemically harder to fall asleep. *Put your phone to bed before you get ready for bed.* Avoid screens for 1-2 hours before bed (minimum thirty minutes if you can't manage more), charge your phone in another room (use an alarm clock if needed), no TV in the bedroom, and if you must use devices, use blue light blocking glasses or night mode.

- **Wind-down routine:** Your body needs a transition from "doing mode" to "sleep mode." Create a 30-60-minute wind-down routine that signals to your nervous system that it's time to rest. Dim lights throughout your home, take a warm bath or shower (the subsequent cooling helps trigger sleep), do gentle stretching or restorative yoga, read a physical book (not a screen), journal or do a brain dump (get worries out of your head), practice deep breathing or meditation, listen to calming music or a sleep meditation, or drink herbal tea (chamomile, passionflower, valerian). The key is consistency—do the same routine every night so your body recognizes the cues.

- **Manage light exposure:** Your circadian rhythm is primarily controlled by light exposure. In the morning, get bright light (ideally sunlight) within thirty minutes of waking. This sets your cortisol rhythm and times your melatonin release 12-16 hours later. Go outside for 10-15 minutes, eat breakfast near a window, or use a light therapy box if you wake before sunrise. Aim for exposure to natural light throughout the day. In the evening, dim lights in your home starting 2-3 hours before bed. Use lamps instead of overhead lights. Consider red or amber bulbs which don't suppress melatonin as much.

- **Limit caffeine:** Caffeine has a half-life of 5-6 hours, meaning if you have coffee at two p.m., half of that caffeine is still in your system at eight p.m. For many people, afternoon caffeine significantly impairs sleep quality even if they don't notice difficulty falling asleep. To be safe, try cutting caffeine off at noon. If you're particularly sensitive, cut off by ten a.m. Remember that caffeine is in coffee, tea (black, green, white, oolong), chocolate, many medications/supplements (check labels), energy drinks, and some pre-workout supplements.

- **Limit alcohol:** While alcohol might help you fall asleep initially (it's a sedative), it significantly disrupts sleep architecture by suppressing REM sleep, increasing nighttime awakenings, worsening hot flashes and night sweats, and causing early morning waking. If you drink, do so earlier in the evening (finishing at least three hours before bed) and limit quantity (one drink maximum if sleep is a priority).

- **Manage bedroom stress:** If your bedroom is associated with stress, worry, or sleeplessness, your brain will resist sleeping there. Don't work in bed. If you can't fall asleep after 20-30 minutes, get up and do something relaxing in another room until you feel sleepy. Don't watch the clock (turn clock face away from bed). If you wake and your mind races, keep a journal bedside to write down thoughts so you can release them.

Supplement Support For Sleep

Sometimes lifestyle changes aren't enough, especially during perimenopause. These supplements can support better sleep:

Magnesium (300-600mg before bed): Calms the nervous system, supports GABA production, relaxes muscles. Forms: glycinate (best for sleep), threonate (crosses blood-brain barrier), or malate.

L-Theanine (200-400mg before bed): Amino acid from green tea, promotes relaxation without sedation, increases GABA, serotonin, and dopamine, and reduces anxiety and racing thoughts.

Glycine (3-5g before bed): Amino acid that lowers body temperature (facilitates sleep), improves sleep quality, non-sedating.

Melatonin (0.5-3mg, 30-60 minutes before bed): Start with the lowest dose (0.5-1mg). More is not better (high doses can cause grogginess). Helps reset circadian rhythm. Particularly helpful for travel or shift work.

Herbs: Valerian, passionflower, lemon balm, ashwagandha, or chamomile can be taken in many forms (tinctures, capsules, teas) to support relaxation and sleep.

Many companies make sleep formulas combining several of these ingredients. Look for clean products without melatonin so you can dose it separately if needed.

The Perimenopause Sleep Challenge

Unfortunately, at the exact life stage when sleep is most critical for metabolism, perimenopause often disrupts sleep quality. Hot flashes and night sweats wake you repeatedly, declining progesterone (which has calming effects) makes it harder to fall asleep, anxiety and racing thoughts increase, cortisol dysregulation creates a "tired but wired" feeling, and declining estrogen affects sleep architecture. This creates a vicious cycle: Hormonal changes disrupt sleep, worsening hormonal imbalances and further disrupting sleep. Breaking this cycle requires addressing both sleep hygiene AND hormone balance.

When To Seek Medical Help

Sometimes sleep problems require medical intervention: sleep apnea (loud snoring, gasping, witnessed pauses in breathing), restless leg syndrome, chronic insomnia despite good sleep hygiene, or severe night sweats disrupting sleep multiple times nightly. Talk to your doctor about a sleep study (to rule out sleep apnea), hormone replacement therapy (can dramatically improve perimenopause sleep disruption which we will talk about in Part 3), or short-term sleep medication (while you work on underlying causes).

WHAT HAPPENS WHEN YOU ADD MORE (Quantity & Quality) SLEEP

You'll burn more fat and preserve more muscle (even when eating the same calories), wake up feeling refreshed instead of exhausted, have stable energy throughout the day without needing excessive caffeine, experience fewer cravings and more natural appetite regulation, think more clearly with reduced brain fog, feel less anxious and more emotionally resilient, recover faster from exercise and feel less sore, have more stable blood sugar and improved insulin sensitivity, balance hormones more effectively (sex hormones, thyroid, and cortisol all improve), and strengthen your immune system.

"Addition Mindset"—by adding more sleep, you naturally reduce hunger, cravings, cortisol, insulin resistance, and inflammation. You're not restricting anything or pushing harder. You're giving your body the single most powerful tool it needs to heal and function optimally.

Your hormones aren't random—they follow a rhythm, a twenty-four-hour pattern known as your circadian rhythm. This internal clock controls the rise and fall of cortisol, insulin, thyroid hormones, sex hormones, and even hunger and fullness signals like ghrelin and leptin. When you get enough consistent, quality sleep, your body will keep that rhythm stable. But when your sleep is shortened, disrupted, or inconsistent, that rhythm gets thrown off—and every major hormone system starts to suffer.

You may be shocked how many women start losing weight again when they fix sleep. The "eat less, move more" crowd will roll their eyes. Let them. We'll be over here quietly getting results.

Client words you'll recognize: *"After a busy, sleep-deprived weekend, I traded my hard workout for a walk and prayer time. I still got my steps in but was kinder to my body."* —**Jenny**

HOME BASE HABIT #4: More Movement

NEAT (non-exercise activity thermogenesis) is the energy you burn doing life: walking the dog, standing, cleaning the kitchen, taking the stairs, strolling after dinner, gardening, running errands. It matters—a lot.

If you are exhausted and inflamed, daily high-intensity workouts can keep you in a stress loop. A season of less formal exercise and more movement may be the kindness your hormones need.

Target: Prioritize daily NEAT (walking, standing, household activities) over intense structured exercise while healing.

Your daily target: Move your body gently and frequently throughout the day. Aim for 7,000-10,000 steps through regular activity (not a single exercise session). Add a 10-20-minute walk after meals, especially dinner. Stand more than you sit. Prioritize consistent, gentle movement over intense workouts while you heal.

Why it works (science, simply):

- **NEAT burns more calories** than structured exercise without the stress response
- **Post-meal walks** reduce blood sugar spikes by 20-30 percent
- **Gentle movement lowers cortisol** instead of raising it like intense exercise

Chapter 7: The Four Habits Of Home Base

THE SCIENCE EXPLAINED:
Why NEAT Matters More Than Exercise for Healing

1. NEAT BURNS MORE CALORIES: The Hidden Metabolic Advantage

Let's talk about something that surprises most women: Formal exercise might be holding you back. If you're dealing with hormonal imbalances, chronic stress, poor sleep, perimenopause symptoms, or unexplained weight gain despite eating well, then intense exercise is likely making things worse, not better.

Exercise is a physical stressor. Don't misunderstand—exercise is incredibly beneficial and important for long-term health. But when your body is already stressed (from hormonal changes, inadequate sleep, life stress, nutrient deficiencies, inflammation), adding MORE stress can push you over the edge into a state where your body cannot recover.

Every time you do intense exercise, cortisol spikes—this is necessary and normal because cortisol mobilizes energy to fuel your workout. Inflammation also increases, which is actually a good thing in the right context because it's part of the muscle adaptation process that makes you stronger. Energy is depleted, and your body requires recovery through sleep, nutrition, and rest to repair and rebuild.

These are all normal, healthy responses to exercise when your body is in a good place metabolically. But if your body is already in a stressed state, these normal exercise responses become problematic. Instead of building you up, they break you down further.

If your baseline cortisol is already elevated from stress, lack of sleep, or hormonal changes, exercise-induced cortisol spikes can keep you chronically elevated. This results in fat storage, muscle breakdown, insulin resistance, and energy depletion. If you're already dealing with chronic inflammation, your body's ability to recover from workouts is strained. Now you're dealing with persistent soreness, joint pain, and feeling worse instead of better.

Here's the game-changer: Non-exercise activity thermogenesis—all the movement that isn't formal exercise—actually accounts for MORE calorie burn than exercise for most people. Research shows structured exercise might burn 200-400 calories (if you do it), but NEAT can burn 500-2,000+ calories daily depending on your lifestyle.

Someone who exercises intensely for one hour but sits the other twenty-three hours burns fewer total calories than someone who never formally exercises but walks frequently, stands often, takes stairs, and stays generally active.

2. POST-MEAL WALKS: The Blood Sugar Hack That Changes Everything

One of the most powerful NEAT habits is a 10-20-minute walk after meals, particularly after dinner. This simple practice reduces post-meal blood sugar spikes by 20-30 percent (massive for insulin sensitivity), improves insulin signaling, aids digestion, lowers cortisol (walking is meditative and stress-reducing), improves sleep quality (especially evening walks), and adds 500-1,000 steps to your daily total.

You don't need to walk fast or far. A leisurely stroll around the block, through your neighborhood, or even around your house if weather is bad—all of it counts.

The glucose-lowering effect is remarkable. Studies show that a fifteen-minute walk after meals lowers blood sugar more effectively than a single forty-five-minute walk at another time of day. The timing matters because you're using the glucose as fuel immediately after it enters your bloodstream, preventing the blood sugar spike that triggers insulin release and fat storage.

Think about what this means: You're eating the same food, but by simply walking for 10-15 minutes afterward, your body processes that food completely differently. Less insulin is released, less fat is stored, more glucose goes into muscle cells for energy, and your metabolism improves. That's a massive return on a tiny investment of time and effort.

You're not restricting what you eat, you're not forcing yourself through exhausting workouts, you're simply adding a pleasant walk after your meal. This single addition can improve your insulin sensitivity, support weight

Chapter 7: The Four Habits Of Home Base

loss, enhance digestion, reduce cortisol, and improve sleep—all from 10-20 minutes of gentle movement.

3. GENTLE MOVEMENT LOWERS CORTISOL: The Anti-Stress Effect

While intense exercise raises cortisol (which is problematic when you're already stressed), gentle movement actually lowers cortisol. Walking, stretching, yoga, leisurely cycling, swimming, gardening—these activities activate your parasympathetic nervous system (rest and digest mode) rather than your sympathetic nervous system (fight or flight mode).

This is crucial for women in perimenopause who are already dealing with elevated cortisol from hormonal changes, life stress, inadequate sleep, and chronic inflammation. Adding high-intensity exercise to this mix is like throwing gasoline on a fire. But adding gentle movement is like applying a soothing balm—it calms your nervous system, reduces inflammation, improves mood, and creates the internal environment your body needs to heal.

Walking is particularly powerful because it's rhythmic, meditative, and gets you outside (sunlight exposure further supports cortisol regulation and circadian rhythm). You don't need a gym membership or fancy equipment. Just move your body in ways that feel good.

Gentle movement also supports lymphatic drainage. Walking, stretching, and general daily activity keep your lymphatic system flowing, reducing puffiness, supporting immune function, and helping your body eliminate waste efficiently.

Pro tip: If the scale has been stuck and you've been going to Boot Camps, Orange Theory, HIIT Training, or Spin Class, consider pausing these for a short season. Get the scale moving with NEAT and heal your hormones first. When your hormones are balanced, you'll have more margin for stress if you love those styles of workouts. It can be powerful for the mind, though, to see how the scale can move WITHOUT intense exercise if you've always connected intense exercise as necessary in order to lose weight. Give yourself time to heal and see what movements bring you joy, results, and help you feel your best.

"Addition Mindset": Instead of forcing yourself through punishing workouts that stress your already-stressed body, add gentle, consistent movement throughout your day. This movement supports healing rather than demanding more from a depleted system. Think "more movement" vs structured exercise. Your body will thank you, and you may be surprised how much better you feel and how much more weight you lose.

HOW TO MAKE IT REAL: Practical Strategies

Increase Your Daily Neat

- **Take the stairs** whenever possible. Park farther away from store entrances. Every extra step counts.
- **Stand more than you sit.** Use a standing desk if possible, fold laundry while standing, pace during phone calls, stand while chopping vegetables or doing dishes.
- **Walk after meals.** Even ten minutes after dinner lowers blood sugar significantly. This is the single most powerful NEAT habit you can build.
- **Move throughout your day.** Dance while cooking, garden, play with your kids or grandkids, clean the house with intention, stretch while watching TV.
- **Walk your dog** (or borrow a neighbor's dog). This builds movement into your daily routine and provides accountability.
- **Have "walking meetings"** instead of sitting at a desk or on video calls. Take phone calls while walking.
- **Set a timer** to stand and move every hour if you work at a desk. Even 2-3 minutes of movement every hour adds up significantly.
- **Make it enjoyable.** Listen to podcasts, audiobooks, or music while walking. Walk with a friend for social connection. Explore new neighborhoods or nature trails. Movement should feel good, not like punishment.

When To Add Back Structured Exercise

Once you've established Home Base (vegetables, water, sleep, movement) and your energy is improving, and the scale is moving, THEN you can consider adding structured exercise back strategically. Here is a model to follow for your midlife training plan:

Strength Training (2-3x per week): This is the most important type of exercise for women in perimenopause because it builds and maintains muscle mass to combat muscle sarcopenia due to aging and increase muscle preservation during weight loss. More muscle increases your metabolic rate: Remember, muscle burns more calories at rest than fat. It also improves insulin sensitivity, supports bone density, and improves functional strength and quality of life.

Focus on compound movements (squats, deadlifts, presses, rows) with proper form to prevent injury. Progressive overload means gradually increasing weight/resistance or reps. This is an effective strategy to build muscle without overstressing the body. Be sure to allow for adequate recovery between sessions. You don't need to spend hours in the gym. 30-45 minutes, 2-3x per week, focusing on major muscle groups, is sufficient.

Low-Intensity Cardio (daily walking): This is your NEAT—walking, hiking, swimming, cycling at conversational pace. Do this every day if possible. It's the foundation of an active lifestyle and doesn't require recovery.

High-Intensity Exercise (optional, 1-2x per week maximum): HIIT, sprints, intense cycling, hard running—these have benefits but also high stress cost. If you enjoy them and recover well, include 1-2 sessions per week maximum. If you're exhausted or struggling with weight loss, skip these entirely until you're in a better place metabolically.

Yoga/Pilates/Stretching (as desired): These modalities support flexibility, stress management, and mind-body connection. They're restorative rather than depleting. Include as often as feels good.

The 80/20 Rule for Exercise

Aim for eighty percent of your movement to be gentle, restorative, and stress-reducing. This includes walking, stretching, yoga, light cycling, swimming, gardening, and play. The remaining twenty percent can be more intense, like strength training, HIIT, running, intense cycling, or sports.

Most women have this backward—they do eighty percent intense exercise and twenty percent gentle movement. Flip it, especially during perimenopause, and watch your body respond.

Listen to Your Body

Your body gives you clear signals about whether exercise is helping or harming. When exercise is helping, you feel energized afterward rather than exhausted. Your sleep improves, your mood lifts, and you're recovering well between sessions with minimal soreness. You feel fresh, not beaten down. You're seeing strength or endurance gains, and your energy remains steady throughout the day.

When exercise is harming you, you feel depleted after workouts instead of energized. Your sleep worsens, you're constantly sore or injured, and you're not recovering between sessions. You find yourself ravenously hungry and craving sugar. Your weight is stuck or even increasing despite all your exercise efforts. You feel burnt out or resentful about workouts, viewing them as punishment rather than something you enjoy. If you're experiencing these warning signs, you're over-exercising for your current metabolic state. Pull back and focus on NEAT and gentle movement, alongside the other Home Base habits. Give your body time to heal. This isn't giving up—it's a strategic addition of what your body actually needs right now.

What Happens When You Add More Movement vs. Exercise

You'll burn more calories throughout the day from consistent movement, not just during a single workout session. Your cortisol will lower, and your stress levels will decrease naturally. Your insulin sensitivity and blood sugar control will improve dramatically, especially from those post-meal walks. You'll maintain more consistent energy without the post-workout crashes that leave you depleted and reaching for caffeine or sugar.

You'll experience less hunger and fewer cravings because gentle movement doesn't spike appetite the way intense exercise does. You'll recover faster and feel less sore because you're not constantly breaking down your body. Your digestion and gut motility will improve. Your lymphatic system will drain more efficiently, reducing puffiness and bloating. You'll sleep better, especially when you add evening walks to your routine. And here's what might surprise you most: You'll feel less resentful about movement because it becomes something you genuinely enjoy rather than something you force yourself to do out of obligation or punishment.

This is the addition mindset at its finest. Instead of forcing yourself through exhausting workouts that deplete your already-stressed body, you're adding gentle, consistent movement that supports healing. You're working with your biology instead of against it. You're giving your body what it needs—gentle, stress-reducing movement—rather than what diet culture says you "should" do, which is intense, punishing exercise that proves your worth through suffering.

When you prioritize NEAT and gentle movement, your body finally feels safe enough to release stored fat, balance hormones, and heal from years of metabolic stress. You're not being lazy—you're being strategic. You're not giving up—you're finally giving your body what it's been asking for all along.

Measuring Progress & Self Reflection

As you work on building up your Home Base habits, remember it's not all or nothing. We can't drink a hundred ounces of water without drinking twenty ounces first. We can't eat 5-6 cups of vegetables in a day if we aren't eating any at all. Start small and keep building. When it comes to establishing a new habit, it is easier to build on existing habits than to create new ones from scratch. Try habit stacking.

Use this habit stacking formula: **After/Before [CURRENT HABIT], I will [NEW HABIT].**

- Before I drink my coffee, I will drink a glass of water.
- Before I eat my pizza, I will eat my salad.

- After I eat dinner, if I'm still hungry, I will eat another serving of vegetables.
- Before I open my laptop, I'll take a five-minute walk.
- After I put the kids to bed, I'll start my wind-down routine.

The Scale Isn't the Enemy — It's Just the Tool

You've probably heard people say, "Throw away the scale; it doesn't tell the whole story." They're right: It doesn't tell the whole story, but it is absolutely a useful tool for weight loss. Here's how we see it: The scale measures weight, not worth. It reflects the sum of your tissues, water, fat, blood, bones, organs, and muscle mass on any given day. It doesn't tell you if you're a good mom, a good partner, or a good human. But it can help you understand how your body is responding to what you're doing. If you have a goal weight and never step on a scale, it's going to be pretty challenging to know whether you're moving in the direction you care about. Pictures and measurements matter; strength and energy matter; how your clothes fit matters. But fearing the scale gives it more power than it deserves. We take that power back by using it—not worshiping it, not avoiding it. The goal isn't to obsess over the number the scale says; it's to learn from it.

Here's what we tell every client:

"You don't lose weight ten pounds at a time. You lose it 0.2 pounds at a time."

Those small wins matter: 0.2 pounds a day might not sound like much, but over seven days, that's 1.4 pounds—and over twelve weeks, it's nearly seventeen pounds. That's not a fantasy number; that's what steady, consistent progress looks like when you're finally working *with* your body instead of against it.

When you get a digital scale that tracks to the tenth of a pound, you start to see those small fluctuations that show you what's happening inside your body. You'll notice how inflammation, water retention, sleep, stress, and food choices affect your weight day to day. You'll see the patterns, not just the peaks and valleys. And the more you understand those patterns, the less emotional power that number holds over you.

Because here's the thing: Fearing the scale gives it control. Using it with understanding gives *you* control.

Understanding Weight Fluctuations

Water retention is one of the biggest culprits. Your sodium intake affects water retention—more salt means your body temporarily holds on to more fluid. Carbohydrate intake also plays a major role because carbs are stored as glycogen with 3-4 grams of water per gram of carbohydrate. Your hormones matter too: Both estrogen and progesterone affect fluid retention, which is why you might feel puffier at certain times of the month. Inflammation from an injury, hard workout, or illness causes your body to retain water as part of the healing process. Poor sleep quality leads to elevated cortisol, which increases water retention. Stress does the same thing—cortisol signals your body to hold on to fluid. Even many common medications cause water retention as a side effect.

Bowel movements (or lack thereof) significantly impact what you see on the scale. You're carrying 5-20 pounds of food and waste in your digestive tract at any given time. If you haven't had a bowel movement, that weight is still inside you, registering on the scale. A large bowel movement can change the scale by 1-2 pounds instantly—not because you lost fat but because you eliminated waste your body was done with.

Your menstrual cycle (if you're still cycling) creates massive fluctuations. You can gain five pounds of water weight during the luteal phase, which is the time after ovulation and before your period starts. Progesterone causes significant fluid retention during this time. This weight drops off quickly once your period starts. This is not fat gain—it's temporary, cyclical, and completely normal.

Exercise causes muscle inflammation from workouts. When you exercise, you create micro-tears in muscle tissue. Your body retains water to repair this damage, which is a normal and necessary part of recovery. You can gain 2-5 pounds after a hard workout, but this resolves within 48-72 hours as you recover. This is part of the muscle-building process, not fat gain. Your muscles are healing and getting stronger.

Time of day matters more than you think. You weigh the least first thing in the morning after using the bathroom because you've fasted overnight and eliminated waste. You weigh more after meals, after drinking water, and later in the day as food moves through your system and you consume fluids. This can vary by 2-5 pounds throughout a single day.

None of these fluctuations are fat gain. Expect normal fluid shifts after salty meals, late nights, or skipping a bowel movement. Understanding the fluctuations will help you take the power back and cash in on trends that are bringing results. So our first challenge to you is to get a scale and step on it first thing every morning (after bathroom, before eating). Let numbers be **information**, not identity.

We already talked about the decimals, but let us speak to your heart for a second. The scale is not your confessional booth. It's not your report card. It's not an opinion on your worth. It's a *number about gravity* on a particular day, with a particular amount of salt and water and fiber and sleep in your system. The "bad" weekend where you had one margarita and two tacos with your girlfriends and gained three pounds on Monday morning? That's almost certainly water, sodium, digestive contents, and glycogen—not three pounds of fat. To gain three pounds of actual fat, you'd need to eat 10,500 calories OVER your maintenance needs in one weekend. Did you do that? Probably not.

Your job is to **come home**—to Home Base. Focus on the habits that will support your body, and watch the scale come right back down. Give it 2-3 days of returning to your normal routine, and that weight will disappear.

Remember, if you gained three pounds of fluid over the two-day weekend, you can lose it over the next two days as well. Keep your head in the game and don't let your emotions take over. When you see the scale trending down while you keep living your life, it cements the new story. Your brain learns, *I can be free and make progress.* That is how the drama ends.

What we measure, we improve. But measurement doesn't have to mean calorie-counting. For many women, that's diet-brain in disguise. Instead,

track behaviors: take photos of meals, check off water, sleep, movement, veggies. Use your digital scale for gentle data. And keep building up your Home Base habits. That's it.

As you start to apply what you're learning, here are a few key takeaways to keep in the front of your mind:

- **You don't have to micromanage your whole plate if you prioritize vegetables first.** The rest settles into place.
- **Ordering double veggies or a salad does not mean you're dieting or missing out.**
- **Eating less is not always better.** Sometimes it's the most stressful thing you could do to your biology.
- **You're never too far from Home Base.** One meal, one glass of water, one walk—reset.
- **We lose weight 0.2 pounds at a time.** Celebrate the decimals.
- **The scale is a tool, not a judge.**
- **There are no bad foods.**

It's easy to overlook Home Base and think that we are eating more vegetables than we are, getting all our water in, sleeping enough, and prioritizing that NEAT. It's easy to slack on these habits, so as you build them, remember to have regular "perception vs. reality" checks if you aren't working with someone who is holding you accountable. Here are some questions to ask yourself:

- How many veggie servings do you actually eat most days?
- How many ounces of water do you actually drink?
- How much sleep do you actually get?
- How much do you actually move?
- Are the things you think you do "occasionally" (grazing, wine, takeout) frequent enough to keep you in maintenance?

Move More:
Movement >
"Exercise"

Drink more: Half
your body weight in
ounces of water

MOVE

Home Base

SLEEP

VEGGIES

Half your plate at
lunch & dinner
should be filled
with veggies

Minimum
of 7 hours
of sleep

Gut Health And Detoxification

You wake up already bloated. You haven't even had breakfast yet, but your stomach feels tight and heavy, like it's holding something it doesn't want to. By the end of the day, you look a few months pregnant, and you're wondering what you could possibly be doing wrong. You've tried cutting dairy, skipping gluten, adding probiotics, drinking greens powders, maybe even taking laxatives when things get desperate, but nothing seems to stick.

You're tired of being told that this, like so many other things, is "just part of getting older." Your energy is flat, your digestion is unpredictable, and you just want to feel light again physically and mentally. That's exactly what this chapter is about.

Your gut is not just about digestion—it's the control center for your hormones, immune system, mood, and metabolism. If your gut isn't healthy, nothing else works right. You can hit your calorie goal, take all the supplements, and still struggle with weight, inflammation, and hormone imbalance if your gut is compromised.

You can't lose weight in an inflamed body. You can't balance hormones when the system that processes them is backed up. And you can't heal if you're constantly reabsorbing the very toxins your body is trying to get rid of.

So let's start with the truth about what's really going on inside—and how you can begin healing from the inside out.

The Gut-Hormone Connection

Here's what most people don't know: Your gut and your hormones are in constant communication. In fact, there's a specific collection of bacteria in your gut called the estrobolome that directly regulates how your body processes and eliminates estrogen. If your gut bacteria are out of balance, you can end up with too much estrogen as a whole or in ratio to other hormones. We call this estrogen dominance which drives weight gain, especially around your midsection.

In addition to the regulation of estrogen, your gut also produces about ninety percent of your body's serotonin—the neurotransmitter that regulates mood, sleep, and appetite. When your gut is unhealthy, serotonin production drops, which is why gut issues often show up as depression, anxiety, insomnia, and intense cravings. About twenty percent of thyroid hormone conversion—from T4 (inactive) to T3 (active)—happens in your gut. If your microbiome is off or you're not having daily healthy bowel movements, your metabolism slows down even if your thyroid labs look "normal."

And here's something that blew our minds when we first learned it: Your gut naturally produces GLP-1, the same hormone that medications like Ozempic mimic. GLP-1 is your body's natural appetite suppressant and blood sugar regulator. But if your gut lining is damaged or your microbiome is out of balance, you produce less of it—which means you're hungrier, your blood sugar is less stable, and weight loss becomes harder. GLP-1 medications can be an incredible tool when used thoughtfully, but they're not the whole solution. The goal is to restore your body's own ability to make and respond to GLP-1 naturally through fiber, protein, sleep, and gut healing.

What Damages Your Gut?

Chronic stress is one of the biggest gut destroyers because it raises cortisol, which directly damages the gut lining. Antibiotics, while sometimes necessary, kill good bacteria right along with the bad, disrupting the delicate balance of your microbiome. NSAIDs like ibuprofen might seem harmless for occasional aches and pains, but with chronic use, they damage the gut lining and contribute to leaky gut.

Processed foods, sugar, and artificial sweeteners feed the bad bacteria in your gut while starving the good bacteria, creating an environment where harmful organisms thrive and beneficial ones struggle. Low fiber intake of the standard American diet compounds this problem because good bacteria need fiber to survive and multiply. Without it, your beneficial bacteria literally starve. Alcohol is both inflammatory and directly damaging to the gut lining, weakening the barrier that's supposed to keep toxins and undigested food particles out of your bloodstream.

And here's something most women don't realize: The hormonal changes in perimenopause directly affect your gut health. Low estrogen weakens the gut lining. This is one more reason why gut health becomes so critical during this life stage: Your declining hormones are literally making your gut more vulnerable.

When your gut lining is damaged, you develop what's called "leaky gut" or intestinal permeability. This means food particles, toxins, and bacteria can pass through your gut lining into your bloodstream, triggering inflammation throughout your body.

Your gut lining is supposed to be a selective barrier, letting nutrients through while keeping harmful substances out. Think of it like a screen door: It allows air in but keeps bugs out. When the gut lining is damaged, it's like having holes in your screen door. Things that should stay outside (partially digested food, bacteria, toxins) get inside.

Your immune system recognizes these foreign invaders and mounts an inflammatory response. This isn't an overreaction—your immune system is doing its job. But when this happens chronically (multiple times per day, every day), you develop systemic inflammation.

That inflammation drives:
- Insulin resistance
- Weight gain and inability to lose fat
- Fatigue and brain fog

- Joint pain and muscle aches
- Skin issues
- Autoimmune flare-ups
- Mood disorders

Healing the gut isn't just about digestion. It's about reducing system-wide inflammation so your hormones can function optimally.

Digestion & Detoxification: Your Body's Natural Process

If your gut feels bloated, distended, or unpredictable, that's your body waving a red flag. It's saying, "Something isn't processing the way it should."

Many women in perimenopause experience low stomach acid without realizing it. That means you're not breaking down protein efficiently, and undigested food sits in the gut fermenting—creating gas, bloating, and discomfort. It also means you're not absorbing the micronutrients your body needs to make hormones, like zinc, magnesium, B vitamins, and iron.

When your digestion slows, toxins and waste linger. If you're not having at least one (ideally two) daily bowel movements, your body's "trash" starts to pile up. Think of it like forgetting to take out your kitchen trash for a week. Everything you were trying to get rid of starts breaking down, releasing odor and bacteria. That's exactly what happens in your intestines when you're constipated.

And here's the kicker: Your liver dumps used hormones and toxins into your intestines to be excreted. When you're not eliminating daily, those excess hormones and toxins can get reabsorbed back into your bloodstream, creating a vicious cycle of hormone imbalance, fatigue, and inflammation.

If you're feeling bloated, constipated, foggy, or heavy, your body isn't working against you—it's communicating with you. It's saying, "Help me get things moving again."

Let's talk about **detox**—one of the most misunderstood concepts in health. When most people hear the word "detox," they picture juice cleanses,

Chapter 8: Gut Health And Detoxification

laxative teas, or expensive supplement kits. But your body already has a built-in detox system—it just needs support, not gimmicks.

Your **liver**, **kidneys**, **lungs**, **lymphatic system**, **skin**, and **bowels** are your body's waste management team. They work together to process and remove toxins like:

- Environmental chemicals and pollutants
- Agricultural pesticides
- Additives and dyes in processed food
- Alcohol, nicotine, and medication residues
- Hormone-disrupting compounds from plastics and personal care products

Every single day, your body is processing thousands of these exposures. When your liver is overloaded or your gut is sluggish, that waste piles up, just like an overflowing trash can. The goal of detox isn't to stop eating and starve your body into "cleaning itself." It's to nourish your detox organs and reduce inflammation so they can do their job effectively.

That's why the ten-day detox plan I'm about to outline for you focuses on *adding*, not removing—adding fiber, hydration, and movement to help your body release what it's been holding on to. You don't need to buy a fancy detox product. You already have the most powerful detox tools inside you—your organs. You just need to support them.

Why The 10-Day Detox Works: The Science Behind the Reset

Let us be clear from the start: This is not a juice cleanse. This is not a starvation protocol. This is not about deprivation or punishment. This is a strategic, science-backed nutritional reset designed specifically for women with hormone imbalances who are struggling to lose weight despite doing "all the right things."

If you've read Part 1 of this book, you understand that your weight struggle isn't about willpower or moral failing—it's about five interconnected hormone imbalances working against you. You know that insulin resistance locks your cells in storage mode. You know that cortisol dysregulation promotes belly fat and breaks down muscle. You know that thyroid dysfunction slows your metabolism. You know that sex hormone imbalances drive weight gain and make fat loss nearly impossible. And you know that vitamin D deficiency affects every system in your body.

What you might not know is this: Chronic inflammation is the common thread connecting all five of these imbalances. Inflammation disrupts insulin signaling, elevates cortisol, suppresses thyroid function, throws sex hormones out of balance, and impairs vitamin D metabolism. It's the fire burning underneath all your symptoms, and until we put out that fire, your body will resist every effort you make to lose weight.

The 10-Day Detox is designed to dramatically reduce inflammation, give your gut a chance to heal, provide your body with the raw materials it needs to create and metabolize hormones properly, and teach you which foods serve your unique biology and which ones work against it.

The Inflammation-Hormone-Weight Loss Connection

Here's what most women don't realize: You can eat perfectly calculated macros, exercise religiously, and take all the right supplements, but if your gut is inflamed and leaky, if your liver is overburdened, and if your body is constantly fighting an inflammatory fire, you will not lose weight. Your body will hold onto every ounce of fat as protective insulation because it perceives that you're under attack.

Chronic inflammation comes from multiple sources: processed foods filled with inflammatory seed oils and additives, sugar that spikes blood glucose and triggers inflammatory cascades, gluten that increases intestinal permeability even in people without celiac disease, dairy that many women cannot properly digest (sixty-five percent of the world population has reduced ability to digest lactose after infancy), artificial sweeteners that disrupt gut bacteria and increase insulin resistance, alcohol that damages the gut lining and burdens the liver, chronic stress that raises cortisol and damages gut integrity, inadequate sleep that elevates inflammatory cytokines, and this is all on top of the hormonal changes in perimenopause we discussed that weakens the gut lining.

Here's the beautiful part: When we remove the inflammatory triggers, even for just ten days, your body can begin to heal. Inflammation drops dramatically. Your gut lining starts to repair. Your liver gets a break from processing inflammatory compounds. Your insulin sensitivity improves. Your cortisol begins to normalize. Your thyroid function optimizes. Your sex hormones can rebalance. And your body finally feels safe enough to release stored fat.

The 10-Day Detox removes the foods that damage your gut lining and disrupt your microbiome while flooding your system with nutrients that actively heal and restore gut integrity. This isn't just about reducing bloating (though you will notice that); it's about restoring the foundation that allows all your other hormones to function optimally.

Providing the Raw Materials Your Body Needs

If you've spent years thinking of food in terms of calories, macros, or "good" and "bad," here's the reframe that changes everything: Food is raw material. Your hormones are built from amino acids and fats. Your detoxification pathways and neurotransmitters rely on vitamins and minerals. Your thyroid conversion, insulin sensitivity, and sex hormone balance all depend on whether your body has the tools to do the job.

Your hormones are physical molecules that must be built from specific components that come from your diet. Think of your body as a construction site and your hormones as the buildings being constructed. You can have the best architectural plans in the world (your DNA), the most skilled construction crew (your cells and enzymes), and the perfect construction schedule (your circadian rhythms), but if you don't deliver the RAW MATERIALS to the job site, nothing gets built.

During the 10-Day Detox, we're going to flood your body with exactly what it needs, and we will continue to expand on your understanding as we go.

PROTEIN provides amino acids—the literal building blocks your body uses for hormone creation, muscle repair (which increases metabolic rate), and stable blood sugar. Amino acids are the LEGO blocks of biology. Your body needs twenty different amino acids to build everything it needs to function. Nine of these are "essential," meaning your body cannot make them; they MUST come from food.

When you don't eat enough protein, your body has to make impossible choices. Do we use this amino acid to make stress hormones so you can survive the day, or do we use it to make sex hormones so you have a regular cycle? Do we repair gut lining so you can absorb nutrients, or do we make thick, shiny hair? Do we make infection-fighting antibodies, or do we make the neurotransmitters that keep you happy and motivated?

Your body will always choose survival over beauty, fertility, or feeling good. Always.

This is why "eating clean" on 1,200 calories doesn't work long-term. You might be eating vegetables and avoiding junk food, but if you're not providing enough raw materials—especially protein—your body goes into rationing mode. It keeps you alive, but it shuts down everything else. You become a shell of yourself, functioning but not thriving.

Specific amino acids have specific roles in your body. Tyrosine is needed to make thyroid hormones that control your metabolism and dopamine that gives you motivation and pleasure. Tryptophan is needed to make serotonin that stabilizes your mood and melatonin that helps you sleep. Arginine is needed for nitric oxide production that supports blood flow, cardiovascular health, and even sexual function. Glutamine is the primary fuel for your intestinal cells, keeping your gut healthy so you can absorb nutrients. Cysteine is needed for glutathione production—your body's master detoxifier that clears toxins and reduces inflammation.

If you're not eating adequate protein—and most women aren't—your body literally cannot build hormones optimally. It's like asking a construction

Chapter 8: Gut Health And Detoxification

crew to build a house but only delivering half the lumber. The crew will do their best, but the house will be incomplete, unstable, and unable to function as intended.

Healthy Fats

Healthy fats are not optional; your body NEEDS fat to make hormones. Here's something that might surprise you: All your sex hormones—estrogen, progesterone, and testosterone—plus your stress hormone cortisol, are made from cholesterol.

Yes, that's right. The same cholesterol you've been told to avoid is actually the essential starting material for every single one of your reproductive and stress hormones. The low-fat diet trend of the 1980s-2000s has left a generation of women with hormone imbalances because they've been eating fat-free everything for decades. Without enough dietary fat (and the ability to digest it), hormone synthesis is hindered.

Think of it like baking. If you want to make cookies, cake, and bread, you need flour as your base ingredient. You can't make any of them without flour. Cholesterol is the "flour" for your hormones—it's the base ingredient your body uses to create all of them.

Your body takes cholesterol and first converts it into something called pregnenolone. We call it the "mother hormone" because every other hormone is born from it. Think of pregnenolone as the raw dough before you decide what you're making.

From pregnenolone, your body can make progesterone (which helps you sleep, stay calm, and have regular cycles), DHEA (which gives you energy and eventually becomes testosterone), and several other important hormones.

Then these hormones get converted again into estrogen, testosterone, and cortisol—depending on what your body needs most at any given moment.

If you don't have enough cholesterol, this entire cascade falters. Your body can make SOME cholesterol in your liver, but when you're under stress (which all of us are) or not eating enough, your body faces a dilemma. It needs cholesterol to make ALL your hormones, but it has to prioritize. And guess which hormone wins? Cortisol—your stress hormone. Because when your body perceives stress (whether that's a work deadline, a hard workout, or simply not eating enough), it thinks you're in danger and needs cortisol to help you survive.

So your body literally steals the cholesterol that should have gone to making estrogen, progesterone, and testosterone, and diverts it all to making more cortisol instead. Like we talked about in Part I, this is called "pregnenolone steal"—your body is stealing the raw materials meant for your sex hormones and using them for stress hormones instead.

This is why women under chronic stress or eating very low-fat diets often experience irregular periods, worse PMS, low libido, mood swings, and difficulty losing weight. It's not that their bodies are broken—they simply don't have enough of the raw material (cholesterol and fats from food) to make both stress hormones AND sex hormones. When forced to choose, the body always picks survival (cortisol) over reproduction (sex hormones).

The solution? Eat enough healthy fats so your body has plenty of cholesterol to work with. When you're not in scarcity mode, your body can make all the hormones you need—both the stress hormones that keep you safe and the sex hormones that keep you feeling like yourself.

Micronutrients from vegetables act as cofactors for almost every metabolic process your body uses to regulate hormones, stabilize blood sugar, burn fat efficiently, detoxify, and produce energy. Magnesium alone is involved in over three hundred enzymatic reactions. Zinc is essential for thyroid function, immune health, and insulin sensitivity. B vitamins are required for energy production and methylation (which affects hormone metabolism). Vitamin C supports adrenal function and stress response.

Fiber from vegetables, fruits, and eventually whole grains binds to excess estrogen and carries it out of your body, feeds beneficial gut bacteria that support hormone metabolism, stabilizes blood sugar by slowing glucose absorption, creates volume in your stomach to trigger satiety, and ensures daily bowel movements (critical for hormone elimination).

Phytonutrients from colorful vegetables influence gene expression, reduce inflammation, support detoxification pathways, and even affect

Chapter 8: Gut Health And Detoxification

hormone receptor sensitivity. Cruciferous vegetables like broccoli and cauliflower contain compounds that help your body convert estrogen into beneficial metabolites rather than harmful ones—this is especially important for women in perimenopause.

During these ten days, you're going to eat MORE than you might expect. This is not a calorie-restriction protocol. We're removing inflammatory foods while providing abundant nutrition. Your body needs adequate calories and nutrients to heal, to produce hormones, to detoxify, and to feel safe enough to release stored fat. Restriction signals scarcity, which triggers your body to hold on to fat. Nourishment signals abundance, which allows your body to let go.

The Scale as a Learning Tool

One of the most valuable outcomes of the 10-Day Detox isn't just the weight you'll lose (though most women lose 5-8 pounds during these ten days)—it's what you'll learn about how YOUR body responds to different foods.

When we remove all the inflammatory triggers and then systematically reintroduce foods one at a time, you become a scientist studying your own biology. You'll discover which foods cause bloating, which ones make you retain water, which ones trigger cravings or energy crashes, which ones affect your sleep quality, which ones cause digestive upset, and which ones make you feel amazing.

As we discussed in the earlier chapter on using the scale as a tool, daily weight fluctuations are normal and expected. Your weight can vary in a single day based on water retention from sodium, carbohydrate intake, hormones, inflammation, exercise, sleep quality, stress, medications, bowel movements, and time of day. None of this is fat gain—it's just your body being a body.

But here's where the detox becomes powerful: When you have a clean baseline (low inflammation, good hydration, regular elimination, stable eating pattern), you can use the scale to identify patterns. If you reintroduce dairy and suddenly gain three pounds overnight along with feeling bloated and congested, that's valuable information. That's not fat gain—it's inflammation and water retention telling you that dairy doesn't serve your body right now. You can choose to eliminate it entirely, or you can choose to have it occasionally knowing it will cause temporary water retention.

This is how you move from generic diet rules to personalized nutrition based on YOUR unique biology. This is food freedom—making informed choices about what you eat based on how it makes you feel and whether it serves your goals, not based on arbitrary rules or moral judgments about "good" and "bad" foods.

Getting Wins on the Scale: Motivation that Compounds

Let's be honest: Seeing results matters. We know you want to lose weight for deeper reasons—to feel confident, to have energy to play with your kids or grandkids, to reduce your disease risk, to feel like yourself again. Those are the reasons that will sustain you long-term.

But in the short term, especially when you've been struggling and feeling defeated, seeing the scale move down is incredibly motivating. It's validation that your efforts are working. It's proof that your body can change. It's momentum that makes you want to keep going.

Most women lose 5-8 pounds during the 10-Day Detox. Some of that is water weight and inflammation (especially in the first 3-4 days), but some of it is actual fat loss. And here's what I've seen working with nearly 1,800 women 1:1—when you get that initial win, when you see the scale drop and feel your energy improve and notice your clothes fitting better, something shifts mentally. You start to believe that change is possible. You start to trust your body again. You start to feel empowered instead of defeated.

That momentum matters. It's not vanity; it's psychology. When you see results, you're more likely to continue the behaviors that created those results. When you feel deprived and nothing is changing, you're more likely to give up and return to old patterns.

The 10-Day Detox is designed to give you quick wins while teaching you sustainable principles. You'll lose weight, but more importantly, you'll learn

Chapter 8: Gut Health And Detoxification

how to eat in a way that supports your hormones, reduces inflammation, and makes weight loss easier long-term.

Client Stories: What's Possible

"In the first week I've already lost five pounds... I crave vegetables now!" —**Amanda**

Amanda came to us after years of yo-yo dieting. She'd lost and regained the same thirty pounds multiple times. She was exhausted, bloated, and convinced her body was broken. Within the first week of the detox, her bloating disappeared. By day ten, she'd lost seven pounds and had more energy than she'd had in years. But what surprised her most was that she actually started craving vegetables. She'd forgotten how naturally sweet and satisfying whole foods could be.

"After just a week of changing my habits, my inflammation went down and my energy improved. My mantra now is, 'I will listen to my body and give it what it needs.'" —**Brianne**

Brianne discovered during the detox that dairy was a major trigger for her. She'd always had sinus congestion, joint pain, and persistent bloating, but she'd never connected it to her daily yogurt, cheese, and milk. When she eliminated dairy for ten days and then reintroduced it, the connection was undeniable. She woke up congested, her joints ached, and she felt bloated and uncomfortable. Now she chooses to avoid dairy most of the time, and when she does have it, she knows exactly what to expect. That awareness is power.

"I lost eight pounds in ten days, my bloating is gone, and I have so much energy!" —**Katelyn**

Katelyn was shocked by how much better she felt without gluten. She didn't have celiac disease, but she definitely had sensitivity. Her digestive issues resolved, her skin cleared up, her brain fog lifted, and she lost significant water weight. She now eats gluten occasionally but has learned that when she does, she needs to be prepared for the consequences. Most of the time, she chooses whole, naturally gluten-free foods because they make her feel so much better.

These women aren't special or uniquely disciplined. They're women just like you who were struggling with the exact same challenges you're facing. The difference is they gave their bodies a chance to communicate by removing the noise (inflammatory foods) and listening to the signals.

The 10-Day Detox Protocol

Now that you understand the science behind the 10-Day Detox, let's talk about the practical details of what you'll eat during these ten days.

The Foundation: Foods that Heal

For all ten days, you'll be eating unlimited amounts of these foundational foods:

Non-Starchy Vegetables (Unlimited)

These are the cornerstone of the detox. Vegetables provide volume, fiber, micronutrients, and phytonutrients while being very low in calories. You literally cannot eat too many vegetables during this detox.

Leafy greens like spinach, kale, arugula, collard greens, Swiss chard, lettuce, and bok choy are rich in folate, magnesium, vitamin K, calcium, and iron. These support estrogen metabolism, bone health, energy production, and detoxification.

Cruciferous vegetables including broccoli, cauliflower, Brussels sprouts, cabbage, and bok choy contain indole-3-carbinol and sulforaphane—compounds that support healthy estrogen metabolism by helping your body convert estrogen into beneficial metabolites rather than harmful ones. This is especially important during perimenopause when estrogen dominance is common.

Colorful vegetables such as bell peppers, tomatoes, carrots, beets, eggplant, and summer squash provide antioxidants like carotenoids, lycopene, and anthocyanins that reduce inflammation and oxidative stress. The more colors on your plate, the more diverse phytonutrients you're getting.

Alliums like onions, garlic, shallots, and leeks contain sulfur compounds that support detoxification and liver function—helping your body process and eliminate used hormones efficiently.

Other approved vegetables include asparagus, green beans, snap peas, snow peas, zucchini, cucumber, celery, radishes, mushrooms, hearts of palm, jicama, and artichokes.

Your target: Half your plate (or more) at lunch and dinner should be vegetables. If you're already doing that, aim for two servings at each meal. Add vegetables at breakfast if possible—spinach in eggs, roasted vegetables on the side, or a green smoothie.

Clean Protein Sources
(4-6 oz per meal, liberal during first three days)

Protein is essential for hormone production, muscle maintenance, satiety, blood sugar stability, and gut repair. During the first three days especially, when cravings and hunger may be strongest, we encourage you to lean into protein—eat six ounces instead of four, have protein at every meal and snack, and don't be afraid of eating too much.

Wild-caught fish including salmon, sardines, mackerel, herring, rainbow trout, and shrimp are excellent sources of omega-3 fatty acids (anti-inflammatory), complete protein, and minerals like selenium (thyroid support).

Pasture-raised eggs provide complete protein, healthy fats, choline (liver and brain health), and fat-soluble vitamins. The yolks contain most of the nutrition—don't skip them.

Organic, pasture-raised poultry such as chicken and turkey offers lean protein with minimal inflammatory potential when sourced well.

Grass-fed, organic red meat like beef, bison, lamb, and venison provides protein, iron, zinc, B vitamins, and when grass-fed, contains beneficial omega-3s and CLA (conjugated linoleic acid).

Conventionally raised animal products contain hormones, antibiotics, and inflammatory compounds from the animals' diet and living conditions. When you're trying to reduce your toxic load and balance your hormones, choosing the cleanest protein sources possible makes a significant difference. Choose organic and pasture raised whenever possible.

Plant-based options including organic tofu and tempeh can work for vegetarians, but ensure you're getting adequate complete protein throughout the day. Don't hate the messenger, but it is hard to get enough protein in and keep your protein higher than your carbs for blood sugar stability through midlife as a vegetarian or vegan. If you aren't supplementing and desire to continue this lifestyle, you'll likely need to make that adjustment.

Healthy Fats (Liberal, especially days 1-3)

Fat is not the enemy—it's essential for hormone production, satiety, nutrient absorption, and reducing inflammation. During the first three days especially, be liberal with healthy fats. Use them to cook your vegetables, dress your salads, and add richness to your meals. This will keep you satisfied and help manage cravings as your body adjusts.

Cooking oils: Avocado oil, coconut oil, olive oil (better for low-heat or finishing), and grass-fed butter or ghee (starting day six if you tolerate dairy).

Whole food fats: Avocados and guacamole (no added sugar), nuts including almonds, walnuts, pecans, macadamia nuts, cashews, pistachios, and pine nuts, seeds such as pumpkin seeds, sunflower seeds, sesame seeds, flax seeds, chia seeds, and hemp hearts, and olives.

Nut and seed butters from the above nuts and seeds (check labels for added sugar or oils).

Target: Use fats liberally in cooking and food preparation. Add a thumb-sized portion of nuts or seeds to salads or snacks. Include avocado or nut butter with meals.

The Phases of Reintroduction

DAYS 1-3: The Foundation Phase

These first three days are the most important and often the most challenging. You're removing all added sugar, all dairy, all grains and starches, all fruit (temporarily), all alcohol, all caffeine (or significantly reducing it), and all processed foods.

What you're eating: Unlimited non-starchy vegetables, 4-6 oz of clean protein per meal (lean toward six ounces during these days with less carbs), liberal amounts of healthy fats for cooking and satiety, water and herbal tea only, and seasonings, herbs, and spices without added sugar.

What to expect: You're removing all the inflammatory foods at once. Your body is adjusting to the absence of caffeine, sugar, processed foods, and carbohydrates. This is typically the hardest phase.

Physical: You may experience detox symptoms like headaches (especially if cutting caffeine), fatigue or low energy, cravings for sugar or carbs, mild irritability or mood swings, digestive changes (could be looser stools or constipation as your gut adjusts), and possible hunger if you're not eating enough protein and fat.

Mental/Emotional: You might feel deprived or resentful, question whether you can do this, think about the foods you're "not allowed" to have, or wonder if it's worth it.

Days 1-3 can be challenging. These are temporary and indicate your body is adjusting and detoxing. They typically resolve by day four.

How to succeed during days 1-3: Eat enough—this is not a calorie-restriction protocol. If you're hungry, eat more protein and vegetables with plenty of healthy fats. Stay hydrated—aim for at least half your body weight in ounces of water daily. If you're experiencing caffeine headaches, try green tea to take the edge off rather than going completely cold turkey if you were drinking large amounts of coffee. Prioritize sleep—your body is working hard to detoxify and heal. Get to bed early and aim for 8-9 hours.

Prepare your food in advance—batch cook proteins, chop vegetables, make a big salad, have convenient options ready.

DAYS 4-5: Adding Fruit

On day four, you can add back low-glycemic fruits. This gives you natural sweetness while keeping blood sugar relatively stable.

Approved fruits (two servings per day): Berries including blueberries, strawberries, raspberries, blackberries, and pomegranate seeds are highest in antioxidants and fiber, lowest in sugar. Citrus like grapefruit, oranges, lemons, and limes provide vitamin C and support detoxification. Other low-glycemic options include green apples, pears, cantaloupe, and small portions of other melons.

Serving size: one cup fresh berries or one medium piece of fruit (about the size of a tennis ball).

Timing: Ideally consume fruit earlier in the day (breakfast, morning snack, or lunch) when you need the energy carbohydrates provide. Fruit is nature's candy—take a moment to appreciate how sweet it tastes when your palate has been cleansed of added sugars. To reduce blood sugar spikes, eat it at the end of your meal or pair it with a protein or fat if it's a snack.

What to expect: By days 4-5, you should be feeling significantly better.

Physical: Energy is returning, headaches resolve, bloating is decreasing, sleep is improving, cravings are diminishing, and you may notice the scale dropping (mostly water weight and inflammation at this point). As you increase carbs with fruit, you can start to decrease fat if you were leaning heavily into it. Find that balance that works for your body by listening. Were you satisfied? Were you still hungry?

Mental/Emotional: You start to believe this is working, feel proud of yourself for sticking with it, notice you're thinking about food less obsessively, and feel hopeful and motivated.

What helps: On day four, you add fruit back, which provides natural sweetness and feels like a treat after three days without. Celebrate your progress. Notice how much better you feel compared to days 1-3.

DAYS 6-10: Strategic Carbohydrate Reintroduction

Starting day six, you can begin adding back grains and starches—but we're going to do this strategically, one food category at a time, so you can learn how your body responds.

Day six also allows: Grass-fed butter or ghee, plain yogurt or kefir (if you tolerate dairy—watch for bloating, congestion, digestive upset), and a small amount of cheese (maximum one serving per day, treated more like a condiment than a food group). Choose one to integrate at a time vs adding grains/starches and dairy all together. My recommended reintroduction order:

REINTRODUCTION PHASE 1 (Days 6-7):
Paleo-Friendly Complex Carbohydrates

Start with starchy vegetables and naturally gluten-free, grain-free carbohydrate sources: sweet potatoes, white potatoes, winter squash (butternut, acorn, spaghetti), beets, green peas, parsnips, and plantains.

Serving size: 1/2 to one cup or one medium potato/sweet potato per day (one serving total).

Why these first: These are whole foods, nutrient-dense, naturally gluten-free, high in fiber, and the least likely to cause inflammatory reactions. They provide clean carbohydrates for energy and thyroid support without the potential issues of grains or dairy.

What to expect: You're in a groove. You've figured out meals you enjoy, your body has adjusted, and you're feeling great.

> *Physical:* Energy is steady and good throughout the day, bloating is minimal or gone, skin starts clearing up and looking brighter, sleep is deep and restorative, digestive issues resolve (regular bowel movements, no bloating), and the scale continues to drop.
>
> *Mental/Emotional:* You feel confident and empowered, food freedom is emerging (you don't feel controlled by cravings), you're proud of your commitment, and you start to believe sustainable change is possible.

What helps: On day six, you can start adding back strategic carbohydrates or dairy. This feels exciting and also allows you to start learning how your body responds to different foods. Stay mindful and observant. Focus on what you CAN have, vs leaning into feelings of restriction.

RENITRODUCTION PHASE 2 (Days 8-9):
Non-Gluten Whole Grains

If you tolerated the starchy vegetables well, add in naturally gluten-free whole grains: brown rice, wild rice, quinoa, oats (certified gluten-free), buckwheat, millet, and legumes like beans, lentils, and chickpeas (which also provide protein and fiber).

Serving size: 1/2 to one cup cooked grains or legumes per day.

Why these second: These are whole, minimally processed grains that provide B vitamins, fiber, minerals, and sustained energy. They're gluten-free, so they're less likely to trigger inflammatory responses than wheat-based products.

What to expect: You're systematically reintroducing foods and gathering data about how your body responds. This is where the real learning happens.

Physical: Continued improvement in energy, mood, sleep, and digestion if you're reintroducing foods your body tolerates well. Possible symptoms if you reintroduce a food that's inflammatory for you (bloating, congestion, digestive upset, water retention, skin breakouts, energy crashes).

Mental/Emotional: Excitement about what you're learning, awareness of how different foods make you feel, confidence in your ability to read your body's signals, and eagerness to continue nourishing yourself well.

What helps: Journal carefully about what you eat and how you feel. Don't rush the reintroduction process. If you react poorly to a food, that's valuable information, not failure. Stay curious and compassionate with yourself.

REINTRODUCTION PHASE 3 (Day ten and beyond):
Dairy or Gluten—Choose Your Priority

If you've been missing dairy more than gluten, reintroduce small amounts of high-quality dairy in its most whole form. If you've been missing bread, pasta, or baked goods more, reintroduce gluten in its most whole, organic form.

Dairy reintroduction: Plain Greek yogurt, kefir, small amounts of cheese (preferably raw, grass-fed), or grass-fed butter/ghee. Watch for symptoms: bloating, gas, congestion, sinus issues, digestive upset, skin breakouts, or water retention. If you experience any of these, dairy is likely inflammatory for you right now.

Gluten reintroduction: Organic whole grain bread, organic pasta, organic oats (if not certified gluten-free), or other whole wheat products. Avoid processed foods with gluten—choose the most whole, minimally processed versions possible. Watch for symptoms: bloating, digestive upset, brain fog, fatigue, joint pain, headaches, or skin issues. If you experience any of these, gluten sensitivity is likely present.

What to expect by day ten: The transformation. Most women report significant changes by the end of ten days: 5-10 pounds lost (combination of water weight, inflammation, and fat), dramatically reduced bloating ("I don't look pregnant anymore!"), significantly improved energy ("I wake up refreshed instead of exhausted"), better sleep quality, clearer skin, reduced joint pain and inflammation, more stable mood, elimination of or major reduction in cravings, improved digestion and regular bowel movements, and most importantly: knowledge about which foods serve your body and which ones don't.

Critical Reintroduction Rules

Introduce ONE new food category at a time—not dairy and gluten on the same day. If you experience any symptoms you're monitoring, wait 48–72 hours before adding another food so you can clearly identify which one caused the reaction. You don't need to reintroduce gluten or dairy yet.

Continue adding foods slowly, one at a time, and extend this phase for as long as you need.

Keep a journal recording what you ate and how you felt—energy, digestion, mood, sleep, bloating, cravings, and scale weight. Choose whole, organic forms of reintroduced foods rather than processed versions. Treat dairy like a condiment, not a food group—a sprinkle of cheese, a dollop of yogurt, not multiple servings per meal.

Remember: This is not about creating a list of "forbidden foods." This is about gathering data on which foods serve your body and your goals and which ones create inflammation, water retention, digestive upset, or other symptoms. You can choose to eat foods that don't serve you, but you'll be making that choice consciously, knowing the consequences, rather than eating unconsciously and wondering why you aren't feeling well.

Approved Foods Reference

For a complete and comprehensive list of approved vegetables, proteins, healthy fats, fruits, and grains/starches with specific serving sizes and timing, please refer to the Detox Approved Foods List found here: https://empoweredweightlossbook.com/.

Strategies to Succeed: Setting Yourself Up for Success

The 10-Day Detox works, but only if you actually do it. And you'll only actually do it if you set yourself up for success from the beginning. Let's talk about how to prepare, when to start, and how to navigate the common pitfalls.

Choosing the Right Time to Start

Timing matters. Don't set yourself up for failure by starting during a week when success is nearly impossible.

Pick a time when you can eat at home most of the time. Restaurants, social events, and travel make the detox significantly harder. You need control over your food environment, especially during the first 3-5 days.

Avoid weeks with holidays, birthdays, weddings, or major social celebrations. It's not that you can never have these things—it's that starting a detox the week of Thanksgiving or your best friend's wedding is setting yourself up to feel deprived and tempted. Choose a quieter week.

Consider your work schedule and stress levels. If you're in the middle of a major work deadline, traveling for business, or experiencing unusual stress, this might not be the ideal time. The detox works best when you can prioritize sleep, stress management, and self-care.

For women still cycling, avoid starting the week before your period when cravings are naturally highest due to hormonal fluctuations. The week after your period ends is often ideal—energy is higher, cravings are lower, and your body is more insulin-sensitive during the follicular phase.

Think about which day of the week to start. Many women prefer starting on a Wednesday, which means they finish on a Friday. This allows them to enter the weekend with completion momentum and confidence. Others prefer starting on a Saturday when they have time to meal prep and adjust without work stress. Choose what works best for your schedule and personality.

The key principle: choose a week when you have the highest likelihood of success. This is a ten-day commitment to yourself. Treat it like an important appointment that you won't reschedule.

Meal Planning: Formula Over Rigidity

You'll notice we haven't given you a rigid meal plan with specific recipes for every meal of every day. That's intentional. We want you to learn the formula so you can apply it to foods you actually enjoy, customize based on your preferences and what's available, and develop food freedom rather than meal-plan dependency.

The formula for every meal during the detox:

Days 1-3:

- Protein (4-6 oz, lean toward six oz)
- Non-starchy vegetables (unlimited, fill half your plate or more)
- Healthy fats (liberal—use for cooking, dressing, or adding richness)

Days 4-5, Add:

- Fruit (up to two servings daily, preferably earlier in the day)

Days 6-10, Add:

- Grains/starches (one serving daily—replace one serving of fruit to start if you were having two—following the strategic reintroduction order)
- Optional dairy (if choosing to test, maximum 1-2 servings daily, treated like a condiment)

Breakfast examples:
- **Vegetable scramble:** 2-3 eggs scrambled with two cups of vegetables like spinach, mushrooms, peppers, and onions. Cook in up to one tablespoon of coconut oil (or butter/ghee day six and on)
- **Protein bowl:** Leftover protein from dinner (chicken, salmon, ground beef) with roasted vegetables and avocado
- **Smoothie:** Clean protein powder, spinach, frozen berries (days 4+), almond butter, unsweetened coconut milk, ice
- **Simple:** Hard-boiled eggs with avocado, cucumber slices, and cherry tomatoes

Lunch examples:
- **Big detox salad:** 3+ cups mixed greens, 4-6 oz grilled chicken or salmon, cucumbers, tomatoes, avocado, pumpkin seeds, olive oil and lemon dressing

- **Leftover dinner:** Protein and vegetables from the night before
- **Stir-fry over cauliflower rice:** Protein of choice with mixed vegetables cooked in sesame or avocado oil with garlic and ginger
- **Lettuce wraps:** Ground turkey or beef cooked with vegetables, wrapped in large lettuce leaves

Dinner examples:
- Grilled salmon with roasted Brussels sprouts and sweet potato (days 6+)
- Chicken stir-fry with broccoli, peppers, and snap peas over cauliflower rice
- Grass-fed burger (no bun days 1-5 or wrapped in lettuce) with side salad and roasted vegetables
- Shrimp and vegetable skewers with side of grilled zucchini and a large salad

Snacks (if needed):
- Raw vegetables with guacamole
- Apple slices (days 4+) with unsweetened almond butter
- Hard-boiled eggs
- Handful of nuts and berries (days 4+)
- Celery with nut butter

For complete meal plans, recipe suggestions, and a sample menu, please refer to the Detox Meal Planning Guide found here: https://empoweredweightlossbook.com/.

The beauty of the formula approach: you can eat foods you already enjoy, you can adapt based on what's available or in season, you can cook once and eat leftovers, and you develop the skill of building balanced meals rather than depending on someone else's meal plan.

Preparing for Success: What to Do Before Day One

The day before you start (or even 2-3 days before), take these steps:

- **Clear your kitchen of temptation.** You don't have to throw things away, but put tempting foods out of sight, in the back of the pantry, or ask family members to keep their snacks in a separate area. Out of sight, out of mind actually works.
- **Grocery shop and meal prep.** Buy all your approved proteins, vegetables, healthy fats, and approved foods for at least the first 3-5 days. Batch cook some proteins—grill several chicken breasts, hard-boil a dozen eggs, cook a big pot of ground turkey or beef. Chop vegetables and store in clear containers at eye level in your fridge. Make a big batch of salad dressing with olive oil, lemon, and herbs.
- **Set up your water system.** Get a water bottle you love (thirty-two ounces or larger). Set reminders on your phone to drink water throughout the day. Put a glass of water on your nightstand to drink first thing in the morning.
- **Plan your wind-down routine.** Decide what you'll do in the evening instead of snacking—herbal tea, reading, journaling, bath, gentle yoga. Have your plan ready.
- **Tell supportive people.** Let your family, close friends, or accountability partners know you're doing this detox. Ask for their support. You don't need to justify or defend your choice—just inform people who might be eating with you or are affected by your food choices.
- **Take "before" measurements.** Weigh yourself, take measurements (chest, waist, hips, thighs), take a progress photo, and note how you're currently feeling (energy, mood, sleep quality, bloating, joint pain, etc.). You'll want this baseline for comparison.

Navigating the Common Pitfalls

Even with perfect preparation, you'll face challenges. Here's how to handle the most common ones:

PITFALL #1: Hunger and Cravings (Especially Days 1-3)

This is the number one reason people struggle or quit early. You feel hungry, deprived, and like you're white-knuckling through cravings.

The solution: EAT MORE. This bears repeating: You should not be hungry during this detox. If you're hungry, you're not eating enough.

During days 1-3 especially, be generous with portions. Eat six ounces of protein instead of four. Cook your vegetables in plenty of healthy fat—coconut oil, avocado oil, grass-fed butter (day 6+). Add avocado to meals. Snack on nuts, seeds, hard-boiled eggs, or vegetables with guacamole. Fill up on volume—eat as many non-starchy vegetables as you want.

Hunger is often a sign you're either not eating enough total food, not eating enough protein, not eating enough fat, or going too long between meals. Fix these issues and hunger resolves.

Cravings for sugar and carbs are normal during the first 2-3 days as your blood sugar stabilizes and your body adjusts to burning fat for fuel instead of glucose. Stay hydrated, keep protein and fat intake high, and remind yourself these cravings are temporary. By day four, they typically diminish significantly.

PITFALL #2: Detox Symptoms (Headaches, Fatigue, Body Aches)

If you're cutting caffeine, added sugar, or processed foods, your body will go through a withdrawal period. This is temporary but can be uncomfortable.

The solution: Support your body through the transition.

For caffeine withdrawal: If you were drinking a lot of coffee (half a pot or more daily), going completely cold turkey can trigger severe headaches. Instead, transition to green tea, which has less caffeine but enough to take the edge off. Reduce gradually over the first 2-3 days if needed. Stay hydrated—dehydration makes headaches worse. Consider taking magnesium, which can help with headache relief.

For fatigue: Prioritize sleep. Go to bed earlier than usual. Take naps if possible. Your body is working hard to detoxify and heal. Rest is productive, not lazy.

For body aches: Gentle movement helps—walking, stretching, yoga. Epsom salt baths can ease muscle soreness. Stay hydrated. These symptoms typically resolve by day four.

Remember: Detox symptoms are a sign that your body was dependent on these substances and is now recalibrating. This is evidence that the detox is needed and working.

PITFALL #3: Social Pressure and Temptation

Friends invite you to dinner. Your spouse orders pizza. Your coworker brings donuts to the office. Social situations and other people's food choices can derail you if you're not prepared.

The solution: Have a plan and set boundaries.

Politely decline invitations or suggest alternative activities that don't revolve around food. "I'm doing a hormone reset right now, but I'd love to go for a walk instead!"

Eat before social events so you're not hungry and tempted.

Bring your own food to gatherings if appropriate.

Practice saying "No thank you, I'm good" without over-explaining or justifying. You don't owe anyone an explanation for your food choices.

Remove yourself from the kitchen or break room if others are eating tempting foods.

Remember your "why"—why are you doing this detox? Reconnect with that reason when temptation arises.

PITFALL #4: All-or-Nothing Thinking

You eat something "off plan" and immediately think, *I ruined it. I'll just start over Monday.* This is diet mentality, and it's destructive.

The solution: Progress over perfection.

If you eat something that wasn't on the approved list, simply return to the protocol at your next meal. Don't punish yourself, don't restrict extra to "make up for it," and don't throw in the towel and binge because "it's already ruined."

One meal or one food choice doesn't undo your progress. Your body doesn't work on a pass/fail grading system. Just get back on track and keep going.

Ask yourself: What triggered this? Were you too hungry? Were you unprepared? Was it emotional eating? Learn from it and adjust your plan to prevent the same trigger next time.

PITFALL #5: Reintroducing Everything Too Quickly

You finish day ten feeling amazing and immediately go out for pizza, ice cream, and margaritas. You add back dairy, gluten, sugar, and alcohol all at once. This defeats the entire purpose of the detox.

The solution: Slow, strategic reintroduction.

The reintroduction phase is just as important as the elimination phase. This is where you learn which foods serve your body and which ones don't.

This isn't a race. Add one new food category at a time. Watch for reactions: bloating, digestive upset, energy crashes, mood changes, skin breakouts, joint pain, congestion, headaches, or water retention. Keep a journal, tracking what you ate and how you felt.

If a food causes a negative reaction, remove it for a few days before testing another food or retesting it to flush fluid retention and inflammation.

Don't view day eleven as "freedom from restriction." View it as "continuing to nourish my body with the addition of learning which foods work well for me."

You can have pizza and margaritas occasionally—but give your body a chance to communicate with you first. Learn what serves you. Then make informed choices.

Detox 2.0: Optional Upgrades to Enhance Your Results

The nutrition protocol is the foundation of the detox and will deliver results on its own. But if you want to take your detox to the next level, here are some optional additions that support your body's natural detoxification processes.

Challenge yourself to choose 1-2 of these per day for an enhanced detox experience if you feel like you've already been eating closely to the protocol. If the protocol already seems overwhelming, skip these add-ons until the next time you revisit the detox. We recommend that our clients revisit the detox quarterly as a way to recalibrate, focus on their health, give their body a break, and never slip too far away from where they feel their best.

Get Your Sweat On

Exercise, sauna, hot yoga, or any activity that makes you sweat helps eliminate toxins through your skin (one of your body's four main detoxification pathways). Sweating also supports lymphatic drainage and improves circulation.

Recommendations: 20-30 minutes of gentle movement that makes you sweat (brisk walking, gentle yoga flow, cycling), infrared sauna session (15-20 minutes), or hot yoga class (be mindful of intensity—we want stress-reducing movement, not high-intensity cortisol-spiking exercise during the detox).

Fiber Boosters For Toxin Binding

Ground flaxseed or chia seeds help bind toxins in your digestive tract and carry them out of your body. They also provide omega-3 fatty acids and support regular bowel movements.

Recommendations: Add 1-2 tablespoons of ground flaxseed or chia seeds to smoothies, salads, or yogurt (days 6+).

Medicinal Detox Foods

Seaweed, chlorella, and spirulina are nutrient-dense foods that support your body's natural detoxification processes and provide minerals and antioxidants.

Recommendations: Add one teaspoon spirulina or chlorella powder to smoothies, or include seaweed salad or nori sheets with meals. You can also grab supplements with these ingredients in capsule form if you prefer.

Detoxifying Herbs And Spices

Garlic, turmeric, ginger, cilantro, rosemary, parsley, basil, and cinnamon all have detoxifying properties and reduce inflammation.

Recommendations: Cook with these herbs and spices liberally. Make golden milk with turmeric, ginger, and unsweetened coconut milk. Add fresh cilantro to salads. Use garlic and ginger in stir-fries.

Detoxifying Teas

Dandelion root tea, green tea, Traditional Medicinals EveryDay Detox Tea, ginger/fennel/peppermint/turmeric/hibiscus teas, or dandy blend (dandelion coffee alternative) support liver function and detoxification.

Recommendations: Drink 1-2 cups daily in place of regular tea or coffee.

Chapter 9: The 10-Day Detox Protocol

Dry Skin Brushing

Dry brushing stimulates your lymphatic system (which doesn't have a pump like your cardiovascular system and relies on muscle movement and external stimulation). This supports detoxification and immune function.

Recommendations: Before showering, use a natural-bristle brush to brush your skin in long strokes toward your heart. Start at your feet and work upward. Takes 3-5 minutes.

Epsom Salt Baths

Epsom salt (magnesium sulfate) helps relax muscles, reduce inflammation, and support detoxification. The warm water also supports lymphatic drainage and stress reduction.

Recommendations: Add 1-2 cups Epsom salt to a warm bath. Soak for 20-30 minutes 2-3 times per week. Add essential oils like lavender for additional relaxation.

Again, these upgrades are optional, not required. If you're feeling overwhelmed by the food protocol alone, skip these for now and consider adding them next time you do the detox. If you want to maximize results and have the capacity, choose 1-2 daily.

The Power of Journaling, Gratitude, and Mindset

This detox is not just about what you eat. It's about how you think, how you talk to yourself, and how you cultivate awareness of your body's signals.

Throughout these ten days, we encourage you to journal daily. Write about how you're feeling physically, emotionally, and mentally. Write about what you're learning about yourself and your relationship with food. Write about challenges you're facing and strategies that are working. Write about wins, no matter how small.

Gratitude practice is also incredibly powerful. Research shows that daily gratitude lowers stress and anxiety, improves sleep quality, reduces depression, strengthens relationships, and even boosts immune function. When you focus on what you're grateful for, your brain literally cannot simultaneously focus on what you're lacking or struggling with.

Reflection helps you learn. At the end of each day, ask yourself: What did I eat today and how did I feel afterward? What was challenging today and how did I handle it? What went well today that I want to repeat? What do I want to adjust tomorrow? What am I learning about my body and my relationship with food?

These practices—journaling, gratitude, and reflection—help you develop the self-awareness and mindset that will serve you long after the detox ends. This is how you move from unconscious eating driven by cravings and habits to conscious, empowered eating driven by self-knowledge and choice.

For daily journaling prompts, gratitude exercises, and reflection questions specific to each day of the detox, please refer to the Detox Daily Journal found here: https://empoweredweightlossbook.com/.

After Day Ten: Transitioning to Sustainable Eating

The 10-Day Detox is not a temporary restriction followed by returning to your old eating patterns. It's a reset that launches you into a sustainable, personalized way of eating that supports your hormones, reduces inflammation, and makes weight loss easier long-term.

After day ten, you transition into "The Well-Rounded Plate" (covered in the next chapter), where you'll learn how to build balanced meals that include all food groups, customize your carbohydrate intake based on your individual insulin sensitivity and activity level, enjoy treats and special occasions without guilt or derailing your progress, and maintain the principles of eating whole, unprocessed foods most of the time while leaving room for flexibility and enjoyment.

The detox taught you which foods make you feel amazing and support your goals. Now you get to choose: Do you want to continue avoiding foods that cause bloating, inflammation, or water retention? Or do you want to include them occasionally, knowing exactly what the consequences will be?

This is food freedom—making conscious, informed choices based on your own body's signals, not arbitrary rules or someone else's diet plan.

Some women discover they feel so much better without dairy or gluten that they choose to avoid them most of the time. Others find they tolerate these foods well in moderation. Some women realize that sugar is their trigger and choose to keep added sugar very low. Others find that occasional treats fit perfectly into their life without causing issues.

There's no single "right" answer. The right answer is what works for YOUR body and YOUR life.

Your Invitation: You Don't Have to Do This— You Get to Do It

We want to leave you with this reframe: You don't have to do this detox. You get to do it.

You get to give your body a break from inflammatory foods that have been creating chaos in your system. You get to flood your cells with the nutrients they've been starving for. You get to learn which foods serve you and which ones work against you. You get to experience what it feels like to have steady energy, restful sleep, and a calm, non-inflamed body. You get to see the scale move and remember that your body is capable of change. You get to prove to yourself that you can commit to something and follow through.

This is not punishment. This is not deprivation. This is a gift you're giving yourself.

Your body has been working so hard to protect you, to keep you alive, to function despite being undernourished and overburdened. It's been doing the best it can with what you've given it. Now you get to give it what it actually needs. And when you do, it will respond. It will heal. It will release

Part II: Nutrition, Foundations & Lifestyle

stored fat. It will produce hormones properly. It will communicate clearly about what it needs.

Your body is not broken. It's been waiting for you to give it the support it needs to thrive.

These ten days are your opportunity to hit the reset button, to quiet the inflammation, to restore hormone balance, and to finally break free from the restrict-binge cycle that has kept you stuck.

You've got this. We believe in you. Your body believes in you. Now it's time to believe in yourself.

Let's begin.

Resources referenced in this chapter

(available at https://empoweredweightlossbook.com/):

- Detox Approved Foods List (comprehensive)
- Detox Meal Planning Guide with Sample Menu
- Detox Daily Journal with Gratitude Prompts and Reflection Questions
- Before & After Tracking Sheet (weight, measurements, symptoms, photos)
- Detox Prep Checklist
- Detox 2.0 Enhancement Guide

The Well-Rounded Plate

Sustainable Eating After Detox

Congratulations—you've made it through the detox. Your gut is healing, your inflammation is down, and you're starting to feel like yourself again. Now what?

This is where most programs fail you. They give you a restrictive protocol, you see results, and then they send you back out into the world with no roadmap for what comes next. You're left wondering: Do I eat like this forever? What if I want pizza? What about birthdays and vacations? And before you know it, you're back where you started.

Not here. This chapter is about building a sustainable, flexible way of eating that supports your goals without making you feel deprived or controlled by food rules.

A well-rounded plate evolves from **Home Base.** Remember: Home Base never goes out of style. We always need water, vegetables, sleep, and movement. But now, we go one level deeper. This is where we identify your *ideal amounts* for each category based on how your unique body responds.

Everyone is different. How insulin resistant you are, how your metabolism functions, and even your genetics (through DNA testing) can determine how well you tolerate different amounts and types of carbohydrates. We call this your **carbohydrate tipping point**—the perfect amount of carbs your body needs to feel good, sleep well, perform well, maintain consistent energy, support hormone production, and still lose weight.

For some women, that means staying closer to a Paleo-style plate—lean proteins, lots of vegetables, berries, starchy vegetables like potatoes or yams, and fewer grains. For others, a Mediterranean-style plate works beautifully—whole grains, legumes, olive oil, and fish.

There's no right or wrong. Your body holds the answers.

My goal for you is to help you write your own manual—one that teaches you how *your* body loses weight and feels its best because there isn't a one-size-fits-all model. You discover this through curiosity and experimentation, by adding foods and watching how your body responds.

With clients, we often pair this process with DNA testing. This gives us insight into how your body processes macronutrients, how efficient your methylation and detox pathways are, and what micronutrients you might need more of to support your hormone balance. It's not a gimmick—it's a shortcut to personalization. But even without it, the principles still work. Thousands of women have found their best results through this exact process before DNA testing ever came into the picture.

So if that's not accessible right now, don't worry. Your body is still your best lab.

This isn't a rigid formula—it's a framework. It ensures you're getting the building blocks your body needs (protein for hormones and muscle, fats for hormones and satiety, vegetables for micronutrients and fiber) while leaving room for flexibility and enjoyment. Half your plate of vegetables and protein at every meal stays true for everyone, but the amount of carbs and fat on your plate are determined by your biology. We will help you uncover that through this process of trial and error as you add foods back in and continue to get progress post detox.

Building Your Plate

Every meal you eat should be a balance of protein, non-starchy vegetables, and either healthy fat or carbohydrates—or a little of both. The more vegetables, the better. Understanding what the different foods on your plate

Chapter 10: The Well-Rounded Plate

are responsible for will help you prioritize them and understand when you need more.

Well-Rounded Plate

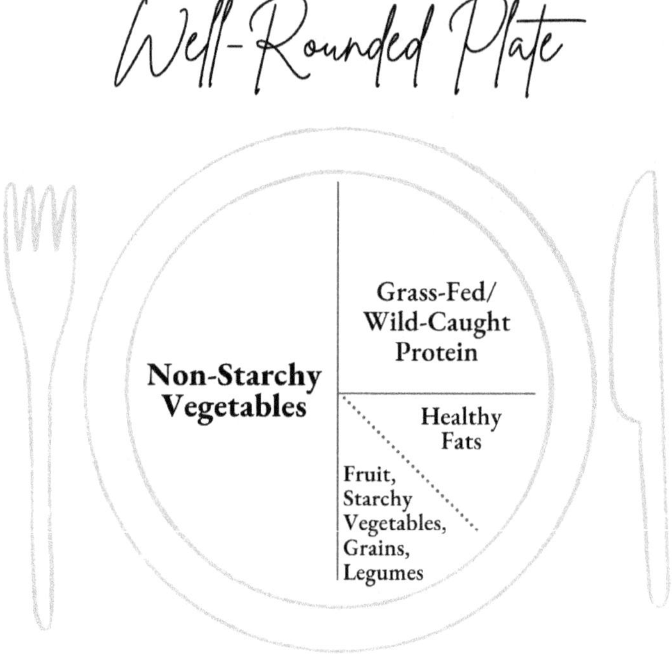

Protein

Most women thrive on 100-140 grams of protein daily, or approximately 0.7-1.0 grams per pound of goal body weight.

If you're shocked by that number, you're not alone. Most women are eating 40-60 grams daily and wondering why they're struggling. They're essentially asking their body to function optimally while providing less than half the building materials needed. It's like hiring a construction crew to build a three-story house but only delivering enough materials for one floor.

When you start eating adequate protein, something magical happens. You'll notice the "optional" functions come back online. Your hair gets thicker and starts growing again. Your nails become strong and healthy. Your skin regains its glow and elasticity. Your menstrual cycles regulate and PMS symptoms decrease. Your mood stabilizes, and you feel more resilient to stress. Your energy returns, and you wake up feeling rested instead of depleted. Your metabolism speeds up, and fat loss becomes easier because your body finally has the resources to build and maintain calorie-burning muscle tissue.

Sources: chicken, turkey, fish, seafood, eggs, Greek yogurt, cottage cheese, lean beef, bison, pork, protein powder

Healthy Fats

Remember fats are required for hormone production. They support cell membranes, aid in absorption of fat soluble vitamins, and support brain health. They are also the nutrient that will help you feel satisfied at meals.

If you've had your gallbladder removed or you're dealing with low stomach acid due to age, stress, or medication, you may struggle to break down fats and absorb fat-soluble vitamins—another reason we take a whole-system view instead of throwing you on a low-fat or low-calorie plan and calling it a day. If this is you, digestive enzymes with HCL and ox bile can be helpful.

Sources: avocado, olive oil, coconut oil, nuts, seeds, fatty fish (salmon, mackerel, sardines), egg yolks, grass-fed butter or ghee

Carbohydrates

Carbs aren't the enemy. They provide energy, support thyroid function, provide fiber, and support gut bacteria. But the amount of carbs your body can handle without storing fat depends on your insulin sensitivity. If your insulin is working well, you can eat more carbs without issue. If you're insulin-resistant (which many perimenopausal women are), too many carbs—especially refined ones—spike your blood sugar and insulin, leading to fat storage.

The good news: as you heal your metabolism by following Home Base, your insulin sensitivity improves. That means you can gradually add back more carbs without sabotaging your progress.

Non-starchy vegetables, which are currently taking up half your plate like we talked about in Home Base, are carbohydrates. You're already creating balance by default, so you don't have to stress about every detail. Keep

Chapter 10: The Well-Rounded Plate

fruit, starches, grains, and legumes to about one-eighth of your plate to start, then adjust as you learn your carbohydrate tipping point and which ones work best for your body.

You don't have to stick to exact ratios. The visual is simply there to help guide you, not to trap you. We're not counting calories, tracking macros, or weighing food. We're focused on building nutrient-dense, satisfying meals that fuel your body and help it work for you instead of against you.

Listen to your body. Eat one plate of food at a time or until your hunger feels truly satisfied—not stuffed but content. Learn the difference between enough and extra. That awareness is a skill, not a rule. Like we talked about with Home Base, if you're still hungry at the end of a meal, go back and eat some more non-starchy vegetables. Still hungry? Now hit up some more protein. It's common to grab seconds on starches first because they are satisfying. It's not that you can't have more, but we are trying to find that ideal balance that works best for your body and determine how much you need. When we haven't had enough protein and fiber, it's easy to "think" we need more starches.

Sources: vegetables (unlimited), fruits, starchy vegetables (sweet potato, squash, beets), legumes (beans, lentils), whole grains (oats, quinoa, rice).

Personalizing Nutrition

The exact ratios aren't as important as the quality of the foods and how they make YOU feel. This is bio-individual. Try to stick to three meals a day, and if you're hungry before that next meal, take a look at your plate from the meal before and see how maybe it could have been adjusted to better serve you. This is where the art meets the science. Everyone's carb tolerance and macronutrient needs are slightly different. You'll learn yours by paying attention to symptoms around sleep, hunger, energy, cravings, and mood.

When the scale is trending down and your energy is high, your body is telling you that your ratio is right. If you're feeling tired, bloated, or craving sugar, that's feedback. It's your body's way of saying something needs adjustment.

Ask yourself:

- **Sleep:** Are you eating enough? Do you need a protein-rich snack before bed to stabilize blood sugar overnight? Do you need a little more carbohydrate at dinner to support your hormones?
- **Hunger and cravings:** Are you getting half your plate vegetables to stay full? Are you eating enough protein? Remember, protein is the only nutrient that can stabilize blood sugar for up to six hours.
- **Energy:** Are you under-eating? Are your workouts overexerting you? Do you need more carbs to support recovery?
- **Mood:** Are you feeling restricted or deprived? Are you eating enough fat and protein to support your hormone production? Are you choosing nutrient-dense foods? Are you having daily bowel movements?

The goal is to stay curious, not critical. If something feels off, make one small tweak and watch what happens.

The Scale Is Still a Tool

After detox, many women panic the first time the scale goes up. They're used to seeing it drop in a straight line during detox, but that was because we were ditching a lot of inflammation. Real weight loss doesn't look like a slide—it looks like a staircase.

You might lose 1.5 pounds during the week, enjoy date night, and see it up half a pound the next morning. That's not failure; that's life. Zoom out, and you're still down one pound overall.

Here's what we want you to remember:

- It takes **3,500 calories** more than your body needs in a day to gain one pound of fat. That's nearly impossible to do overnight.
- Most daily fluctuations are water retention, inflammation, or skipping a bowel movement—not fat gain.
- When the number goes up, go back to your Home Base habits and your well-rounded plate. It will come down again, and each time it does, you build confidence. If you get right back to what you know

works—hydration, vegetables, protein, sleep, and movement—you'll see that little blip disappear. That's how you develop trust in your body and peace with food. You stop believing the lie that one meal ruins everything. You start believing the truth that you can enjoy life and still see progress.

You can lose weight as fast as you gain it because what goes up quickly usually comes down just as fast as long as we don't let our emotions get involved. The key is to separate data from emotion. The scale is information, not judgment.

The Freedom Mindset

You might be able to lose weight by being very restrictive, but when you add back your favorite foods, the weight will return if you never learned how to incorporate them wisely. The goal isn't to live without joy—it's to live with intention.

This is where food freedom becomes real. The best weight loss plan is the one that looks most like how you want to eat forever.

If your family eats pizza every Friday night, we don't want you to avoid it for ninety days and then binge on day ninety-one. We want you to enjoy it *with* them. That's what margin looks like.

Maybe your fat and carb portion that night comes from two slices of pizza—but you still fill half your plate with vegetables and add a little protein. You enjoy your meal, you connect with your family, and the next day, you go right back to your well-rounded plate.

When you learn to lose weight while eating the foods you love, maintenance looks almost identical to weight loss—it just includes a little more margin for things like a glass of wine, dessert, or date night.

Weight loss isn't linear; it's rhythmic. It's a dance between consistency and flexibility.

"Is It Worth It?"

You'll hear us say this often: Ask yourself two questions before you eat something that might impact your progress:

Do I really want it?

Is it worth it?

If you can answer "yes" to both, then enjoy it—without guilt.

Here's Abbey's personal example: For me, a grocery store birthday cake is *not worth it.* I don't even like the taste, and I know I'll feel off afterward. But I used to say yes to it because I didn't want to feel left out. Now I know there will always be another opportunity.

But when it's something special—like my favorite carrot cake from the local bakery—I say yes without hesitation. I enjoy every bite, and I'm not mad at all if the scale goes up the next day. I know it's temporary, and I know exactly what to do to bring it back down.

That's the difference between reaction and intention.

We live in a world where we have access to almost anything, anytime. We can't even isolate a seasonal item to just a season. If it is Thanksgiving and you are trying to stay focused on your weight loss, you can say no to pumpkin pie knowing you could still always find one or make one when you really want it, even if it's not Thanksgiving.

Gone is the thought process of "you're missing out" or "it's your only opportunity." When you feel like it's *your choice*, not a rule, that's freedom.

Rewriting the Story

To live a balanced, free lifestyle, we have to make shifts mentally. We've been building toward this all along—breaking up with food rules, focusing on addition instead of subtraction, and giving your body what it needs instead of punishing it for what it's not.

But now we go deeper.

The hardest work we do when it comes to sustainable weight loss is the work between your ears. It starts with your thoughts. You can't always control your circumstances, but you can control your thoughts about them. And your thoughts create your feelings, your feelings drive your actions, and your actions ultimately determine your results.

So let's rewrite the story:

Old thought:	New thought:
"I struggle to lose weight."	"My body wants to release the weight."
"I can't eat carbs."	"Carbs bring me energy."
"I hate the scale."	"The scale is my friend. It helps me navigate how my body responds to food, sleep, and stress."
"I have to clean my plate."	"I listen to my body for signs of satisfaction."
"Food choices are out of my control."	"I always have a choice in what I eat."
"That's a bad food. I was bad for eating it."	"There are no bad foods. There are only habits that serve me and habits that don't."

At first, it feels awkward—like walking through tall grass. But every time you repeat these new truths, you're clearing the path. Over time, it becomes second nature. Your goals become standards, and your standards become your normal.

Your brain runs on evidence. It believes what you prove to it over and over again.

Every time you step on the scale, choose curiosity instead of judgment, return to Home Base, or enjoy food intentionally instead of impulsively, you're collecting evidence that this works. You're retraining your mind to believe something new: that you can lose weight, live freely, and never diet again.

Real-Life Freedom

Food isn't just fuel—it's comfort, culture, and connection. Sometimes nourishment looks like a perfectly balanced meal and sometimes it looks like a small slice of cake at your grandchild's first birthday or a glass of wine overlooking the rolling hills of Tuscany on your anniversary.

It's not about avoiding those moments—it's about being present for them.

Your body can handle flexibility when it's grounded in consistency. Stressing about the treat does more damage than enjoying it ever could. Your results are the sum of all the small choices, not the one choice it's easy to get hung up on.

Ask yourself: "Do I really want it? Is it worth it?" If the answer is yes, and you know how to get back to your baseline afterward, you can enjoy anything.

That's true freedom.

Client Reflections

"Twenty pounds!! Wow, I can't believe I have twenty pounds in the rearview mirror! Not only do I just feel lighter, I feel good all over. All of this seems less of a fight, and more like I'm finally hearing my body."—**Moya**

"I'm down ten pounds! Not only that, but I don't have a 44 oz Diet Coke every day (although I still have one as a treat here and there), I'm sleeping through the night, and here's my four-year-old eating a kale and cabbage salad for lunch with me."—**Heather**

"Over eight weeks of implementing all of these principles—through the holidays—I've lost 7.8 pounds. While I'm elated the scale is finally moving, more than anything, I've learned balance and grace, which I realized I needed more than weight loss."—**Jenny**

"Freeing my mind: Old belief—'Hypothyroidism makes it impossible for me to lose weight.' New belief—'Nourishing my body with the foods it needs supports thyroid health.'"—**Betsy**

This is what freedom looks like. It's not perfection, it's about being present and making progress. When you eat in a way you love while losing weight, maintenance doesn't feel like a struggle; it becomes natural.

You're building your forever way of eating: one well-rounded plate, one conscious choice, one rewrite at a time. Welcome to the place where healing becomes freedom—and freedom becomes your new normal.

The Comprehensive Approach

Introduction

You made it.

You've journeyed through Part I, where you learned exactly what's happening in your body—the five specific hormone imbalances sabotaging your weight, your energy, your sleep, your mood, and your quality of life. You understand insulin resistance, cortisol dysregulation, thyroid dysfunction, sex hormone imbalance, and vitamin D deficiency. You've taken the quizzes. You've identified your patterns. You know what's broken.

In Part II, you discovered the foundational lifestyle interventions that support all five hormone systems simultaneously—how to nourish your body, move in ways that heal rather than stress your system, manage stress, optimize sleep, and create the conditions for hormonal balance. You have tools you can implement immediately, regardless of where you are in your testing or treatment journey. By completing the 10-Day Detox, you lowered inflammation and identified the food triggers that were holding you back. The Well-Rounded Plate guided you in building a simple, sustainable eating style tailored to your body. You've broken up with dieting once and for all.

And now you're ready for the specific treatment protocols that will be the final tweaks to heal each imbalance, optimize your lab values, and reverse your symptoms.

If you're feeling both hopeful and perhaps a bit overwhelmed by the volume of information you've absorbed, that's completely normal. Here's what we want you to know: While the science behind these hormone imbalances is complex, the treatments are straightforward. We've taken everything we've learned from working with thousands of women and distilled them into clear, actionable protocols you can follow.

This part of the book will give you exactly what you need to work effectively with healthcare providers who understand whole-person medicine and to guide your own healing journey with appropriate support.

Understanding the Foundation: Normal vs. Optimal

Remember back in Part I when we introduced the critical distinction between "normal" and "optimal" lab values? This concept is so fundamental to everything we do that it's worth revisiting here because it's what makes our treatment approach different from conventional medicine.

When your doctor runs labs and tells you everything is "normal," what they're really saying is that your values fall within the laboratory's reference range—a range determined by testing thousands of people and identifying the middle ninety-five percent. If you're not in the bottom 2.5 percent or the top 2.5 percent, you're considered "normal."

But here's the problem: That reference range includes sick people. It includes people with undiagnosed conditions. It includes people who feel terrible but haven't yet crossed the threshold into disease. Being "normal" simply means you don't have a diagnosable disease state—yet.

Optimal ranges are different. Optimal ranges represent where your lab values should be for you to feel your best, function at your peak, and prevent future disease. These are the ranges associated with healthy metabolism, stable energy, balanced mood, restful sleep, and sustainable weight management.

Throughout Part III, each treatment protocol chapter will include the optimal ranges we use with our clients—not just the lab's reference range but the specific values we're targeting to achieve symptom resolution and metabolic health. This is where functional medicine diverges from conventional care, and it's why women who've been told their labs are "fine" can still feel terrible and struggle with weight.

When you treat to optimal ranges rather than just avoiding disease ranges, transformation becomes possible.

Introduction

The Investment That Matters Most

Before we dive into the specific treatment protocols, we need to have an honest conversation about investing in your health.

Here's a truth that might be uncomfortable but is critically important: Health insurance in the United States is like car insurance. Think about it—you've been paying for car insurance your entire life, but not once has it gotten you a better vehicle. Car insurance is there for accidents, for breakdowns, for catastrophic events. But if you want a car that won't break down on the side of the road, a vehicle that's reliable and dependable, you need to invest in a better quality car.

Health insurance works the same way.

Health insurance is there after you get sick, after you've progressed so far in your disease state that you qualify for medications, after things have gone wrong. It's reactive, not proactive. It won't help you get your health back. It won't get you a better body. It won't pay for organic whole foods, gym memberships, high-quality supplements, or support to treat problems before they become diseases.

If you want a better, healthier body—one that serves you well through perimenopause, menopause, and for decades beyond—you need to invest.

And here's what makes this investment different from every diet program, every fitness challenge, every quick-fix solution you've tried before: You're not just buying a temporary result. You're investing in knowledge. You're investing in understanding your body so deeply that you can make informed decisions for the rest of your life. You're investing in skills that compound over time.

That's why we named this book *Empowered*.

For too long, women have been dismissed, gaslit, and told their symptoms are "just part of getting older" or "all in their head." You've been made to feel like you're being difficult when you push back against inadequate care. You've been told to just "eat less and exercise more" when you're already doing both. You've accepted "your labs are normal" even when you feel terrible because you didn't know what else to ask for.

That ends now.

You deserve to feel good in your body. You deserve to have energy to do the things you love. You deserve to sleep peacefully and wake refreshed. You deserve mental clarity and emotional stability. You deserve to love the body you live in.

These aren't luxuries. These aren't unreasonable expectations. These are basic markers of health that should be accessible to every woman navigating perimenopause and menopause.

We're teaching you to learn what's happening in your body so you can have educated discussions with medical providers. We're showing you how to eat, move, sleep, and manage stress in ways that support healthy aging. We're giving you the lab values and treatment options so you can advocate effectively for appropriate care.

Most importantly, we're helping you understand that this—all of this struggle you've been experiencing—is not your fault.

You haven't failed. Your body hasn't betrayed you. You've been navigating a profound hormonal transition without adequate medical support, accurate information, or effective tools. But now you have all three.

Now you can take control of your health and feel great as you age and move through menopause.

What to Expect in Part III

In the chapters that follow, we'll walk through comprehensive treatment protocols for each of the five hormone imbalances. Each chapter will include:

- **Optimal Lab Ranges:** The specific values we target with our clients—not just "normal" but truly optimal. These are the ranges associated with symptom resolution, metabolic health, and long-term vitality.
- **Medical Interventions:** The medications, hormones, and prescription treatments that can restore balance when lifestyle alone isn't enough. We'll cover what's available, how they work, who benefits most, and how to use them safely and effectively.

- **Supplement Protocols:** Targeted supplementation to support each hormone system, including quality considerations, and which supplements provide the most benefit based on research.
- **Lifestyle Integration:** How the foundational strategies from Part II specifically support each imbalance and any additional targeted lifestyle interventions that enhance treatment effectiveness.
- **The Interconnections:** Because these five hormone systems don't exist in isolation, we'll show you how optimizing one system supports the others and why comprehensive treatment produces results that single interventions cannot achieve.
- **Retesting Timelines:** When to retest, what to look for, and how to adjust your protocol based on results.

Here's how we recommend you approach implementing these protocols:

- **Start with comprehensive lab testing.** Before you begin any targeted treatment, you need to know what's actually happening in your body. The symptom quizzes from Part I give you valuable information about which imbalances are likely present, but you cannot diagnose based on symptoms alone. Work with a healthcare provider to order comprehensive testing for all five hormone systems.
- **Based on your results, prioritize healing the abnormal imbalances.** Some women will discover all five systems are out of balance and need support. Others may find only two or three imbalances that require targeted intervention. If it's not broken, don't fix it. Focus your efforts and resources on the systems that testing reveals need optimization.
- **Layer in Part II foundations.** Regardless of which specific imbalances you're treating, the lifestyle foundations from Part II—nutrition, movement, stress management, sleep optimization—support all five hormone systems. These aren't optional "nice to haves." They're essential components that make every medical intervention more effective and help prevent future imbalances.

Part III: The Comprehensive Approach

- **Work with a healthcare provider who understands and supports you on this journey.** Whether that's a functional medicine provider, an integrative physician, or even your primary care provider, find someone who gets it. You need a medical provider (physician, nurse practitioner, or physician associate) who will test comprehensively, utilize your insurance for everything it will cover, treat to optimal ranges, and partner with you rather than dismissing your concerns.

- **Be patient with the process.** Hormonal healing doesn't happen overnight. It took time for these imbalances to develop, and it takes time to restore balance. Some women see dramatic improvements within weeks—significant weight loss, restored energy, better sleep. Others experience more gradual changes over months as their systems rebalance. Trust the process, stay consistent with your protocols, and retest to track progress objectively.

- **Remember the goal.** This isn't just about losing weight or eliminating hot flashes. This is about training for aging. This is about establishing the metabolic health, hormonal balance, and physiological resilience that will serve you for decades to come. You're not just surviving perimenopause—you're setting yourself up to thrive in your sixties, seventies, eighties, and beyond.

Let's get started.

Understanding Your Treatment Options

You've been doing this alone for too long, and that changes now. What if someone handed you a personalized plan? Not a generic diet or one-size-fits-all protocol, but a comprehensive roadmap built specifically from YOUR lab results, YOUR symptoms, and YOUR goals. A plan that shows you exactly what to do, in what order, and why—based on your actual data, not guesswork.

What if you finally had access to treatments that actually work? Medical interventions, targeted supplements, and strategic lifestyle modifications that address the root cause of your struggles instead of just treating symptoms. What if you had a team of experts—medical providers, nutritionists, fitness coaches—all working together, rowing in the same direction, focused on getting you results in the shortest amount of time possible?

That's exactly what this chapter is about.

Think of it this way: You now have access to a comprehensive toolbox filled with every treatment option available to balance your hormones and transform your health. But having all these tools doesn't matter if you don't know which ones to use for your specific situation, in what order, and for what purpose.

You wouldn't try to hammer a nail with a screwdriver. The right tool for the right job, used in the right sequence, gets the project done efficiently and effectively. The same is true for your health. When you use the right interventions—personalized to your labs, your symptoms, and your goals—you accelerate your timeline to results.

This isn't about chasing a number on the scale anymore. This is about feeling in charge of your health again. It's about waking up with energy, sleeping through the night, having mental clarity, feeling confident in your body, and showing up as the best version of yourself for the people you love.

It's about reclaiming control. It's about being empowered.

You've done the hard work of understanding your body in Part I. You've established the foundational habits in Part II that support all five hormone systems. Now you're ready to layer in the targeted treatments that will optimize your hormones, reverse your symptoms, and help you finally achieve the transformation you've been working toward.

Let's talk about what's in your toolbox.

The Spectrum of Treatment Options

When we work with clients at our practice, we have five primary categories of interventions we can use to restore hormonal balance and optimize health. Each has its place, and the art of effective treatment is knowing which to use, when, and in what combination. Here's what's available:

1. Foundational Supplements: What Everyone Needs

Before we even talk about targeted hormone support, every woman—regardless of which hormone imbalances she's dealing with—needs a solid nutritional foundation.

Think of these as the nutritional insurance policy for your body. Even if you're eating well (and we know from Part II that you're working on your Home Base habits), modern agriculture, soil depletion, food processing, and lifestyle stressors make it nearly impossible to get optimal amounts of every nutrient from food alone.

Here's an uncomfortable truth: Even if you're eating a nutrient-dense diet, you're likely not getting all the vitamins and minerals your body needs for optimal function.

Chapter 11: Understanding Your Treatment Options

Why? Our soil is depleted. Modern agricultural practices have stripped nutrients from the earth, which means the food grown in that soil—no matter how organic or well-sourced—contains fewer vitamins and minerals than the same foods did fifty or a hundred years ago. Studies show that today's fruits and vegetables contain significantly less magnesium, iron, zinc, calcium, and other essential nutrients compared to decades past.

This is why foundational supplementation isn't optional—it's essential for filling gaps that diet alone cannot address.

The foundational supplements virtually every client needs include:

- **A high-quality multivitamin:** Provides baseline coverage of essential vitamins and minerals your body needs for thousands of biochemical reactions, including hormone production and metabolism. Look for formulas with methylated B vitamins (including methylfolate and B12) for energy production, stress response, and proper methylation—critical for detoxification and hormone metabolism.

- **Omega-3 fatty acids:** Support cellular health, reduce inflammation, improve insulin sensitivity, and provide the building blocks for hormone production. You need both EPA and DHA (the active forms found in fish oil) daily for optimal hormonal and cardiovascular health.

- **Magnesium:** Critical for over 300 enzymatic reactions in your body, including blood sugar regulation, stress response, sleep quality, and muscle function. Most women are deficient. Comprehensive mineral support including calcium and trace minerals is essential for hundreds of enzymatic reactions in the body.

- **Vitamin D3 with K2:** As we discussed in Part I, vitamin D is actually a hormone, not a vitamin, and it's essential for immune function, bone health, hormone production, and metabolic health. Most women need a daily maintenance dose to maintain optimal levels, and include vitamin K2 to ensure that calcium is directed into your bones rather than your arteries.

- **Targeted minerals for thyroid function:** Zinc, selenium, and iodine are essential for optimal thyroid hormone production and conversion.

These aren't optional "nice to haves." They're essential building blocks that make every other intervention more effective. You can't build a house on a cracked foundation, and you can't optimize hormones without adequate nutritional support.

2. Targeted Supplements: Addressing Specific Imbalances

Beyond the foundation, we use specific supplements to support each of the five hormone systems. These are chosen based on your lab results and symptoms:

- **For insulin resistance:** Berberine, Ceylon cinnamon, alpha-lipoic acid, chromium, inositol
- **For cortisol dysregulation:** Adaptogenic herbs like ashwagandha, rhodiola, holy basil, L-theanine; phosphatidylserine for elevated evening cortisol
- **For thyroid dysfunction:** Selenium for T4 to T3 conversion, zinc for thyroid hormone production, L-tyrosine, targeted iodine when indicated
- **For sex hormone balance:** DIM, calcium D-glucarate, milk thistle for healthy estrogen metabolism, vitex for progesterone support, and herbal options like black cohosh, maca, and EstroG-100 Blend
- **For vitamin D deficiency:** Additional therapeutic dosing of vitamin D3 beyond the foundation, often at higher doses with cofactors

We'll dive deep into each of these in the individual protocol chapters. For now, just know that targeted supplementation can be remarkably effective—but only when you're taking the right supplements for YOUR specific imbalances, at the right doses, at the right times.

This isn't about taking random supplements you heard were "good for you." This is about systematically addressing the specific deficiencies and imbalances that testing has revealed in YOUR body.

3. Prescription Medications

When lifestyle and supplements aren't enough—and often they aren't for women with significant hormone imbalances—prescription medications become essential tools for healing.

The good news: most prescription medications for hormone imbalances are covered by insurance and available at your local pharmacy. This includes:

- **For insulin resistance:** Metformin, GLP-1 medications (semaglutide, tirzepatide)
- **For thyroid dysfunction:** Levothyroxine (T4), liothyronine (T3), combination therapies, natural desiccated thyroid
- **For sex hormone support:** FDA-approved bioidentical (also called body identical) hormone replacement therapy including estradiol and progesterone preparations. Testosterone is not yet FDA approved in women and does not have a female dosing schedule, so this one is a bit more nuanced at the writing of this book.

To access these medications, you'll need to work with a prescribing provider—a physician (MD or DO), nurse practitioner (NP), or physician assistant (PA)—who understands treating to optimal ranges rather than just avoiding disease. The key is finding someone who will:

- Order comprehensive testing for all five hormone systems
- Interpret results using optimal ranges, not just lab reference ranges
- Prescribe appropriate medications when indicated
- Retest regularly to adjust dosing
- Utilize your insurance for everything it will cover

Prescription medications are powerful tools, but they must be prescribed by a licensed medical provider who can monitor your response and adjust dosing as needed.

4. Compounded Medications

Compounded medications are custom-formulated prescriptions made specifically for you by a specialized pharmacy. Unlike mass-produced pharmaceuticals that come in standard doses, compounded medications can be tailored to your exact needs.

This is particularly valuable for hormone replacement therapy. Compounded bioidentical hormones allow us to:

- Adjust dosing precisely to your individual needs
- Combine multiple hormones in a single preparation
- Use delivery methods (creams, troches, capsules) that work best for your body and lifestyle
- Avoid fillers or additives you may be sensitive to

Compounded medications are typically outside what insurance will cover, but they can be useful—and sometimes more cost-effective—in specific situations. For example:

- GLP-1 medications in compounded form can be significantly less expensive than brand-name options and allow for customized dosing (including the microdosing strategies we'll discuss in Chapter 10)
- Low-dose naltrexone (LDN) for inflammation and immune support isn't available in the low doses we use therapeutically, so compounding is necessary
- Bioidentical hormone combinations that allow precise customization of estrogen-progesterone-testosterone ratios

Compounded medications require a prescription from a licensed provider and must come from a reputable compounding pharmacy. We'll discuss specific applications in the individual hormone chapters.

5. Lifestyle Interventions

Finally—and this is crucial—every treatment plan includes the lifestyle foundations you learned in Part II. These aren't "extras" you add if you have time. They're non-negotiable components that make every medical intervention more effective.

Proper nutrition, adequate sleep, stress management, and appropriate movement patterns don't just support hormone balance—they determine whether your treatments will work optimally or only marginally.

We've seen it repeatedly: two women with identical lab values, identical prescriptions, identical supplements—but one follows the Home Base principles and one doesn't. The woman who prioritizes nutrition, hydration, sleep and movement sees dramatically better results. Every. Single. Time.

The women who get the best results are the ones who implement comprehensive treatment: appropriate medications + targeted supplements + foundational nutrition + lifestyle support. Not one or the other—all of it, working together.

Quality and Safety: Not All Supplements Are Created Equal

Here's something most women don't realize: The supplement industry in the United States is largely unregulated. Unlike prescription medications, which must undergo rigorous testing and FDA approval before reaching consumers, supplements can be manufactured and sold with minimal oversight.

This creates a significant problem: When you walk into a drugstore or order supplements online, you have no guarantee that what's on the label is actually in the bottle. Studies have found supplements contaminated with heavy metals, undisclosed ingredients, allergens, or fillers. Some contain far less of the active ingredient than claimed. Others contain potentially harmful additives.

This is why understanding how to evaluate supplement quality isn't just about getting better results—it's about safety.

What to Look for in High-Quality Supplements

When evaluating any supplement, ask these five critical questions:

1. Is it manufactured in an FDA-registered, cGMP-certified facility?

While supplements themselves aren't FDA-approved, the facilities that manufacture them can be registered with the FDA. cGMP (current Good Manufacturing Practices) certification means the facility follows strict protocols for quality control, ingredient verification, and contamination prevention.

This certification isn't required, which means many supplement manufacturers don't bother. Look for supplements that explicitly state they're manufactured in FDA-registered facilities that follow cGMP standards.

2. Does it have third-party testing?

This is perhaps the most important quality indicator. Third-party testing means an independent laboratory—not the company selling the supplement—has verified that the supplement contains what the label claims and is free from contaminants.

Here's why this matters: The supplement company can claim anything on their label. They can say their product contains 1,000mg of a particular ingredient when it actually contains 200mg. They can claim purity when their product contains heavy metals or undisclosed fillers. Without third-party verification, you're taking their word for it.

Third-party testing removes that uncertainty. An independent lab tests every batch, every time. If the supplement doesn't meet the standards—if it doesn't contain what it claims or if contaminants are found—that batch is discarded and not sold to consumers.

This is important because supplements aren't regulated by the FDA the way medications are. Third-party testing fills that regulatory gap, giving you confidence that you're getting exactly what you're paying for and nothing you don't want.

Look for certifications from reputable organizations. When you see these seals on a supplement bottle, it means the manufacturer has invested in verification because they care about quality:

- **NSF International** (NSF Certified for Sport is particularly rigorous)
- **USP** (United States Pharmacopeia)
- **ConsumerLab**
- **Informed Choice** (particularly important for athletes concerned about banned substances)

These certifications cost manufacturers money, which is why many cheap supplements skip this step. But third-party testing is your assurance that you're getting what you're paying for—and that what you're taking is safe.

3. What's the bioavailability?

Bioavailability refers to how well your body can actually absorb and use the supplement. You can take all the supplements in the world, but if your body can't absorb them and put them to use, you're just making expensive urine—literally excreting the nutrients you paid for without getting any benefit.

The cheapest form of a nutrient isn't always the most effective. In fact, it rarely is.

Here's why bioavailability matters: Let's say you take a magnesium supplement. Magnesium oxide—the least expensive form—has very poor absorption. Studies show only about four percent of magnesium oxide is actually absorbed by your body. The rest passes through your digestive system unused, often causing digestive upset along the way.

Contrast that with magnesium glycinate, which has much better absorption and is well-tolerated by the digestive system. Yes, it costs more to manufacture. Yes, the supplement will be more expensive. But you're actually getting the magnesium into your body where it can be used.

The same principle applies across all nutrients:

- **Folic acid** is the synthetic form of folate. Many women—especially those with MTHFR gene variations—can't convert folic acid efficiently into the active form their bodies need. **Methylfolate (5-MTHF)** is the active form your body can use immediately without conversion.
- **Cyanocobalamin** is cheap synthetic B12. **Methylcobalamin** or **adenosylcobalamin** are the bioavailable forms your body actually uses.
- Different forms of **vitamin D** (D2 vs. D3), different mineral chelates, different omega-3 sources—both have different absorption rates and effectiveness.

Quality supplements use the most bioavailable forms of nutrients, even when they cost more to manufacture. This is reflected in the price—but it's also reflected in your results.

If your body can't absorb and utilize the supplements you're taking, they're not worth taking. You're wasting your money regardless of how cheap they were.

4. Is it backed by research?

Legitimate supplement companies invest in research demonstrating that their products actually do what they claim. This doesn't mean testimonials from customers or claims on their website—it means peer-reviewed scientific studies, clinical trials, and published research.

For example: Does taking vitamin D3 actually increase your serum vitamin D levels and provide the health benefits we know vitamin D supports? If the answer is *yes—there's extensive research demonstrating this*, then that is a research-backed supplement claim.

Contrast that with proprietary blends that claim miraculous results but don't have any published studies supporting those claims. Or supplements making outrageous health promises without scientific backing.

When evaluating supplements, look for:

- Published clinical studies (not just "clinical testing")
- Research on the specific form and dose used in the supplement
- Studies published in reputable journals
- Transparency about what research supports their formulation

Be wary of supplements that rely entirely on testimonials, use vague language like "clinically inspired" rather than "clinically tested," or make claims that sound too good to be true.

The active ingredients in quality supplements are backed by science showing they actually work—they help with what they claim to help with.

5. What are the inactive ingredients?

Check the "other ingredients" list on any supplement label. This tells you what fillers, binders, and additives are included beyond the active ingredients.

Chapter 11: Understanding Your Treatment Options

High-quality supplements minimize fillers, binders, and unnecessary additives. They avoid common allergens when possible (gluten, dairy, soy). They use vegetarian capsules rather than gelatin when appropriate. They're typically non-GMO and free from artificial colors, flavors, and preservatives.

If a supplement has a long list of artificial ingredients, questionable additives, or potential allergens, that's a red flag about the manufacturer's priorities.

The Cost-Benefit Reality

Yes, high-quality supplements cost more upfront. But low-quality supplements that your body can't absorb are a complete waste of money—no matter how cheap they are. When you invest in quality supplementation:

- You actually get the nutrients you're paying for.
- Your body can absorb and utilize them effectively.
- You see results in your lab values and symptoms.
- You avoid potential contamination or safety issues.
- You're not throwing money away on products that don't work.

Think of it this way: Would you rather spend $30 on a supplement that does nothing or $60 on one that actually improves your hormone function and helps you feel better? The higher-quality option is actually the better value.

The Matrix Method: Why You Need a Team Approach

Throughout this book, we've referenced The Matrix Method—our comprehensive approach to healing hormone imbalances and reversing symptoms. Now let's talk about what that actually means and why it works when isolated interventions fail.

What Is The Matrix Method?

The Matrix Method is our proven system to reverse metabolic damage, eliminate or significantly improve symptoms, and get the scale moving in the right direction. It's not a one-size-fits-all protocol or a generic treatment plan. It's a personalized, comprehensive approach that addresses YOUR unique hormonal picture. Here's what makes it different from conventional care:

- **It's comprehensive, not isolated.** Instead of treating one hormone or one symptom, we address all five hormone imbalances that testing reveals need support. We use medications, supplements, nutrition, fitness, and lifestyle interventions—all working together in a coordinated protocol. When you treat all the imbalances simultaneously, the synergistic effects produce results that far exceed what any single intervention could achieve.

- **It's personalized, not one-size-fits-all.** Your treatment plan is built from YOUR specific lab results, YOUR symptom patterns, YOUR health history, YOUR goals, and YOUR lifestyle. What works for one woman may not work for another. Some women need aggressive intervention with multiple medications. Others get excellent results with targeted supplements and lifestyle modifications. The art of medicine is knowing which tools to use for which person at which time.

- **It's team-based, not siloed.** When you work with a comprehensive team—medical provider, nutritionist, personal trainer, and support coach—everyone knows your complete hormone profile, understands what the other team members are doing, and coordinates their recommendations. You're not getting conflicting information from different providers who don't communicate with each other. Everyone is rowing in the same direction, working from the same blueprint: YOUR personalized plan.

- **It's data-driven, not guesswork.** We test comprehensively to establish your baseline. We implement targeted protocols based on what your labs reveal. Then we retest at ninety days to see how your body

Chapter 11: Understanding Your Treatment Options

has responded. We adjust based on objective data—how your labs have changed and how your symptoms have improved. We're not throwing interventions at the wall to see what sticks. We're using data to guide decisions and track progress.

- **It's advanced, not generic.** We use cutting-edge strategies to accelerate results and solve complex cases that conventional providers can't. Our proprietary DNA testing panel uncovers genetic variations that affect how your body processes caffeine and alcohol, how efficiently your methylation and detoxification pathways function, whether you're genetically predisposed to vitamin or mineral deficiencies, and what your optimal sleep window is.

This isn't guesswork or generic recommendations—it's precision medicine that identifies your unique genetic blueprint so we can personalize everything from your eating style (low carb, Paleo, Mediterranean, vegetarian) to your supplement protocols to your exercise programming.

For women with complex medical histories—cancer survivors, autoimmune conditions, severe metabolic dysfunction, celiac disease, or multiple failed weight loss attempts—we employ advanced interventions including specialized protocols for food sensitivities and inflammatory triggers, reverse dieting strategies to repair metabolic damage from years of restriction, custom compounded hormone formulations when standard options aren't sufficient, and comprehensive functional testing beyond basic hormone panels.

When standard approaches fail, advanced strategies create breakthroughs, and we've refined these protocols through thousands of complex cases.

What Makes Us Different

We can use every tool available. Need supplements? We've got evidence-based protocols refined over thousands of patients. Need prescription medications? We can prescribe them. Need compounded bioidentical hormones? We work with specialized pharmacies. Need thyroid optimization that goes beyond "your TSH is normal"? We know exactly how to do it. Need someone to look at your complete picture—labs, symptoms, health history, genetic testing—and create a truly personalized protocol? That's what we do, every single day.

And here's the game-changer: We work as a team. When you work with our approach, you're not bouncing between providers who don't communicate. Everyone is on the same page, reviewing the same labs, discussing cases together, and making coordinated decisions.

This teamwork isn't just convenient—it's why we get results when other approaches fail.

Can You Do This Without a Full Team?

We understand that not everyone can access or afford comprehensive team-based care. So let's be realistic about what's possible if you're implementing this book on your own:

1. **Minimum viable approach:**
   » Find a medical provider willing to order comprehensive testing and treat to optimal ranges.
   » Use Part II of this book to implement the nutrition and fitness foundations yourself.
   » Join support communities (online groups, local meetups) for accountability.
   » Be diligent about retesting and adjusting based on results.

2. **What to prioritize if you can only add one support person:**
   » If you struggle with nutrition and need meal planning guidance → nutritionist
   » If you need accountability and get stuck when implementing alone → coach
   » If you need exercise programming and struggle with consistency → personal trainer

3. **Where to find support:**
   » Look for board certified and licensed providers. Certified nutrition specialists® (CNS) or registered dietitians (RD) with hormone specialization
   » Seek certified personal trainers with experience working with perimenopausal women
   » Join online communities focused on perimenopause and hormone health

---

The truth is this: The more support you have, the faster and more sustainably you'll see results. After helping thousands of women, we know that those who work with a coordinated team get results in the shortest amount of time.

But even if you're doing this on your own with just your medical provider and this book as your guide, you can still heal. It may take longer. You may hit more obstacles. You may need to troubleshoot on your own. But the protocols work—and you're capable of implementing them.

The question isn't whether you can do this alone. It's whether you want to, and whether investing in support might get you to your goals faster with less frustration.

Only you can answer that question for yourself.

Setting Realistic Expectations: What Success Actually Looks Like

One additional point as we dive into the specific treatment protocols for each hormone imbalance. We need to have an honest conversation about timelines, results, and what "success" actually means.

This matters because unrealistic expectations are the biggest source of discouragement we see in women trying to heal their hormones and lose weight. When you expect to lose eighty pounds in ninety days and you "only" lose twenty-five, you feel like a failure—even though twenty-five pounds is remarkable progress and exactly what we'd expect for safe, sustainable weight loss.

So let's set the record straight about what's realistic, what's safe, and what you should actually expect from implementing these protocols.

The Timeline: Be Patient, Trust the Process

Here's the first thing you need to understand: Healing takes time. It depends entirely on where you are when you start working with us or on your own.

- **Less damage = quicker results.** If you're catching your hormone imbalances relatively early—maybe your HbA1c is 5.3 instead of 6.5, your thyroid is only slightly sluggish rather than severely hypothyroid, your cortisol pattern shows mild dysregulation rather than complete adrenal exhaustion—you'll likely see results faster. Your body hasn't been in crisis mode for as long. The metabolic damage is less severe. Recovery happens more quickly.

- **More damage = longer healing phase.** If you've been struggling for years or decades—if you've been yo-yo dieting for twenty years, if you've been on thyroid medication for ten years but never optimized, if your HbA1c has crept up to pre-diabetic or diabetic range, if you've gained sixty pounds during perimenopause—your body has more healing to do. This isn't a judgment. It's just reality. Your metabolism has adapted to survive in crisis mode. It takes time to restore trust and rebuild healthy function.

- **Everything we do is low, slow, and steady.** Women are sensitive to changes—in hormones, in medications, in dosing. We start low and increase gradually. We make one or two changes at a time rather than overhauling everything at once. This minimizes side effects and allows your body to adjust.

You should see improvement over a three-month period. The exact timeline depends on your symptoms, your goals, and how much damage we're reversing. But ninety days is the window where we consistently see significant transformation.

The Weight Loss Reality

Here's the truth about weight loss in perimenopausal and menopausal women: It's slower at first, then accelerates as healing happens.

In the first 4-6 weeks of implementing comprehensive treatment protocols, you might lose five pounds—less if you have significant metabolic damage. This isn't because the protocols aren't working. It's because a damaged, hormonally imbalanced body will not release weight until healing begins.

Your body is smart. When it's dealing with insulin resistance, elevated cortisol, sluggish thyroid function, sex hormone chaos, and chronic inflammation, it perceives threat. And when your body perceives threat, it holds on to every calorie, stores fat protectively (especially around your midsection), and refuses to let go of weight no matter how little you eat or how much you exercise.

This is the metabolic damage we've been talking about throughout this book.

But here's what happens as healing progresses: As your insulin sensitivity improves, your cortisol patterns normalize, your thyroid function optimizes, your sex hormones balance, and inflammation decreases, your body begins to feel safe. Your metabolism starts to trust that it has the resources it needs. Your cells become responsive to hormonal signals again.

And that's when weight starts to consistently drop.

Our ninety-day outcomes: Women who implement comprehensive treatment protocols—addressing all identified hormone imbalances with medications, supplements, and lifestyle interventions—lose between 12-36 pounds in ninety days, with an average of 22.7 pounds.

That's safe, steady, sustainable weight loss without starvation, without restrictive dieting, and without killing yourself at the gym. More importantly, it's weight loss that happens because you're reversing underlying metabolic dysfunction—which means it's weight loss you can maintain.

Let's look at what that timeline actually looks like:

Weeks 1-6: Foundation and Early Healing (5-8 pounds typical)
- Initial weight loss as inflammation decreases

- Modest changes as medications and supplements begin working
- Energy starting to improve
- Sleep quality getting better
- Some symptom reduction

Weeks 7-12: Accelerated Healing (additional 15-25 pounds typical)
- Metabolism beginning to respond
- More consistent week-to-week weight loss
- Energy significantly improved
- Sleep normalized in most cases
- Most bothersome symptoms resolving
- Body composition changing (losing inches even when scale doesn't move as fast)

This pattern—slow initial progress followed by acceleration—is exactly what we expect when healing metabolic damage. If you lose two pounds in your first month and feel discouraged, remember: You're laying the foundation. Your body is beginning to trust. The momentum is building.

Beyond the Scale: What Else Defines Success

Here's something critical to understand: The number on the scale is not the only—or even the most important—measure of success.

We see women who are discouraged because they've "only" lost twelve pounds in ninety days. But when we review their symptom checklist, they've gone from experiencing intense, life-crippling symptoms to complete resolution. Their energy has transformed. Their sleep has normalized. Their brain fog is gone. Their mood is stable. Their hot flashes have disappeared. Their joint pain has vanished.

That's not "only" anything. That's profound healing.

Yes, you want to lose weight. We understand that. Weight matters—both for how you feel in your body and for long-term health outcomes. But weight loss is a byproduct of metabolic healing, not the goal itself.

When you optimize your hormones, reverse insulin resistance, heal your thyroid function, balance your sex hormones, and reduce inflammation, weight loss becomes almost inevitable. But it happens as part of comprehensive healing, not in isolation.

So when we talk about success, we're measuring:

Symptom resolution:

- How have your top three symptoms improved or disappeared?
- Are you sleeping through the night?
- Is your energy restored?
- Is your mood stable?
- Is your brain fog gone?
- Have your hot flashes reduced or stopped?

Lab optimization:

- Are your hormone levels moving toward optimal ranges?
- Is your insulin sensitivity improving?
- Are your inflammatory markers decreasing?
- Is your thyroid function optimizing?

Functional improvements:

- Can you do activities you couldn't do before?
- Do you have energy for your life?
- Are you building muscle and improving strength?
- Is your cardiovascular fitness improving?

Quality of life:

- Do you feel like yourself again?
- Are you enjoying life rather than just surviving it?
- Do you feel empowered and in control of your health?
- Are you confident in your ability to maintain these changes long-term?

Part III: The Comprehensive Approach

If you've achieved these things—even if you haven't lost all the weight you want to lose yet—you are succeeding. The weight will continue to come off as you maintain the protocols. But you've already reclaimed your health, your vitality, and your sense of self.

That's what we mean by transformation.

The Ninety-Day Retest and Refinement

At the end of ninety days, we recommend retesting your labs. This gives objective data to answer critical questions:

- Are your hormone levels improving and moving toward optimal ranges?
- Is your insulin sensitivity better?
- Has your thyroid function optimized?
- Are your sex hormones more balanced?
- Has your vitamin D reached optimal levels?

This data—combined with your symptom improvement and weight loss—tells definitively whether the protocols are working and what adjustments we need to make moving forward.

Then re-evaluate:

- Review your lab results and compare them to your initial results
- Celebrate your progress
- Refine your protocol based on how your body has responded
- Adjust medications or supplements if needed
- Create your new plan for the next phase

This is the test-treat-retest cycle in action. Instead of guessing, use data to guide every decision.

Some women at this point have optimized their labs, resolved their symptoms, and achieved their weight loss goals. They transition to maintenance protocols. Others still have work to do—more weight to lose, labs that haven't quite reached optimal ranges yet, lingering symptoms. They continue with an adjusted active treatment phase.

Chapter 11: Understanding Your Treatment Options

Either way, you're not doing this blindly. You have data. You have a plan. You have support.

The Importance of Patience and Consistency

Hormonal healing doesn't happen overnight. It took time for these imbalances to develop—often years or even decades of accumulated metabolic damage, chronic stress, poor sleep, inflammatory diets, and hormonal decline.

It takes time to reverse that damage.

This is where patience becomes your superpower. The women who see the most dramatic, lasting results are the ones who stay consistent even when progress feels slow. They trust the process. They keep implementing the protocols. They don't give up after thirty days because they haven't lost forty pounds.

Think of it this way: If you could consistently lose one pound per week for the next year, you'd lose fifty-two pounds. If you lost two pounds per week for the next year, that would be 104 pounds! That's a life-changing transformation. But it requires staying the course week after week, month after month, trusting that the small consistent actions compound into remarkable results.

The alternative—yo-yo dieting, extreme restriction followed by regaining the weight, trying quick fixes that don't address root causes—doesn't work. You've probably already proven that to yourself over the years.

This approach works. But it requires patience, consistency, and commitment to the process rather than obsession with immediate results.

The Long Game: Training for Aging

Remember why you're doing this: Yes, you want to lose weight and feel better now. But more importantly, you're establishing the metabolic health, hormonal balance, and physiological resilience that will serve you for decades to come.

You're not just surviving perimenopause—you're training for aging.

The eighty-year-old woman who lives independently, remains physically active, maintains cognitive sharpness, and enjoys tremendous quality of life didn't get there by accident. She established the foundations during perimenopause and maintained them through menopause and beyond.

That's you. That's what you're building right now with every protocol you implement, every lab test you complete, every adjustment you make.

So when you feel frustrated that you haven't lost all the weight in ninety days, zoom out. You're building something much bigger than short-term weight loss. You're building the foundation for your next 40+ years.

That's worth patience. That's worth consistency. That's worth the investment.

Chapter Summary

You now understand the full spectrum of treatment options available to heal your hormone imbalances:

- Foundational supplements to address nutrient deficiencies that impair hormone function
- Targeted supplements based on your specific imbalances
- Prescription medications to restore hormone levels and improve metabolic function
- Compounded medications when customization or cost savings are beneficial
- Lifestyle interventions that make everything else more effective

You know how to evaluate supplement quality and safety—looking for FDA-registered cGMP facilities, third-party testing, bioavailable forms, research backing, and minimal fillers. You understand why cheap supplements are often a waste of money and why investing in quality matters.

You understand The Matrix Method—our comprehensive, team-based approach that creates synergistic effects and produces results that isolated interventions cannot achieve. You know how we personalize treatment based

Chapter 11: Understanding Your Treatment Options

on your labs, symptoms, goals, and lifestyle. And you understand how to implement these protocols even if you don't have access to a full team.

Most importantly, you have realistic expectations about what success looks like: steady weight loss averaging 22.7 pounds in ninety days (with a range of 12-36 pounds based on your starting point and level of metabolic damage), symptom improvement over time, lab optimization, and the establishment of sustainable habits that will serve you for life.

You understand that this takes time—that less damage means quicker results and more damage means a longer healing phase. You know that everything we do is low, slow, and steady because women are sensitive to changes. And you know that patience and consistency are your superpowers.

Now you're ready for what comes next: the specific treatment protocols for each of the five hormone imbalances.

Treatment Protocols for the Five Hormone Imbalances

This chapter contains the complete toolkit—every evidence-based intervention we use with clients to restore hormone balance. But here's what's critical to understand: **Not every tool is right for every woman.** Some women need medications. Others achieve optimal results with supplements and lifestyle alone. Some require aggressive intervention across all five systems. Others need to focus on just one or two imbalances.

Work with your healthcare provider to determine which interventions are appropriate for your specific lab results, symptoms, medical history, and goals. The protocols in this chapter give you the knowledge to have informed, empowered conversations with your medical team—not to self-diagnose or self-treat.

MEDICAL DISCLAIMER: The information provided in this chapter is for educational purposes only and is not intended as medical advice, diagnosis, or treatment. All treatment protocols, medications, supplements, and lifestyle interventions discussed here should be implemented under the supervision of qualified healthcare providers who can order appropriate testing, determine proper dosing based on your individual needs, monitor your response, adjust protocols as needed, and manage potential side effects or interactions. Do not attempt to self-diagnose or self-treat based on this information. Always consult with licensed medical professionals before starting, stopping, or changing any treatment regimen.

Protocol 1: Cortisol Regulation

As you learned in Part I, when cortisol rhythm becomes disrupted during perimenopause, insulin stops working properly, thyroid conversion slows, progesterone plummets, estrogen becomes erratic, testosterone and DHEA drop, and inflammation increases.

This is why treating cortisol first is non-negotiable. If cortisol doesn't get back into rhythm, nothing else you do—no supplement, no medication, no diet—will give you the results you deserve. Your body cannot heal in a stress chemistry environment.

You've already established the lifestyle foundations in Part II—sleep, adequate nourishment, movement, and stress management strategies that calm your nervous system. Now we add the targeted treatments that work with your biology to regulate cortisol so your body feels safe enough to release weight, balance hormones, and repair.

Optimal Lab Ranges

Unlike the other four hormone imbalances, cortisol dysregulation is primarily diagnosed based on your symptoms rather than lab testing. As you learned in Part I, the symptom patterns tell us what we need to know: waking between 2-4 a.m., afternoon crashes, belly fat accumulation, sugar and salt cravings, anxiety, irritability, and difficulty losing weight despite doing everything right.

That said, some providers may choose to order cortisol testing to confirm HPA axis dysfunction:

Morning Cortisol (serum)

- **Optimal range:** 10-18 µg/dL
- **Standard lab range:** 6-23 µg/dL

Four-Point Salivary Cortisol—Tests cortisol at four times throughout the day to reveal your cortisol curve pattern.

DUTCH Complete (Dried Urine Test for Comprehensive Hormones)—Assesses cortisol and cortisol metabolites over twenty-four hours, includes cortisol awakening response, and also measures sex hormones and neurotransmitter metabolites.

Cortisol testing is optional. We don't retest cortisol—we treat based on symptoms and adjust protocols based on how you feel. When sleep improves, energy stabilizes, cravings diminish, and weight loss becomes consistent, you know your cortisol rhythm is normalizing.

Prescription Medications

Cortisol dysregulation is best addressed by treating the root cause—the chronic stress, poor sleep, blood sugar instability, and lifestyle patterns that keep your HPA axis in overdrive. However, when symptoms significantly impair your quality of life, healthcare providers may prescribe medications to help mitigate symptoms while the deeper healing occurs.

Medications that may be prescribed include:

- Sleep medications to restore restful sleep when cortisol surges prevent you from falling or staying asleep
- Anti-anxiety medications to reduce acute anxiety and nervous system reactivity
- Antidepressants (SSRIs or SNRIs) when cortisol dysregulation manifests as depression or mood instability

These medications are not addressing the root cause of cortisol dysregulation, but they can provide critical relief while you implement the lifestyle strategies, stress management techniques, and supplements that will restore your HPA axis function. Think of them as a bridge—temporary support that allows your body to get out of survival mode so the real healing work can take effect.

The goal is always to address the root cause. Medications can help you function while you're building the foundation, but lasting cortisol regulation comes from the comprehensive approach outlined in this protocol.

Supplement and Nutritional Support Options

The following are evidence-based adaptogenic herbs and nutrients that support cortisol regulation and HPA axis function. **These are options to discuss with your provider—not a requirement to use them all.** Your healthcare team will help you determine which are appropriate for your specific situation.

Adaptogenic Herbs:

Ashwagandha (Sensoril®)—One of the most studied adaptogens for hormone health. Supports healthy cortisol levels, improves sleep onset and quality, reduces stress-related cravings, supports thyroid hormone conversion (T4 → T3), and supports progesterone during perimenopause.

> *Best for: Elevated cortisol, difficulty falling asleep, anxiety*
>
> *Safety: Not recommended during pregnancy; use caution in hyperthyroidism*

Rhodiola rosea—Reduces stress-related fatigue without overstimulation. Improves mental performance under stress, reduces "wired but tired" fatigue, and is particularly helpful when cortisol is low in the morning.

> *Best for: Morning fatigue, burnout, low cortisol patterns*
>
> *Safety: Best taken in the morning; may be too stimulating for anxiety-prone women unless combined with L-theanine*

Magnolia Bark & Phellodendron Bark (Relora®)—Researched extensively for stress-related eating and nighttime cortisol surges. Reduces stress-induced cravings, supports healthy evening cortisol levels, and improves sleep onset.

> *Best for: Evening cravings, nighttime cortisol spikes, stress eating*

Maral Root (*Rhaponticum carthamoides*)—Supports stress adaptation and metabolic resilience. Promotes healthy glucose and lipid metabolism and helps with fatigue and recovery.

> *Best for: Physical & metabolic recovery, stamina, and libido*

L-Theanine (Suntheanine®)—An amino acid that increases alpha brain waves. Promotes calm without drowsiness, improves sleep quality, reduces stress reactivity, and enhances focus.

> *Best for: Daytime stress, mental clarity, sleep quality, and anxiety without drowsiness*

Phosphatidylserine—A phospholipid that modulates the HPA axis. Reduces cortisol spikes after physical or emotional stress, enhances memory and concentration, and supports mood regulation.

Best for: Cortisol spikes, emotional reactivity, brain fog

Valerian root—quiets an overactive nervous system by supporting GABA activity, allowing cortisol to come down naturally—especially at night.

Best for: Feeling wired but exhausted, racing thoughts, anxiety, and trouble falling or staying asleep. It can also be supportive for hot flashes.

Holy basil (Tulsi)—a powerful adaptogen that helps the body respond to stress more efficiently, smoothing out cortisol spikes and lowering stress-driven inflammation.

Best for: Chronic stress, emotional overwhelm, irritability, and mood changes tied to cortisol imbalance

Licorice root—supports cortisol by slowing its breakdown in the body, making it especially helpful when cortisol is too low and energy feels depleted.

Best for: Low morning energy, burnout, afternoon crashes, dizziness on standing, and symptoms of adrenal underperformance

Why combined formulas work: Clinically, the best outcomes occur when adaptogens are used in combination. Each botanical supports a different checkpoint in the HPA axis, creating a synergistic effect that helps restore rhythm and reduce symptoms. Look for blends that include herbs that target your symptoms.

Important: Choose high-quality, standardized extracts from reputable manufacturers. Look for patented forms (Sensoril®, Relora®, Suntheanine®), cGMP manufacturing, and third-party testing.

Lifestyle Integration: The Part II Foundation

Cortisol regulation requires addressing the root cause—the chronic stress, poor sleep, blood sugar instability, and lifestyle patterns keeping your HPA axis in overdrive. The supplements above support your body, but lifestyle creates the environment where healing can occur.

Chapter 12: Treatment Protocols for the Five Hormone Imbalances

Sleep Optimization, Blood Sugar Stability, Movement, and Hydration

As you learned in Part II, the Home Base habits—adequate sleep, protein-rich meals, regular movement, and hydration—are foundational for cortisol regulation. Consistent sleep schedules, a cool, dark bedroom, eating regular meals (never skipping breakfast), avoiding long fasting windows, and staying hydrated are all essential. These aren't optional additions—they're the soil in which cortisol healing grows.

For comprehensive strategies on sleep, nutrition, movement, and hydration, refer back to Part II.

Stress Management Techniques

Beyond the foundational habits, specific stress management techniques have powerful research supporting their ability to lower cortisol and restore HPA axis function. Here's the empowering truth: You may not be able to eliminate all stress from your life, but you CAN dramatically change how your body responds to stress.

Mindfulness Meditation

Research demonstrates that mindfulness meditation lowers cortisol levels. Even a four-day mindfulness program significantly decreased morning cortisol in medical students. Longer-term studies show that participants with extensive meditation experience have progressively lower morning cortisol.

Practical application:

- **Start small:** 5-10 minutes daily is better than thirty minutes occasionally
- **Use guided meditations (apps like Headspace, Calm, Insight Timer)**
- **Focus on breath:** Simply bringing attention to your breathing activates the parasympathetic nervous system
- **Practice mindful moments:** Bring full attention to routine activities (eating, walking, showering)

Deep Breathing and Breathwork

Controlled breathing directly activates your parasympathetic nervous system ("rest and digest") and inhibits your sympathetic nervous system ("fight or flight"). Techniques:

- **Box Breathing:** Inhale for four counts, hold four, exhale four, hold four. Repeat for five minutes. This technique is used by Navy SEALs to manage stress in high-pressure situations.
- **4-7-8 Breathing:** Inhale for four counts, hold seven, exhale slowly for eight. The extended exhale activates the vagus nerve and triggers relaxation. Particularly effective before bed or during acute stress.
- **Morning breathing practice:** 5-10 minutes upon waking helps set your cortisol rhythm for the day

Nature Exposure

Time in nature reduces cortisol, lowers blood pressure, decreases heart rate, and improves mood. Even twenty minutes in a natural setting produces measurable stress reduction. Combine this with gentle movement (walking) for synergistic benefits.

Social Connection

Positive social relationships buffer stress responses. Time with supportive friends and family, meaningful conversation, and physical touch (hugs release oxytocin, which counteracts cortisol) all help regulate your stress response.

Conversely, toxic relationships and social isolation elevate cortisol. Sometimes stress management means setting boundaries with people who deplete you.

Boundaries and Saying No

High-performing women often struggle with this. You've been conditioned to meet everyone's needs, say yes to every request, take on more responsibility. But chronic overcommitment is a direct path to adrenal burnout.

Learning to say no, to set boundaries, to protect your time and energy—this isn't selfish. It's essential for regulating cortisol and restoring adrenal function.

Therapy and Counseling

If chronic stress stems from trauma, relationship issues, or unresolved psychological patterns, therapy isn't optional—it's essential. Cognitive Behavioral Therapy (CBT) has strong research support for stress and anxiety reduction. EMDR can help process trauma that's driving chronic stress responses.

What Success Looks Like

When cortisol dysregulation is properly addressed, the transformation extends far beyond just "feeling less stressed." Here's the empowering truth: Even if you can't escape a demanding, high-stress lifestyle, you CAN change how stress impacts your body and reverse the symptoms you identified in Part I. Women report feeling calm and in control of their emotions rather than "on edge and ready to snap." Energy becomes sustained and stable throughout the day. Sleep is restorative. Mental clarity returns. And perhaps most importantly, when cortisol demands decrease, your adrenal glands can finally shift resources toward producing sex hormones—particularly progesterone and DHEA—instead of being stuck in survival mode producing cortisol. The pregnenolone steal reverses, and your entire hormonal cascade begins functioning properly again. The symptoms that drove you to take the quiz in Part I begin to disappear. Your body remembers how to function.

Protocol 2: Insulin Resistance

Insulin resistance is the most common hormone imbalance in women over thirty-five, and it's the primary reason for midlife weight gain—even when you're eating "healthy" and exercising consistently. As you learned in Part I, insulin is a storage hormone. When cells stop responding efficiently to insulin, the body produces more and more of it to push glucose inside. Chronically high insulin keeps you in fat-storing mode and creates the stubborn belly fat, constant cravings, afternoon crashes, and "nothing works for me" frustration you identified in your quiz results.

Here's what's critical: Insulin is deeply interconnected with every other hormone system. When insulin resistance improves, cortisol stabilizes, progesterone finds rhythm, thyroid hormones convert more efficiently, inflammation drops, and weight loss becomes predictable again.

Optimal Lab Ranges

Insulin resistance assessment reveals your metabolic health status and guides treatment decisions.

Hemoglobin A1c (HbA1c)

- **Optimal:** 4.8-5.1%
- **Insulin Resistant:** 5.1-5.7%
- **Pre-diabetes:** 5.8-6.3%
- **Diabetes:** ≥6.4%

  Why it matters: Reflects average blood sugar over three months

Fasting Insulin

- **Low:** 0-2 µIU/mL
- **Optimal:** 2-5 µIU/mL
- **Above optimal:** 7-12 µIU/mL
- **Elevated:** 12-15 µIU/mL
- **High:** >15 µIU/mL

  Why it matters: Insulin rises long before glucose does. This is one of the earliest markers of insulin resistance.

HOMA-IR (Homeostatic Model Assessment of Insulin Resistance)

- **Optimal:** <1.5
- **Above optimal:** 1.5-2.4
- **Insulin resistant:** >2.4

- **Calculated from:** HOMA-IR = (fasting glucose mg/dL × fasting insulin μIU/mL) ÷ 405

  Why it matters: HOMA-IR is a more accurate measure of insulin resistance than fasting insulin alone. It requires both fasting glucose and fasting insulin to calculate. This is the gold standard for assessing insulin resistance.

Fasting Glucose

- **Optimal range:** 70-85 mg/dL
- **Standard lab range:** 70-99 mg/dL

  Why it matters: Needed to calculate HOMA-IR; also shows glucose regulation, though glucose elevates later than insulin in the progression of insulin resistance

---

Retesting typically occurs at three months to assess response to treatment.

Prescription Medications

When insulin resistance is moderate to severe, or when lifestyle and supplements alone aren't sufficient, prescription medications can be transformative. These are powerful tools that address the root metabolic dysfunction—but they're also complex interventions that require careful medical supervision.

GLP-1 Medications

GLP-1 (glucagon-like peptide-1) medications represent one of the most significant advances in metabolic medicine for treating insulin resistance and achieving sustainable weight loss. The two FDA-approved medications are semaglutide (Wegovy) and tirzepatide (Zepbound). How it works:

- Slows gastric emptying, keeping you fuller longer after meals
- Reduces appetite and food cravings at the brain level (hypothalamus)
- Stabilizes blood sugar by stimulating insulin production when glucose is elevated

- Improves insulin sensitivity throughout the body
- Enhances pancreatic beta-cell function
- Tirzepatide activates both GIP and GLP-1 receptors, providing enhanced metabolic benefits

Why it's helpful: GLP-1 medications address multiple aspects of metabolic dysfunction simultaneously—insulin resistance, appetite dysregulation, and weight loss resistance. They're particularly effective for perimenopausal and menopausal women because hormonal changes during this transition damage the GI tract lining and lower natural GLP-1 production precisely when insulin resistance is developing. GLP-1 medications can reverse years of metabolic damage, but they work most effectively when combined with comprehensive hormone optimization. Research demonstrates that women using both GLP-1 medications and hormone therapy achieve significantly better outcomes than those using GLP-1s alone.

What you need to know:
- Weekly injections with gradual dose titration
- Common side effects: nausea, constipation, reduced appetite (typically improve with proper dosing)
- Rare but serious side effects: gastroparesis, pancreatitis, vision changes
- Must be combined with adequate protein intake (90-120g daily) and resistance training to preserve muscle mass
- Require ongoing medical supervision and monitoring
- Compounded versions exist but lack FDA approval and regulatory oversight
- Insurance coverage varies significantly

Treatment Approach: We use a microdosing strategy with most patients—starting at lower doses than standard FDA titration and increasing gradually based on individual response. This minimizes side effects while maximizing results. Our goal is always the lowest effective dose combined with comprehensive hormone optimization, nutrition, and lifestyle interventions.

Chapter 12: Treatment Protocols for the Five Hormone Imbalances

GLP-1 medications are considered when:
- Any early insulin resistance with elevated HbA1c
- Weight loss resistance despite addressing other hormone imbalances
  - » In our practice, we offer GLP1 medications even if someone doesn't meet BMI requirements and only has twenty pounds to lose using a microdosing strategy and very close medical oversight

- Stubborn visceral adiposity
- Strong family history of type 2 diabetes
- Moderate to severe metabolic dysfunction

Combined therapy (GLP-1 with metformin) is appropriate for more advanced disease states (prediabetic or type 2 diabetic) or when HbA1c remains elevated on single-agent therapy.

Treatment duration varies: Some women use GLP-1 medications for 12-24 months to reverse insulin resistance and establish sustainable habits, then discontinue successfully. Others benefit from long-term maintenance doses, especially those with lifelong metabolic dysfunction. Your provider determines the appropriate duration based on your metabolic response, symptom resolution, and lab improvements.

Success with GLP-1 medications depends on addressing all hormone imbalances simultaneously, maintaining adequate protein and resistance training, and building sustainable habits—not just taking the medication. When integrated into comprehensive treatment, these medications produce transformative results that are maintainable long-term.

Metformin

Metformin is one of the oldest and most studied diabetes medications, frequently used for insulin resistance even when diabetes isn't present.

How it works:
- Reduces glucose production in the liver
- Improves insulin sensitivity in muscle tissue
- Decreases intestinal glucose absorption
- May support modest weight loss

Why it's helpful: Metformin addresses the root problem—insulin resistance—not just the symptoms. It's generally well-tolerated, has decades of safety data, is inexpensive, and has demonstrated cardiovascular benefits. It's particularly useful when HbA1c is more elevated or when there's a family history of type 2 diabetes.

What you need to know:

- Typically started at low dose and gradually increased
- Extended-release formulation (Metformin ER) significantly reduces GI side effects
- Take with food to minimize digestive upset
- May cause vitamin B12 deficiency with long-term use (your provider will monitor and recommend supplementation if needed)
- Generally very safe with decades of use data

Treatment Approach:

In clinical practice, treatment decisions depend on your individual situation:

- **GLP-1 medications** are often considered first-line for significant insulin resistance with elevated HbA1c, especially when weight loss is a primary goal
- **Metformin** may be started first for milder insulin resistance or as a cost-effective option
- **Combined therapy** (both GLP-1 and metformin) is appropriate for more severe insulin resistance or when HbA1c remains elevated on monotherapy

Your provider will determine the appropriate strategy based on your lab results, symptoms, medical history, insurance coverage, and personal preferences.

Supplement and Nutritional Support Options

The following are evidence-based nutrients and compounds that support insulin sensitivity, glucose metabolism, and metabolic health. **These are options to discuss with your provider—not a mandate to use them all.**

Chapter 12: Treatment Protocols for the Five Hormone Imbalances

Your healthcare team will help determine which are appropriate for your specific situation.

Insulin-Sensitizing Compounds:

Berberine—A botanical compound studied extensively for metabolic health. Research shows it improves insulin sensitivity, supports healthy blood sugar and HbA1c levels, reduces fasting insulin, helps lower inflammatory markers, and activates AMPK (your metabolic "master switch"). Some studies show berberine performs comparably to metformin for certain metabolic markers.

>*Best for: Mild to moderate insulin resistance, women preferring natural options, or as complement to medications*
>*Safety: Avoid during pregnancy; may cause mild digestive changes initially; take with meals*

Ceylon Cinnamon Extract (4:1 Concentrate)—The 4:1 extract is four times more concentrated than raw cinnamon, ensuring therapeutic dosing. Research shows it supports healthy fasting glucose, improves insulin receptor sensitivity, reduces oxidative stress, and helps with cravings.

>*Best for: Mild insulin resistance, blood sugar stability, cravings*
>*Safety: Use Ceylon (not cassia) to avoid high coumarin content*

Myo-Inositol—Supports insulin signaling, particularly beneficial for women with PCOS. Also helps with cravings, supports ovulation, and helps stabilize mood.

>*Best for: PCOS, insulin resistance with hormonal imbalance*

Chromium—A trace mineral that improves insulin receptor sensitivity and helps reduce sugar cravings.

>*Best for: Carbohydrate cravings, glucose metabolism*

Omega-3 Fatty Acids—Reduce inflammation, improve insulin sensitivity, support thyroid hormone receptor sensitivity, improve triglycerides, and activate cell membrane fluidity (making insulin receptors more responsive).

>*Best for: Inflammation, insulin resistance, cardiovascular health*
>*Safety: Choose pharmaceutical-grade, tested for purity and heavy metals*

Gut-Directed Metabolic Support:

Your gut microbiome is one of the most important regulators of metabolic health. Certain bacterial strains directly influence GLP-1 production, appetite, insulin sensitivity, fat storage, and inflammation.

Clinically validated probiotic strains for metabolic health include:

- **Akkermansia muciniphila AH39:** Strengthens gut barrier, improves insulin sensitivity, reduces inflammation
- **Bifidobacterium animalis (HN019& B420):** Supports healthy body composition, regulates glucose metabolism
- **Lactobacillus rhamnosus GG:** Reduces inflammation, strengthens gut lining
- **Clostridium butyricum 10:** Produces butyrate (key short-chain fatty acid), supports GLP-1 release

Why this matters: These bacteria produce short-chain fatty acids (SCFAs) that activate GLP-1—the same pathway used by GLP-1 medications. Higher GLP-1 naturally increases satiety, reduces cravings, stabilizes blood sugar, and supports weight management.

Best for: Anyone with insulin resistance, especially when using GLP-1 medications

Digestive Enzyme Support:

Digestive enzymes help break down food effectively, relieving discomfort and improving nutrient absorption—essential for thyroid function, energy production, and hormone synthesis. This is particularly important when using GLP-1 medications, which slow gastric emptying.

Best for: Bloating, early satiety, fatigue after meals; essential when using GLP-1 medications

Protein Supplement Support:

As you learned in Part II, adequate protein (90-120g daily for most women) is one of the most powerful metabolic levers available. Protein stabilizes blood sugar, lowers insulin response, supports muscle mass, improves metabolic

Chapter 12: Treatment Protocols for the Five Hormone Imbalances

rate, and reduces cravings. High-quality protein powders can help you hit daily targets, especially when appetite is low or schedules are tight.

Best for: Meeting protein goals, post-workout recovery, blood sugar stability

Lifestyle Integration: The Part II Foundation

Insulin resistance treatment works when combined with the nutritional strategies from Part II. The Home Base habits—MORE water, sleep, vegetables, movement. For insulin resistance protein at every meal for blood sugar stability, eating veggies first for reduced post meal blood sugar spikes accelerate healing. These begin reversing insulin resistance naturally. These aren't optional additions; they create the environment where medications and supplements can work effectively.

Key Principles from Part II:

- **Protein priority:** 90-120g daily, protein at every meal
- **Build your plate:** Half non-starchy vegetables, quarter protein, quarter complex carbs
- **Veggies first:** Eating veggies first, then protein, fat, and carbs last will reduce post meal blood sugar spikes.
- **Limit refined carbs:** Minimize added sugars, white flour, and processed foods
- **Eat regularly:** Don't skip meals; blood sugar crashes trigger insulin surges
- **Post-meal walks:** 10-20-minute walks after meals is better than one sixty-minute walk for insulin resistance.
- **Resistance training:** Build insulin-sensitive muscle tissue—non-negotiable for long-term metabolic health
- **Sleep optimization:** Poor sleep worsens insulin resistance
- **Stress management:** Chronic stress drives cortisol, which worsens insulin resistance

Part III: The Comprehensive Approach

For comprehensive strategies on nutrition, movement, sleep, and stress management, refer back to Part II.

What Success Looks Like:

When insulin resistance improves, the symptoms you identified in Part I begin to disappear. You burn stored fat easily. Cravings disappear. Food noise quiets. Appetite normalizes. Energy stabilizes throughout the day. Belly fat shrinks. Sleep improves. Mood lifts. And critically, downstream hormone balance improves—thyroid conversion becomes more efficient, sex hormones stabilize, and inflammation drops. Women say, *"For the first time in years, my body is responding again."*

Insulin resistance is not a moral failing or a lack of willpower. It's a physiologic pattern you can reverse with the right tools.

Protocol 3: Thyroid Optimization

Your thyroid is your metabolic master regulator. As you learned in Part I, thyroid hormones control the rate at which every cell in your body burns energy—your metabolism, body temperature, heart rate, digestion, brain function, and more. When thyroid function declines during perimenopause, everything slows down: Weight gain becomes effortless, energy disappears, brain fog settles in, hair thins, skin dries, and you feel cold all the time.

Here's what makes thyroid dysfunction particularly frustrating: You can have "normal" lab values and still feel terrible. Standard thyroid testing often misses subclinical hypothyroidism, suboptimal Free T3 levels, elevated Reverse T3, and autoimmune thyroid disease. And even when thyroid dysfunction is diagnosed, conventional treatment often involves T4-only medication without addressing the conversion to active T3 or the root causes driving dysfunction.

The good news: when thyroid function is optimized—not just "normal" but truly optimal—the transformation is remarkable. Energy returns, weight loss becomes possible again, mental clarity improves, mood stabilizes, and your body remembers how to function efficiently.

Chapter 12: Treatment Protocols for the Five Hormone Imbalances

Optimal Lab Ranges

Comprehensive thyroid assessment requires multiple markers—not just TSH. Your healthcare provider should order:

TSH (Thyroid Stimulating Hormone)

- **Low:** 0-0.45 mIU/L
- **Below optimal:** 0.45-0.8 mIU/L
- **Optimal:** 0.8-1.8 mIU/L (ideally close to 1.0, always less than 1.8)
- **Above optimal:** 1.8-4.5 mIU/L
- **High:** 4.5-20 mIU/L

  Why it matters: TSH is a pituitary hormone that signals the thyroid to produce more hormone. However, TSH alone is insufficient for diagnosis—you must check Free T4 and Free T3.

Free T4 (Free Thyroxine)

- **Low:** 0-0.7 ng/dL
- **Below optimal:** 0.7-0.9 ng/dL
- **Optimal:** 0.9-1.2 ng/dL
- **Above optimal:** 1.2-1.8 ng/dL
- **High:** >1.8 ng/dL

  Why it matters: T4 is the inactive form of thyroid hormone produced by your thyroid gland. It must be converted to T3 (the active form) to work in your cells.

Free T3 (Free Triiodothyronine)

- **Low:** <2.5 pg/mL
- **Below optimal:** 2.5-3.5 pg/mL
- **Optimal:** 3.6-4.2 pg/mL
- **Above optimal:** 4.3-5.0 pg/mL
- **High:** >5.0 pg/mL

Why it matters: T3 is the active thyroid hormone that actually does the work in your cells. This is the most important marker for how you feel. Many women have adequate T4 but insufficient T3 due to poor conversion.

Reverse T3 (RT3)

- **Optimal:** 8-12 ng/dL, (15-16 can still be ok if fT3 is optimized)
- **Elevated:** >16 ng/dL

Why it matters: Reverse T3 is an inactive form of thyroid hormone that blocks T3 receptors. High stress, inflammation, and insulin resistance all increase RT3 production, creating "thyroid resistance" even when Free T3 levels appear adequate.

Thyroid Peroxidase Antibodies (TPO)

- **Optimal:** <2 IU/mL
- **Ideal (functional medicine):** <14 IU/mL
- **Normal:** <24 IU/mL
- **Elevated:** 25-35 IU/mL
- **High:** >35 IU/mL
- **Lab cutoff (conventional):** <35 IU/mL (conventionally considered negative)

Why it matters: Elevated antibodies indicate Hashimoto's thyroiditis—autoimmune thyroid disease. Approximately ninety percent of hypothyroidism is autoimmune. If you have elevated antibodies, you need additional strategies to reduce autoimmune activity and inflammation.

Thyroglobulin Antibodies (TgAb)

- **Optimal:** <2 IU/mL
- **Lab cutoff may be around 9 IU/mL**

Why it matters: Another marker for autoimmune thyroid disease. Some women have elevated TgAb even when TPO is normal.

Chapter 12: Treatment Protocols for the Five Hormone Imbalances

Key Principle: Treat the Person, Not Just the Numbers

Even when labs fall in "optimal" ranges, if you still have hypothyroid symptoms (fatigue, weight gain, brain fog, cold intolerance, hair loss, constipation), your thyroid may need further optimization. Conversely, if you feel great and your symptoms have resolved, that's the goal, regardless of where your numbers fall within the optimal range.

Your provider will determine which tests are most appropriate for your situation. Education regarding sudden onset of symptoms indicating overcorrection (such as rapid heart rate, sweating, difficulty sleeping) is important and warrants earlier evaluation and repeat testing. **Otherwise, retesting typically occurs at 8-12 weeks after starting or adjusting thyroid medication, then every 3-6 months once stable.**

Prescription Medications

Thyroid hormone replacement is the cornerstone of treatment for hypothyroidism. The goal is to restore optimal thyroid hormone levels—not just bring TSH into "normal" range but achieve Free T3 and Free T4 levels where you feel your best and symptoms resolve.

Levothyroxine (Synthroid, Levoxyl, Tirosint)

Levothyroxine is synthetic T4 (thyroxine), the inactive form of thyroid hormone that your body must convert to active T3.

How it works:
- Provides T4, which your body converts to T3 in the liver, gut, and peripheral tissues
- Requires approximately twenty percent conversion to happen in the gut (which is why gut health matters)
- Takes 6-8 weeks to reach steady state in your system

Why it's helpful: Levothyroxine is the most commonly prescribed thyroid medication and works well for many women, especially those whose bodies efficiently convert T4 to T3. It's covered by insurance, has decades of safety data, and is FDA-approved.

What you need to know:
- Must be taken on an empty stomach, 30-60 minutes before food
- Coffee, calcium, iron, and magnesium can interfere with absorption (wait at least four hours)
- Consistency matters—take at the same time daily
- Brand matters for some women (Tirosint is a gel cap with fewer fillers that some tolerate better)
- Dosing is highly individualized

Liothyronine (Cytomel)

Liothyronine is synthetic T3—the active form of thyroid hormone.

How it works:
- Provides T3 directly, bypassing the need for conversion
- Works quickly (you may feel effects within hours to days)
- Has a shorter half-life than T4 (needs to be taken 1-2 times daily)

Why it's helpful: Some women don't convert T4 to T3 efficiently due to inflammation, stress, nutrient deficiencies, or gut issues. Adding T3 can dramatically improve symptoms even when TSH and Free T4 are "optimal." T3 is particularly helpful for persistent fatigue, brain fog, and weight loss resistance despite adequate T4 levels.

What you need to know:
- Can be added to levothyroxine or used alone
- May be split into two doses daily (morning and early afternoon) for more stable levels
- Requires careful titration—too much T3 can cause anxiety, palpitations, or insomnia
- Not all providers are comfortable prescribing T3

Combination T4/T3 Therapy

Many functional medicine providers prescribe both T4 and T3 together to achieve optimal Free T3 levels while maintaining adequate T4.

Why it works: This approach mimics what a healthy thyroid gland produces naturally (approximately eighty percent T4 and twenty percent T3). For women with conversion issues—common during perimenopause due to inflammation, stress, and gut dysfunction—adding T3 ensures adequate active hormone reaches cells.

Natural Desiccated Thyroid (NDT): Armour Thyroid, Nature-Throid, WP Thyroid

NDT is derived from porcine (pig) thyroid glands and contains both T4 and T3 in a roughly 4:1 ratio, plus small amounts of T2, T1, and calcitonin.

How it works:

- Provides both T4 and T3 naturally
- Some patients report feeling better on NDT than synthetic hormones
- Contains the same thyroid hormones humans produce

Why some providers prescribe it: Women who don't feel optimal on levothyroxine alone sometimes experience significant improvement on NDT. The combination of T4 and T3, plus the additional thyroid components, may provide benefits for certain patients.

What you need to know:

- Not all endocrinologists prescribe NDT (many prefer synthetic hormones).
- Requires compounding in some cases due to manufacturing issues with commercial brands.
- Dosing can be less predictable than synthetic hormones.
- Some insurance doesn't cover it.
- Quality and potency can vary between manufacturers.

Reverse T3 Considerations

When Reverse T3 is elevated, it blocks thyroid hormone receptors even when Free T3 is adequate. Treatment focuses on:

- Addressing root causes: stress (cortisol), inflammation, insulin resistance

- Optimizing Free T3 levels higher in the range
- Some providers use sustained-release T3 or adjust T4/T3 ratios

Treatment Approach:

Your provider will determine the best thyroid medication strategy based on:

- Your lab results (TSH, Free T4, Free T3, Reverse T3, antibodies)
- Your symptoms
- How well you convert T4 to T3
- Whether you have Hashimoto's or other autoimmune conditions
- Your response to previous thyroid medications
- Your insurance coverage and preferences

Many women start with levothyroxine alone. If symptoms persist despite optimal TSH and Free T4, adding T3 or switching to combination therapy often produces dramatic improvement.

The most important principle: Thyroid optimization is not one-size-fits-all. Work with a provider who listens to your symptoms, tests comprehensively, and is willing to adjust your medication until you feel optimal—not just until your TSH is "normal."

Hashimoto's Thyroiditis Considerations

Hashimoto's thyroiditis is the most common cause of hypothyroidism in the United States, accounting for approximately ninety percent of cases. As discussed in Part I, it's an autoimmune condition where the immune system mistakenly attacks the thyroid gland, causing chronic inflammation and progressive destruction of thyroid tissue. This attack is mediated by antibodies—primarily thyroid peroxidase (TPO) antibodies and thyroglobulin (TG) antibodies—that can be measured in blood tests.

Standard treatment focuses on thyroid hormone replacement to address the hypothyroidism, but this approach doesn't address the underlying autoimmune attack. The thyroid continues to be destroyed even when thyroid hormone levels are optimized with medication.

Chapter 12: Treatment Protocols for the Five Hormone Imbalances

For women with Hashimoto's who have completed comprehensive treatment including thyroid medication optimization, elimination of inflammatory triggers, targeted supplementation, and gut healing but still have elevated antibodies or persistent symptoms, Low Dose Naltrexone (LDN) offers an additional therapeutic option that targets the autoimmune process itself. When used in **low, micro-dosed amounts**, GLP-1 medications can also provide powerful anti-inflammatory support, helping calm immune overactivation and reduce systemic inflammation that often drives autoimmune thyroid flares.

Low Dose Naltrexone (LDN)

Low Dose Naltrexone (LDN) is an off-label treatment that has shown promise in managing autoimmune thyroid conditions, particularly Hashimoto's thyroiditis. While originally FDA-approved at higher doses for opioid and alcohol addiction, low doses have demonstrated immune-modulating properties that may benefit autoimmune conditions.

How it works:
- Acts as a Toll-like receptor 4 (TLR4) antagonist, reducing glial cell activation and pro-inflammatory cytokine production
- Modulates immune function by decreasing inflammatory markers including IL-6, TNF-alpha, and interferon-alpha
- May improve T4 to T3 conversion through reduced inflammation at both pituitary and peripheral tissue levels
- Helps balance Th1/Th2 immune response and supports regulatory T cell function

Why it's helpful: For women with Hashimoto's thyroiditis, LDN addresses the autoimmune process driving thyroid destruction rather than just replacing thyroid hormone. Clinical observations show significant reductions in thyroid antibodies (TPO and TG) in approximately 40-50 percent of patients with some experiencing drops from levels exceeding 1000 IU/mL to under 100 IU/mL within 3-6 months. Beyond antibody reduction, patients report improvements in energy (sixty-six percent), mood (sixty-one percent), pain (forty percent), and overall well-being.

LDN is particularly valuable when thyroid antibodies remain stubbornly elevated despite dietary modifications and supplement protocols or when autoimmune symptoms persist even with optimized thyroid hormone replacement. It may slow or halt the progressive destruction of thyroid tissue, and in some cases, restore thyroid function sufficiently to allow reduction in thyroid medication dosing.

What you need to know:

- Available only through compounding pharmacies (most local pharmacies don't stock low-dose formulations)
- **Common side effects:** vivid dreams, insomnia (usually resolve within 2-3 weeks)
- **Less common:** transient nausea, headaches, feeling "flat" emotionally (indicates dose is too high)
- **Contraindications:** concurrent opioid use, severe liver or kidney disease, immunosuppressive medications
- Requires regular thyroid function monitoring—successful treatment may necessitate thyroid medication dose reductions
- Takes 8-12 weeks to see antibody changes; symptom improvements may occur earlier
- Generally well-tolerated with minimal side effects at appropriate dosing
- Relatively inexpensive ($30-60/month typically)

Treatment Approach: We use a conservative titration strategy to minimize side effects and allow the body to adjust gradually. Patients with Hashimoto's are often particularly sensitive to LDN, so we start lower than with other autoimmune conditions.

LDN is considered when:

- Thyroid antibodies remain elevated (TPO >100 IU/mL or TG >100 IU/mL) despite comprehensive treatment
- Autoimmune symptoms persist despite optimized thyroid medication
- Other autoimmune conditions coexist (multiple autoimmune syndrome)

Chapter 12: Treatment Protocols for the Five Hormone Imbalances

- Patient prefers immune-modulating approach over symptom management alone
- Conventional approaches have plateaued but symptoms continue

Critical monitoring requirements:
- Monitor thyroid antibodies (TPO, TG) every three months
- Watch for signs of hyperthyroidism (anxiety, palpitations, tremors, insomnia)—may indicate thyroid function improving and medication dose needs reduction
- Some patients experience rapid antibody reduction with dramatic restoration of thyroid function, requiring prompt medication adjustments

LDN works synergistically with comprehensive Hashimoto's treatment including thyroid medication optimization, targeted supplementation (selenium, vitamin D, zinc), inflammatory food elimination, and stress management. It's an adjunct therapy, not a replacement for thyroid hormone when hypothyroidism is present.

Success with LDN varies significantly between individuals. Some experience complete remission of autoimmune activity with normalized antibodies and restored thyroid function. Others see moderate antibody reductions and symptom improvements.

Supplement and Nutritional Support Options

The following are evidence-based nutrients that support thyroid function, hormone conversion, and reduce autoimmune activity. **These are options to discuss with your provider—not a mandate to use them all.** Your healthcare team will help determine which are appropriate for your specific situation.

Essential Nutrients for Thyroid Function:

Selenium—Critical for converting T4 to T3. Your body needs selenium-dependent enzymes (deiodinases) to activate thyroid hormone. Research shows selenium supplementation can reduce TPO antibodies in Hashimoto's patients and improve thyroid function.

Best for: Poor T4 to T3 conversion, elevated thyroid antibodies, Hashimoto's

Safety: Don't exceed 400 mcg daily; excessive selenium can be toxic

Zinc—Required for thyroid hormone production and T4 to T3 conversion. Zinc deficiency is common in hypothyroid patients and can worsen thyroid function.

Best for: Low Free T3, hair loss, immune dysfunction

Safety: Take with food; can cause nausea on empty stomach

Magnesium—Supports thyroid hormone production and helps convert T4 to T3. Magnesium deficiency is extremely common and worsens both thyroid and metabolic function.

Best for: Everyone with thyroid dysfunction, also supports sleep and stress response

Forms: Magnesium glycinate (best absorbed, calming) or magnesium citrate

Vitamin D—Low vitamin D is associated with autoimmune thyroid disease and worsens thyroid function. Vitamin D acts as an immune modulator and supports thyroid hormone receptor sensitivity.

Best for: Hashimoto's, autoimmune conditions, anyone with vitamin D deficiency (which is most perimenopausal women)

Omega-3 Fatty Acids (EPA/DHA)—Reduce inflammation, support thyroid hormone receptor sensitivity, and help modulate autoimmune activity. Essential for anyone with Hashimoto's or elevated antibodies.

Best for: Inflammation, Hashimoto's, autoimmune conditions

Safety: Choose pharmaceutical-grade, tested for purity and heavy metals

Methylated B vitamins play a key role in thyroid hormone production and conversion, particularly by supporting methylation pathways needed to convert T4 into the metabolically active T3. They also aid in reducing inflammation and optimizing cellular energy, both of which improve thyroid function. Because methylated forms bypass common genetic blocks like

MTHFR mutations, they ensure your thyroid gets the nutrients it needs to function efficiently.

Making sure there are adequate methylated B vitamins in your multivitamin supplement is a great way to reduce supplement "capsule burden" from having to take more supplements while supporting your thyroid function.

Reminder: All of these supplements do not need to be taken individually. Taking a high-quality multivitamin and mineral supplement that includes all of these nutrients is typically our starting recommendation. Need help identifying one? Visit empoweredweightlossbook.com for specific supplements that will check all these boxes.

Gut Support for Thyroid Function:

Your gut is responsible for approximately twenty percent of T4 to T3 conversion. When gut health is compromised—through inflammation, dysbiosis, leaky gut, or poor nutrient absorption—thyroid function suffers even when thyroid hormone levels appear adequate.

Gut-directed probiotics that support thyroid function and reduce inflammation include strains like Lactobacillus and Bifidobacterium species that strengthen the gut lining, reduce inflammatory cytokines, and support healthy immune function.

Digestive enzymes can improve nutrient absorption—particularly important for selenium, zinc, and other thyroid-supporting nutrients. When digestion is impaired, you can't absorb the building blocks your thyroid needs.

Best for: Anyone with digestive issues, bloating, or suspected nutrient malabsorption

For Hashimoto's and Elevated Antibodies:

If you have elevated TPO or TgAb antibodies, additional strategies to reduce autoimmune activity include:

- **Elimination Diet:** Certain foods can trigger inflammation/autoimmune flares in susceptible individuals. Doing the 10-Day Detox can help you identify which foods are triggers for you.

- **Anti-inflammatory support:** Omega-3s, curcumin, and antioxidants help reduce autoimmune activity
- **Gut healing:** Addressing leaky gut and dysbiosis reduces systemic inflammation and autoimmune triggers. Immunolin® is a serum-derived bovine immunoglobulin/protein isolate that works by binding, neutralizing, and removing toxins from the gut. Using a supplement with this key ingredient promotes healthy immune activation responses and gut permeability.
- **Stress management:** Chronic stress worsens autoimmune conditions through cortisol dysregulation. Stress relieving activities: walking, yoga, breathwork, meditation, baths, reading etc.

Lifestyle Integration: The Part II Foundation

Thyroid optimization requires the foundational strategies from Part II. The Home Base habits—adequate protein, nutrient-dense vegetables, quality sleep, stress management, and consistent movement—all support thyroid function.

Key Principles from Part II:

- **Adequate protein:** Supports thyroid hormone production and metabolism
- **Nutrient density:** Thyroid function depends on micronutrients (selenium, zinc, magnesium, B vitamins, iron)
- **Blood sugar stability:** Insulin resistance worsens T4 to T3 conversion and increases Reverse T3
- **Sleep optimization:** Poor sleep increases cortisol, which worsens thyroid function
- **Stress management:** Chronic stress increases Reverse T3 and inhibits thyroid hormone conversion
- **Avoid extreme caloric restriction:** Severe calorie deficit signals your body to slow metabolism by reducing T3 production

Chapter 12: Treatment Protocols for the Five Hormone Imbalances

Additional Thyroid-Specific Considerations:

- **Timing thyroid medication properly:** Take 30-60 minutes before food, away from coffee, supplements (especially calcium, iron, magnesium)
- **Consistent schedule:** Take at the same time daily for stable hormone levels
- **Monitor symptoms:** Track energy, body temperature, hair quality, weight, mood—these tell you if optimization is working
- **Retest appropriately:** 6-8 weeks after medication changes, then every 3-6 months once stable

For comprehensive strategies on nutrition, movement, sleep, and stress management, refer back to Part II.

What Success Looks Like:

Thyroid optimization is not just about getting TSH into range. It's about achieving Free T3 levels where your cells can function optimally, addressing conversion issues, reducing autoimmune activity if present, and supporting your thyroid with the nutrients it needs to work efficiently.

When thyroid function is optimized, the symptoms you identified in Part I begin to disappear. Energy returns—real, sustained energy that lasts throughout the day. Mental clarity improves; brain fog lifts. Body temperature normalizes; you stop feeling cold all the time. Hair stops falling out and begins growing back thicker. Weight loss becomes possible again when combined with the other protocols. Mood stabilizes. Your metabolism wakes up. Women say, *"I feel like myself again."*

Protocol 4: Sex Hormone Balance

Estrogen, progesterone, and testosterone—your sex hormones—are declining during perimenopause and will eventually reach menopausal levels. As you learned in Part I, this isn't just about hot flashes and missed periods. These hormones regulate metabolism, muscle mass, bone density, brain function, mood, sleep, libido, skin quality, cardiovascular health, and more. When they decline, the effects ripple through every system in your body.

Here's what makes sex hormone treatment different from the other protocols: The approach depends entirely on where you are in your transition. A woman in early perimenopause with erratic estrogen swings needs different support than a woman in late perimenopause with plummeting progesterone, and both are different from a postmenopausal woman who's been without ovarian hormone production for years.

The goal isn't to restore hormones to age twenty-five levels—that's neither possible nor appropriate. The goal is to provide adequate hormone support to maintain quality of life, protect long-term health (bone density, cardiovascular function, cognitive health), and allow your body to function optimally during and after this transition.

Optimal Lab Ranges

Sex hormone assessment during perimenopause and menopause focuses on **ratios and relationships between hormones** rather than absolute values. Unlike cycling women who need to test at specific cycle points, perimenopausal and menopausal women can test at any time because we're evaluating overall hormone patterns and imbalances.

Progesterone/Estrogen Ratio (P/E2 Ratio)

- **Optimal:** <200

    Why it matters: This ratio of serum progesterone to estradiol reveals whether you're experiencing estrogen dominance (common in early perimenopause when progesterone drops before estrogen) or overall low sex hormones (late perimenopause/menopause when both are declining). A high ratio indicates estrogen dominance relative to progesterone. A very low ratio with low absolute values suggests both hormones are depleted.

Total Testosterone (females)

- **Optimal range:** 20-45 ng/dL

  Why it matters: Testosterone supports libido, muscle mass, bone density, energy, motivation, and metabolic function. Levels naturally decline with age and drop significantly during perimenopause

DHEA-S (Dehydroepiandrosterone Sulfate)

- **Optimal range:** 125-200 mcg/dL

  Why it matters: DHEA is the precursor hormone from your adrenal glands that converts to both estrogen and testosterone. When DHEA is low, your body has less raw material to produce sex hormones

Additional Markers Your Provider May Order:

- **FSH (Follicle Stimulating Hormone):** Rises as ovarian function declines
- **LH (Luteinizing Hormone):** Helps confirm menopausal status
- **SHBG (Sex Hormone Binding Globulin):** Affects how much testosterone and estrogen are available to your cells

Key Principle: Symptoms Matter More Than Numbers

Two women can have similar lab results but dramatically different symptom profiles. The goal isn't just normalizing numbers—it's addressing your specific symptoms while maintaining hormonal balance. Hot flashes, night sweats, vaginal dryness, painful sex, mood changes, brain fog, sleep disruption, weight gain, muscle loss—these symptoms guide treatment decisions alongside lab values.

Your provider will determine which tests are appropriate for your situation.

Prescription Medications: Hormone Replacement Therapy (HRT)

IMPORTANT DISCLAIMER: Hormone replacement therapy should only be prescribed and managed by qualified healthcare providers experienced in HRT. Proper evaluation, monitoring, dosing, and individualized treatment require medical expertise. This section is designed to help you understand what options exist and have informed conversations with your healthcare team—not to guide self-treatment.

Hormone replacement therapy is often the final piece that brings everything together for perimenopausal and menopausal women—but HRT alone won't reverse insulin resistance, fix thyroid conversion, rebuild lost muscle, or correct cortisol dysregulation. Comprehensive treatment addressing all five hormone systems produces the results women are seeking.

Understanding "Bioidentical" Hormones

Bioidentical hormones look almost exactly the same from a chemical and molecular structure standpoint as the hormones your body produces naturally. This is different from synthetic hormones, which have altered molecular structures.

Bioidentical estradiol (17-beta estradiol) is similar to the primary estrogen your body produced during your reproductive years. Bioidentical progesterone (micronized progesterone) is similar to the progesterone your ovaries produced. Both are available as FDA-approved preparations.

The term "bioidentical" does NOT mean "natural" or "unprocessed." Even though these hormones are derived from plant sources (typically yams or soy), they must be chemically processed in laboratories to become bioidentical to human hormones. They're pharmaceutical preparations with specific molecular structures, not simply ground-up plants.

Why bioidentical matters: Research shows that transdermal estradiol combined with micronized progesterone represents one of the optimal HRT regimens with better safety profiles than older synthetic formulations.

Chapter 12: Treatment Protocols for the Five Hormone Imbalances

Estrogen Replacement

Forms available:
- **Transdermal patches:** Applied to skin, changed once or twice weekly depending on brand (Climara, Vivelle-Dot, Alora, Menostar)
- **Gels or creams:** Applied daily to skin (Estrogel, Divigel, Elestrin)
- **Vaginal estradiol:** Creams (Estrace), tablets (Vagifem), or rings (Estring) for urogenital symptoms

Why transdermal estradiol is preferred: Transdermal estrogen (patches or gels) is not associated with increased risk of venous thromboembolism (blood clots), unlike oral estrogen. It can be safely given to women with history of migraines, gallbladder disease, diabetes, or obesity. Transdermal delivery bypasses the liver, avoiding the "first-pass effect" that increases clotting factors.

Why estradiol specifically: Estradiol is the primary, most potent estrogen your body produced during your reproductive years. We use bioidentical estradiol rather than synthetic estrogens or conjugated equine estrogens (derived from horse urine, used in the Women's Health Initiative study that created widespread HRT fears).

Vaginal estrogen: Vaginal estrogen is safe for everyone and specifically addresses urogenital symptoms including recurrent urinary tract infections, vaginal dryness and painful intercourse, difficulty with arousal and climax, and urinary urgency and frequency. Even women who cannot take systemic HRT can safely use vaginal estrogen, which has minimal systemic absorption.

Progesterone Replacement

Forms available:
- **Oral micronized progesterone:** FDA-approved
- **Compounded progesterone creams:** Custom-made by compounding pharmacies

Why continuous dosing: We use oral micronized progesterone taken continuously (daily) rather than cyclically. Continuous progesterone provides consistent endometrial protection (preventing overgrowth of uterine lining from estrogen), supports sleep and mood, and is easier for compliance—you take it every day rather than trying to cycle it.

When progesterone is critical: Any woman with a uterus who takes estrogen MUST take progesterone to protect the endometrium. Unopposed estrogen (estrogen without progesterone) significantly increases endometrial cancer risk. Progesterone is also essential for women experiencing estrogen dominance symptoms (heavy bleeding, breast tenderness, anxiety, sleep disruption) common in early perimenopause.

Safety data: Large observational data from the French E3N cohort showed that breast cancer risk was lower with micronized progesterone regimens compared with synthetic progestins, suggesting micronized progesterone may be safer.

Testosterone Considerations

Testosterone is not yet FDA-approved for women. There are no standardized women's doses available. This creates significant challenges for treatment.

Because of this limitation, we focus primarily on supporting your body's own testosterone production through DHEA supplementation (the precursor hormone that converts to both estrogen and testosterone) and adrenal support, which we'll discuss in the supplement section.

When testosterone replacement is used, it requires:

- Custom compounding or careful titration of male-dose preparations
- Frequent testing due to risks of levels getting too high
- Close monitoring for side effects (acne, increased hair growth, voice changes, clitoral enlargement)
- Working with a provider experienced in female testosterone replacement

The lack of FDA approval doesn't mean testosterone isn't important. It means treatment requires careful, individualized management by experienced providers.

Chapter 12: Treatment Protocols for the Five Hormone Imbalances

The Women's Health Initiative: What Really Happened

The 2002 Women's Health Initiative (WHI) study created widespread fear about HRT that persists today. Let's clarify what this study actually showed—and what it got wrong. Major issues with the WHI study:

- **Wrong hormones:** Used conjugated equine estrogens (from horse urine) combined with synthetic medroxyprogesterone acetate—NOT bioidentical estradiol and micronized progesterone
- **Wrong timing:** Average participant age was sixty-three years—more than ten years past menopause for most women
- **Wrong population:** Many participants were overweight, sedentary, with existing health conditions—not representative of healthy perimenopausal women seeking symptom relief

What we've learned since:

The "timing hypothesis" or "window of opportunity" has emerged from reanalysis of WHI data and subsequent studies. **Starting HRT within ten years of menopause leads to significant reduction in death and cardiovascular disease.** Women who start HRT early in menopause experience cardiovascular protection rather than increased risk.

Recent data from the Menopause Society shows that starting HRT within two years of menopause decreases risks up to sixty percent for:

- Cardiovascular disease
- Cancers
- Dementia
- Osteoporosis

A 2024 study showed that estrogen-only HRT in women over sixty-five was linked to significant reductions in mortality (nineteen percent) and risks for breast cancer, lung cancer, colorectal cancer, heart failure, blood clots, atrial fibrillation, heart attack, and dementia.

Current guidelines from major medical societies:

Four major North American medical societies—the American College of
Obstetricians and Gynecologists, American Association of Clinical Endocrinology, the Endocrine Society, and the North American Menopause
Society—now recommend HRT in appropriate patients for management
of menopausal symptoms. For women younger than sixty or within ten
years of menopause who have no contraindications, **the benefits of HRT
outweigh the risks.**

Breast cancer risk context:

For the first five years of taking estrogen with micronized progesterone,
there is no increased risk of breast cancer. Women taking estrogen-only
HRT (women who've had hysterectomies) do not have a greater risk of
breast cancer. The absolute risk increase seen in some studies is extremely
small—smaller than the increased risk from obesity, alcohol consumption,
or lack of exercise.

FDA-Approved vs. Compounded HRT

The estrogen and progesterone forms discussed above are available as FDA-approved preparations at traditional pharmacies and are often covered by
insurance.

 Compounded bioidentical hormones are custom-made by compounding pharmacies, are NOT covered by insurance, and cost more out-of-pocket.
Compounded hormones are not subject to the same quality control, testing
for safety and efficacy, or dosing consistency as FDA-approved preparations.
They may contain inconsistent amounts of active ingredients or undesirable
additives.

 When to consider compounded:
- Allergic to inactive ingredients in FDA-approved preparations (Pro-
  metrium contains peanut oil, for example)
- Need a specific dose or combination not available commercially
- Prefer cream formulations over pills or patches

Important: Work closely with your provider and use a trusted compounding pharmacy with good manufacturing practices. Compounded doesn't automatically mean better or safer—it simply means custom-made.

Supplement and Nutritional Support Options

Herbal Support for Estrogen-Related Symptoms:

EstroG-100®—A patented blend of three herbs (Cynanchum wilfordii, Phlomis umbrosa, and Angelica gigas) studied specifically for menopausal symptoms. Research shows it reduces hot flashes, night sweats, sleep disturbances, and mood changes without estrogenic effects on reproductive tissues.

> *Best for: Hot flashes, night sweats, mood swings in women who cannot or prefer not to use HRT*

Black Cohosh—One of the most studied herbs for menopausal symptoms. Research shows it may help reduce hot flashes and support mood, though results vary between individuals. Works through serotonin pathways rather than acting as a phytoestrogen.

> *Best for: Hot flashes, mood support, sleep disturbances*
> *Safety: Generally well-tolerated; avoid if you have liver disease*

Maca Root—An adaptogenic herb that supports hormonal balance without containing plant estrogens. Research shows benefits for energy, libido, mood, and hot flash reduction in perimenopausal and postmenopausal women.

> *Best for: Energy, libido, mood, overall hormone balance, hormone receptor sensitivity*

Supporting Testosterone and DHEA Production:

Longjack (Tongkat Ali)—Supports healthy testosterone production and may improve libido, energy, and body composition. Research shows benefits for sexual function and hormone balance in aging populations.

> *Best for: Low libido, low energy, supporting testosterone levels*

Tribulus Terrestris—Traditionally used to support libido and sexual function. May help support healthy testosterone levels and sexual satisfaction in women.

Best for: Low libido, sexual dysfunction

DHEA Supplementation—DHEA is the precursor hormone from your adrenal glands that converts to both estrogen and testosterone. When DHEA-S levels are low (typically <125 mcg/dL), supplementation can help support sex hormone production.

Best for: Low DHEA-S, low testosterone, adrenal support

Safety: Requires monitoring; can convert to estrogen or testosterone depending on your body's needs; may cause acne or unwanted hair growth if dose is too high

Supports: Energy, libido, and low sex hormones

Liver Support for Estrogen Metabolism:

Milk Thistle (Silymarin)—Supports healthy liver function and estrogen metabolism. The liver processes and clears excess estrogen; when liver function is impaired, estrogen can accumulate. Milk thistle supports Phase I and Phase II liver detoxification pathways.

Best for: Estrogen dominance, supporting healthy estrogen metabolism

Additional Support:

DIM (Diindolylmethane) and **I3C (Indole-3-Carbinol)**—Compounds from cruciferous vegetables that support healthy estrogen metabolism, promoting conversion to less potent estrogen metabolites.

Best for: Estrogen dominance, supporting healthy estrogen metabolism

Vitamin D and Omega-3s—Both support hormone receptor sensitivity and reduce inflammation. Adequate vitamin D is essential for hormone production and function (see Protocol 5).

Best for: Inflammation, mood, hormone production and regulation

Chapter 12: Treatment Protocols for the Five Hormone Imbalances

Lifestyle Integration: The Part II Foundation

Sex hormone balance requires the foundational strategies from Part II. Adequate protein and fat supports hormone production. Getting enough vegetables supports micronutrients needed for hormone production, conversion, metabolism, and receptor sensitivity. Strength training preserves muscle mass and bone density—both critically affected by declining estrogen and testosterone. Sleep optimization supports hormone regulation. Stress management prevents cortisol from further disrupting sex hormone production (remember the pregnenolone steal from Part I).

For comprehensive strategies on nutrition, movement, sleep, and stress management, refer to Part II.

What Success Looks Like:

When sex hormones are optimized—whether through HRT, supplements, or both—the symptoms you identified in Part I begin to disappear. Hot flashes and night sweats diminish or resolve completely. Sleep becomes restorative. Brain fog lifts and mental clarity returns. Libido rebounds. Vaginal dryness improves and sex becomes comfortable again. Mood stabilizes; anxiety and irritability quiet down. Energy returns. Body composition improves when combined with the other protocols. Women say, *"I feel like myself again. I didn't realize how much I'd lost until I got it back."*

Sex hormone balance is not about returning to age twenty-five. It's about providing adequate hormone support to maintain quality of life, protect long-term health (bone density, cardiovascular function, cognitive health), and allow your body to function optimally during and after this profound transition.

Protocol 5: Vitamin D

Optimal Lab Ranges

25-Hydroxyvitamin D [25(OH)D]

- **Deficient:** <35 ng/mL
- **Insufficient:**35-59 ng/mL
- **Optimal (for hormones & metabolism): 60-80 ng/mL**
- **High:** >100 ng/mL

  Why it matters: Standard labs report anything within the range of 30-100 ng/mL as "normal," but research shows optimal hormone function, immune health, bone density, cardiovascular protection, and metabolic health occur between 60-80 ng/mL. Most perimenopausal women test below 30 ng/mL—well below optimal.

Your provider will test your baseline 25(OH)D level before starting supplementation. **Retesting occurs at three months after starting or adjusting vitamin D supplementation to ensure you've reached optimal range without over-correction.**

Treatment Approach

Vitamin D3 with K2: The Essential Combination

Vitamin D should never be supplemented alone at therapeutic doses—it must be paired with vitamin K2. Here's why:

Vitamin D3 (Cholecalciferol):

- The form your skin produces from sun exposure
- Superior absorption compared to D2 (ergocalciferol)
- Increases calcium absorption from your gut

- Supports bone density, immune function, hormone production, mood regulation, and cardiovascular health

Vitamin K2 (Menaquinone):

- Directs calcium to bones and teeth where it belongs
- Prevents calcium from depositing in arteries, soft tissues, and kidneys
- Essential for cardiovascular protection when taking vitamin D

Why K2 is non-negotiable: The Rotterdam Study—a large, long-term study—showed that higher vitamin K2 intake was associated with reduced arterial calcification and reduced cardiovascular mortality. When you take vitamin D without K2, you increase calcium absorption but don't direct where that calcium goes. This can lead to arterial calcification, kidney stones, and soft tissue calcium deposits.

K2 activates proteins (osteocalcin and matrix Gla-protein) that ensure calcium ends up in bones rather than arteries. This is especially critical for perimenopausal and menopausal women who are already at increased risk for both osteoporosis and cardiovascular disease.

Safety considerations for K2:

- Speak with your provider about vitamin K2 if you're taking warfarin (Coumadin), as it can interfere with the medication
- Safe with other anticoagulants like rivaroxaban (Xarelto), apixaban (Eliquo), or aspirin
- Inform your provider of all medications before starting K2

Magnesium: The Essential Cofactor

Magnesium is required for vitamin D metabolism—your body cannot convert vitamin D to its active form without adequate magnesium. Magnesium deficiency is extremely common (estimated 50%+ of Americans) and worsens during perimenopause.

Why magnesium matters for vitamin D:

- Required for vitamin D activation in the liver and kidneys
- Without adequate magnesium, vitamin D supplementation is far less effective
- Magnesium also supports sleep, stress response, blood sugar regulation, muscle function, and cardiovascular health

Forms: Magnesium glycinate (best absorbed, calming) or magnesium citrate. This can be a combination of diet and supplementation. A diet of Home Base behaviors and a multivitamin should get you enough for absorption.

Why Vitamin D Matters:

Vitamin D functions as a hormone that influences every system you're treating—insulin sensitivity, thyroid function, sex hormone effectiveness, cortisol regulation, immune function, mood, bone health, and cardiovascular health. Deficiency makes optimal results nearly impossible regardless of other interventions. Over forty percent of Americans are deficient, with rates higher in perimenopausal women. Standard ranges are insufficient for optimal function—therapeutic levels should be maintained between 50-80 ng/mL.

Sun Exposure and Natural Production

As you learned in Part I, your skin produces vitamin D when exposed to UVB rays from sunlight. However, geography, age, skin tone, sunscreen use, and indoor lifestyles make sun exposure alone insufficient for most perimenopausal women to achieve optimal levels. While sensible sun exposure during warmer months can contribute to vitamin D status, supplementation is necessary for most women to achieve and maintain optimal levels year-round.

Lifestyle Integration: The Part II Foundation

Vitamin D optimization works synergistically with the foundational strategies from Part II. The Home Base habits you've already established—adequate

Chapter 12: Treatment Protocols for the Five Hormone Imbalances

protein, nutrient-dense foods, movement (especially outdoor activity), stress management, and sleep optimization—all support vitamin D metabolism and receptor function.

What Success Looks Like:

When vitamin D is optimized, the improvements often surprise women because they didn't realize how much vitamin D deficiency was affecting them. Energy improves—that heavy, exhausted feeling lifts. Mood stabilizes; seasonal depression lessens or resolves. Immune function strengthens; you stop catching every cold. Muscle and joint pain decrease. And critically, every other hormone protocol becomes more effective. Insulin sensitivity improves. Thyroid hormones work better. Cortisol regulates more easily. Sex hormones function more efficiently.

Women say, *"I thought I was depressed or this was just how I was supposed to feel at my age. I didn't know I could feel this good."*

Vitamin D optimization is simple, inexpensive, and profoundly effective. It's the foundation that allows every other intervention to work optimally.

Bringing It All Together:
The Interconnected Web

You've now learned the complete treatment protocols for all five hormone imbalances affecting perimenopausal and menopausal women.

There is no prescribed order. There is no "fix this first, then that." Your treatment plan is entirely individualized:

- A woman with severe insulin resistance (HbA1c 6.0, fasting insulin 18) and mild cortisol dysregulation will emphasize insulin resistance treatment while supporting cortisol.
- A woman with crippling anxiety, insomnia, and high cortisol alongside moderate insulin resistance will prioritize cortisol regulation while addressing metabolic dysfunction.

- A woman with subclinical hypothyroidism (TSH 3.5, Free T3 low-normal) and Hashimoto's will focus on thyroid optimization while simultaneously addressing the inflammation and insulin resistance driving autoimmune activity.
- A woman in full menopause with debilitating hot flashes but otherwise optimal labs will emphasize HRT while maintaining the lifestyle foundations that support all five systems.

Your labs tell us what's broken. Your symptoms tell us what's most impactful to your quality of life. Your goals determine where we focus intensity and resources.

The beauty of comprehensive treatment is that improvements in one system support improvements in all the others. When insulin comes down, cortisol stabilizes. When cortisol regulates, thyroid conversion improves. When thyroid optimizes, sex hormones function better. When vitamin D reaches optimal levels, everything works more efficiently.

Looking Ahead

You now have the knowledge to understand what's happening in your body, the lab values to know what optimal looks like, the treatment options available for each hormone system, and the framework for working effectively with your healthcare team.

You are empowered.

The symptoms you've been experiencing—the weight gain, fatigue, brain fog, mood swings, sleep disruption, loss of libido—are not inevitable parts of aging. They're not character flaws or lack of willpower. They're physiologic consequences of hormone imbalances that can be identified, tested, and treated.

Your body is not broken. Your hormones are out of balance. And balance can be restored.

Chapter 12: Treatment Protocols for the Five Hormone Imbalances

Take this knowledge. Use it to advocate for yourself. Demand comprehensive testing. Insist on optimal treatment. Find providers who will partner with you. Implement the strategies from Part II while pursuing appropriate medical interventions from Part III.

Julie's Story—From Impossible to Inevitable

A year ago, I was planning to end my life. Today, I'm planning a baby shower to welcome my first grandchild.

The Breaking Point

When Julie began treatment in June 2024, she carried more than fifty extra pounds. She carried the weight of trauma that nearly destroyed her. Here's how Julie describes where she was:

"A year ago in mid-September, I was literally suicidal. I had gone through two years of torturous cancer treatment that had worn me down to a nub physically and emotionally. I had osteoporosis from chemo. I'd fractured four vertebrae in my back. My knees have zero cartilage remaining, and I need knee replacement. I was fifty pounds overweight. Everything hurt. I'd also had a personal situation occur that had devastated me further emotionally and spiritually. I was beaten down and scarred from the inside out. Exhausted. In pain heart and body and spirit. And I'd actually considered that it was all too much, and I was done."

The medical trauma Julie endured:
- Stage 3 invasive breast cancer with a seven-centimeter mass
- Double mastectomy
- Six rounds of chemotherapy
- Thirty-five rounds of radiation
- Multiple reconstructive surgeries

- Full hysterectomy with removal of both ovaries
- Chemotherapy-induced osteoporosis at age fifty
- Four fractured vertebrae
- Severe arthritis requiring future knee replacements

And through it all, tremendous personal hardship that left her emotionally and spiritually devastated.

Post-cancer treatment, she was trapped on Letrozole—a medication that prevents breast cancer recurrence but makes weight gain almost inevitable. She'd tried Wegovy with no success. Despite working a farm and being incredibly active—wrangling animals, hauling feed, working outdoors for hours every day—her body refused to respond.

"I had also tried all the things. Weight Watchers, Noom, Atkins, Mediterranean Diet, online programs, Facebook groups, church weight loss groups, just drinking protein shakes ... I'd tried it all and was terrified I'd pay the money and fail."

Her oncologist had looked her in the eye and said it flat out: "Losing fifty pounds would be impossible with your medical history."

She came to us at 207 pounds, convinced she was broken beyond repair.

Her three biggest struggles:

- Complete weight loss resistance no matter what she tried
- Brain fog so severe that simple tasks felt impossible
- Constant, debilitating pain throughout her entire body

"I was beaten down and scarred from the inside out. Exhausted. In pain heart and body and spirit."

What Julie's Body Was Trying To Tell Her

Julie's story illustrates everything you've learned in this book. Her symptoms—the ones she thought were inevitable consequences of cancer treatment, aging, and impossible odds—were actually a roadmap. Her body was speaking a specific language. It was just that no one had bothered to learn it.

Let's look at what Julie was experiencing through the lens of Part I:

The weight loss resistance despite extreme physical activity? That's insulin resistance combined with thyroid dysfunction. Her body was in fat-storage mode, unable to access stored energy no matter how many calories she burned.

The crushing fatigue and brain fog? Classic hypothyroidism, compounded by severe vitamin D deficiency and the metabolic stress of surgical menopause (remember, they'd removed her ovaries).

The constant, debilitating pain? Inflammation driven by hormone imbalance, insulin resistance, and the lingering effects of chemotherapy—all creating a perfect storm of chronic pain.

The loss of libido and feeling "not like herself"? Testosterone had crashed to nearly undetectable levels after her hysterectomy. Sex hormones aren't just about reproduction—they're metabolic hormones that affect energy, mood, muscle mass, bone density, and vitality.

Julie didn't have one problem. She had all five hormone imbalances working against her simultaneously, amplified by the medical trauma her body had endured.

And here's what made her case so complex: Because her breast cancer was strongly estrogen AND progesterone receptor positive, traditional hormone replacement therapy was completely off the table.

This is where personalized medicine becomes absolutely critical—not just "nice to have" but potentially life-saving.

The Collaborative Approach: Working With Her Oncology Team

Here's what many people don't understand about comprehensive hormone optimization: **It's not about replacing your existing medical care; it's about filling in the gaps and working collaboratively with your current providers.**

Julie's oncologist was managing her cancer treatment and prevention brilliantly. He understood oncology. But hormone optimization during cancer survivorship—particularly with the complexity of surgical menopause, multiple metabolic imbalances, and severe medication side effects—wasn't within his typical expertise. And that's completely understandable. Oncologists focus on keeping you cancer-free. That's their priority.

Our role was different: Optimize the hormone systems that were creating debilitating symptoms and metabolic dysfunction, while ensuring everything we did was safe and appropriate given her cancer history.

From day one, we established direct communication with Julie's oncologist. This wasn't optional; it was essential. Before implementing any treatment, we:

- **Reviewed her complete medical records** including pathology reports, treatment history, and current medications
- **Researched current literature** on hormone optimization in breast cancer survivors, particularly those with ER+/PR+ tumors
- **Submitted our proposed treatment protocol** to her oncologist for review and approval
- **Requested clearance** for each supplement and medication we intended to use
- **Established ongoing communication** for monitoring and adjustments

This collaborative approach is how personalized medicine should work. Her oncologist maintained oversight of cancer prevention. We focused on metabolic optimization and quality of life. Both teams communicated regularly to ensure every intervention was safe, appropriate, and didn't compromise her cancer treatment.

Why this matters for you: If you have a complex medical history—cancer, autoimmune disease, cardiac issues, or other serious conditions—comprehensive hormone optimization requires this level of coordination. It's not about one provider "taking over." It's about creating a team approach where each specialist contributes their expertise while ensuring all interventions work together safely.

The Investigation: Comprehensive Testing

We ran comprehensive lab work—the kind you learned about in Part I. Not just TSH and fasting glucose. We tested all five hormone systems to understand the complete picture. What we discovered:

- **Vitamin D:** Severely deficient—below 20 ng/mL. Remember from Chapter 5 that vitamin D deficiency affects insulin sensitivity, thyroid function, immune health, bone density, mood, and inflammation. Julie's deficiency was worsening every other imbalance.
- **Testosterone:** Crashed to nearly undetectable levels after surgical menopause. This explained her loss of energy, muscle weakness, bone density issues, and complete absence of libido.
- **Thyroid function:** Struggling. Her TSH was creeping up, Free T3 was in the lower end of the range, and her symptoms screamed hypothyroidism—fatigue, brain fog, cold intolerance, weight gain, constipation.
- **Insulin resistance:** Present. Her fasting insulin was elevated, HgbA1c showed insulin resistance, and her body composition—particularly the stubborn abdominal fat—told the metabolic story.
- **Cortisol dysregulation:** After years of cancer treatment, surgical trauma, emotional trauma, chronic pain, and sleep disruption, her HPA axis was exhausted.

Plus, Julie carries the CHEK2 gene mutation—a genetic variant that affects how her body processes hormones and responds to stress, making hormone optimization even more critical.

Her lab results revealed a body in complete hormonal chaos. But to us, it wasn't chaos. It was a clear map showing exactly where we needed to go.

The Protocol: Working with Limitations, Not Against Them

This is where everything you've learned in Parts II and III comes together—and where personalized medicine becomes absolutely essential.

We couldn't use a standard approach. Julie needed something designed specifically for her unique situation—one that respected her medical limitations while addressing every root cause.

Here's where research and staying current with medical literature became crucial. Treatment recommendations for cancer survivors are constantly evolving. What was considered contraindicated five years ago might now have supporting evidence. What's considered safe today might be reconsidered tomorrow as new research emerges. We reviewed:

- Current oncology guidelines for ER+/PR+ breast cancer survivors
- Recent studies on metabolic health in Letrozole users
- Safety data on various supplements and medications in cancer survivors
- Emerging research on hormone optimization without traditional HRT

Every decision was evidence-based and approved by her oncology team. Here's exactly what we created:

Protocol 1: Cortisol Regulation

We didn't need to test her twenty-four-hour cortisol (remember, it's symptom-based), because Julie's history told us everything we needed to know. Years of trauma, chronic pain, and sleep disruption had dysregulated her HPA axis. Treatment focused on:

- Sleep optimization strategies from Part II
- Stress management techniques (breathing exercises, boundaries, therapeutic support for processing her trauma)
- Adaptogenic support to help regulate her stress response

- Low Dose Naltrexone (LDN) at 4.5mg—not standard weight loss
  protocol but exactly what Julie's inflamed, pain-ridden body needed.
  LDN modulates the immune system, reduces inflammation, and
  helps regulate the stress response.

Oncologist approval: LDN was reviewed and cleared as it doesn't interact with Letrozole and has emerging evidence for reducing inflammation in cancer survivors and the adaptogen support didn't interfere with drug metabolism.

Protocol 2: Insulin Resistance

Julie's insulin resistance was significant, and it was sabotaging every other system. Treatment included:

- The Home Base nutrition from Part II—adequate protein (we aimed
  for 100-120g daily), half-plate vegetables, blood sugar stability
- Tirzepatide injections starting at a microdose, dosed weekly
- Berberine for additional blood sugar control and AMPK activation
- Gut-directed probiotics to support GLP-1 production naturally

Oncologist approval: We provided research showing GLP-1 medications don't increase cancer recurrence risk and may actually have protective metabolic effects. Berberine was cleared as it doesn't interfere with Letrozole metabolism.

Protocol 3: Thyroid Optimization

Julie's thyroid function was suboptimal, and hypothyroidism was crushing her energy and metabolism. Treatment included:

- NP Thyroid (natural desiccated thyroid) at 30mg daily—providing
  both T4 and T3
- Methylated B vitamins her body could actually utilize (important
  given her genetic variant)
- Selenium and Brazil nuts for optimal thyroid hormone conversion

Chapter 13: Julie's Story—From Impossible to Inevitable

- Addressing gut health to support the twenty percent of T4 to T3 conversion that happens in the gut

Oncologist approval: Thyroid optimization was fully supported as hypothyroidism is common post-chemotherapy and doesn't interact with cancer treatment.

Protocol 4: Sex Hormone Balance

This was the trickiest piece. Julie's cancer history meant we couldn't use estrogen or progesterone replacement. But we could support her body's production of hormones that were safe. Initial treatment included:

- Herbal testosterone support supplement (with herbs like tribulus and longjack)
- DHEA support—the precursor hormone that converts to both estrogen and testosterone
- Herbal estrogen support supplement (with EstroG-100, ashwagandha, milk thistle)
- Vaginal estrogen cream (since it stays locally and improves urogenital symptoms of menopause)

Oncologist approval: Each herbal supplement was reviewed for potential estrogenic activity. We provided research on each ingredient and their safety profile in ER+ cancer survivors.

Important note: This is where treatment evolved over time (more on this below).

Protocol 5: Vitamin D Optimization

We implemented an aggressive vitamin D protocol:

- High dose prescription D2 from her local pharmacy, dosed weekly for twelve weeks
- Daily D3/K2 supplementation at maintenance dosing
- Essential multivitamin and foundational nutrient support

Oncologist approval: Strongly supported given Julie's chemotherapy-induced osteoporosis. Vitamin D optimization is standard of care for bone health in cancer survivors.

The Part II Foundation

None of this would have worked without the lifestyle foundation from Part II:

- Home Base habits: adequate protein, vegetables, water, sleep
- Working with a nutritionist to break dieting behaviors and encourage lifestyle changes
- Movement that supported healing rather than adding stress—farm work provided natural activity
- Stress management and boundaries
- Community support through weekly check-ins and 24/7 access to our medical team

Every single piece was chosen to work around her cancer treatment limitations while addressing the root causes everyone else had missed.

The Transformation: Month by Month

What happened next was remarkable to witness.

Month 1—The Awakening

Weight: 202-207 pounds (fluctuating, no significant loss yet)

But something profound was happening. Julie reported, *"I don't know what you've done, but I haven't felt this energetic in years. The farm work that used to exhaust me? I'm handling it like my old self."*

This is what happens when you address cortisol and vitamin D first. Energy returns before the scale moves. The body starts feeling safe enough to function properly.

Month 2—The Breakthrough

Weight: 197 pounds—DOWN TEN POUNDS

But the real victory wasn't the scale. Julie reported, *"That constant noise in my head about food? The cravings that used to drive me crazy? They're just… gone. I'm in complete control for the first time in years."*

This is insulin resistance reversing. This is GLP-1 working. This is what happens when blood sugar stabilizes and your brain stops sending constant hunger signals.

Month 3—Coming Alive

Weight: 193.2 pounds—DOWN FOURTEEN POUNDS

Julie said, *"My libido is back! I feel sassy again! I actually want to be intimate with my husband for the first time since my diagnosis. I feel like myself again."*

Testosterone support was working. Her body was producing hormones again. She wasn't just losing weight—she was reclaiming her vitality, her sensuality, her sense of self.

Month 4—Pain-Free Living

Weight: 185.6 pounds—DOWN TWENTY-ONE POUNDS

Julie's words: *"The pain is GONE. I used to dread getting out of bed every morning because everything hurt. Today I bounced up and thought, what's different? Then I realized—nothing hurts. I can wrangle my farm animals again!"*

This is inflammation resolving. This is what happens when insulin resistance improves, vitamin D reaches optimal levels, cortisol regulates, and chronic pain pathways finally quiet down.

Month 6—The Impossible Made Possible

Current weight: 160 pounds

TOTAL TRANSFORMATION:
FORTY-SEVEN POUNDS LOST

From a size sixteen to a size ten. A weight she hadn't seen since college—twenty-eight years ago.

But the numbers don't capture the real transformation.

Beyond The Scale: What Really Changed

Let us share what Julie posted on social media:

"A year ago I was literally planning to end my life. I was beaten down and scarred from the inside out. My pain from juvenile arthritis plus arthritis from age PLUS arthritis from chemo... it's gone. When I get a twinge now, Advil can handle it. I bounce out of bed in the morning instead of creaking like an old door.

"My weight is down forty-seven pounds. I've learned so much from this program. I have our first grandbaby coming in October, and not only am I going to be able to help physically chase after her... I'm still here. That was seriously in question a year ago. I don't even recognize the broken woman I was in that dark place."

This woman went from planning her own funeral to planning a baby shower to welcome her first grandchild.

From barely surviving each day to thriving as the energetic grandmother she always wanted to be.

From believing she was broken beyond repair to understanding her body was simply waiting for someone who spoke its language.

The Ongoing Journey: Why Treatment Evolves

Here's what many people don't understand about hormone optimization: **It's not a "set it and forget it" protocol. It's an ongoing process that requires regular monitoring, lab retesting, and adjustments based on how your body responds and how research evolves.**

Julie's treatment didn't stay static. Over the eighteen months since we began working together, we've made several significant adjustments:

Six-Month Lab Recheck

We retested all five hormone systems to see how her body was responding:

- **Vitamin D:** Improved dramatically to 65 ng/mL (optimal range). We adjusted her maintenance dose accordingly.
- **Thyroid:** Free T3 had improved but still had room for optimization. We increased NP Thyroid slightly to 45mg daily.
- **Insulin markers:** Fasting insulin normalized. HgbA1c showed significant improvement. This confirmed the GLP-1 and lifestyle modifications were working.
- **Testosterone:** Showed modest improvement with herbal support but still suboptimal.

The Testosterone Conversation

This is where ongoing collaboration with her oncologist became crucial again—and where staying current with evolving research made a significant difference.

Recent studies have provided new data on testosterone use in breast cancer survivors. Unlike estrogen and progesterone, testosterone doesn't appear to increase recurrence risk in ER+/PR+ breast cancer, and some research suggests it may actually have protective effects.

We presented this emerging research to Julie's oncologist, including:

- Studies showing testosterone doesn't stimulate ER+ breast tissue the way estrogen does
- Data on testosterone's role in bone density (critical given her osteoporosis)
- Evidence of testosterone's metabolic benefits
- Quality of life improvements in cancer survivors using testosterone

Her oncologist reviewed the literature, consulted with colleagues, and made a decision based on current evidence: **Testosterone replacement was approved.**

This is personalized medicine in action. Treatment decisions evolving as research progresses. A willingness to reconsider previous limitations when new evidence emerges. Ongoing collaboration between providers to ensure patient safety while optimizing quality of life.

We initiated bioidentical testosterone cream at a conservative dose with close monitoring by both our team and her oncologist.

Twelve-Month Lab Recheck

- **Testosterone:** Now in optimal range. Julie reported even better energy, continued libido improvement, and noticeable muscle strength gains.
- **All other markers:** Remained stable and optimized.
- **Cancer surveillance:** Her oncologist confirmed no concerns. All cancer markers remained stable. Imaging clear.

Eighteen-Month Check-In (Current)

Julie has now maintained her weight loss for over a year. She's 160 pounds—stable and sustainable. But more importantly:

- Energy remains high
- Pain remains minimal

- Brain fog completely resolved
- Libido healthy
- Mood stable
- Able to do farm work without limitation
- Playing with her granddaughter actively
- Living the life she thought she'd lost

Recent protocol adjustments:
- Fine-tuned GLP-1 dosing based on appetite and weight stability
- Adjusted some supplements based on updated labs
- Continued collaboration with oncology for cancer surveillance

The Medical Validation

Six months into treatment, Julie went back to see her oncologist for her regular follow-up. His jaw dropped when he saw her.

He said, *"In twenty years of oncology practice, I've never seen results like this in a cancer patient on your medications. What are you doing?"*

Julie told him about our comprehensive hormone optimization approach—the testing, the protocols, the medical supervision, the community support.

He looked at her labs—every single marker dramatically improved—and said, *"I don't know how they did it, but whatever they're doing, keep doing it."*

The man who told her weight loss was "medically impossible" was now telling her to continue the protocol that proved him wrong.

And then he did something remarkable: He asked for copies of her treatment protocol to share with other patients facing similar challenges and now regularly refers patients to our practice.

This is what happens when providers work collaboratively rather than territorially. When we focus on patient outcomes rather than ego. When we're willing to learn from each other and adapt based on results.

What Made The Difference

Julie's transformation didn't happen by accident. It happened because we applied everything you've learned in this book:

- **Part I:** We identified all five hormone imbalances through comprehensive testing and symptom analysis. We didn't just treat the obvious (weight). We treated the root causes (insulin resistance, thyroid dysfunction, vitamin D deficiency, sex hormone imbalance, cortisol dysregulation).
- **Part II:** We built the foundation with the Home Base habits—adequate protein, vegetables, hydration, sleep optimization, stress management, appropriate movement. No supplement or medication works without this foundation.
- **Part III:** We implemented targeted treatment protocols individualized to Julie's unique situation—her labs, her symptoms, her medical limitations, her goals. Not a standardized program. Not a one-size-fits-all approach. A medical protocol designed specifically for her.

Ongoing collaboration: We worked directly with her oncologist, obtained clearance for every intervention, stayed current with evolving research, and adjusted treatment as new evidence emerged.

Regular monitoring: We retested labs every 3-6 months, adjusted protocols based on response, and refined treatment continuously rather than assuming the initial protocol would work indefinitely.

Personalized adjustments: As Julie's body healed and changed, we changed with it. Doses adjusted. Supplements modified. Approaches refined based on her individual response and evolving research.

This is what comprehensive, personalized, collaborative medical care looks like.

This is what becomes possible when you treat the whole person, not just the symptoms.

This is what happens when providers work together rather than in silos.

This is what happens when you understand that "impossible" often just means "no one's tried the right approach yet."

The Lessons From Julie's Journey

If you're reading Julie's story and seeing yourself in her struggles, here's what you need to understand:

- **Complex medical histories require personalized approaches.** If you have cancer, autoimmune disease, or other serious health conditions, you need providers who will work collaboratively with your existing care team—not replace them but fill in the gaps.
- **Research is constantly evolving.** What was considered contraindicated years ago might now be safe and beneficial. Staying current with medical literature matters. Finding providers who actively research and adapt their approach based on new evidence is crucial.
- **Treatment must evolve as you heal.** The protocol that gets you started isn't necessarily the protocol that maintains your results. Regular retesting, honest assessment of how you're responding, and willingness to adjust are essential.
- **All five hormone systems matter.** Julie had all five imbalances. Your pattern might be different—maybe you have three out of five, or four out of five. But you won't know unless you test comprehensively. And you can't optimize what you don't measure.
- **The foundation always matters.** Supplements and medications don't work without the Part II foundation. Julie did the nutritional work. She prioritized sleep. She managed stress. She moved her body appropriately. The protocols worked because the foundation was solid.
- **Collaboration produces better outcomes than isolation.** Julie's oncologist had expertise we didn't have. We had expertise he didn't have. Together, we created a care plan that optimized her health while protecting her from cancer recurrence. This is how medicine should work.

- **"Impossible" is often negotiable.** Julie was told her weight loss was impossible. It wasn't. It just required the right approach with the right support addressing the right root causes.

Your Path Forward

You now have the knowledge Julie didn't have when she started. You understand the five hormone imbalances. You know optimal lab ranges. You've learned treatment protocols.

What matters now is applying this knowledge to your unique situation. If you have a complex medical history, find providers who:

- Test comprehensively
- Work collaboratively with your existing care team
- Stay current with research
- Personalize treatment rather than applying standardized protocols
- Monitor regularly and adjust based on your response
- Communicate transparently about risks, benefits, and alternatives

If your current providers aren't willing or able to provide this level of care, you may need to expand your team. This doesn't mean abandoning your existing doctors—it means adding specialists who can fill specific gaps.

Julie's oncologist remains her primary cancer doctor. We work alongside him, not instead of him. This collaborative model is how complex medical cases should be managed.

You deserve the same comprehensive, personalized, collaborative approach.

Your body isn't broken. It's speaking a language. Sometimes you need someone who can translate.

Julie went from planning her funeral to planning a baby shower for her first grandbaby.

She's 160 pounds now—a weight she hasn't seen in twenty-eight years. She has energy to chase her granddaughter. She's pain-free for the first time since chemotherapy. Her libido is back. Her brain fog is gone. Her lab markers are optimal.

She's not just surviving. She's thriving.

And she did it by understanding what you now understand: Hormone imbalances are identifiable, testable, and treatable. Symptoms are your body's language, not your destiny. Comprehensive treatment addressing root causes produces results that single interventions cannot achieve.

You have the knowledge now. You understand the five hormone imbalances. You know the optimal lab ranges. You've learned the treatment protocols. You have the tools.

What you do with this knowledge is up to you.

Julie chose empowerment over resignation. She chose comprehensive treatment over "it's just aging." She chose to trust that her body wasn't broken—it was just waiting for the right approach.

What will you choose?

Welcome to empowered hormone health.

Your transformation story could be the next one we tell.

Conclusion

The Woman You're Becoming

There's a moment that happens with every single woman we work with. It's not when the scale finally moves. It's not when the pants fit again. It's not even when the labs come back optimal.

It's the moment she realizes she was never broken.

That moment might be happening for you right now.

Maybe it's happening as you realize that every symptom you thought was "normal aging" actually had a name. A cause. A solution.

Maybe it's happening as you understand that your body wasn't refusing to cooperate—it was desperately trying to communicate in the only language it had: symptoms.

Maybe it's happening as the shame you've carried for years—the shame of "failing" at every diet, of not being disciplined enough, of somehow being the one person this didn't work for—finally begins to lift.

Because now you know the truth: The diets didn't fail because of you. They failed because they never addressed what was actually broken.

Your willpower was never the problem. Your hormones were.

What You Now Understand That Most Women Never Will

You now possess knowledge that most women in perimenopause will never have. Knowledge that could have saved you years of struggle if someone had just told you sooner.

Weight gain in midlife isn't about calories. It's about five specific hormone imbalances that create a perfect metabolic storm. When your body refuses to release weight despite "doing everything right," it's not being stubborn—it's protecting you from what it perceives as a threat.

Optimal isn't the same as normal. You can have "normal" labs and still be suffering because the reference ranges on standard testing were never designed to optimize female health. Insulin resistance, thyroid dysfunction, vitamin D deficiency, sex hormone imbalance, and cortisol dysregulation don't exist in isolation; they cascade into each other, each one making the others worse.

Comprehensive testing reveals what's actually happening in your body, not just what's "bad enough" to treat. Treatment isn't one-size-fits-all. What works for your friend, your sister, your coworker might not work for you because your hormone pattern is uniquely yours.

Nutrition, supplements, lifestyle changes, and medication aren't competing approaches; they're collaborative tools that work exponentially better together. Home Base isn't a punishment or a starting point you'll eventually graduate from; it's the foundation that makes everything else possible. Adequate protein, abundant vegetables, proper hydration, quality sleep, stress management, and appropriate movement aren't optional extras; they're non-negotiable requirements for healing.

Healing takes time. You didn't develop these imbalances overnight, and you won't reverse them overnight. The protocols that change your life aren't the ones that promise instant results; they're the ones that address root causes and restore function.

Symptoms are your body's language, not your destiny. Fatigue, weight gain, brain fog, low libido, mood swings, and insomnia aren't things you have to accept as "just part of aging"; they're treatable conditions with identifiable causes.

Most importantly, you understand that you're not crazy. You're not lazy. You're not broken.

You're a woman in perimenopause whose body is going through profound hormonal changes and who has been failed by a medical system that doesn't understand how to optimize female health in midlife.

But that changes now.

The Two Paths from Here

You're standing at a crossroads.

One path is familiar. It's the path of resignation. The path of accepting that "this is just how it is now." The path of shrinking your life to accommodate your symptoms instead of treating them. The path of watching other women transform and wondering why it's not happening for you.

It's the path of collecting more information but never taking action. Of waiting for the "perfect time" that never comes. Of staying stuck in the same patterns that brought you here, hoping somehow the results will be different this time.

It's the path of another year of feeling invisible in your own body. Another birthday where you look in the mirror and barely recognize the exhausted woman staring back. Another vacation spent hiding in oversized clothes and avoiding photos. Another holiday season watching from the sidelines because you just don't have the energy.

The other path is different.

It's the path Jennifer took when she finally tested her thyroid comprehensively and discovered the dysfunction that no one had found in decades of normal TSH tests. When she addressed her insulin resistance, optimized her vitamin D, balanced her sex hormones, and managed her cortisol. When she lost twenty pounds in three months after years of gaining weight despite training for a marathon.

It's the path Lisa took when she refused to accept that diabetes medication was inevitable. When she got the right testing, found all five hormone imbalances, treated them comprehensively, and not only lost thirty-five pounds but reversed her pre-diabetic markers completely.

It's the path Julie took when her oncologist said weight loss was medically impossible given her cancer treatment history. When she found providers who would collaborate instead of dismiss her. When she lost forty-seven pounds and her oncologist asked for our protocols to share with other patients.

It's the path of women who decided that their health was worth fighting for. Who refused to accept "normal for your age" as a diagnosis. Who found providers willing to dig deeper, test comprehensively, and treat aggressively.

Women who built their Home Base and never abandoned it, even when the protocols took time to work. Who understood that healing isn't linear—that some months you see dramatic changes and other months you just hold steady while your body catches up.

Women who stopped comparing their journey to everyone else's and started honoring their unique hormone pattern, their unique challenges, their unique timeline.

Women who transformed not just their weight but their entire relationship with their body.

Which path will you take?

Your Next Steps: The Action Plan That Changes Everything

Knowledge without action is just entertainment. You've read this entire book. You understand the five hormone imbalances. You've learned optimal lab ranges and treatment protocols.

Now what? Here's exactly what to do next, in order:

STEP 1: Start Home Base Today
(Not Monday, Not January First—Today)

Don't wait for testing. Don't wait for a doctor's appointment. Don't wait until you "feel ready."

Start with the four non-negotiables:

- **More Water**: Calculate your body weight in pounds, divide by two, and drink that many ounces daily. Set reminders. Get a water bottle you actually like. Add lemon or cucumber if plain water bores you. Just drink it.
- **More Vegetables**: Add vegetables to every meal. Not instead of what you're eating—in addition to it. Roast a pan of mixed vegetables every Sunday. Keep pre-washed salad and cut vegetables on hand. Make it easy.
- **More Sleep**: Aim for 7-9 hours. Create a bedtime routine. Make your bedroom actually dark—blackout curtains, cover all lights. Keep it cool. Put your phone in another room. Prioritize this like your life depends on it, because your hormones do.
- **More Movement**: Walk thirty minutes daily. Not HIIT. Not marathon training. Just consistent, moderate movement that doesn't spike cortisol. Walk during lunch. Walk after dinner. Walk first thing in the morning. Make it non-negotiable.

These four habits prepare your body for healing. They create metabolic flexibility. They restore insulin sensitivity. They support thyroid function. They reduce inflammation. They regulate cortisol.

Everything else we've talked about works better when Home Base is solid.

STEP 2: Get Comprehensive Testing (This Week)

Schedule an appointment with your primary care provider this week. Not next month. This week.

Use the comprehensive testing protocols outlined throughout this book. We've made it easy for you—visit https://empoweredweightlossbook.com

where you can download a printable PDF of all the tests you need, organized by hormone system. You can hand this directly to your provider, or you can order labs directly through us if that's more convenient.

The key is getting complete testing, not just the standard panels that miss most hormone imbalances. This means testing for all five hormone systems comprehensively: insulin resistance, thyroid dysfunction, vitamin D deficiency, sex hormone imbalance, and cortisol dysregulation.

Your health is too important to fight for crumbs of attention from someone who won't order comprehensive lab work. Find a provider who will listen to you, take your symptoms seriously, and order the testing that reveals what's actually happening in your body. This might be your current doctor. It might not be. Either way, align yourself with someone who sees you as a partner in your health, not a problem to manage.

STEP 3: Review Your Results Against Optimal Ranges

When your results come back, don't just accept "everything's normal." Compare your results to the optimal ranges outlined in Part 3 of this book, not just the reference ranges on the lab report. Remember that "normal" and "optimal" are completely different standards. Fasting insulin under 25 might be normal, but under 5 is optimal. TSH between 0.5 and 4.5 might be normal, but between 0.5 and 2.5 is optimal for most women. Free T3 in range isn't enough—it should be in the upper third of that range for optimal thyroid function.

We've created a free resource to help you interpret your results. Visit https://empoweredweightlossbook.com to download comprehensive guides showing exactly what optimal looks like for each hormone system, what it means when values are suboptimal, and what questions to ask your provider about treatment. Write down every value that's not optimal, even if it's "in range," because these are the clues your body is giving you about what needs to be addressed.

STEP 4: Find a Provider Who Will Treat Comprehensively

This might be your current doctor. It might not be. The provider who's willing to order comprehensive testing might not be the same provider who's equipped to treat all five hormone imbalances optimally. That's okay. You're building a team, not replacing your entire medical care.

The ideal provider takes your symptoms seriously, tests comprehensively, treats to optimal ranges rather than just normal ranges, understands that multiple imbalances exist simultaneously, and is willing to use every tool available—nutrition, supplements, lifestyle changes, and medication—to restore your health. They monitor regularly and adjust treatment based on your response, not just your initial labs. They see hormone optimization as an ongoing process of refinement, not a one-time prescription.

If your current provider checks all these boxes, that's wonderful. Work with them. If not, it's time to expand your team. You don't have to abandon your current doctors. You're adding specialists who can fill specific gaps—a provider skilled in thyroid optimization, another who understands insulin resistance and metabolic health, perhaps a hormone specialist who can manage your sex hormone replacement. These providers work alongside your existing care team, not instead of them. The goal is collaborative, comprehensive care that addresses all five hormone systems simultaneously.

STEP 5: Implement Your Personalized Treatment Protocol

Based on your testing, work with your provider to create a comprehensive treatment plan that addresses all of your imbalances simultaneously. This is critical—treating one imbalance while ignoring the others rarely produces the transformation you're looking for. The five hormone systems influence each other so profoundly that addressing them together creates exponential improvements that isolated treatments cannot achieve.

Your protocol will be unique to you because your hormone pattern is unique to you. One woman might need aggressive thyroid treatment, moderate insulin resistance protocols, and minimal sex hormone support. Another might need significant progesterone replacement, vitamin D optimization, and cortisol management strategies but only minor thyroid adjustments. There's no standard protocol that works for everyone, which is exactly why comprehensive testing matters so much.

The foundation, however, is universal: Home Base. Every woman, regardless of her specific hormone pattern, needs adequate protein, abundant vegetables, proper hydration, quality sleep, stress management, and appropriate movement. These aren't optional recommendations that you'll implement "when you have time"—they're non-negotiable requirements that determine whether your treatment protocols actually work. Supplements don't compensate for terrible sleep. Medications don't override chronic stress. Hormone replacement doesn't fix inadequate nutrition.

Your provider will help you layer in targeted interventions on top of this foundation: thyroid medication optimized to bring Free T3 into the upper third of range, not just TSH into normal range. Insulin-sensitizing medications or supplements if your fasting insulin is elevated or your HOMA-IR indicates resistance. Vitamin D supplementation dosed appropriately for your current deficiency level with a plan to retest and adjust. Bioidentical hormone replacement for deficient sex hormones, carefully monitored and adjusted. Cortisol support strategies tailored to whether you're running high or low.

The key is addressing everything simultaneously while monitoring how your body responds. Some protocols work immediately. Others take months to show full effect. Some need dose adjustments. Others work perfectly from the start. This is why regular retesting matters—you're not guessing whether treatments are working. You're measuring, adjusting, and refining based on objective data combined with how you actually feel.

For detailed protocols for each hormone system, including specific supplement recommendations, medication options, and lifestyle interventions, visit https://empoweredweightlossbook.com where you'll find comprehensive guides you can review with your provider.

STEP 6: Monitor, Adjust, and Refine

Retest every 3-6 months. Your initial protocol isn't your forever protocol. As your body heals, your needs change. Thyroid medication doses that work at first might need adjustment as your thyroid function improves or as your weight changes. Vitamin D supplementation that brings you to optimal levels might be higher than what maintains you there long-term. Insulin sensitivity improves, potentially allowing you to reduce or eliminate berberine or metformin. Cortisol patterns shift as sleep improves and stress management becomes consistent.

Your body is dynamic. Your treatment should be too. Work with providers who understand that optimization is an ongoing process of monitoring and refinement, not a one-time intervention. The women who get the best results are the ones who commit to regular testing, honest assessment of how they're responding, and willingness to adjust protocols based on objective data.

STEP 7: Connect with Women Who Understand This Journey

Healing happens faster in community. Find other women who understand hormone optimization. Who celebrate lab improvements as much as scale victories. Who support you on hard days and cheer you on successful ones.

We've created a space specifically for this. Visit https:// empoweredweightlossbook.com to join women who are walking this same path—implementing Home Base, getting comprehensive testing, treating all five hormone imbalances, and experiencing the transformation that comes from finally addressing root causes instead of just managing symptoms.

This community understands that healing takes time. That your body is responding even when you can't see it yet. That comparing your journey to someone else's is pointless because your hormone pattern is uniquely yours. That some months bring dramatic changes while other months you just hold steady while your body catches up. That celebrating a Free T3 level moving into the upper third of range is just as exciting as celebrating pounds lost.

On the days when you feel discouraged, when the results aren't coming as fast as you want, when you question whether any of this is working, you need people who can remind you that healing is happening, that your body is responding, that you're doing exactly what you need to be doing. That's what community provides.

The Cost of Waiting

Let's be honest about what happens if you don't take action.

You'll wake up six months from now in the exact same place. Same weight. Same symptoms. Same frustration.

You'll try another diet that doesn't work because it doesn't address your hormones. You'll spend more money on supplements that can't compensate for untreated insulin resistance or thyroid dysfunction. You'll exercise harder and eat less and wonder why nothing changes.

You'll watch other women transform and tell yourself it's too late for you. That you're too broken. That this might work for them but won't work for you.

You'll resign yourself to "this is just my life now." You'll make peace with exhaustion, brain fog, weight gain, low libido, mood swings, and insomnia. You'll shrink your life to fit your symptoms instead of treating your symptoms so you can live your life.

You'll look back a year from now and wish you had started today.

Or.

You'll start today.

You'll implement Home Base immediately. You'll get comprehensive testing this week. You'll find a provider who takes you seriously. You'll treat all five hormone imbalances comprehensively. You'll monitor, adjust, and refine.

And six months from now, you'll be a completely different woman.

Not just because the weight came off—though it will.

Not just because your energy returned—though it will.

Not just because the brain fog lifted, the sleep improved, the libido came back, the mood stabilized—though all of that will happen.

But because you'll know in your bones that you were never broken.

That your body was speaking, and you finally learned to listen.

That the medical system failed you, but you didn't fail you.

That healing was possible all along—you just needed the right information, the right testing, and the right treatment.

The Ripple Effect of Your Transformation

Here's what we don't talk about enough: Your healing doesn't just change you.

It changes your daughter who's been watching you criticize your body in the mirror. Who's learning from you what it means to be a woman in midlife. Who will either inherit your resignation or your resilience.

It changes your partner who gets back the woman they fell in love with—not because you're smaller but because you're vibrant again. Present. Engaged with life instead of just surviving it.

It changes your friends who've been struggling silently with the same symptoms, too afraid to speak up, too ashamed to ask for help. Who will see your transformation and think, *If she can do it, maybe I can too.*

It changes your coworkers who've noticed you showing up differently—with more energy, more confidence, more joy. Who will ask what you're doing differently. Who you'll be able to help with the knowledge you now possess.

It changes the medical system one doctor at a time, as you refuse to accept "everything's normal" and insist on comprehensive testing and optimal treatment. As you become an informed advocate for your own health. As you show them that treating hormones comprehensively produces results that symptom management never could.

Your transformation isn't just about you.

It's about every woman whose life you'll impact by refusing to accept that suffering is inevitable.

It's about the new standard you're setting for what's possible in midlife.

It's about the legacy you're creating—not of diets and restriction and shame but of knowledge and empowerment and healing.

Our Invitation

We wrote this book because we've been where you are.

Sarah stood in her bathroom at two a.m., sixty pounds overweight despite training for a marathon, knowing something was profoundly wrong but unable to find anyone who would listen.

Abbey watched her most dedicated gym members work out religiously and eat clean yet unable to lose weight and couldn't find answers for why.

We each had half the puzzle. Medical expertise without the functional medicine framework. Nutrition and lifestyle knowledge without prescribing authority.

Together, we created The Matrix Method.

And over the past few years, we've helped more than 1,800 women lose weight, balance hormones, and reclaim themselves.

Not by giving them another diet.

Not by telling them to try harder.

But by teaching them what you now understand: That hormone imbalances are identifiable, testable, and treatable. That symptoms are your body's language, not your destiny. That comprehensive treatment addressing root causes produces results that single interventions cannot achieve.

This book is our invitation to join those 1,800 women.

Not just as someone who read our book and learned some information.

But as someone who took action. Who got tested. Who found the right providers. Who treated comprehensively. Who transformed.

We want to hear your story.

We want to know which hormone imbalances you discovered. Which protocols worked best for you. How your life changed when your symptoms finally resolved.

We want you to be the woman who, two years from now, tells another struggling woman, *"I was exactly where you are. And here's what changed everything."*

The Last Thing We Want You to Understand

You picked up this book for a reason.

Maybe you're desperate. Maybe you're skeptical. Maybe you're cautiously hopeful that this time will be different.

Whatever brought you here, we're grateful you trusted us with your time and attention.

We understand you've tried everything. We understand you've been disappointed before. We understand hope feels dangerous when you've been let down so many times.

But here's what we need you to grasp:

This isn't another diet book promising quick fixes that don't last.

This isn't another guru telling you the secret is just eating less and moving more.

This isn't another program blaming you for your lack of results.

This is evidence-based medicine. This is comprehensive hormone optimization. This is treating root causes instead of managing symptoms.

This is what we wish someone had told us years ago.

This is what we do every single day with real women getting real results.

This is the difference between struggling for years and finally understanding why.

You're not broken.

You never were.

Your body has been speaking in the only language it has: symptoms.

And now you finally understand what it's been trying to tell you all along.

The question is: What will you do with this knowledge?

Will you close this book, nod thoughtfully, and return to the same patterns that brought you here?

Or will you take the first step today?

Your body is waiting.

It's been waiting for you to listen. To test. To treat. To heal.

It's been waiting for you to stop accepting "normal" and start demanding optimal.

It's been waiting for you to understand that you deserve better than resignation, better than symptom management, better than shrinking your life to accommodate your hormones.

Your body has been waiting for you to realize that healing is possible.

That transformation is available to you.

That the woman you're becoming—the vibrant, energized, confident version of yourself—isn't gone forever.

She's been here all along.

Just waiting for you to balance the five hormone systems that have been keeping her hidden.

Welcome home.

Your transformation starts now.

The knowledge is yours.

The protocols are proven.

The results are waiting.

All you have to do is take the first step.

Will you?

Resources and Next Steps

Congratulations on taking this important step toward healing and reclaiming your health.

Reading this book is just the beginning. To support you beyond these pages, we've created a collection of resources designed to help you implement what you've learned and stay supported as you move forward.

By visiting our resource hub, you'll gain access to:

- The tools, guides, and checklists referenced throughout this book
- Additional education to help you better understand your hormones and metabolism
- Ongoing support and updates created specifically for women in perimenopause

Simply scan the QR code below or visit:
www.empoweredweightlossbook.com to get started

About the Authors

Sarah Gibson, MPAS, HWC, PAC

Sarah Gibson is a board-certified physician associate with over twenty years of clinical experience and a nationally recognized expert in hormone optimization and metabolic weight loss for women in perimenopause. After earning her Masters of Physician Assistant Studies and spending years in trauma and emergency medicine, Sarah became a pioneer in comprehensive hormone health when conventional medicine failed to address her own dramatic midlife weight gain and metabolic dysfunction.

Sarah is a featured medical expert in BALANCE: A Perimenopause Journey, the groundbreaking documentary series executive produced by Alyssa Milano that premiered on Apple TV and Amazon Prime in January 2026. She has appeared in multiple media outlets as an authority on perimenopausal weight loss and hormone optimization and has established her evidence-based protocols in medical and wellness practices nationwide.

As the medical architect behind The Matrix Method, Sarah has developed comprehensive diagnostic and treatment protocols that address the five hormone imbalances affecting midlife women. Her approach combines traditional medical expertise with functional medicine principles, utilizing prescription medications, bioidentical hormone therapy, thyroid optimization beyond standard TSH ranges, and personalized treatment plans based on comprehensive lab testing. Sarah specializes in complex cases including cancer survivors, women with multiple comorbidities, and patients dismissed by conventional providers as "medically impossible" to treat.

Sarah's clinical outcomes speak for themselves: Her patients lose an average of 22.7 pounds in ninety days while experiencing dramatic improvements in energy, sleep, mental clarity, and overall quality of life. Her protocols have been adopted by healthcare providers across the country seeking effective, evidence-based solutions for their perimenopausal patients.

Abbey Walsh, MS, CNS, LDN

Abbey Walsh holds a Masters of Science in Nutrition, is a Certified Nutrition Specialist®, and is a nationally recognized expert in personalized nutrition protocols for hormone optimization. After opening her first boutique fitness studio in 2012, Abbey dedicated her career to solving the metabolic puzzle facing women in midlife who were exercising intensely and eating clean yet seeing no results.

Abbey is the innovative force behind The Matrix Method's cutting-edge diagnostic and supplement protocols. She developed proprietary DNA testing panels that identify individual genetic variations affecting hormone metabolism, detoxification pathways, and nutrient needs, allowing for unprecedented personalization in treatment approaches. As the creator of specialized supplement formulations and bioidentical hormone cream protocols refined through years of clinical application with over 1,800 women, Abbey bridges the gap between functional nutrition and pharmaceutical intervention.

Her expertise extends far beyond standard nutritional counseling. Abbey has developed evidence-based protocols for the 10-Day Detox that identifies inflammatory triggers and food sensitivities, strategic supplementation targeting specific hormone imbalances, and personalized macronutrient ratios based on individual metabolic response. Her work has helped women avoid unnecessary hysterectomies by bringing severe menstrual bleeding under control through targeted nutritional and supplement interventions, achieve successful pregnancies after years of infertility by optimizing hormonal balance, and reverse metabolic dysfunction that conventional medicine deemed permanent.

As a nationally recognized speaker alongside Sarah, Abbey educates healthcare providers and women nationwide on the critical intersection of nutrition, supplementation, and hormone optimization. Her protocols have been implemented in wellness practices across the country, providing practitioners with systematic approaches to complex hormone cases.

Together: Transforming Women's Health

Sarah and Abbey have established themselves as the go-to experts for weight loss in perimenopause, combining Sarah's medical authority and prescribing capabilities with Abbey's advanced nutritional science and supplement development expertise. Their comprehensive team-based approach—integrating medical providers, nutritionists, personal trainers, and success coaches—produces results that isolated interventions cannot achieve.

Through The Matrix Method, they have helped over 1,800 women achieve transformative results, including women told by oncologists that weight loss was "medically impossible," patients dismissed by endocrinologists despite debilitating symptoms, and women with decades of failed diet attempts. Their systematic approach to identifying and treating all five hormone imbalances simultaneously has proven effective across diverse populations and complex medical histories.

As nationally recognized speakers and thought leaders in women's hormone health, Sarah and Abbey continue to expand the reach of their evidence-based protocols through practitioner training, media appearances, and their comprehensive treatment programs. Their mission: ensuring that every woman in perimenopause receives the comprehensive, personalized care required to thrive during this critical life transition.

To learn more about working with Sarah and Abbey, visit our website https://empoweredweightlossbook.com/.

References

Part 1 References

Chapter 1: Insulin Resistance

1. De Paoli M, Zakharia A, Werstuck GH. The Role of Estrogen in Insulin Resistance: A Review of Clinical and Preclinical Data. *Am J Pathol.* 2021;191(9):1490-1498.
2. Carr MC. The emergence of the metabolic syndrome with menopause. *J Clin Endocrinol Metab.* 2003;88(6):2404-2411.
3. Mauvais-Jarvis F, Clegg DJ, Hevener AL. The role of estrogens in control of energy balance and glucose homeostasis. *Endocr Rev.* 2013;34(3):309-338.
4. Salpeter SR, Walsh JM, Ormiston TM, Greyber E, Buckley NS, Salpeter EE. Meta-analysis: effect of hormone-replacement therapy on components of the metabolic syndrome in postmenopausal women. *Diabetes Obes Metab.* 2006;8(5):538-554.
5. Wildman RP, Sowers MR. Adiposity and the menopausal transition. *Obstet Gynecol Clin North Am.* 2011;38(3):441-454.
6. Lovejoy JC, Champagne CM, de Jonge L, Xie H, Smith SR. Increased visceral fat and decreased energy expenditure during the menopausal transition. *Int J Obes (Lond).* 2008;32(6):949-958.
7. American Diabetes Association. Classification and Diagnosis of Diabetes: Standards of Medical Care in Diabetes—2024. *Diabetes Care.* 2024;47(Suppl 1):S20-S42.
8. Matthews DR, Hosker JP, Rudenski AS, Naylor BA, Treacher DF, Turner RC. Homeostasis model assessment: insulin resistance and beta-cell function from fasting plasma glucose and insulin concentrations in man. *Diabetologia.* 1985;28(7):412-419.
9. Freeman EW, Sammel MD, Lin H, Gracia CR. Obesity and reproductive hormone levels in the transition to menopause. *Menopause.* 2010;17(4):718-726.

10. Kapoor E, Collazo-Clavell ML, Faubion SS. Weight Gain in Women at Midlife: A Concise Review of the Pathophysiology and Strategies for Management. *Mayo Clin Proc.* 2017;92(10):1552-1558.

11. Gavin KM, Bessesen DH. Sex Differences in Muscle Mass and Insulin Resistance After Menopause. *Curr Opin Endocr Metab Res.* 2020;12:20-26.

12. International Diabetes Federation. The IDF consensus worldwide definition of the metabolic syndrome. 2006.

13. Nathan DM, Kuenen J, Borg R, Zheng H, Schoenfeld D, Heine RJ; A1c-Derived Average Glucose Study Group. Translating the A1C assay into estimated average glucose values. *Diabetes Care.* 2008;31(8):1473-1478.

14. Reaven GM. Banting lecture 1988. Role of insulin resistance in human disease. *Diabetes.* 1988;37(12):1595-1607.

15. Skov V, Glintborg D, Knudsen S, et al. Reduced expression of nuclear-encoded genes involved in mitochondrial oxidative metabolism in skeletal muscle of insulin-resistant women with polycystic ovary syndrome. *Diabetes.* 2007;56(9):2349-2355.

Chapter 2: Cortisol Dysregulation

1. McEwen BS. Stress, adaptation, and disease. Allostasis and allostatic load. *Ann N Y Acad Sci.* 1998;840:33-44.

2. Epel ES, McEwen B, Seeman T, et al. Stress and body shape: stress-induced cortisol secretion is consistently greater among women with central fat. *Psychosom Med.* 2000;62(5):623-632.

3. Lupien SJ, McEwen BS, Gunnar MR, Heim C. Effects of stress throughout the lifespan on the brain, behaviour and cognition. *Nat Rev Neurosci.* 2009;10(6):434-445.

4. Sapolsky RM, Krey LC, McEwen BS. The neuroendocrinology of stress and aging: the glucocorticoid cascade hypothesis. *Endocr Rev.* 1986;7(3):284-301.

5. Chrousos GP. Stress and disorders of the stress system. *Nat Rev Endocrinol.* 2009;5(7):374-381.

6. Pasquali R, Vicennati V, Cacciari M, Pagotto U. The hypothalamic-pituitary-adrenal axis activity in obesity and the metabolic syndrome. *Ann N Y Acad Sci.* 2006;1083:111-128.

7. Björntorp P, Rosmond R. Obesity and cortisol. *Nutrition.* 2000;16(10):924-936.

8. Raikkonen K, Matthews KA, Kuller LH. The relationship between psychological risk attributes and the metabolic syndrome in healthy women: antecedent or consequence? *Metabolism.* 2002;51(12):1573-1577.

9. Hewagalamulage SD, Lee TK, Clarke IJ, Henry BA. Stress, cortisol, and obesity: a role for cortisol responsiveness in identifying individuals prone to obesity. *Domest Anim Endocrinol.* 2016;56 Suppl:S112-S120.

10. Hannibal KE, Bishop MD. Chronic stress, cortisol dysfunction, and pain: a psychoneuroendocrine rationale for stress management in pain rehabilitation. *Phys Ther.* 2014;94(12):1816-1825.

11. Nicolaides NC, Kyratzi E, Lamprokostopoulou A, Chrousos GP, Charmandari E. Stress, the stress system and the role of glucocorticoids. *Neuroimmunomodulation.* 2015;22(1-2):6-19.

12. Dallman MF, Pecoraro N, Akana SF, et al. Chronic stress and obesity: a new view of "comfort food". *Proc Natl Acad Sci U S A.* 2003;100(20):11696-11701.

13. Rosmond R. Role of stress in the pathogenesis of the metabolic syndrome. *Psychoneuroendocrinology.* 2005;30(1):1-10.

14. Kadmiel M, Cidlowski JA. Glucocorticoid receptor signaling in health and disease. *Trends Pharmacol Sci.* 2013;34(9):518-530.

15. Nieuwenhuizen AG, Rutters F. The hypothalamic-pituitary-adrenal-axis in the regulation of energy balance. *Physiol Behav.* 2008;94(2):169-177.

Chapter 3: Thyroid Dysfunction

Thyroid Hormone Production and Conversion

1. Bianco AC, Salvatore D, Gereben B, Berry MJ, Larsen PR. Metabolism of Thyroid Hormone. *Endotext [Internet].* January 2017. NCBI Bookshelf. Available at: https://www.ncbi.nlm.nih.gov/books/NBK285545/

2. Visser TJ, Peeters RP. Role of hepatic deiodinases in thyroid hormone homeostasis and liver metabolism, inflammation, and fibrosis. *European Thyroid Journal.* 2023;12(3). Available at: https://etj.bioscientifica.com/view/journals/etj/12/3/ETJ-22-0211.xml

3. Hagmeyer R. Thyroid Conversion Issues—Everything You Ever Wanted To Know. November 2024. Available at: https://www.drhagmeyer.com/thyroid-conversion-issues-everthing-you-ever-wanted-to-know/

4. Campbell P. Improving Thyroid Hormone Conversion. *Cytoplan Blog.* March 2018. Available at: https://blog.cytoplan.co.uk/improving-thyroid-hormone-conversion/

5. Nomura S, Pittman CS, Chambers JB Jr, Buck MW, Shimizu T. Reduced peripheral conversion of thyroxine to triiodothyronine in patients with hepatic cirrhosis. *Journal of Clinical Investigation.* 1975;56(3):643-652. Available at: https://pubmed.ncbi.nlm.nih.gov/1159078/

Hashimoto's Thyroiditis

1. Shi SR, Zhang JA, Liu CJ, et al. Global prevalence and epidemiological trends of Hashimoto's thyroiditis in adults: A systematic review and meta-analysis. *Frontiers in Public Health.* 2022;10:1020709. Available

at: https://www.frontiersin.org/journals/public-health/articles/10.3389/
fpubh.2022.1020709/full

2. Caturegli P, De Remigis A, Rose NR. Hashimoto thyroiditis: Clinical and
diagnostic criteria. *Autoimmunity Reviews*. 2014;13(4-5):391-397.

3. Ralli M, Angeletti D, Fiore M, et al. Hashimoto Thyroiditis. *StatPearls
[Internet]*. February 2025. NCBI Bookshelf. Available at: https://www.
ncbi.nlm.nih.gov/books/NBK459262/

4. Gierach M, Gierach J, Junik R. Hashimoto's thyroiditis and
cardiometabolic risk. *Polish Archives of Internal Medicine*.
2022;132(3):16222. Available at: https://www.mp.pl/paim/issue/
article/16222/

5. National Institute of Diabetes and Digestive and Kidney Diseases
(NIDDK). Hashimoto's Disease. August 2025. Available at: https://www.
niddk.nih.gov/health-information/endocrine-diseases/hashimotos-disease

6. Autoimmune Association. Hashimoto's Thyroiditis. October 2024.
Available at: https://autoimmune.org/disease-information/hashimotos-
thyroiditis/

MTHFR Gene and Thyroid Function

1. MTHFR Support Australia. The Role of MTHFR in Thyroid Conditions:
A Deep Dive into the Connection. December 2024. Available at: https://
www.mthfrsupport.com.au/2024/12/the-role-of-mthfr-in-thyroid-
conditions-a-deep-dive-into-the-connection/

2. Paloma Health. MTHFR Gene Variations, Hashimoto's Thyroiditis,
and Hypothyroidism. September 2024. Available at: https://www.
palomahealth.com/learn/mthfr-gene-variations-hashimotos-thyroiditis-
hypothyroidism

3. Arakhamia T, Iobadze M, Meparishvili M, et al.
Methylenetetrahydrofolate Reductase (MTHFR) C677T and A1298C
Polymorphisms in Georgian Females with Hypothyroidism. *Georgia
Medical News*. 2020. PMC7490122. Available at: https://pmc.ncbi.nlm.
nih.gov/articles/PMC7490122/

4. Al-Kuraishy HM, Batiha GE, Al-Gareeb AI, et al. Genetic
predisposition of MTHFR and TNFSF4 gene polymorphism related to
hypothyroidism—A meta-analysis. *Gene*. 2024. Available at: https://www.
sciencedirect.com/science/article/abs/pii/S2452014424002140

5. Methyl-Life. MTHFR and Thyroid. Available at: https://methyl-life.com/
blogs/mthfr/mthfr-thyroid

6. Gronick C. MTHFR and Thyroid Disorders. Dr. Chelsea Gronick ND.
August 2023. Available at: https://drchelseagronick.com/mthfr-and-
thyroid-disorders/

7. Holtorf Medical Group. Methyl Tetrahydrofolate Reductase (MTHFR): The Thyroid Connection. May 2023. Available at: https://holtorfmed.com/articles/methyl-tetrahydrofolate-reductase-mthfr-the-thyroid-connection/

8. Advanced Functional Medicine. Can MTHFR affect your thyroid and cause Hashimoto's disease? September 2023. Available at: https://advancedfunctionalmedicine.com.au/mthfr-and-hashimotos-disease/

9. Al-Batayneh KM, Zoubi MSA, Shudifat AE, et al. MTHFR gene polymorphisms in hypothyroidism and hyperthyroidism among Jordanian females. *Endocrine*. 2023;82(1):176-184. PMC10522201. Available at: https://pmc.ncbi.nlm.nih.gov/articles/PMC10522201/

Estrogen and Thyroid Function

1. Marqusee E, Hill JA, Mandel SJ. The effect of droloxifene and estrogen on thyroid function in postmenopausal women. *Journal of Clinical Endocrinology and Metabolism*. 2000;85(11):4407-4410. Available at: https://pubmed.ncbi.nlm.nih.gov/11095487/

2. Arafah BM. Interaction of Estrogen Therapy and Thyroid Hormone Replacement in Postmenopausal Women. *Thyroid*. 2001;11(8):1127-1134. Available at: https://www.liebertpub.com/doi/pdf/10.1089/105072504323024561

3. Ain KB, Refetoff S, Sarne DH, Murata Y. Effect of Estrogen on the Synthesis and Secretion of Thyroxine-Binding Globulin by a Human Hepatoma Cell Line, HEP G2. *Molecular Endocrinology*. 1988;2(4):313-323. Available at: https://academic.oup.com/mend/article-pdf/2/4/313/9088457/mend0313.pdf

4. Refetoff S, Weiss RE, Usala SJ. Thyroid Hormone Serum Transport Proteins. *Endotext [Internet]*. March 2023. NCBI Bookshelf. Available at: https://www.ncbi.nlm.nih.gov/books/NBK285566/

5. Wikipedia. Thyroxine-binding globulin. October 2024. Available at: https://en.wikipedia.org/wiki/Thyroxine-binding_globulin

6. Medscape. Thyroid-Binding Globulin: Reference Range, Interpretation, Collection and Panels. Available at: https://emedicine.medscape.com/article/2089554-overview

7. Mayo Clinic Laboratories. Thyroxine-Binding Globulin (TBG), Serum. Available at: https://endocrinology.testcatalog.org/show/TBGI

8. ScienceDirect. Thyroxine Binding Globulin—an overview. Available at: https://www.sciencedirect.com/topics/medicine-and-dentistry/thyroxine-binding-globulin

9. D'Elia AV, Tell G, Russo D, Arturi F, Puglisi F, Filetti S, Damante G. Support for the upregulation of serum thyrotropin by estrogens coming from the increased requirement of levothyroxine in one gynecomastic patient with excess of thyroxine-binding globulin secondary to exposure to exogenous estrogens. *Endocrine Connections*. 2018;7(10):EC-18-

0247. Available at: https://www.sciencedirect.com/science/article/pii/
S2214624518300388

Factors Affecting T4 to T3 Conversion

1. Cleuet N. Factors Affecting Thyroid Hormone Conversion. November
    2020. Available at: https://www.nikicleuet.com/blog-1/2020/4/11/factors-
    affecting-thyroid-hormone-conversion
2. Campbell P. Improving Thyroid Hormone Conversion. *Cytoplan Blog.*
    March 2018. Available at: https://blog.cytoplan.co.uk/improving-thyroid-
    hormone-conversion/
3. Campbell P. Low Thyroid Conversion of T4 to T3. *Pippa Campbell Health.*
    July 2024. Available at: https://www.pippacampbellhealth.com/blog/
    low-thyroid/
4. Hagmeyer R. Thyroid Conversion Issues. November 2024. Available at:
    https://www.drhagmeyer.com/thyroid-conversion-issues-everthing-you-
    ever-wanted-to-know/
5. Walk-In Lab. T3, T4, and TSH Explained Simply | Thyroid Hormones.
    September 2025. Available at: https://resources.walkinlab.com/thyroid/
    thyroid-hormones-explained/
6. MTHFR Doctors. The MTHFR Gene Mutation. May 2025. Available at:
    https://www.mthfrdoctors.com/the-mthfr-mutation/

Chapter 4: Sex Hormone Imbalance

1. Lennartsson AK, Jonsdottir IH. Prolactin in response to acute
    psychosocial stress in healthy men and women. *Psychoneuroendocrinology.*
    2011;36(10):1530-1539.
2. Havlikova H, Hill M, Kancheva L, Vrbikova J, Pouzar V, Cerny I,
    Kancheva R, Novak Z, Starka L. Serum profiles of free and conjugated
    neuroactive pregnanolone isomers in nonpregnant women of fertile age. *J
    Clin Endocrinol Metab.* 2006;91(8):3092-3099.
3. Maninger N, Wolkowitz OM, Reus VI, Epel ES, Mellon SH.
    Neurobiological and neuropsychiatric effects of dehydroepiandrosterone
    (DHEA) and DHEA sulfate (DHEAS). *Front Neuroendocrinol.*
    2009;30(1):65-91.
4. Carr MC. The emergence of the metabolic syndrome with menopause. *J
    Clin Endocrinol Metab.* 2003;88(6):2404-2411.
5. Mauvais-Jarvis F, Clegg DJ, Hevener AL. The role of estrogens in
    control of energy balance and glucose homeostasis. *Endocr Rev.*
    2013;34(3):309-338.
6. Shi H, Seeley RJ, Clegg DJ. Sexual differences in the control of energy
    homeostasis. *Front Neuroendocrinol.* 2009;30(3):396-404.

7. Palmer BF, Clegg DJ. The sexual dimorphism of obesity. *Mol Cell Endocrinol.* 2015;402:113-119.

8. Lovejoy JC, Champagne CM, de Jonge L, Xie H, Smith SR. Increased visceral fat and decreased energy expenditure during the menopausal transition. *Int J Obes (Lond).* 2008;32(6):949-958.

9. Bonds DE, Lasser N, Qi L, et al. The effect of conjugated equine oestrogen on diabetes incidence: the Women's Health Initiative randomised trial. *Diabetologia.* 2006;49(3):459-468.

10. Yan H, Yang W, Zhou F, et al. Estrogen improves insulin sensitivity and suppresses gluconeogenesis via the transcription factor Foxo1. *Diabetes.* 2019;68(2):291-304.

11. Brinton RD, Yao J, Yin F, Mack WJ, Cadenas E. Perimenopause as a neurological transition state. *Nat Rev Endocrinol.* 2015;11(7):393-405.

12. Rocca WA, Bower JH, Maraganore DM, et al. Increased risk of cognitive impairment or dementia in women who underwent oophorectomy before menopause. *Neurology.* 2007;69(11):1074-1083.

13. Henderson VW, Brinton RD. Menopause and mitochondria: windows into estrogen effects on Alzheimer's disease risk and therapy. *Prog Brain Res.* 2010;182:77-96.

14. Iorga A, Cunningham CM, Moazeni S, Ruffenach G, Umar S, Eghbali M. The protective role of estrogen and estrogen receptors in cardiovascular disease and the controversial use of estrogen therapy. *Biol Sex Differ.* 2017;8(1):33.

15. Rossouw JE, Anderson GL, Prentice RL, et al. Risks and benefits of estrogen plus progestin in healthy postmenopausal women: principal results from the Women's Health Initiative randomized controlled trial. *JAMA.* 2002;288(3):321-333.

16. Manson JE, Chlebowski RT, Stefanick ML, et al. Menopausal hormone therapy and health outcomes during the intervention and extended poststopping phases of the Women's Health Initiative randomized trials. *JAMA.* 2013;310(13):1353-1368.

17. Khosla S, Oursler MJ, Monroe DG. Estrogen and the skeleton. *Trends Endocrinol Metab.* 2012;23(11):576-581.

18. Sözen T, Özışık L, Başaran NÇ. An overview and management of osteoporosis. *Eur J Rheumatol.* 2017;4(1):46-56.

19. Pfeilschifter J, Köditz R, Pfohl M, Schatz H. Changes in proinflammatory cytokine activity after menopause. *Endocr Rev.* 2002;23(1):90-119.

20. Straub RH. The complex role of estrogens in inflammation. *Endocr Rev.* 2007;28(5):521-574.

21. Schüle C, Nothdurfter C, Rupprecht R. The role of allopregnanolone in depression and anxiety. *Prog Neurobiol.* 2014;113:79-87.

22. Backstrom T, Haage D, Löfgren M, et al. Paradoxical effects of GABA-A modulators may explain sex steroid induced negative mood symptoms in some persons. *Neuroscience.* 2011;191:46-54.

23. Lancel M, Faulhaber J, Holsboer F, Rupprecht R. Progesterone induces changes in sleep comparable to those of agonistic GABAA receptor modulators. *Am J Physiol.* 1996;271(4 Pt 1):E763-E772.

24. Baker FC, Driver HS. Circadian rhythms, sleep, and the menstrual cycle. *Sleep Med.* 2007;8(6):613-622.

25. Bunevicius R, Kazanavicius G, Zalinkevicius R, Prange AJ Jr. Effects of thyroxine as compared with thyroxine plus triiodothyronine in patients with hypothyroidism. *N Engl J Med.* 1999;340(6):424-429.

26. L'Hermite M, Simoncini T, Fuller S, Genazzani AR. Could transdermal estradiol + progesterone be a safer postmenopausal HRT? A review. *Maturitas.* 2008;60(3-4):185-201.

27. Stanczyk FZ, Hapgood JP, Winer S, Mishell DR Jr. Progestogens used in postmenopausal hormone therapy: differences in their pharmacological properties, intracellular actions, and clinical effects. *Endocr Rev.* 2013;34(2):171-208.

28. Fournier A, Berrino F, Clavel-Chapelon F. Unequal risks for breast cancer associated with different hormone replacement therapies: results from the E3N cohort study. *Breast Cancer Res Treat.* 2008;107(1):103-111.

29. Sipilä S, Narici M, Kjaer M, et al. Sex hormones and skeletal muscle weakness. *Biogerontology.* 2013;14(3):231-245.

30. Davis SR, Wahlin-Jacobsen S. Testosterone in women--the clinical significance. *Lancet Diabetes Endocrinol.* 2015;3(12):980-992.

31. Santoro N, Torrens J, Crawford S, et al. Correlates of circulating androgens in mid-life women: the study of women's health across the nation. *J Clin Endocrinol Metab.* 2005;90(8):4836-4845.

32. Kingsberg SA, Simon JA, Goldstein I. The current outlook for testosterone in the management of hypoactive sexual desire disorder in postmenopausal women. *J Sex Med.* 2008;5 Suppl 4:182-193.

33. Davis SR, Davison SL, Donath S, Bell RJ. Circulating androgen levels and self-reported sexual function in women. *JAMA.* 2005;294(1):91-96.

34. Vanderschueren D, Vandenput L, Boonen S, Lindberg MK, Bouillon R, Ohlsson C. Androgens and bone. *Endocr Rev.* 2004;25(3):389-425.

35. Navarro G, Allard C, Xu W, Mauvais-Jarvis F. The role of androgens in metabolism, obesity, and diabetes in males and females. *Obesity (Silver Spring).* 2015;23(4):713-719.

36. Prior JC. Progesterone for symptomatic perimenopause treatment—progesterone politics, physiology and potential for perimenopause. *Facts Views Vis Obgyn.* 2011;3(2):109-120.

37. Lee JR. What your doctor may not tell you about menopause: the breakthrough book on natural progesterone. Warner Books. 1996.

38. Manson JE, Aragaki AK, Rossouw JE, et al. Menopausal hormone therapy and long-term all-cause and cause-specific mortality: the Women's Health Initiative randomized trials. *JAMA.* 2017;318(10):927-938.

39. Schierbeck LL, Rejnmark L, Tofteng CL, et al. Effect of hormone replacement therapy on cardiovascular events in recently postmenopausal women: randomised trial. *BMJ*. 2012;345:e6409.

40. Hodis HN, Mack WJ, Henderson VW, et al. Vascular Effects of Early versus Late Postmenopausal Treatment with Estradiol. *N Engl J Med*. 2016;374(13):1221-1231.

41. The NAMS 2017 Hormone Therapy Position Statement Advisory Panel. The 2017 hormone therapy position statement of The North American Menopause Society. *Menopause*. 2017;24(7):728-753.

42. ACOG Practice Bulletin No. 141: management of menopausal symptoms. *Obstet Gynecol*. 2014;123(1):202-216.

43. Stuenkel CA, Davis SR, Gompel A, et al. Treatment of symptoms of the menopause: an Endocrine Society Clinical Practice Guideline. *J Clin Endocrinol Metab*. 2015;100(11):3975-4011.

44. Teede HJ, Misso ML, Costello MF, et al. Recommendations from the international evidence-based guideline for the assessment and management of polycystic ovary syndrome. *Fertil Steril*. 2018;110(3):364-379.

45. Legro RS, Arslanian SA, Ehrmann DA, et al. Diagnosis and treatment of polycystic ovary syndrome: an Endocrine Society clinical practice guideline. *J Clin Endocrinol Metab*. 2013;98(12):4565-4592.

46. Marshall JC, Dunaif A. Should all women with PCOS be treated for insulin resistance? *Fertil Steril*. 2012;97(1):18-22.

47. Legro RS, Driscoll D, Strauss JF 3rd, Fox J, Dunaif A. Evidence for a genetic basis for hyperandrogenemia in polycystic ovary syndrome. *Proc Natl Acad Sci U S A*. 1998;95(25):14956-14960.

48. Revised 2003 consensus on diagnostic criteria and long-term health risks related to polycystic ovary syndrome. *Fertil Steril*. 2004;81(1):19-25.

49. Santoro N, Randolph JF Jr. Reproductive hormones and the menopause transition. *Obstet Gynecol Clin North Am*. 2011;38(3):455-466.

50. Prior JC. Perimenopause: The Complex Endocrinology of the Menopausal Transition. *Endocr Rev*. 1998;19(4):397-428.

51. Burger HG, Hale GE, Robertson DM, Dennerstein L. A review of hormonal changes during the menopausal transition: focus on findings from the Melbourne Women's Midlife Health Project. *Hum Reprod Update*. 2007;13(6):559-565.

52. Orentreich N, Brind JL, Rizer RL, Vogelman JH. Age changes and sex differences in serum dehydroepiandrosterone sulfate concentrations throughout adulthood. *J Clin Endocrinol Metab*. 1984;59(3):551-555.

53. Gupte AA, Pownall HJ, Hamilton DJ. Estrogen: an emerging regulator of insulin action and mitochondrial function. *J Diabetes Res*. 2015;2015:916585.

54. Livingstone C, Collison M. Sex steroids and insulin resistance. *Clin Sci (Lond)*. 2002;102(2):151-166.

55. Arafah BM. Increased need for thyroxine in women with hypothyroidism during estrogen therapy. *N Engl J Med*. 2001;344(23):1743-1749.

56. Santin AP, Furlanetto TW. Role of estrogen in thyroid function and growth regulation. *J Thyroid Res.* 2011;2011:875125.

57. Young EA, Altemus M, Parkison V, Shastry S. Effects of estrogen antagonists and agonists on the ACTH response to restraint stress in female rats. *Neuropsychopharmacology.* 2001;25(6):881-891.

58. Handa RJ, Weiser MJ, Zuloaga DG. A role for the androgen metabolite, 5alpha-androstane-3beta,17beta-diol, in modulating oestrogen receptor beta-mediated regulation of hormonal stress reactivity. *J Neuroendocrinol.* 2009;21(4):351-358.

59. Maltais ML, Desroches J, Dionne IJ. Changes in muscle mass and strength after menopause. *J Musculoskelet Neuronal Interact.* 2009;9(4):186-197.

60. Karastergiou K, Smith SR, Greenberg AS, Fried SK. Sex differences in human adipose tissues—the biology of pear shape. *Biol Sex Differ.* 2012;3(1):13.

61. Toth MJ, Tchernof A, Sites CK, Poehlman ET. Effect of menopausal status on body composition and abdominal fat distribution. *Int J Obes Relat Metab Disord.* 2000;24(2):226-231.

62. Dulloo AG, Jacquet J, Montani JP, Schutz Y. How dieting makes the lean fatter: from a perspective of body composition autoregulation through adipostats and proteinstats awaiting discovery. *Obes Rev.* 2015;16 Suppl 1:25-35.

63. Fothergill E, Guo J, Howard L, et al. Persistent metabolic adaptation 6 years after "The Biggest Loser" competition. *Obesity (Silver Spring).* 2016;24(8):1612-1619.

64. Rosenbaum M, Leibel RL. Adaptive thermogenesis in humans. *Int J Obes (Lond).* 2010;34 Suppl 1(Suppl 1):S47-S55.

CHAPTER 5: VITAMIN D DEFICIENCY

1. Purishh. "Vitamin D: Not Actually a Vitamin." Available at: https://purishh.com

2. Quora. "Why is vitamin D considered a hormone?" Available at: https://quora.com

3. AHA Journals. "Vitamin D and Cardiovascular Disease." Available at: https://ahajournals.org

4. Amchara. "Vitamin D and Hormone Function." Available at: https://amchara.com

5. Diabetes Journals. "Vitamin D supplementation and insulin secretion." Available at: https://diabetesjournals.org

6. PubMed Central. "Vitamin D deficiency and thyroid function." Available at: https://pmc.ncbi.nlm.nih.gov

7. F1000Research. "Vitamin D treatment alters adrenal steroidogenesis." Available at: https://f1000research.com

8. Frontiers. "Vitamin D and PCOS." Available at: https://frontiersin.org

9. Wikipedia. "Vitamin D Receptor." Available at: https://en.wikipedia.org/wiki/Vitamin_D_receptor

10. GeneCards. "VDR Gene." Available at: https://genecards.org

11. MDPI. "Vitamin D Receptor Interactions." Available at: https://mdpi.com

12. Nature. "Vitamin D supplementation increases VDR gene expression." Available at: https://nature.com

13. ScienceDirect. "Vitamin D regulates steroid hormone production." Available at: https://sciencedirect.com

14. Elara. "Vitamin D and aromatase activity." Available at: https://elara.com

15. Amegroups. "Vitamin D stimulates estrogen and progesterone production." Available at: https://amegroups.com

16. PubMed Central. "Vitamin D and SHBG levels." Available at: https://pmc.ncbi.nlm.nih.gov

17. Diabetes Journals. "Vitamin D deficiency and weight loss." Available at: https://diabetesjournals.org

18. PubMed. "Vitamin D levels normalize after weight loss." Available at: https://pubmed.ncbi.nlm.nih.gov

19. Healthline. "Vitamin D and Weight Loss." Available at: https://healthline.com

20. PubMed. "Vitamin D and serotonin synthesis." Available at: https://pubmed.ncbi.nlm.nih.gov

21. PubMed Central. "Vitamin D induces TPH2 expression." Available at: https://pmc.ncbi.nlm.nih.gov

22. ScienceDirect. "Vitamin D supplementation improves depression." Available at: https://sciencedirect.com

23. Psychiatry Times. "Vitamin D and Depression." Available at: https://psychiatrytimes.com

24. WHO EMRO. "Effect of latitude on seasonal variations of vitamin D." Available at: https://www.emro.who.int

25. PubMed. Webb AR, Kline L, Holick MF. "Influence of season and latitude on the cutaneous synthesis of vitamin D3: exposure to winter sunlight in Boston and Edmonton will not promote vitamin D3 synthesis in human skin." *J Clin Endocrinol Metab.* 1988 Aug;67(2):373-8.

26. The Journal of Clinical Endocrinology & Metabolism. Levis S, Gomez A, Jimenez C, et al. "Vitamin D Deficiency and Seasonal Variation in an Adult South Florida Population." Volume 90, Issue 3, March 2005.

27. PMC. "Seasonal variations in serum vitamin D according to age and sex." Available at: https://pmc.ncbi.nlm.nih.gov/articles/PMC3755860/

28. PubMed. "Sunlight and dietary contributions to the seasonal vitamin D status of cohorts of healthy postmenopausal women living at northerly latitudes." Available at: https://pubmed.ncbi.nlm.nih.gov/21085934/

29. Consensus. "Can People North of 35deg Latitude Get Enough Vitamin D via the Sun in Winter?" Available at: https://consensus.app

30. Oxford Academic. Webb AR, Kline L, Holick MF. "Influence of Season and Latitude on the Cutaneous Synthesis of Vitamin D3." *The Journal of Clinical Endocrinology & Metabolism*, Volume 67, Issue 2, August 1988.

31. PubMed. "Vitamin D deficiency prevalence in summer compared to winter in a city with high humidity." Available at: https://pubmed.ncbi.nlm.nih.gov/21717408/

32. PubMed. "The effect of season and latitude on in vitro vitamin D formation by sunlight in South Africa." Available at: https://pubmed.ncbi.nlm.nih.gov/8955733/

33. PMC. "Is Sunlight Exposure Enough to Avoid Wintertime Vitamin D Deficiency in United Kingdom Population Groups?" Available at: https://pmc.ncbi.nlm.nih.gov/articles/PMC6121420/

34. PMC. "The role of vitamin D in menopausal women's health." Available at: https://pmc.ncbi.nlm.nih.gov/articles/PMC10291614/

35. Femgevity Health. "The Vitamin D Paradox: Understanding Deficiency and Its Impact on Health." Available at: https://www.femgevityhealth.com

36. PMC. "Vitamin D supplementation after the menopause." Available at: https://pmc.ncbi.nlm.nih.gov/articles/PMC7278294/

37. PubMed. "Impact of Vitamin D on Skin Aging, and Age-Related Dermatological Conditions." Available at: https://pubmed.ncbi.nlm.nih.gov/39862075/

38. PubMed. "Aging decreases the capacity of human skin to produce vitamin D3." Available at: https://pubmed.ncbi.nlm.nih.gov/2997282/

39. Sage Journals. Pérez-López FR, Chedraui P, Pilz S. "Vitamin D supplementation after the menopause." Available at: https://journals.sagepub.com/doi/full/10.1177/2042018820931291

40. PMC. "Unravelling of hidden secrets: The role of vitamin D in skin aging." Available at: https://pmc.ncbi.nlm.nih.gov/articles/PMC3583884/

41. Balance Menopause. "All about vitamin D, menopause and hormone health." Available at: https://www.balance-menopause.com

42. IMR Press. "Impact of Vitamin D on Skin Aging, and Age-Related Dermatological Conditions." Available at: https://www.imrpress.com/journal/FBL/30/1/10.31083/FBL25463/htm

43. Nutrition & Metabolism. "Effects of high fat diet-induced obesity on vitamin D metabolism and tissue distribution." Available at: https://nutritionandmetabolism.biomedcentral.com/articles/10.1186/s12986-020-00463-x

44. PubMed. "Unraveling the Connection: Visceral Adipose Tissue and Vitamin D Levels in Obesity." Available at: https://pubmed.ncbi.nlm.nih.gov/37836543/

45. PMC. "Vitamin D and Visceral Obesity in Humans: What Should Clinicians Know?" Available at: https://pmc.ncbi.nlm.nih.gov/articles/PMC9332747/

46. Wiley Online Library. Hengist A, et al. "Mobilising vitamin D from adipose tissue: The potential impact of exercise." *Nutrition Bulletin*. 2019.

47. Oxford Academic. Di Nisio A, et al. "Impaired Release of Vitamin D in Dysfunctional Adipose Tissue: New Cues on Vitamin D Supplementation in Obesity." *The Journal of Clinical Endocrinology & Metabolism*, Volume 102, Issue 7, July 2017.

48. PMC. "Vitamin D regulation of adipogenesis and adipose tissue functions." Available at: https://pmc.ncbi.nlm.nih.gov/articles/PMC7683208/

49. Medscape. "Does Vitamin D Deficiency Cause Obesity or Vice Versa?" Available at: https://www.medscape.com/viewarticle/985973

50. PMC. "Vitamin D Storage in Adipose Tissue of Obese and Normal Weight Women." Available at: https://pmc.ncbi.nlm.nih.gov/articles/PMC5577589/

51. PMC. "Vitamin D Deficiency: Consequence or Cause of Obesity?" Available at: https://pmc.ncbi.nlm.nih.gov/articles/PMC6780345/

52. PubMed. "Vitamin D deficiency in the aetiology of obesity-related insulin resistance." Available at: https://pubmed.ncbi.nlm.nih.gov/30801902/

53. PMC. Grant WB, et al. "Does the High Prevalence of Vitamin D Deficiency in African Americans Contribute to Health Disparities?" *Nutrients*. 2021 Feb 3;13(2):499.

54. PubMed. Grant WB, et al. "Does the High Prevalence of Vitamin D Deficiency in African Americans Contribute to Health Disparities?" Available at: https://pubmed.ncbi.nlm.nih.gov/33546262/

55. The Cooper Institute. "African Americans At Greatest Risk of Vitamin D Deficiency." Available at: https://www.cooperinstitute.org/blog

56. University of Houston. "Study Finds Low Vitamin D Levels in Young People of Color." Available at: https://www.uh.edu/news-events

57. MDPI. Grant WB, et al. "Does the High Prevalence of Vitamin D Deficiency in African Americans Contribute to Health Disparities?" Available at: https://www.mdpi.com/2072-6643/13/2/499

58. ScienceDirect. "The prevalence of vitamin D deficiency among dark-skinned populations according to their stage of migration and region of birth: A meta-analysis." Available at: https://www.sciencedirect.com/science/article/abs/pii/S0899900715002932

59. News Center (Northwestern). Murphy AB, et al. "One Size Doesn't Fit All When It Comes To Vitamin D for Men." Available at: https://news.feinberg.northwestern.edu/2011/09/20/vitamin-d/

60. PubMed. Harris SS. "Vitamin D and African Americans." *J Nutr.* 2006 Apr;136(4):1126-9.

61. Afriscitech. "The Myth of chronic Black Vitamin D deficiency." Available at: https://www.afriscitech.com/en/blogs/afroscientific-en/343

62. PMC. Kumar J, et al. "Impact of season and diet on vitamin D status of African American and Caucasian children." Available at: https://pmc.ncbi.nlm.nih.gov/articles/PMC3296802/

63. PMC. Lucas RM, et al. "Globally Estimated UVB Exposure Times Required to Maintain Sufficiency in Vitamin D Levels." *Nutrients*. 2024 May 15;16(10):1489.

64. UCLA Health. "Ask the Doctors—How much sunshine do I need for enough vitamin D?" Available at: https://www.uclahealth.org/news/article/ask-the-doctors

65. Overcoming MS. "UV Index Calculator—How much sunlight you need for Vitamin D." Available at: https://overcomingms.org/program/sunlight-vitamin-d/uv-index-calculator

66. Consensus. "Is 5 Minutes of Summer Sun a Safe Amount of Time for Vitamin D?" Available at: https://consensus.app

67. Healthline. "How to Safely Get Vitamin D From Sunlight." Available at: https://www.healthline.com/nutrition/vitamin-d-from-sun

68. Consensus. "Vitamin D Synthesis And Time Of Day." Available at: https://consensus.app/questions/vitamin-d-synthesis-and-time-of-day/

69. PMC. "Moderate Sun Exposure Is the Complementor in Insufficient Vitamin D Consumers." Available at: https://pmc.ncbi.nlm.nih.gov/articles/PMC8957913/

70. Harvard Health. "Time for more vitamin D." Available at: https://www.health.harvard.edu/staying-healthy/time-for-more-vitamin-d

71. Wikipedia. "Health effects of sunlight exposure." Available at: https://en.wikipedia.org/wiki/Health_effects_of_sunlight_exposure

72. MDPI. Lucas RM, et al. "Globally Estimated UVB Exposure Times Required to Maintain Sufficiency in Vitamin D Levels." Available at: https://www.mdpi.com/2072-6643/16/10/1489

73. GrassrootsHealth. "Can You Benefit from Having Vitamin D Levels Over 60 ng/ml? 100 ng/ml?" Available at: https://www.grassrootshealth.net/blog

74. Medical News Today. "Normal vitamin D levels by age, sources, and toxicity." Available at: https://www.medicalnewstoday.com/articles/normal-vitamin-d-levels

75. GrassrootsHealth. "Over 40% of Vitamin D Results have been Above 60 ng/ml Among GrassrootsHealth Participants for the Past 3 Years." Available at: https://www.grassrootshealth.net/blog

76. Harvard Health. "Vitamin D: What's the 'right' level?" Available at: https://www.health.harvard.edu/blog/vitamin-d-whats-right-level-2016121910893

77. ZRT Laboratory. "Vitamin D: What Level is Normal vs Optimal?" Available at: https://www.zrtlab.com/blog/archive/vitamin-d-reference-ranges-optimal/

78. OptimalDX. "Vitamin D: Optimal Levels and How to Get There." Available at: https://www.optimaldx.com/blog/vitamin-d-optimal-levels-and-how-to-get-there

79. StatPearls (NCBI). "Vitamin D." Available at: https://www.ncbi.nlm.nih.gov/books/NBK441912/

80. Office of Dietary Supplements. "Vitamin D." Available at: https://ods.od.nih.gov/factsheets/VitaminD-Consumer/

81. Endocrinología, Diabetes y Nutrición. "Recommended vitamin D levels in the general population." Available at: https://www.elsevier.es/en-revista-endocrinologia-diabetes-nutricion-english-ed--413

82. SSM Health. "Achieving optimal levels of vitamin D can help you live your best life." Available at: https://www.ssmhealth.com/newsroom/blogs/ssm-health-matters

83. National Cancer Institute. "Vitamin D and Cancer." Available at: https://www.cancer.gov/about-cancer/causes-prevention/risk/diet/vitamin-d-fact-sheet

84. GrassrootsHealth. "'Prevention is better than a Cure!'—Vitamin D Reduces Autoimmune Disease." Available at: https://www.grassrootshealth.net/blog

85. PMC. Wimalawansa SJ. "Vitamin D's Impact on Cancer Incidence and Mortality: A Systematic Review." Available at: https://pmc.ncbi.nlm.nih.gov/articles/PMC12298439/

86. PMC. Keum N, Giovannucci E. "Vitamin D in Cancer Prevention: Gaps in Current Knowledge and Room for Hope." Available at: https://pmc.ncbi.nlm.nih.gov/articles/PMC9657468/

87. PMC. Wimalawansa SJ, et al. "Vitamin D: Evidence-Based Health Benefits and Recommendations for Population Guidelines." Available at: https://pmc.ncbi.nlm.nih.gov/articles/PMC11767646/

88. PMC. Holick MF. "Vitamin D and Sunlight: Strategies for Cancer Prevention and Other Health Benefits." Available at: https://pmc.ncbi.nlm.nih.gov/articles/PMC4571149/

89. PMC. Fleet JC, Schoch RD. "Influence of vitamin D on cancer risk and treatment: Why the variability?" Available at: https://pmc.ncbi.nlm.nih.gov/articles/PMC6201256/

90. PMC. Zhang Y, Fang F, Tang J, et al. "Vitamin D supplementation and total cancer incidence and mortality: a meta-analysis of randomized controlled trials." *Ann Oncol.* 2019 May 1;30(5):733-743.

91. ScienceDirect. Grant WB. "Vitamin D and viral infections: Infectious diseases, autoimmune diseases, and cancers." Available at: https://www.sciencedirect.com/science/article/abs/pii/S1043452623001018

92. PMC. Gupta D, Vashi PG, Trukova K, Lammersfeld CA. "Vitamin D and Cancer." Available at: https://pmc.ncbi.nlm.nih.gov/articles/PMC3355893/

References

Part 3: Complete Reference List

Insulin Resistance Protocol References

1. De Paoli M, Zakharia A, Werstuck GH. The Role of Estrogen in Insulin Resistance: A Review of Clinical and Preclinical Data. *Am J Pathol.* 2021;191(9):1490-1498.
2. Carr MC. The emergence of the metabolic syndrome with menopause. *J Clin Endocrinol Metab.* 2003;88(6):2404-2411.
3. Mauvais-Jarvis F, Clegg DJ, Hevener AL. The role of estrogens in control of energy balance and glucose homeostasis. *Endocr Rev.* 2013;34(3):309-338.
4. Salpeter SR, Walsh JM, Ormiston TM, Greyber E, Buckley NS, Salpeter EE. Meta-analysis: effect of hormone-replacement therapy on components of the metabolic syndrome in postmenopausal women. *Diabetes Obes Metab.* 2006;8(5):538-554.
5. Wildman RP, Sowers MR. Adiposity and the menopausal transition. *Obstet Gynecol Clin North Am.* 2011;38(3):441-454.
6. Lovejoy JC, Champagne CM, de Jonge L, Xie H, Smith SR. Increased visceral fat and decreased energy expenditure during the menopausal transition. *Int J Obes (Lond).* 2008;32(6):949-958.
7. American Diabetes Association. Classification and Diagnosis of Diabetes: Standards of Medical Care in Diabetes—2024. *Diabetes Care.* 2024;47(Suppl 1):S20-S42.
8. Matthews DR, Hosker JP, Rudenski AS, Naylor BA, Treacher DF, Turner RC. Homeostasis model assessment: insulin resistance and beta-cell function from fasting plasma glucose and insulin concentrations in man. *Diabetologia.* 1985;28(7):412-419.
9. Freeman EW, Sammel MD, Lin H, Gracia CR. Obesity and reproductive hormone levels in the transition to menopause. *Menopause.* 2010;17(4):718-726.
10. Kapoor E, Collazo-Clavell ML, Faubion SS. Weight Gain in Women at Midlife: A Concise Review of the Pathophysiology and Strategies for Management. *Mayo Clin Proc.* 2017;92(10):1552-1558.
11. Gavin KM, Bessesen DH. Sex Differences in Muscle Mass and Insulin Resistance After Menopause. *Curr Opin Endocr Metab Res.* 2020;12:20-26.
12. International Diabetes Federation. The IDF consensus worldwide definition of the metabolic syndrome. 2006.
13. Nathan DM, Kuenen J, Borg R, Zheng H, Schoenfeld D, Heine RJ; A1c-Derived Average Glucose Study Group. Translating the A1C assay into estimated average glucose values. *Diabetes Care.* 2008;31(8):1473-1478.

14. Reaven GM. Banting lecture 1988. Role of insulin resistance in human disease. *Diabetes*. 1988;37(12):1595-1607.

15. Skov V, Glintborg D, Knudsen S, et al. Reduced expression of nuclear-encoded genes involved in mitochondrial oxidative metabolism in skeletal muscle of insulin-resistant women with polycystic ovary syndrome. *Diabetes*. 2007;56(9):2349-2355.

Cortisol Dysregulation Protocol References

1. McEwen BS. Stress, adaptation, and disease. Allostasis and allostatic load. *Ann N Y Acad Sci*. 1998;840:33-44.

2. Epel ES, McEwen B, Seeman T, et al. Stress and body shape: stress-induced cortisol secretion is consistently greater among women with central fat. *Psychosom Med*. 2000;62(5):623-632.

3. Lupien SJ, McEwen BS, Gunnar MR, Heim C. Effects of stress throughout the lifespan on the brain, behaviour and cognition. *Nat Rev Neurosci*. 2009;10(6):434-445.

4. Sapolsky RM, Krey LC, McEwen BS. The neuroendocrinology of stress and aging: the glucocorticoid cascade hypothesis. *Endocr Rev*. 1986;7(3):284-301.

5. Chrousos GP. Stress and disorders of the stress system. *Nat Rev Endocrinol*. 2009;5(7):374-381.

6. Pasquali R, Vicennati V, Cacciari M, Pagotto U. The hypothalamic-pituitary-adrenal axis activity in obesity and the metabolic syndrome. *Ann N Y Acad Sci*. 2006;1083:111-128.

7. Björntorp P, Rosmond R. Obesity and cortisol. *Nutrition*. 2000;16(10):924-936.

8. Raikkonen K, Matthews KA, Kuller LH. The relationship between psychological risk attributes and the metabolic syndrome in healthy women: antecedent or consequence? *Metabolism*. 2002;51(12):1573-1577.

9. Hewagalamulage SD, Lee TK, Clarke IJ, Henry BA. Stress, cortisol, and obesity: a role for cortisol responsiveness in identifying individuals prone to obesity. *Domest Anim Endocrinol*. 2016;56 Suppl:S112-S120.

10. Hannibal KE, Bishop MD. Chronic stress, cortisol dysfunction, and pain: a psychoneuroendocrine rationale for stress management in pain rehabilitation. *Phys Ther*. 2014;94(12):1816-1825.

11. Nicolaides NC, Kyratzi E, Lamprokostopoulou A, Chrousos GP, Charmandari E. Stress, the stress system and the role of glucocorticoids. *Neuroimmunomodulation*. 2015;22(1-2):6-19.

12. Dallman MF, Pecoraro N, Akana SF, et al. Chronic stress and obesity: a new view of "comfort food". *Proc Natl Acad Sci U S A*. 2003;100(20):11696-11701.

13. Rosmond R. Role of stress in the pathogenesis of the metabolic syndrome. *Psychoneuroendocrinology*. 2005;30(1):1-10.

14. Kadmiel M, Cidlowski JA. Glucocorticoid receptor signaling in health and disease. *Trends Pharmacol Sci.* 2013;34(9):518-530.

15. Nieuwenhuizen AG, Rutters F. The hypothalamic-pituitary-adrenal-axis in the regulation of energy balance. *Physiol Behav.* 2008;94(2):169-177.

Thyroid Dysfunction Protocol References

1. Bianco AC, Salvatore D, Gereben B, Berry MJ, Larsen PR. Metabolism of Thyroid Hormone. *Endotext [Internet].* January 2017. NCBI Bookshelf. Available at: https://www.ncbi.nlm.nih.gov/books/NBK285545/

2. Visser TJ, Peeters RP. Role of hepatic deiodinases in thyroid hormone homeostasis and liver metabolism, inflammation, and fibrosis. *European Thyroid Journal.* 2023;12(3). Available at: https://etj.bioscientifica.com/view/journals/etj/12/3/ETJ-22-0211.xml

3. Hagmeyer R. Thyroid Conversion Issues—Everything You Ever Wanted To Know. November 2024. Available at: https://www.drhagmeyer.com/thyroid-conversion-issues-everthing-you-ever-wanted-to-know/

4. Campbell P. Improving Thyroid Hormone Conversion. *Cytoplan Blog.* March 2018.

5. Campbell P. Low Thyroid Conversion of T4 to T3. *Pippa Campbell Health.* July 2024. Available at: https://www.pippacampbellhealth.com/blog/low-thyroid/

6. Walk-In Lab. T3, T4, and TSH Explained Simply | Thyroid Hormones. September 2025. Available at: https://resources.walkinlab.com/thyroid/thyroid-hormones-explained/

7. MTHFR Doctors. The MTHFR Gene Mutation. May 2025. Available at: https://www.mthfrdoctors.com/the-mthfr-mutation/

8. Arafah BM. Increased need for thyroxine in women with hypothyroidism during estrogen therapy. *N Engl J Med.* 2001;344(23):1743-1749.

9. Santin AP, Furlanetto TW. Role of estrogen in thyroid function and growth regulation. *J Thyroid Res.* 2011;2011:875125.

10. Toljan K, Vrooman B. Low-Dose Naltrexone (LDN)-Review of Therapeutic Utilization. Med Sci (Basel). 2018;6(4):82.

11. Younger J, Parkitny L, McLain D. The use of low-dose naltrexone (LDN) as a novel anti-inflammatory treatment for chronic pain. Clin Rheumatol. 2014;33(4):451-459.

12. Li Z, You Y, Griffin N, Feng J, Shan F. Low-dose naltrexone (LDN): A promising treatment in immune-related diseases and cancer therapy. Int Immunopharmacol. 2018;61:178-184.

13. Raknes G, Småbrekke L. No change in the consumption of thyroid hormones after starting low dose naltrexone (LDN): a quasi-experimental before-after study. BMC Endocr Disord. 2020;20(1):151.

14. Brown N, Panksepp J. Low-dose naltrexone for disease prevention and quality of life. Med Hypotheses. 2009;72(3):333-337.

15. Cant R, Dalgleish AG, Allen RL. Naltrexone Inhibits IL-6 and TNFα Production in Human Immune Cell Subsets following Stimulation with Ligands for Intracellular Toll-Like Receptors. Front Immunol. 2017;8:809.

16. Zagon IS, McLaughlin PJ. Endogenous opioid systems and immune function: clinical implications. Immunol Today. 1987;8(12):385-386.

17. Ludwig MD, Zagon IS, McLaughlin PJ. Serum [Met5]-enkephalin levels are reduced in multiple sclerosis and restored by low-dose naltrexone. Exp Biol Med (Maywood). 2017;242(15):1524-1533.

18. Hutchinson MR, Zhang Y, Brown K, et al. Non-stereoselective reversal of neuropathic pain by naloxone and naltrexone: involvement of toll-like receptor 4 (TLR4). Eur J Neurosci. 2008;28(1):20-29.

19. Srivastava AB, Gold MS. Naltrexone: A History and Future Directions. Cerebrum. 2018 Jul-Aug;2018:cer-13-18.

Sex Hormone Balance Protocol References

1. Lennartsson AK, Jonsdottir IH. Prolactin in response to acute psychosocial stress in healthy men and women. *Psychoneuroendocrinology*. 2011;36(10):1530-1539.

2. Havlikova H, Hill M, Kancheva L, Vrbikova J, Pouzar V, Cerny I, Kancheva R, Novak Z, Starka L. Serum profiles of free and conjugated neuroactive pregnanolone isomers in nonpregnant women of fertile age. *J Clin Endocrinol Metab*. 2006;91(8):3092-3099.

3. Maninger N, Wolkowitz OM, Reus VI, Epel ES, Mellon SH. Neurobiological and neuropsychiatric effects of dehydroepiandrosterone (DHEA) and DHEA sulfate (DHEAS). *Front Neuroendocrinol*. 2009;30(1):65-91.

4. Shi H, Seeley RJ, Clegg DJ. Sexual differences in the control of energy homeostasis. *Front Neuroendocrinol*. 2009;30(3):396-404.

5. Palmer BF, Clegg DJ. The sexual dimorphism of obesity. *Mol Cell Endocrinol*. 2015;402:113-119.

6. Bonds DE, Lasser N, Qi L, et al. The effect of conjugated equine oestrogen on diabetes incidence: the Women's Health Initiative randomised trial. *Diabetologia*. 2006;49(3):459-468.

7. Margolis KL, Bonds DE, Rodabough RJ, et al. Effect of oestrogen plus progestin on the incidence of diabetes in postmenopausal women: results from the Women's Health Initiative Hormone Trial. *Diabetologia*. 2004;47(7):1175-1187.

8. Gambacciani M, Ciaponi M, Cappagli B, et al. Body weight, body fat distribution, and hormonal replacement therapy in early postmenopausal women. *J Clin Endocrinol Metab*. 1997;82(2):414-417.

9. Davis SR, Castelo-Branco C, Chedraui P, et al. Understanding weight gain at menopause. *Climacteric*. 2012;15(5):419-429.

10. Sites CK, Toth MJ, Cushman M, et al. Menopause-related differences in inflammation markers and their relationship to body fat distribution and insulin-stimulated glucose disposal. *Fertil Steril.* 2002;77(1):128-135.

11. Writing Group for the Women's Health Initiative Investigators. Risks and benefits of estrogen plus progestin in healthy postmenopausal women: principal results from the Women's Health Initiative randomized controlled trial. *JAMA.* 2002;288(3):321-333.

12. Canonico M, Fournier A, Carcaillon L, et al. Postmenopausal hormone therapy and risk of idiopathic venous thromboembolism: results from the E3N cohort study. *Arterioscler Thromb Vasc Biol.* 2010;30(2):340-345.

13. Scarabin PY, Oger E, Plu-Bureau G; EStrogen and THromboEmbolism Risk Study Group. Differential association of oral and transdermal oestrogen-replacement therapy with venous thromboembolism risk. *Lancet.* 2003;362(9382):428-432.

14. Rossouw JE, Anderson GL, Prentice RL, et al. Risks and benefits of estrogen plus progestin in healthy postmenopausal women: principal results From the Women's Health Initiative randomized controlled trial. *JAMA.* 2002;288(3):321-333.

15. North American Menopause Society. The 2017 hormone therapy position statement of The North American Menopause Society. *Menopause.* 2017;24(7):728-753.

16. Manson JE, Chlebowski RT, Stefanick ML, et al. Menopausal hormone therapy and health outcomes during the intervention and extended poststopping phases of the Women's Health Initiative randomized trials. *JAMA.* 2013;310(13):1353-1368.

17. Khosla S, Oursler MJ, Monroe DG. Estrogen and the skeleton. *Trends Endocrinol Metab.* 2012;23(11):576-581.

18. Sözen T, Özışık L, Başaran NÇ. An overview and management of osteoporosis. *Eur J Rheumatol.* 2017;4(1):46-56.

19. Pfeilschifter J, Köditz R, Pfohl M, Schatz H. Changes in proinflammatory cytokine activity after menopause. *Endocr Rev.* 2002;23(1):90-119.

20. Straub RH. The complex role of estrogens in inflammation. *Endocr Rev.* 2007;28(5):521-574.

21. Schüle C, Nothdurfter C, Rupprecht R. The role of allopregnanolone in depression and anxiety. *Prog Neurobiol.* 2014;113:79-87.

22. Backstrom T, Haage D, Löfgren M, et al. Paradoxical effects of GABA-A modulators may explain sex steroid induced negative mood symptoms in some persons. *Neuroscience.* 2011;191:46-54.

23. Lancel M, Faulhaber J, Holsboer F, Rupprecht R. Progesterone induces changes in sleep comparable to those of agonistic GABAA receptor modulators. *Am J Physiol.* 1996;271(4 Pt 1):E763-E772.

24. Baker FC, Driver HS. Circadian rhythms, sleep, and the menstrual cycle. *Sleep Med.* 2007;8(6):613-622.

25. Bunevicius R, Kazanavicius G, Zalinkevicius R, Prange AJ Jr. Effects of thyroxine as compared with thyroxine plus triiodothyronine in patients with hypothyroidism. *N Engl J Med.* 1999;340(6):424-429.

26. L'Hermite M, Simoncini T, Fuller S, Genazzani AR. Could transdermal estradiol + progesterone be a safer postmenopausal HRT? A review. *Maturitas.* 2008;60(3-4):185-201.

27. Stanczyk FZ, Hapgood JP, Winer S, Mishell DR Jr. Progestogens used in postmenopausal hormone therapy: differences in their pharmacological properties, intracellular actions, and clinical effects. *Endocr Rev.* 2013;34(2):171-208.

28. Fournier A, Berrino F, Clavel-Chapelon F. Unequal risks for breast cancer associated with different hormone replacement therapies: results from the E3N cohort study. *Breast Cancer Res Treat.* 2008;107(1):103-111.

29. Sipilä S, Narici M, Kjaer M, et al. Sex hormones and skeletal muscle weakness. *Biogerontology.* 2013;14(3):231-245.

30. Goodpaster BH, Park SW, Harris TB, et al. The loss of skeletal muscle strength, mass, and quality in older adults: the health, aging and body composition study. *J Gerontol A Biol Sci Med Sci.* 2006;61(10):1059-1064.

31. Prior JC. Progesterone for Symptomatic Perimenopause Treatment— Progesterone politics, physiology and potential for perimenopause. *Facts Views Vis Obgyn.* 2011;3(2):109-120.

32. Caufriez A, Leproult R, L'Hermite-Balériaux M, Kerkhofs M, Copinschi G. Progesterone prevents sleep disturbances and modulates GH, TSH, and melatonin secretion in postmenopausal women. *J Clin Endocrinol Metab.* 2011;96(4):E614-E623.

33. Halbreich U, Kahn LS. Role of estrogen in the aetiology and treatment of mood disorders. *CNS Drugs.* 2001;15(10):797-817.

34. Soares CN, Almeida OP, Joffe H, Cohen LS. Efficacy of estradiol for the treatment of depressive disorders in perimenopausal women: a double-blind, randomized, placebo-controlled trial. *Arch Gen Psychiatry.* 2001;58(6):529-534.

35. Young EA, Altemus M, Parkison V, Shastry S. Effects of estrogen antagonists and agonists on the ACTH response to restraint stress in female rats. *Neuropsychopharmacology.* 2001;25(6):881-891.

36. Handa RJ, Weiser MJ, Zuloaga DG. A role for the androgen metabolite, 5alpha-androstane-3beta,17beta-diol, in modulating oestrogen receptor beta-mediated regulation of hormonal stress reactivity. *J Neuroendocrinol.* 2009;21(4):351-358.

37. Maltais ML, Desroches J, Dionne IJ. Changes in muscle mass and strength after menopause. *J Musculoskelet Neuronal Interact.* 2009;9(4):186-197.

38. Karastergiou K, Smith SR, Greenberg AS, Fried SK. Sex differences in human adipose tissues—the biology of pear shape. *Biol Sex Differ.* 2012;3(1):13.

39. Toth MJ, Tchernof A, Sites CK, Poehlman ET. Effect of menopausal status on body composition and abdominal fat distribution. *Int J Obes Relat Metab Disord*. 2000;24(2):226-231.

40. Dulloo AG, Jacquet J, Montani JP, Schutz Y. How dieting makes the lean fatter: from a perspective of body composition autoregulation through adipostats and proteinstats awaiting discovery. *Obes Rev*. 2015;16 Suppl 1:25-35.

41. Fothergill E, Guo J, Howard L, et al. Persistent metabolic adaptation 6 years after "The Biggest Loser" competition. *Obesity (Silver Spring)*. 2016;24(8):1612-1619.

42. Rosenbaum M, Leibel RL. Adaptive thermogenesis in humans. *Int J Obes (Lond)*. 2010;34 Suppl 1(Suppl 1):S47-S55.

43. Lee J. *What Your Doctor May Not Tell You About Premenopause: Balance Your Hormones and Your Life from Thirty to Fifty*. Warner Books. 1996.

44. Manson JE, Aragaki AK, Rossouw JE, et al. Menopausal hormone therapy and long-term all-cause and cause-specific mortality: the Women's Health Initiative randomized trials. *JAMA*. 2017;318(10):927-938.

45. Schierbeck LL, Rejnmark L, Tofteng CL, et al. Effect of hormone replacement therapy on cardiovascular events in recently postmenopausal women: randomised trial. *BMJ*. 2012;345:e6409.

46. Hodis HN, Mack WJ, Henderson VW, et al. Vascular Effects of Early versus Late Postmenopausal Treatment with Estradiol. *N Engl J Med*. 2016;374(13):1221-1231.

47. ACOG Practice Bulletin No. 141: management of menopausal symptoms. *Obstet Gynecol*. 2014;123(1):202-216.

48. Stuenkel CA, Davis SR, Gompel A, et al. Treatment of symptoms of the menopause: an Endocrine Society Clinical Practice Guideline. *J Clin Endocrinol Metab*. 2015;100(11):3975-4011.

49. Teede HJ, Misso ML, Costello MF, et al. Recommendations from the international evidence-based guideline for the assessment and management of polycystic ovary syndrome. *Fertil Steril*. 2018;110(3):364-379.

50. Legro RS, Arslanian SA, Ehrmann DA, et al. Diagnosis and treatment of polycystic ovary syndrome: an Endocrine Society clinical practice guideline. *J Clin Endocrinol Metab*. 2013;98(12):4565-4592.

51. Marshall JC, Dunaif A. Should all women with PCOS be treated for insulin resistance? *Fertil Steril*. 2012;97(1):18-22.

52. Legro RS, Driscoll D, Strauss JF 3rd, Fox J, Dunaif A. Evidence for a genetic basis for hyperandrogenemia in polycystic ovary syndrome. *Proc Natl Acad Sci U S A*. 1998;95(25):14956-14960.

53. Revised 2003 consensus on diagnostic criteria and long-term health risks related to polycystic ovary syndrome. *Fertil Steril*. 2004;81(1):19-25.

54. Santoro N, Randolph JF Jr. Reproductive hormones and the menopause transition. *Obstet Gynecol Clin North Am*. 2011;38(3):455-466.

55. Prior JC. Perimenopause: The Complex Endocrinology of the Menopausal Transition. *Endocr Rev*. 1998;19(4):397-428.

56. Burger HG, Hale GE, Robertson DM, Dennerstein L. A review of hormonal changes during the menopausal transition: focus on findings from the Melbourne Women's Midlife Health Project. *Hum Reprod Update*. 2007;13(6):559-565.

57. Orentreich N, Brind JL, Rizer RL, Vogelman JH. Age changes and sex differences in serum dehydroepiandrosterone sulfate concentrations throughout adulthood. *J Clin Endocrinol Metab*. 1984;59(3):551-555.

58. Gupte AA, Pownall HJ, Hamilton DJ. Estrogen: an emerging regulator of insulin action and mitochondrial function. *J Diabetes Res*. 2015;2015:916585.

59. Livingstone C, Collison M. Sex steroids and insulin resistance. *Clin Sci (Lond)*. 2002;102(2):151-166.

Vitamin D Deficiency Protocol References

1. Purishh. "Vitamin D: Not Actually a Vitamin." Available at: https://purishh.com

2. Quora. "Why is vitamin D considered a hormone?" Available at: https://quora.com

3. AHA Journals. "Vitamin D and Cardiovascular Disease." Available at: https://ahajournals.org

4. Amchara. "Vitamin D and Hormone Function." Available at: https://amchara.com

5. Diabetes Journals. "Vitamin D supplementation and insulin secretion." Available at: https://diabetesjournals.org

6. PubMed Central. "Vitamin D deficiency and thyroid function." Available at: https://pmc.ncbi.nlm.nih.gov

7. F1000Research. "Vitamin D treatment alters adrenal steroidogenesis." Available at: https://f1000research.com

8. Frontiers. "Vitamin D and PCOS." Available at: https://frontiersin.org

9. Wikipedia. "Vitamin D Receptor." Available at: https://en.wikipedia.org/wiki/Vitamin_D_receptor

10. GeneCards. "VDR Gene." Available at: https://genecards.org

11. MDPI. "Vitamin D Receptor Interactions." Available at: https://mdpi.com

12. Nature. "Vitamin D supplementation increases VDR gene expression." Available at: https://nature.com

13. ScienceDirect. "Vitamin D regulates steroid hormone production." Available at: https://sciencedirect.com

14. Elara. "Vitamin D and aromatase activity." Available at: https://elara.com

15. Amegroups. "Vitamin D stimulates estrogen and progesterone production." Available at: https://amegroups.com

16. PubMed Central. "Vitamin D and SHBG levels." Available at: https://pmc.ncbi.nlm.nih.gov

17. Diabetes Journals. "Vitamin D deficiency and weight loss." Available at: https://diabetesjournals.org

18. PubMed. "Vitamin D levels normalize after weight loss." Available at: https://pubmed.ncbi.nlm.nih.gov

19. Healthline. "Vitamin D and Weight Loss." Available at: https://healthline.com

20. PubMed. "Vitamin D and serotonin synthesis." Available at: https://pubmed.ncbi.nlm.nih.gov

21. PubMed Central. "Vitamin D induces TPH2 expression." Available at: https://pmc.ncbi.nlm.nih.gov

22. ScienceDirect. "Vitamin D supplementation improves depression." Available at: https://sciencedirect.com

23. Psychiatry Times. "Vitamin D and Depression." Available at: https://psychiatrytimes.com

24. WHO EMRO. "Effect of latitude on seasonal variations of vitamin D." Available at: https://www.emro.who.int

25. PubMed. Webb AR, Kline L, Holick MF. "Influence of season and latitude on the cutaneous synthesis of vitamin D3: exposure to winter sunlight in Boston and Edmonton will not promote vitamin D3 synthesis in human skin." *J Clin Endocrinol Metab.* 1988 Aug;67(2):373-8.

26. The Journal of Clinical Endocrinology & Metabolism. Levis S, Gomez A, Jimenez C, et al. "Vitamin D Deficiency and Seasonal Variation in an Adult South Florida Population." Volume 90, Issue 3, March 2005.

27. PMC. "Seasonal variations in serum vitamin D according to age and sex." Available at: https://pmc.ncbi.nlm.nih.gov/articles/PMC3755860/

28. PubMed. "Sunlight and dietary contributions to the seasonal vitamin D status of cohorts of healthy postmenopausal women living at northerly latitudes." Available at: https://pubmed.ncbi.nlm.nih.gov/21085934/

29. Consensus. "Can People North of 35deg Latitude Get Enough Vitamin D via the Sun in Winter?" Available at: https://consensus.app

30. Oxford Academic. Webb AR, Kline L, Holick MF. "Influence of Season and Latitude on the Cutaneous Synthesis of Vitamin D3." *The Journal of Clinical Endocrinology & Metabolism*, Volume 67, Issue 2, August 1988.

31. PubMed. "Vitamin D deficiency prevalence in summer compared to winter in a city with high humidity." Available at: https://pubmed.ncbi.nlm.nih.gov/21717408/

32. PubMed. "The effect of season and latitude on in vitro vitamin D formation by sunlight in South Africa." Available at: https://pubmed.ncbi.nlm.nih.gov/8955733/

33. PMC. "Is Sunlight Exposure Enough to Avoid Wintertime Vitamin D Deficiency in United Kingdom Population Groups?" Available at: https://pmc.ncbi.nlm.nih.gov/articles/PMC6121420/

34. PMC. "The role of vitamin D in menopausal women's health." Available at: https://pmc.ncbi.nlm.nih.gov/articles/PMC10291614/

35. Femgevity Health. "The Vitamin D Paradox: Understanding Deficiency and Its Impact on Health." Available at: https://www.femgevityhealth.com

36. PMC. "Vitamin D supplementation after the menopause." Available at: https://pmc.ncbi.nlm.nih.gov/articles/PMC7278294/

37. PubMed. "Impact of Vitamin D on Skin Aging, and Age-Related Dermatological Conditions." Available at: https://pubmed.ncbi.nlm.nih.gov/39862075/

38. PubMed. "Aging decreases the capacity of human skin to produce vitamin D3." Available at: https://pubmed.ncbi.nlm.nih.gov/2997282/

39. Sage Journals. Pérez-López FR, Chedraui P, Pilz S. "Vitamin D supplementation after the menopause." Available at: https://journals.sagepub.com/doi/full/10.1177/2042018820931291

40. PMC. "Unravelling of hidden secrets: The role of vitamin D in skin aging." Available at: https://pmc.ncbi.nlm.nih.gov/articles/PMC3583884/

41. Balance Menopause. "All about vitamin D, menopause and hormone health." Available at: https://www.balance-menopause.com

42. IMR Press. "Impact of Vitamin D on Skin Aging, and Age-Related Dermatological Conditions." Available at: https://www.imrpress.com/journal/FBL/30/1/10.31083/FBL25463/htm

43. Nutrition & Metabolism. "Effects of high fat diet-induced obesity on vitamin D metabolism and tissue distribution." Available at: https://nutritionandmetabolism.biomedcentral.com/articles/10.1186/s12986-020-00463-x

44. PubMed. "Unraveling the Connection: Visceral Adipose Tissue and Vitamin D Levels in Obesity." Available at: https://pubmed.ncbi.nlm.nih.gov/37836543/

45. PMC. "Vitamin D and Visceral Obesity in Humans: What Should Clinicians Know?" Available at: https://pmc.ncbi.nlm.nih.gov/articles/PMC9332747/

46. Wiley Online Library. Hengist A, et al. "Mobilising vitamin D from adipose tissue: The potential impact of exercise." *Nutrition Bulletin*. 2019.

47. Oxford Academic. Di Nisio A, et al. "Impaired Release of Vitamin D in Dysfunctional Adipose Tissue: New Cues on Vitamin D Supplementation in Obesity." *The Journal of Clinical Endocrinology & Metabolism*, Volume 102, Issue 7, July 2017.

48. PMC. "Vitamin D regulation of adipogenesis and adipose tissue functions." Available at: https://pmc.ncbi.nlm.nih.gov/articles/PMC7683208/

49. Medscape. "Does Vitamin D Deficiency Cause Obesity or Vice Versa?" Available at: https://www.medscape.com/viewarticle/985973

50. PMC. "Vitamin D Storage in Adipose Tissue of Obese and Normal Weight Women." Available at: https://pmc.ncbi.nlm.nih.gov/articles/PMC5577589/

51. PMC. "Vitamin D Deficiency: Consequence or Cause of Obesity?" Available at: https://pmc.ncbi.nlm.nih.gov/articles/PMC6780345/

52. PubMed. "Vitamin D deficiency in the aetiology of obesity-related insulin resistance." Available at: https://pubmed.ncbi.nlm.nih.gov/30801902/

53. PMC. Grant WB, et al. "Does the High Prevalence of Vitamin D Deficiency in African Americans Contribute to Health Disparities?" *Nutrients*. 2021 Feb 3;13(2):499.

54. PubMed. Grant WB, et al. "Does the High Prevalence of Vitamin D Deficiency in African Americans Contribute to Health Disparities?" Available at: https://pubmed.ncbi.nlm.nih.gov/33546262/

55. The Cooper Institute. "African Americans At Greatest Risk of Vitamin D Deficiency." Available at: https://www.cooperinstitute.org/blog

56. University of Houston. "Study Finds Low Vitamin D Levels in Young People of Color." Available at: https://www.uh.edu/news-events

57. MDPI. Grant WB, et al. "Does the High Prevalence of Vitamin D Deficiency in African Americans Contribute to Health Disparities?" Available at: https://www.mdpi.com/2072-6643/13/2/499

58. ScienceDirect. "The prevalence of vitamin D deficiency among dark-skinned populations according to their stage of migration and region of birth: A meta-analysis." Available at: https://www.sciencedirect.com/science/article/abs/pii/S0899900715002932

59. News Center (Northwestern). Murphy AB, et al. "One Size Doesn't Fit All When It Comes To Vitamin D for Men." Available at: https://news.feinberg.northwestern.edu/2011/09/20/vitamin-d/

60. PubMed. Harris SS. "Vitamin D and African Americans." *J Nutr*. 2006 Apr;136(4):1126-9.

61. Afriscitech. "The Myth of chronic Black Vitamin D deficiency." Available at: https://www.afriscitech.com/en/blogs/afroscientific-en/343

62. PMC. Kumar J, et al. "Impact of season and diet on vitamin D status of African American and Caucasian children." Available at: https://pmc.ncbi.nlm.nih.gov/articles/PMC3296802/

63. PMC. Lucas RM, et al. "Globally Estimated UVB Exposure Times Required to Maintain Sufficiency in Vitamin D Levels." *Nutrients*. 2024 May 15;16(10):1489.

64. UCLA Health. "Ask the Doctors—How much sunshine do I need for enough vitamin D?" Available at: https://www.uclahealth.org/news/article/ask-the-doctors

65. Overcoming MS. "UV Index Calculator—How much sunlight you need for Vitamin D." Available at: https://overcomingms.org/program/sunlight-vitamin-d/uv-index-calculator

66. Consensus. "Is 5 Minutes of Summer Sun a Safe Amount of Time for Vitamin D?" Available at: https://consensus.app

67. Healthline. "How to Safely Get Vitamin D From Sunlight." Available at: https://www.healthline.com/nutrition/vitamin-d-from-sun

68. Consensus. "Vitamin D Synthesis And Time Of Day." Available at: https://consensus.app/questions/vitamin-d-synthesis-and-time-of-day/

69. PMC. "Moderate Sun Exposure Is the Complementor in Insufficient Vitamin D Consumers." Available at: https://pmc.ncbi.nlm.nih.gov/articles/PMC8957913/

70. Harvard Health. "Time for more vitamin D." Available at: https://www.health.harvard.edu/staying-healthy/time-for-more-vitamin-d

71. Wikipedia. "Health effects of sunlight exposure." Available at: https://en.wikipedia.org/wiki/Health_effects_of_sunlight_exposure

72. MDPI. Lucas RM, et al. "Globally Estimated UVB Exposure Times Required to Maintain Sufficiency in Vitamin D Levels." Available at: https://www.mdpi.com/2072-6643/16/10/1489

73. GrassrootsHealth. "Can You Benefit from Having Vitamin D Levels Over 60 ng/ml? 100 ng/ml?" Available at: https://www.grassrootshealth.net/blog

74. Medical News Today. "Normal vitamin D levels by age, sources, and toxicity." Available at: https://www.medicalnewstoday.com/articles/normal-vitamin-d-levels

75. GrassrootsHealth. "Over 40% of Vitamin D Results have been Above 60 ng/ml Among GrassrootsHealth Participants for the Past 3 Years." Available at: https://www.grassrootshealth.net/blog

76. Harvard Health. "Vitamin D: What's the 'right' level?" Available at: https://www.health.harvard.edu/blog/vitamin-d-whats-right-level-2016121910893

77. ZRT Laboratory. "Vitamin D: What Level is Normal vs Optimal?" Available at: https://www.zrtlab.com/blog/archive/vitamin-d-reference-ranges-optimal/

78. OptimalDX. "Vitamin D: Optimal Levels and How to Get There." Available at: https://www.optimaldx.com/blog/vitamin-d-optimal-levels-and-how-to-get-there

79. StatPearls (NCBI). "Vitamin D." Available at: https://www.ncbi.nlm.nih.gov/books/NBK441912/

80. Office of Dietary Supplements. "Vitamin D." Available at: https://ods.od.nih.gov/factsheets/VitaminD-Consumer/

81. Endocrinología, Diabetes y Nutrición. "Recommended vitamin D levels in the general population." Available at: https://www.elsevier.es/en-revista-endocrinologia-diabetes-nutricion-english-ed--413

82. SSM Health. "Achieving optimal levels of vitamin D can help you live your best life." Available at: https://www.ssmhealth.com/newsroom/blogs/ssm-health-matters

83. National Cancer Institute. "Vitamin D and Cancer." Available at: https://www.cancer.gov/about-cancer/causes-prevention/risk/diet/vitamin-d-fact-sheet

84. GrassrootsHealth. "'Prevention is better than a Cure!'—Vitamin D Reduces Autoimmune Disease." Available at: https://www.grassrootshealth.net/blog

85. PMC. Wimalawansa SJ. "Vitamin D's Impact on Cancer Incidence and Mortality: A Systematic Review." Available at: https://pmc.ncbi.nlm.nih.gov/articles/PMC12298439/

86. PMC. Keum N, Giovannucci E. "Vitamin D in Cancer Prevention: Gaps in Current Knowledge and Room for Hope." Available at: https://pmc.ncbi.nlm.nih.gov/articles/PMC9657468/

87. PMC. Wimalawansa SJ, et al. "Vitamin D: Evidence-Based Health Benefits and Recommendations for Population Guidelines." Available at: https://pmc.ncbi.nlm.nih.gov/articles/PMC11767646/

88. PMC. Holick MF. "Vitamin D and Sunlight: Strategies for Cancer Prevention and Other Health Benefits." Available at: https://pmc.ncbi.nlm.nih.gov/articles/PMC4571149/

89. PMC. Fleet JC, Schoch RD. "Influence of vitamin D on cancer risk and treatment: Why the variability?" Available at: https://pmc.ncbi.nlm.nih.gov/articles/PMC6201256/

90. PMC. Zhang Y, Fang F, Tang J, et al. "Vitamin D supplementation and total cancer incidence and mortality: a meta-analysis of randomized controlled trials." *Ann Oncol*. 2019 May 1;30(5):733-743.

91. ScienceDirect. Grant WB. "Vitamin D and viral infections: Infectious diseases, autoimmune diseases, and cancers." Available at: https://www.sciencedirect.com/science/article/abs/pii/S1043452623001018

92. PMC. Gupta D, Vashi PG, Trukova K, Lammersfeld CA. "Vitamin D and Cancer." Available at: https://pmc.ncbi.nlm.nih.gov/articles/PMC3355893/